Norbert Pohlmann | Helmut Reimer | Wolfgang Schneider (Eds.)

ISSE 2010 Securing Electronic Business Processes

T0238957

By the author:

Future of Trust in Computing
by D. Grawrock, H. Reimer, A.-R. Sadeghi and C. Vishik

Autonomous Land Vehicles
by K. Berns and E. v. Puttkamer

Microsoft Dynamics NAV
by P. M. Diffenderfer and S. El-Assal

Using Microsoft Dynamics AX 2009
by A. Luszczak

From Enterprise Architecture to IT Governance
by K. D. Nieman

The New PL/I
by E. Sturm

www.viewegteubner.de

Norbert Pohlmann | Helmut Reimer |
Wolfgang Schneider (Eds.)

ISSE 2010
Securing Electronic
Business Processes

Highlights of the Information Security Solutions
Europe 2010 Conference

With 80 Figures

**VIEWEG+
TEUBNER**

Bibliographic information published by the Deutsche Nationalbibliothek
The Deutsche Nationalbibliothek lists this publication in the Deutsche Nationalbibliografie;
detailed bibliographic data are available in the Internet at http://dnb.d-nb.de.

1st Edition 2011

Editorial Office: Dr. Christel Roß | Andrea Broßler

Vieweg+Teubner Verlag is a brand of Springer Fachmedien.
Springer Fachmedien is part of Springer Science+Business Media.
www.viewegteubner.de

Cover design: KünkelLopka Medienentwicklung, Heidelberg
Typesetting: Oliver Reimer, Jena

Printed on acid-free paper

ISBN 978-3-8348-1438-8

Contents

About this Book

The Information Security Solutions Europe Conference (ISSE) was started in 1999 by eema and TeleTrusT with the support of the European Commission and the German Federal Ministry of Technology and Economics. Today the annual conference is a fixed event in every IT security professional's calendar.

The integration of security in IT applications was initially driven only by the actual security issues considered important by experts in the field; currently, however, the economic aspects of the corresponding solutions are the most important factor in deciding their success. ISSE offers a suitable podium for the discussion of the relationship between these considerations and for the presentation of the practical implementation of concepts with their technical, organisational and economic parameters.

From the beginning ISSE has been carefully prepared. The organisers succeeded in giving the conference a profile that combines a scientifically sophisticated and interdisciplinary discussion of IT security solutions while presenting pragmatic approaches for overcoming current IT security problems.

An enduring documentation of the presentations given at the conference which is available to every interested person thus became important. This year sees the publication of the eighth ISSE book – another mark of the event's success – and with about 40 carefully edited papers it bears witness to the quality of the conference.

An international programme committee is responsible for the selection of the conference contributions and the composition of the programme:

- **Ammar Alkassar,** Sirrix AG and GI e.V. (Germany)
- **Gunter Bitz,** SAP (Germany)
- **Ronny Bjones,** Microsoft (Belgium)
- **Lucas Cardholm,** Ernst&Young (Sweden)
- **Roger Dean,** eema (United Kingdom)
- **Steve Purser,** ENISA
- **Jan De Clercq,** HP (Belgium)
- **Marijke De Soete,** Security4Biz (Belgium)
- **Jos Dumortier,** K.U. Leuven (Belgium)
- **Walter Fumy,** Bundesdruckerei (Germany)
- **Robert Garskamp,** Everett (The Netherlands)
- **Riccardo Genghini,** S.N.G. (Italy)

The editors have endeavoured to allocate the contributions in these proceedings – which differ from the structure of the conference programme – to topic areas which cover the interests of the readers.

Norbert Pohlmann   *Helmut Reimer*   *Wolfgang Schneider*

TeleTrusT Deutschland e.V.
www.teletrust.de

TeleTrusT Germany ("TeleTrusT Deutschland e.V.") was founded in 1989 as a not-for-profit organisation promoting the trustworthiness of information and communication technology in open systems environments.

Today, as an IT security association, TeleTrusT counts more than 100 members from industry, science and research as well as public institutions. Within the last 20 years TeleTrusT evolved to a well known and highly regarded competence network for IT security whose voice is heard throughout Germany and Europe.

In various TeleTrusT working groups ICT security experts, users and interested parties meet each other in frequent workshops, round-tables and expert talks. The activities focus on reliable and trustworthy solutions complying with international standards, laws and statutory requirements.

TeleTrusT is keen to promote the acceptance of solutions supporting identification, authentification and signature (IAS) schemes in electronic business and its processes.

TeleTrusT facilitates information and knowledge exchange between vendors, users and authorities. Subsequently, innovative ICT security solutions can enter the market more quickly and effectively. TeleTrusT aims on standard compliant solutions in an interoperable scheme.

Keeping in mind the raising importance of the European security market, TeleTrusT seeks co-operation with European and international organisations and authorities with similar objectives.

Thus, this year's European Security Conference ISSE is being organized in collaboration with eema, ENISA and the German Federal Ministry of the Interior.

Contact:
Dr. Holger Muehlbauer
Managing Director of TeleTrusT Deutschland e.V.
holger.muehlbauer@teletrust.de

eema
www.eema.org

For 23 years, **eema** has been Europe's leading independent, non-profit e-Identity & Security association, working with its European members, governmental bodies, standards organisations and interoperability initiatives throughout Europe to further e-Business and legislation.

eema's remit is to educate and inform over 1,500 Member contacts on the latest developments and technologies, at the same time enabling Members of the association to compare views and ideas. The work produced by the association with its Members (projects, papers, seminars, tutorials and reports etc) is funded by both membership subscriptions and revenue generated through fee-paying events. All of the information generated by eema and its members is available to other members free of charge.

Examples of recent EEMA events include The European e-ID interoperability conference in Brussels (Featuring STORK, PEPPOL, SPOCS & epSOS) and The European e-Identity Management Conference in London in partnership with OASIS

EEMA and its members are also involved in many European funded projects including STORK, ICEcom and ETICA

Any organisation involved in e-Identity or Security (usually of a global or European nature) can become a Member of eema, and any employee of that organisation is then able to participate in eema activities. Examples of organisations taking advantage of eema membership are *Volvo, Hoffman la Roche, KPMG, Deloitte, ING, Novartis, Metropolitan Police, TOTAL, PGP, McAfee, Adobe, Magyar Telecom Rt, BBS, National Communications Authority, Hungary, Microsoft, HP,* and the *Norwegian Government Administration Services* to name but a few.

Visit www.eema.org for more information or contact the association on +44 1386 793028 or at info@eema.org.

Welcome

Ladies and gentlemen,

It is a particular honour to invite you to the twelfth ISSE Conference, taking place in Berlin on 5 - 7 October 2010, this year hosted by the Federal Ministry of the Interior.

The independent ISSE Conference focuses on secure information systems solutions in a globally networked world. Since the advent of the Internet, countless business, administrative and consumer solutions have transformed our society and the base of economic cooperation around the world. Without doubt, secure and trustworthy information systems are key for the reliability of any ICT infrastructure and future economic prosperity, particularly since more and more fixed and mobile business processes use the Internet.

The ISSE Conference offers the best environment to discuss innovations and new technical solutions for IT security in Europe. We expect more than 400 specialists, researchers, business leaders and policy makers from all over Europe to join us at ISSE to share information and best practices through thoughtful discussions and thorough debates.

Best wishes for a successful and productive conference. I look forward to seeing you in Berlin!

Thomas de Maizière
Federal Minister of the Interior

Germany on the Road to Electronic Proof of Identity

Ulrich Hamann

Bundesdruckerei GmbH
Oranienstrasse 91
10969 Berlin, Germany
email: info@bdr.de

Fast, efficient and convenient – that's how we would like the digital service society to be. Starting 1 November 2010, citizens in Germany will have a new medium for electronic proof of identity and will take an important step towards greater ID security in the online world.

Only a few small details on the outside hint at the multi-functionality of the new German ID card. The technical centre, in the form of a contactless high-security chip, lies inside the document.

High security in miniature format

The new ID card will provide German citizens for the first time ever with a document-based electronic identity that can also be used for private online activities.

To make use of this functionality, a citizen must deliberately choose to activate the electronic functions of the new ID card. Moreover, they must also release their personal data, such as first name and family name, date of birth, address, academic title or pseudonym, if any, during each concrete online application using a personal identification number (PIN).

Source: Federal Ministry of the Interior

Fig. 1: Sample of the new German ID card

Security in many layers

Technically speaking, the new polycarbonate card that is centrally produced at Berlin-based Bundesdruckerei is designed according to the multi-layer principle. The document chip is embedded in several layers of security foil placed on top of each other. These individual layers of foil are irreversibly bonded together in a special production process and using a colour personalisation method, so that the chip, the printed data and the card body form a self-contained unit. Any attempt to manipulate the data would involve damaging the material and hence destroying the document as a whole.

Trust based on reciprocity

According to BITKOM, the German Federal Association for Information Technology, Telecommunications and New Media, more than 70 percent of all Germans go online on a regular basis. In Germany, just like in any other country around the globe, the Internet has become one of the most important sources of information and social platforms for many people. In order to be able to make the best possible use of the growing digital diversity, reliable information regarding the identity of the process participants is becoming increasingly important. At the same time, the sometimes very complex and error-prone control processes are limiting the efficiency and economic feasibility of many online applications, not just in Germany, and are resulting in a sheer endless flood of data.

This is all set to change fundamentally when the new ID card is introduced in November 2010. All new document holders over the age of 16 will have the option to also use the handy card in ID-1 format – comparable to the size of a credit card – for everyday online shopping, to register on online platforms and for digital communications with public authorities. This is based on the principle of mutual authentication, i.e. the user and supplier must identify themselves to each other and hence clearly prove that they are who they claim to be (refer also to Fig. 3).

More than 170 German companies and institutions who have been preparing their new online services since October 2009 in various application tests will be ready to start regular business when the new document is officially launched. Citizens will then be able to experience for themselves the security and convenience which the new eID card (eID: electronic identity) has to offer.

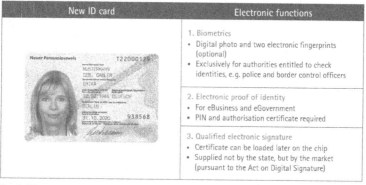

Fig. 2: The new German ID card combines the conventional function of the photo ID card with new electronic functions – in handy ID-1 document format

Give and take – the principle of networked system chains

By today's standards, the German model is now already seen to be one of the most secure and demanding solutions in Europe.

This is primarily due to the *eCard API Framework* developed in Germany, an IT framework structure that has been specified by the German Federal Office for Information Security (BSI). The framework defines new interfaces for electronic identity and signature cards (Application Programming Interface / API) and enables simple platform-independent communication between different eCards and their applications. The so-called *PACE* (Password Authenticated Connection Establishment) method, another component of the new eID infrastructure, will permit additional password-based data release.

This will make it possible to have personal data read directly from the integrated chip of the document and used for online transactions. These transactions are only possible when both the document holder and the online supplier selected by the holder use the same system components and when both partners have identified themselves to each other.

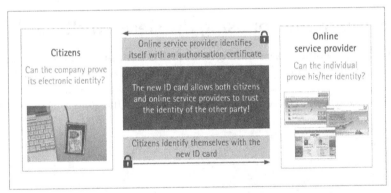

Fig. 3: The electronic functions and security mechanisms bring security to a new level and generate more trust in transactions and communication in the digital world

Full control over data for citizens

The main goal of the new German ID card system is to warrant the informational self-determination of each citizen that is anchored in German constitutional law. Extended Access Control (EAC), for instance, a security protocol already in use in the German electronic passport, will be used. This means that before any data is exchanged, Terminal Authentication and Chip Authentication first check the scope and type of access authorisation as well as the integrity and authenticity of the document chip (refer to diagram).

Protocol	Description	ePassport	New ID card
BAC (Basic Access Control)	Protection against unauthorised reading Communication encrypted	✓	
PA (Passive Authentication)	Proof of the integrity and authenticity of data groups	✓	✓
PACE (Password Authenticated Connection Establishment)	Protection against unauthorised reading Communication encrypted		✓
CA (Chip Authentication)	Proof of the authenticity of the chip	✓	✓
TA (Terminal Authentication)	Proof of the terminal's authorisation	✓	✓

Fig. 4: Security protocols of the German electronic passport and the new ID card

But unlike the passport which is exclusively meant for official use, the electronic proof of identity now possible can also be used for private and commercial purposes. In order to warrant highest data protection and ID security standards in such applications, the PACE method already mentioned requires that the user has a valid document and knows the PIN before data can be accessed or transferred.

Other components for using the German eID card

In addition to a new ID card, citizens wishing to use their document-based personal data for online applications will need an EAC and PACE-compatible card reader and the driver software of the so-called *AusweisApp* – "Ausweis" is the German word for "ID document". The "Tasks of AusweisApp" section describes in more detail how this software and the underlying systems work.

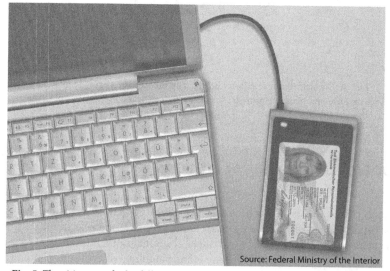

Source: Federal Ministry of the Interior

Fig. 5: The citizen needs the following components to use the online ID function:
- Activated online ID function
- Contactless reading device for secure communication with the new ID card
- AusweisApp driver software for communication between the citizen and online suppliers as well as release of the stored data

That's what authorisation certificates warrant

For online suppliers, the principle of mutual authentication means that they must have special access rights in order to be able to access the ID card data. If, in the future, a company requests a customer's personal data and wishes to have this data transmitted in a reliable manner, it must first prove that it is authorised to read out the document-based data.

This comes in the form of an official *authorisation certificate* that contains details of the business purposes as well as precise information about the necessary scope of the data request. This information is transmitted directly to the online customer's own computer via AusweisApp.

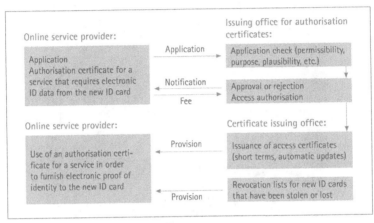

Fig. 6: Before the online service provider can perform a data request, he must first apply for authorisation from the certificate issuing office

The type and scope of data access rights are determined exclusively by the Federal Administration Office (BVA), as the sole German registration agency, with its subordinate *Issuing office for authorisation certificates* (VfB). The technical provision of certificates may only be carried out on the basis of positive VfB notification and exclusively by approved providers of certification services (e.g. trust centers).

In concrete situations, the document holder can always further restrict the amount of data requested by the supplier. On the other hand, the supplier is authorised to make the performance of his services contingent upon the completeness of the data requested. Give and take – and the principle of mutual authentication is fulfilled. Suppliers and users both know who they are dealing with and that all the data provided is correct and complete. A win-win situation for all.

Tasks of AusweisApp

With the new German ID card, identifying oneself on the Internet will be just as clear as presenting a traditional photo document. This is especially due to AusweisApp at the user end. Available as a download from November 2010, the software package permits protected access to the new digital ID system and also allows the user to selectively choose data.

Users who log on in the future using their own computer, a card reader and AusweisApp will be able to immediately recognise by the authorisation certificate of the selected online service provider which information will in fact be needed for the service to be performed.

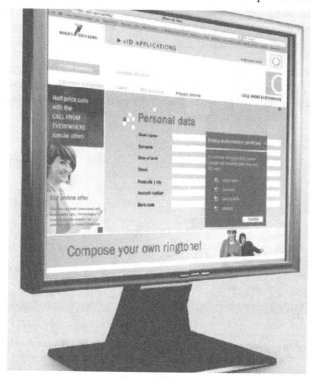

Fig. 7: An intuitive user interface takes users of the electronic ID function by the hand

In the next step, users can activate individual data fields using a simple input mask in AusweisApp. Users who decide to pass on personal information can deliberately select certain data and release this data for further processing simply by using their PIN. The document thus offers completely new possibilities when it comes to active data thriftiness.

eID service as a trust authority

The new ID card, AusweisApp and authorisation certificate, along with the underlying technical and organisational security structures, form the pillars of the new German eID architecture.

This new concept, however, would be incomplete without powerful eID management which cleverly links the aforesaid elements and assumes the role of a higher-order trust authority for all the process participants. This means that the user's incoming information and the supplier information must be carefully checked, compared and further processed according to the respective requirements.

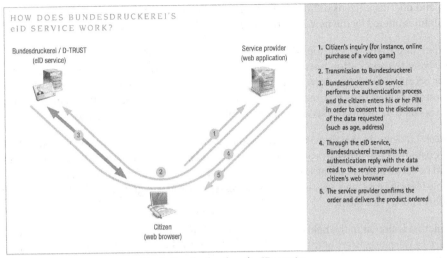

HOW DOES BUNDESDRUCKEREI'S
eID SERVICE WORK?

Bundesdruckerei / D-TRUST
(eID service)

Service provider
(web application)

1. Citizen's inquiry (for instance, online purchase of a video game)

2. Transmission to Bundesdruckerei

3. Bundesdruckerei's eID service performs the authentication process and the citizen enters his or her PIN in order to consent to the disclosure of the data requested (such as age, address)

4. Through the eID service, Bundesdruckerei transmits the authentication reply with the data read to the service provider via the citizen's web browser

5. The service provider confirms the order and delivers the product ordered

Citizen
(web browser)

Fig. 8: Bundesdruckerei's eID service

In order to cover this range of tasks and to meet with the technical guidelines specified by BSI, also at the supplier end, two solutions will be offered in the future.

First of all, the supplier himself implements the BSI-accredited components of a so-called *eID Server* and takes care of both communication with his customers' client software as well as all the necessary administration processes for using valid authorisation certificates.

Secondly, the supplier uses the services of an external, BSI-accredited certificate provider who operates an *eID Service* with client capability for several services. In this scenario, the eID Service commissioned manages the entire AusweisApp communication and performs the comparison of authorisation certificates and revocation lists valid on the day for each data exchange.

Within the scope of application tests and in regular operations, Bundesdruckerei is relying on the latter solution because many suppliers would not be able to set up and operate independent eID servers at short notice. In the long term, however, it can be assumed that both solutions will become established on the market – also in order to ensure optimum availability and stability of the infrastructures created.

Who will benefit from the new eID architecture?

In recent months, discussions about possible applications for electronic ID have been widespread – not just in Germany. These discussions were not limited to aspects of data protection law, but were also related to the economic relevance of state-of-the-art eID solutions in the commercial Internet world.

The work conducted by the Berlin-based *"New identity card: test and demonstration centre"*, which looks after the more than 170 participants in the German application tests, can now be used to derive a number of important areas of focus for the use of new multi-function cards. The area of *eGovernment* especially is at the centre of this interest. Germany's federal states and municipalities are already organising many public-agency administration processes in electronic form and offering citizens online platforms for media-consistent transmission of their data. The possibilities offered by the new ID card are to enhance and expand services in this sector further.

Another important area of focus can be seen with German *insurance companies* who are also involved in the application tests. The use of electronic identities is particularly important in this sector because in order to draw up an insurance offer, insurance companies usually need a lot of data on the person to be insured. Via trustworthy, electronic proof of identity, many routine procedures could be organised faster, more conveniently and more secure than before.

Interest, however, is also growing in the field of classical *eCommerce*. It is equally important for both customers and providers of commercial online platforms to know who they are dealing with and to be certain that all of the information supplied is correct and complete. This also means that reliable identification and age verification processes can lead to significantly better cost efficiency, comfort and service quality.

The picture is similar in the field of *online banking*. Unlike the complicated PostIdent method customary in Germany, users of the online ID function of the new ID card can simply transmit their personal data directly to the selected bank, saving themselves numerous trips and paperwork. This also applies to all companies that handle booking and payment transactions via dedicated user accounts. Airlines and rail companies, as well as car rental and tourism companies, for instance, will be able to offer their online customers much greater convenience and higher service quality through optimised *eTicketing* and *eContracting* processes.

Security for the digital handshake

The new ID card can make matters much simpler everywhere where sensitive data is exchanged or where contracts can only be finalised on the basis of clear proof of identity and legally binding signatures. This is made possible by a qualified electronic signature (QES) which can be optionally integrated. Each citizen can choose to use this option which will not be directly offered by the ID card authorities in charge but by approved providers of certification services (trust centers).

In technical terms, the new ID card is in any case prepared for the QES function which will be of enormous importance not just when it comes to entering into online contracts, but also for the secure signing of digital documents or e-mails. Many online services already see considerable efficiency and security gains in this solution too.

Citizens are the ones who will determine the success of the new concept

But it doesn't matter which possibilities are to be made available in the future and preferred by suppliers – in the end, it is citizens who will decide whether and to what extent they wish to use their electronic identity and disclose this to others.

However, recent forecasts already paint a promising picture. At the beginning of the year, more than half of all German Internet users stated that they would like to use their new multi-function card not just for eGovernment and online banking but also for secure identification when using different online services (source: BITKOM). This also highlights one of the key technical challenges: The success of concepts like the new German ID card system can only be guaranteed if the availability and stability of the infrastructures created are warranted, even for large amounts of data.

A consortium of three highly specialised companies has been commissioned to master this challenge in the run-up to the official launch and during the first three years of regular operations: *Siemens IT Solutions and Services* is the Federal Government's general contractor and is responsible for setting up the new eID architectures and integrating AusweisApp which is being developed and maintained by software specialists *OpenLimit SignCubes AG*. *Bundesdruckerei GmbH*, which had a key role to play in the implementation of the German ePassport project, will produce the new documents. The company will also provide and operate Germany's first eID Service in a high-security trust center environment.

Outlook

The introduction of the new ID card is Germany's response to the ongoing fusion of the online and offline world.

The next step towards greater identity security and around-the-clock online transactions could soon be taken in mobile application scenarios. At this year's CeBIT, Bundesdruckerei already presented first approaches towards such scenarios for the future and is hoping to link state-of-the-art eCard strategies with Near Field Communication (NFC) technology components. This would make it possible for NFC-enabled mobile phones to become part of the innovative ID card system and to be used as a trustworthy environment for transmitting data.

A persistent approach in an online world marked by availability no matter where no matter when – this is also the case when it comes to overcoming the restrictions of national eID concepts in heterogeneous IT landscapes. With this in mind, the interoperable pilot applications by the EU's *STORK (Secure Identity Across Borders Linked)* research project, for instance, will be interesting. The eCard API framework developed in Germany could provide important impetus here.

Conclusion

Beginning in November 2010, the new functions of the German ID card will provide German Internet users with an online identity. What goes without saying in the real world can hence provide greater security, clarity and trustworthiness in the world of the Internet too.

"This new ID card is the most secure electronic ID card available on the market," German Minister of the Interior Thomas de Maizière noted in June of this year when he visited Bundesdruckerei. He hoped that as many companies as possible would pave the way for their customers to use this new online communication and hence actively contribute towards greater efficiency, convenience and security on the Internet.

Identity and
Security Management

Security Analysis of OpenID, followed by a Reference Implementation of an nPA-based OpenID Provider

Sebastian Feld · Norbert Pohlmann

Institute for Internet-Security
Gelsenkirchen University of Applied Sciences
{feld | pohlmann}@internet-sicherheit.de

Abstract

OpenID is an open, decentralized and URL-based standard for Single Sign-On (SSO) on the Internet. In addition, the new electronic identity card ("Neuer Personalausweis", nPA) will be introduced in Germany in November 2010. This work shows the problems associated with OpenID and addresses possible solutions. There is also a discussion on how to improve the OpenID protocol by the combination of the nPA respectively the Restricted Identification (RI) with an OpenID identity. The concept of an OpenID provider with nPA support will be presented together with its precondition. The added value created by the combination of the two technologies nPA and OpenID in different directions is discussed.

1 OpenID as a standard for SSO on the Internet

1.1 Problem

Today, users of IT systems in both the private and the business environment have to memorize more and more access information.

In the private environment this arises from the fact that more and more services move into the Internet. The served applications range from e-mail clients and office suites to social networks. There is a login (the claim and the subsequent proof of identity) in almost every service before it can be used. This becomes a problem if a user chooses too short or simple passwords, uses the same password for different services (for convenience) or writes down the passwords.

But even in business environment, employees have to take care of the subject Identity Management (IdM) and its implications. Through the personal use of services an employee will perform various logins often several times a day. Examples are the login to the operating system, to customer databases and e-mail accounts or the use of the corporation's Internet. A company may establish password policies that define a minimum length for certain passwords or the need to change them at regular intervals. According to experience an increase in security often leads to a decline in user friendliness or efficiency as well. In addition, there are costs resulting from non-productive time (an employee returns from vacations and forgot the password), or the operation of a user help-desk (a central place to restore forgotten passwords amongst others).

There are different remedy approaches for the problem described. This work deals in particular with the idea of Web Single Sign-On (Web SSO) and the so-called strong authentication. On Web SSO there is only one identifier and a unique authentication using, for example, a strong password. The disadvantage is the single point of failure (the identity manager's service) and the urgent risk of phishing. OpenID is an example of a Web SSO protocol. On strong authentication (also multi-factor authentication), multiple factors like knowledge, possession and property are used to determine identity. A classic example is the use of smart cards with digital certificates. A concrete implementation of this strategy is the eID feature of the new electronic identity card in Germany.

1.2 Overview of OpenID

OpenID is an open, decentralized and URL-based standard for SSO on the Internet [ReRe06]. In version 2.0 of the specification (since 2007), a user can freely choose both the identity and the identity manager [ReRe07]. The identification of a user takes place via the proof of the possession of a URL, called OpenID identity.

The great benefits of Web SSO in general, and OpenID in particular is the one-time login at the identity manager (OpenID provider, OP) and the subsequent use of any OpenID-supporting services (relying party, RP). The credentials of a user (client, C) are not longer deposited at many points on the Internet, but only at a central and trusted authority, the OP. Consequently, the digital identity of a user is no longer distributed and redundant, there is only one identifier – the OpenID identity (Identifier, I).

The biggest danger in context of OpenID is the high vulnerability to phishing when using passwords. If an attacker acquires the password of an OpenID identity, all connected services are available to him or her. This can be done, for example, through phishing or by the fact that a user chooses a weak password. Another problem is the possibility of profiling on the part of the OP. The OP knows both the services utilized by the user and the frequency of use and thus could sell these information as user profiles.

1.3 Course of the protocol

The execution of OpenID consists of seven steps which are described more detailed below (see Figure 1):

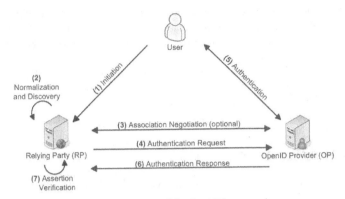

Figure 1: Course of the OpenID protocol

Initiation is the transfer of the user-chosen identifier to the relying party which starts the login process. A user calls the website of the service provider (RP), and names only an OpenID identity (the identifier) instead of a user name and password. An example could be *https://openid.internet-sicherheit.de/johnDoe*. The submission of the HTML form to the RP ends the first step.

Normalization/Discovery describe the process by which the relying party converts the OpenID identity entered by the user in a standardized form on the one hand and obtains information about the responsible OpenID provider on the other hand. The RP starts with normalizing the identifier entered by the user (see [BeFM05], chapter 6). An example is the addition of a missing schema such as *https://* to *openid.internet-sicherheit.de/johnDoe*. Subsequently, the RP executes the Discovery in which the information needed for generating an authentication request are determined. The XRDS or HTML document identified by the Discovery contains information about the location of the OpenID service on the part of the OP (OP Endpoint URL), the version of the supported OpenID protocol (Protocol Version), the name of the claimed identity (Claimed Identifier) and an alternative representation of the identifier (OP-Local Identifier).

Association Negotiation (optional) establishes a communication link with secured integrity between relying party and OpenID provider. RP and OP negotiate a shared secret in order to digitally sign and verify subsequent OpenID messages. If a RP is not capable of creating or saving associations (optionality of this step), the so-called "stateless mode" is used. For this, the OP creates a private secret for signing OpenID messages. The RP verifies messages received through direct communication with the OP (see [ReRe07], chapter 11.4.2).

Authentication Request is the request of the relying party to the OpenID provider to authenticate the user. The RP forwards the user's web browser together with the OpenID authentication request to the OP.

Authentication is the actual verification of the user's identity. The OP checks whether the user is in possession of the OpenID identity and whether he or she wishes to perform the current authentication. The characteristic of the user's authentication is not specified in the standard ([ReRe07], chapter 3). The responsibility is entirely with the OP, on whose statement a RP has confidence in. The execution of authentication is effectively outsourced. These days the combination of user name and password is a common mechanism for authentication.

Authentication Response is the response of the OpenID provider to the relying party together with the statement whether the user's authentication was successful or not. For this purpose, the OP forwards the user's web browser with a positive or negative response to the RP.

Assertion Verification is testing the integrity of the received authentication response by the relying party. The RP reviews the OP's response using the previously negotiated association or via direct request (stateless mode). In case of a correct and positive response from the OP the user is successfully logged in to the service of the RP.

1.4 Possible fields of application

The protocol OpenID, originally arisen from the "blogosphere", can be used for private or commercial websites and in business environment as well.

Personal websites created with content management systems or blog software such as Drupal, Joomla, TYPO3, WordPress, and the like, can be made OpenID-enabled using plug-ins. From now on, a user can not only use authentication methods offered by the software, but in addition the methods of the applied OpenID provider. The administration of personal websites or blogs can therefore easily be secured with multi-factor authentication if this is offered by the OP.

Commercial service provider on the Internet can offer various authentication methods as well through the integration of an OpenID interface. In addition, the user's inhibition to login is reduced and the registration is accelerated respectively made unnecessary. The service provider offers the user a direct login, in case he or she has an OpenID identity. The chosen OpenID identity is integrated in the list of registered users and also defined as the visible user name. Furthermore, the service provider can request additional user information from the OpenID provider such as the e-mail address. The user can grant or refuse this request.

But even in business environment, the use of OpenID is conceivable. A company defines a closed domain (for example the websites and services of the intranet) and a dedicated identity manager (the OpenID provider). From now on, employees no longer login to each service and each application individually, but centralized using the company-wide OpenID identity.

2 Security evaluation of using OpenID

2.1 The main threats: Phishing and profiling

The OpenID protocol is highly vulnerable to phishing. In step "Authentication Request" the user is forwarded from the relying party to the OpenID provider via a simple HTTP redirect. There are two basic categories of phishing attacks.

On the one hand phishing is possible by a relying party. A malicious RP does not forward the user to the "correct" OP, but to an imitation which is also under the control of the attacker. The appearance of the original OP can be copied using proxying. The user enters his or her credentials on the fake OP (the phishing happens), whereby a take-over of the OpenID identity through the attacker is possible.

On the other hand a phishing attack is possible by a malicious or compromised URL-host. The user's OpenID identity does not necessarily need to be at the responsible OpenID provider, but can be located at any other host (the URL-host). It is only important that the user controls the URL. An attacker has to exchange the declaration of the responsible OP in the HTML tags of the OpenID identity. In this scenario, the RP sends a user unwittingly to a wrong OP, which can potentially perform a phishing attack.

The use of strong authentication is a remedy for the main threat of OpenID, "phishing". An attacker can no longer intercept the secret between user and OpenID provider, if the user utilizes, for example, the new German identity card.

The creation of user profiles is a further problem in using OpenID. The OpenID provider is a central authority for the user's logins. An OP can potentially monitor the user's activities on the Internet, as it has the knowledge of the services utilized and the frequency of use.

The knowledge of the used services is unavoidable, as the RP requests the OP to perform an authentication. This temporary data is always available. The human factor "trust" is of importance here. A trustworthy OpenID provider should convince users that its central position is not utilized for misuse of information and profiling. An OP should assure that no profiling is made using mandatory policies, terms and conditions and the like. These aspects can be verified via certification after Common Criteria or a publication of the source code, for example.

2.2 Additional risks and concerns

Basically, a user has to trust the chosen OpenID provider. Aspects of trust relate to the use of provided personal data, for example. A user should choose an OpenID provider which points out explicitly that the stored data is not used elsewhere. In addition, a user should determine which business model the OP follows. Another aspect of trust is the measure of the services' vulnerability. A user should consider whether the OP's offered security features are in accord with the own security awareness or not. The choice of the OP is an important step because from now on it is responsible for the security of the own digital identity.

Entering personal information is a security-relevant step as well. An OpenID provider can hold various information such as full name, birthday and the like and transmit them to relying parties on user's request. The protocol extension "OpenID Attribute Exchange" [HaBH08] can accelerate the registration process, for example. A user has to decide how much data he or she will provide. One possibility is an indication of numerous data, resulting in a complete user profile for a single digital identity. Alternatively, a user can specify only a pseudonym, if just the functionality of authentication is required.

A relying party may, depending on the implementation of the OpenID interface, be victim of a denial-of-service attack (DoS attack). An attacker declares a large file or a malicious script instead of a regular OpenID identity. The attacker hopes that the RP overstresses and limits or completely refuses the intended service by loading the entire file or running the script. As a measure against the abuse, a relying party can define time and data limits as well as restrict the allowed protocols and ports for the OpenID identity.

To establish a communication link with secured integrity, RP and OP negotiate a shared secret (the association). To avert a man-in-the-middle attack (MITM attack) on OpenID messages sent, the exchange of the shared secret and, whenever possible, all communication should base on transport encryption (e.g. SSL/TLS).

At each authentication request a RP communicates a kind of URL (the so-called realm) to the OP, for which the request is valid. With this realm a user can determine that he or she trusts this RP and grants future authentication requests automatically. A malicious RP can effect by specifying an overly general realm (e.g. *http://*.de*), that henceforth all authentication requests from relying parties with a certain domain (in this case a German top-level domain) are granted automatically. An OpenID provider should restrict the use of the wildcard * well directed. In addition, it is advisable that the automated trust should not be utilized by users and not be offered by OPs.

The step of the actual authentication is, as described, particularly vulnerable to phishing attacks and profiling.

A positive authentication response can be the target of a replay attack. An attacker intercepts the message of a successful authentication (the redirect) by sniffing. Inserting the message anew causes the authentication of the attacker as the victim. The OpenID specification recommends the use of nonces (number used once) and timestamps as a countermeasure against replay attacks [ReRe07]. An OP integrates nonces into the authentication response in order to make it unique. A RP accepts responses only if the nonce contained is unknown so far. If a RP receives a response with a nonce already used, the message will be discarded suspected of a replay attack. Timestamps can also be used to restrict the period between authentication request and response. Through this, too old answers will be discarded. Furthermore, the period for holding nonces already used is shortened, saving the RP's resources. The fact that an attacker could be "faster" than the victim is a problem. During a MITM attack, an attacker can intercept the victim's redirect to the OP, reject it and execute it instead of the victim (see [TsTs07]).

The step "assertion verification" is of great importance for a relying party, as it checks the integrity of the authentication response. A RP should verify that it accepts no two authentication responses with the same nonce (replay attack). Furthermore, it should determine whether the responding OpenID provider is authorized to provide assertions for the confirmed identity. This leads the RP to perform a new discovery on the identifier of the response. If the OP of the authentication request is equal to the OP of the determined information using discovery, the authentication request is legitimate.

Another attacking scenario focuses on the Domain Name System (DNS). The name resolution is used several times on discovery and the redirections (authentication request and response). If an attacker is capable of, for example, manipulating the DNS cache of the victim, a seemingly correct redirect can lead the user to a copy of the OpenID provider. A phishing attack takes place. The use of strong authentication such as the eID feature of the German new electronic identity card prevents the interception of credentials.

When implementing an OpenID provider the procedure of "recycling" identities of an OP has to be discussed in order to deal correctly with any possible overlap. The services of a user who deletes an OpenID identity at an OP must not be used by another user, who then registers this exact identifier.

3 The new identity card (nPA) in Germany

3.1 Overview of the nPA

The new identity card ("Neuer Personalausweis", nPA) will be introduced in Germany on November 1, 2010. It supports the Federal Government's eCard strategy, which was decided on March 9, 2005 by the Federal Cabinet. Thus, the nPA is part of the nationwide introduction of the use of smart cards in the federal administration. The eCard-API-Framework is a technical frame for implementing the eCard strategy and is specified in the technical guideline BSI TR-03112 of the Federal Office for Information Security (BSI) [BSI10b]. The basic goal is to expand the conventional use of the identity card to the electronic world, thus enabling a secure and legally binding communication on the Internet [Marg09].

The new ID card has the size of a credit card (form factor ID-1), so it visually and physically differs to the current identity card. In addition, a contactless chip (RF chip) of the interface ISO 14443 is integrated, which communicates by radio with an RF reader. The chip's three electronic functions are described briefly below.

The first functionality "ePass" consists of the well-known identity determination as with the current ID card. A person attests to another person that he or she is actually the one he or she claims to be. The biometric feature is designed as an exclusive sovereign application in which a digital photograph and optionally two fingerprints can be stored on the card. This biometric identity function together with cryptographic mechanisms and optical security features on the card body ensure an increased protection against counterfeiting [Reis09].

The second functionality "online authentication" represents the electronic identity verification (also: eID feature). A mutual authentication between two communication partners is realized over the Internet, resulting in both parties knowing with whom they communicate. The right on informational self-determination was included because only the user decides whether a service provider can access certain data inside the nPA or not [Reis09]. This feature is intended for eBusiness and eGovernment.

The third functionality "qualified electronic signature" (QES) in accordance with the German Signature Law (SigG) is also intended for eBusiness and eGovernment. A QES represents the equivalent of a handwritten signature in electronic legal and business processes [Marg09]. This functionality must be enabled with costs on the nPA.

The data's authenticity and integrity must be ensured both in stored form and during the transmission. The mechanism Extended Access Control (EAC) is to implement these requirements. The protocol aims at ensuring that only authorized readers can access the personal and biometric data of the nPA. The mechanism EAC described by the German BSI is similar to the encryption protocol TLS, and consists of three protocols, "Password Authenticated Connection Establishment" (PACE), "Terminal Authentication" (TA) and "Chip Authentication" (CA). PACE is a procedure that permits a reader to access the radio channel to the nPA after entering a correct PIN. Technically this is an encrypted Diffie-Hellman key agreement (see [BSI10a], chapter 4.2.1). In TA the permissions of the reader are checked by means of a challenge-response procedure (see [BSI10a], chapter 4.4.1). Finally, CA is the process of examining the chip's authenticity and the implicit authentication of data supplied by the chip. From cryptographic point of view, this is a Diffie-Hellman key agreement with a static chip key (see [BSI10a], chapter 4.3.1). Just if all three procedures (PACE, TA and CA) of the mechanism EAC are completed, a secure and encrypted end-to-end-channel is established.

When verifying an identity in the electronic world, the check of an document's authenticity is performed using appropriate cryptographic verification methods (see the method EAC just described). This represents the analogy to the visual inspection of the security features in the real word. Instead of comparing the facial image, a secret PIN is required to be entered. The PIN is used for local activation of the ID card's electronic features and therefore is not transmitted over the Internet. The mutual authentication of communication partners is fully completed, after the service provider proved its identity through the so-called terminal certificate. This certificate contains information regarding the validity, the owner, the corresponding public key as well as information about the data the service provider is allowed to read from the nPA's chip. The certificate is issued by a governmental authority ("Vergabestelle für Berechtigungszertifikate", VfB), after a necessity test has confirmed the legitimate interest of personal data.

3.2 Course of an online authentication

Below the course of the functionality "online authentication" is explained (see Figure 2), since it will be found in connection with the yet to be explained OpenID provider. It is considered an exemplary scenario in which the user performs a registration to a service provider, including the first and last name is read from the new identity card.

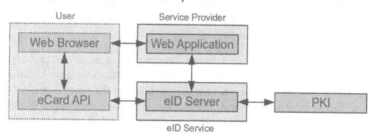

Figure 2: Course of an online authentication, based on [BSI10b], Figure 4

The user directs his or her web browser to the service provider's web application and calls a script which offers a registration using the nPA. The service provider is in possession of a valid terminal certificate which states that the first and last name of a user can be read for registration purposes. The need for the information to be read has been demonstrated when applying for the certificate in the appropriate governmental agency. Then the web application contacts the eID server. The eID server is a simple interface for web applications and encapsulates the complexity of electronic authentication [BSI10b]. Specifically, this means that the eID server will perform the concrete communication with the nPA. The service provider instructs the eID server to read the nPA's information using its terminal certificate and transmit them as a response. For this, the eID server sends certain information to the web application that will be forwarded directly to the user's web browser. This information leads to the invocation of the so-called "AusweisApp" (formerly "Bürgerclient") on the part of the user's PC. AusweisApp is a middleware that implements the communication between card reader, nPA and eID server. This is realized through the eCard-API. The user lays down the identity card on the connected card reader and confirms the current transaction (in this case the reading of first and last name) by entering the secret PIN.

AusweisApp now performs the interaction between nPA and eID server. The information – in this example the user's first and last name – are subsequently available on the eID server. In the meantime, the service provider's web application asks at regular intervals, whether there is a response on the request at the eID server or not. If there is a response, the eID server securely transmits the information to the web application. The web application may use the information for the business logic which is, in this example, the continuation of registration using the identity card's original data.

3.3 Recognition via Restricted Identification

The nPA's specifications provide the recognition of an already registered user. The non-ambiguous identification using the ID card's serial number is legally not permitted in Germany, so the sector-specific identification (Restricted Identification, RI) was introduced.

The RI has two special properties (see [BSI10a], chapter 2.1.5): On the one hand, the RI of a chip is unique within a sector. This means that a user will be recognized without knowing the actual identity. On the other hand, practically it is impossible to connect the RI of a chip between two sectors. This means that accumulated RIs cannot be compared with those of other services and therefore no associations of persons can be made beyond application boundaries.

The protocols CA and TA must have been successfully carried out in order to read the RI. Thus, there is a mutual authentication. The actual protocol for calculating the RI is a key exchange based on Diffie-Hellman algorithm.

4 An nPA-based OpenID provider (OP)

4.1 Fundamental Concept

An OpenID provider supporting the German new ID card was designed and implemented in the course of this work. The realization is based on two basic ideas.

The first idea covers the proof of the possession of a URL, thus the process of authentication. A user no longer logs in using a user name and password combination prone to brute-forcing and phishing in particular, but by means of strong authentication. Specifically, the nPA's eID feature is accessed. When registering an OpenID identity, the chip's Restricted Identification (RI) is linked with the OpenID identity. The only information of the identity card read out – the RI – is used only to recognize the user and never leaves the OP.

The second idea describes the OP's proxy functionality for the new Identity card. Using the OpenID interface will allow service provider without a terminal certificate to use the eID feature. A user can utilize a strong authentication also at service provider that do not have the necessary financial or organizational resources for the deployment of an eID interface. There are several possible scenarios: "Small" web services without the required resources, closed systems in intranets, but also private applications such as blogs can be designed nPA-compatible using an appropriate OpenID interface.

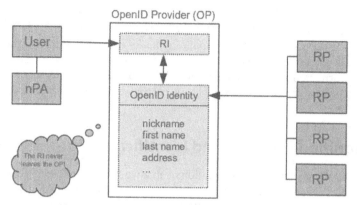

Figure 3: Interface online authentication and OpenID

The schematic connection of the RI to the OpenID identity or rather the interaction of user, OpenID provider and service provider is shown in Figure 3.

4.2 OP's communication sequence

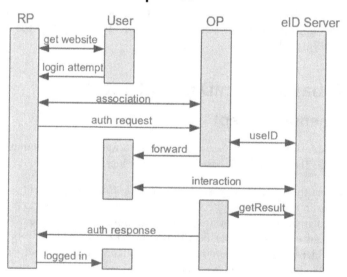

Figure 4: Communication sequence of a login attempt, based on [BSI10b], Figure 6

Figure 4 shows the communication sequence when a user attempts to login to a web service using his or her OpenID identity. The user calls the login form of the service and just enters his or her OpenID identity. After service provider (RP) and OpenID provider (OP) have negotiated a shared secret (the association), the RP sends an authentication request to the OP. The OP contacts the eID server (function "useID") and applies for reading the Restricted Identification (RI) from the user's nPA. The eID server responds with information that the OP will forward directly to the user. The interaction between eID server and user takes places. The user confirms the reading of the RI and enters a secret PIN. The OP checks periodically, whether the results of the requested action are already available (function "getResult"). If the result is available the determined RI is used to authenticate the user and the OP sends a positive or negative authentication response to the RP. Depending on the result, the service can consider the user to be logged in from now on.

4.3 Precondition for user and services

The integration and use of an OpenID provider with nPA support is simple.

From the user's view only the method of authentication changes. The user has still to prove that he or she actually is in possession of the OpenID identity. For this purpose, a strong authentication based on the nPA is performed instead of requesting a password. The RI read out from the nPA never leaves the OP. The principles of data avoidance and data economy are met.

Service provider need to integrate an appropriate interface into their application in order to use OpenID. Depending on the application's general implementation (modularity, and the like) the integration is relatively little extensive. There are libraries for various programming languages, so that the OpenID interface can be implemented quickly. There are no additional costs coming up to the service provider, since no other conditions have to be fulfilled beside the integrated interface.

In order to use an OpenID provider with nPA support, a service provider needs not to make other modifications. Such an OP does not only allow "outsourcing" of authentication, but also the use of the nPA's eID feature via the proxy functionality.

4.4 Added value in different directions

OpenID has the overall value that a user has to prove his or her identity at only a single point. The authority of authentication can be selected more consciously and the effort for a secure configuration can be concentrated. There is only one identifier and one set of credentials to be secured.

The integration of the eID feature as an OP's authentication method create added value in different directions.

From the perspective of the OpenID protocol the authentication, which is not treated in the specification, is made more secure. The user is no longer able to choose weak passwords (too short, easy to guess, etc.) through the use of the nPA. Furthermore, the biggest problem of OpenID when using a user name and password combination, "phishing", no longer exists. On the one hand no secret is sent over the Internet when using multi-factor authentication with the nPA. On the other hand there is an authentication of the OpenID provider through the eID feature. Only an OP which is in possession of a valid terminal certificate is able to read information from the nPA – in this case the Restricted Identification (RI).

A user gets the added value that him or her is not only provided an infrastructure for Web SSO, but also for multi-factor authentication. Since the existing nPA is used, no additional smart cards or readers are required. With the OpenID provider's terminal certificate, a user can verify the identity of the OP.

One advantage from the perspective of the new identity card is a certain degree of "internationalization" of the eID feature. Basically, the nPA's use is intended for applications of German service provider. Service provider without a terminal certificate are not able to use the nPA for authentication, for example. A service provider just has to implement an OpenID interface to use the proxy functionality of an nPA-based OP. From now on, users with a German nPA can login to certain (international) services using that OpenID provider. The service provider can not read information from the nPA (not even the RI), but indirectly use the eID feature via the OpenID provider.

5 Outlook

Since the release of OpenID version 2.0 in 2007, there was a rapid development in terms of web standards. Besides OAuth, Facebook Connect or Google Friend Connect, many other "social" protocols have been established in the Web 2.0. The draft of "OpenID Connect" develops a new generation of OpenID. The protocol based on OAuth 2.0 is to simplify the implementation, make OpenID available for desktop applications and introduce other functionalities. It will be seen how the OpenID community will promote and substantiate this draft.

In relation to the new identity card only guesses can be made as well. The Federal Ministry of the Interior (BMI) has supported the introduction of the nPA through a centrally coordinated and an open application test. From November 1, 2010 only the new ID card will be issued. The reaction of the general population and the nPA's acceptance together with its functions are difficult to assess.

6 Summary

The issue of identity management on the Internet is increasingly important in today's world. And in conjunction with that, the need for verifying the identity must be made as safe as possible. Open standards for Web Single Sign-On, such as OpenID, offer a simple way.

The weaknesses of the OpenID protocol can be compensated by the use of the eID feature of the German electronic new identity card. By combining the two technologies added value are generated in different ways. On the one hand an OpenID provider with authentication using the nPA removes the greatest danger of OpenID "phishing". On the other hand the use of the nPA can be expanded, virtually internationalized, by the proxy functionality of such an OpenID provider.

The OpenID provider presented in this work will be the first of its kind – or at least one of the first – offering a combination of OpenID with the German new identity card. As currently almost all OPs provide just an authentication via user name and password, an OpenID provider with nPA support will be a welcome and also a safe alternative. Transferring a user to another OP is possible without problems through the decentralized architecture of OpenID.

References

[ReRe06]   Recordon, David; Reed, Drummond: OpenID 2.0: a platform for user-centric identity management. In: DIM '06: Proceedings of the second ACM workshop on Digital identity management. ACM, 2006, p. 11-16.

[ReRe07]   Recordon, David; Reed, Drummond: OpenID Authentication 2.0 - Final. http://openid.net/specs/openid-authentication-2_0.html, 2007.

[Marg09]   Margraf, Marian: Der elektronische Identitätsnachweis des zukünftigen Personalausweises. SIT-SmartCard Workshop 2009, Darmstadt, 2009.

[BSI10a]   BSI: Advanced Security Mechanisms for Machine Readable Travel Documents; Extended Access Control (EAC), Password Authenticated Connection Establishment (PACE), and Restricted Identification (RI); Version 2.03. Technische Richtlinie TR-03110, 2010.

[BeFM05]   Berners-Lee, T.; Fielding, R.; Masinter, L.: RFC 3986, Uniform Resource Identifier (URI): Generic Syntax. http://www.ietf.org/rfc/rfc3986.txt, 2005.

[Reis09]   Reisen, Andreas: Die Architektur des elektronischen Personalausweises. 11. Deutscher IT-Sicherheitskongress des BSI, Bonn-Bad Godesberg, 2009.

[HaBH07]   Hardt, D.; Bufu, J.; Hoyt, J.: OpenID Attribute Exchange 1.0 – Final. http://openid.net/specs/openid-attribute-exchange-1_0.html, 2007.

[TsTs07]   Tsyrklevich, E.; Tsyrklevich, V.: Single Sign-On for the Internet: A Security Story. BlackHat USA, 2007.

[BSI10b]   BSI: Technische Richtlinie eID-Server; Version 1.3. Technische Richtlinie TR-03130, 2010.

New Authentication Concepts for Electronic Identity Tokens

Jan Eichholz[1] · Dr. Detlef Hühnlein[2] · Dr. Gisela Meister[1]
Johannes Schmölz[3]

[1] Giesecke & Devrient GmbH
Prinzregentenstraße 159, 81677 München, Germany
{jan.eichholz | gisela.meister}@gi-de.com

[2] secunet Security Networks AG
Sudetenstraße 16, 96247 Michelau, Germany
detlef.huehnlein@secunet.com

[3] Hochschule Coburg
Friedrich-Streib-Straße 2, 96450 Coburg, Germany
schmoelz@hs-coburg.de

Abstract

The national funded project [BioP@ss] researches the possibilities of an IP based smart card interface based on the international smart card application interface standards [CEN 15480] and [ISO/IEC 24727]. Instead of the classical APDU based communication a TCP/IP based web service communication with the smart card is established. This solution offers the benefit that this interface relies on well established standardized Internet protocols and hence reduces the necessity of an intermediate middleware implementation which translates web service calls into APDU's. Additionally, we define a [SAML(v2.0)] profile, which allows the implementation of an Identity Provider directly on a smart card.

1 Introduction

In the area of electronic identity management there are currently two major European projects. While the EU funded project [STORK] is dealing with the interoperability aspects of the existing eID solutions in Europe, the national funded project [BioP@ss] researches new concepts for smart cards to enhance the performance and interoperability for the next generation of electronic identity tokens and electronic passports. The German part of the [BioP@ss] project is funded by the German Federal Ministry of Education and Research.

Within the [BioP@ss] project Giesecke & Devrient researches the possibilities of a new smart card interface based on a HTTP(S) communication using SOAP based web services as interface to the outside world.

Federated Identity Management solutions which are often based on the Security Assertion Markup Language (SAML) [SAML(v2.0)], are increasingly used in practice as they allow to implement Single Sign-On, facilitate the integration of individual Service Providers and heterogeneous national Identity Management solutions using so called Pan-European Proxy Services (PEPS) (e.g. [STORK]). Today's IDM solutions integrating with an eID offer the main drawback of introducing an Identity Provider entity, which may break the end-to-end security. Therefore we sketch a solution, how a SAML Identity Provider can be realized directly on a smart card.

The rest of the paper is structured as follows: Section 2 contains the necessary background and motivation. Within Section 3 we describe the Service Access Layer as a new smart card interface and introduce new concepts for authentication protocols based on web services. Section 4 proposes a new eID-specific SAML-profile. Finally, in Section 5 we draw conclusions.

2 Background and motivation

This section carries together the background information, which is necessary to understand the new concepts presented in the sequel.

2.1 Standardized interfaces in the context of electronic Identity Cards

During the last years, the smart card middleware standards [ISO/IEC 24727] and [CEN 15480] (European Citizen Card) have been developed in order to allow a Client Application to access arbitrary cryptographic tokens through a generic Service Access Interface defined in Part 3 of [ISO/IEC 24727].

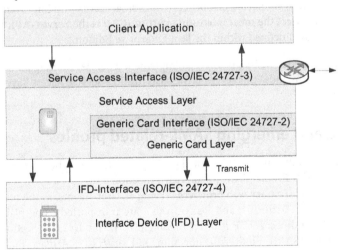

Figure 1: ISO/IEC 24727 Architecture

This interface comprises generic functions which allow to establish (cryptographically protected) connections to card-applications, manage card-applications, store and retrieve data, perform cryptographic operations, manage the related key material (so called Differential-Identities (DID)) and manage access rights for data, keys and services provided by card-applications.

The Service Access Layer (SAL) maps the generic requests at the Service Access Interface to AP-DUs of the Generic Card Interface defined in Part 2 of [ISO/IEC 24727], which allows a subset of the commands and options defined in [ISO/IEC 7816] (Part 4, 8 and 9). If the cryptographic token does not support those standard-commands directly they may be translated by the Generic Card Layer before they are sent to the Interface Device (IFD) Layer using the `<Transmit>`-command defined in Part 4 of [ISO/IEC 24727].

An important feature of the [ISO/IEC 24727] architecture is that it supports arbitrary authentication protocols using the generic `<DIDAuthenticate>`-function, which contains an "open type", which allows to "plug in" protocol-specific elements and hence support arbitrary authentication protocols.

The [ISO/IEC 24727] standard defines different possibilities how the components can be distributed among the network. In this paper we concentrate on the so called ICC-resident-stack configuration, which assumes that the SAL is implemented directly on the smart card. As a consequence, only a minimal IFD-layer and no GCAL at all is necessary.

The European Citizen Card standard [CEN 15480] extends [ISO/IEC 24727] with respect to specific requirements in the context of electronic health and identity cards. Furthermore it clarifies the communication processes in a distributed middleware scenario, where a server and a client PC together with an eID are involved.

2.2 Java Card 3.0 connected

The Java Card 3.0 ([JC30]) connected platform provides smart cards with improved connectivity. Within the BioP@ss project the most interesting part of JC3.0 is the Servlet-API, which is very similar to the Servlet-API defined within the Java Enterprise Edition.

With the help of the Servlet-API it's possible to implement a Servlet running on the card, which can react on HTTP commands. This serves as the basis to add a Service Access Layer Web Service to the smart card.

2.3 Existing and emerging SAML-related profiles

Currently there are the following SAML-related profiles, which need to be considered here:
- **Web Browser SSO Profile** [SAML-Prof(v2.0)] (Section 4.1)
  can be used with arbitrary web browsers serving as User Agents, as the relevant SAML-messages (`AuthnRequest` and `Response`) are transported using plain HTTP and the following bindings: *HTTP Redirect Binding* [SAML-Bind(v2.0)] (Section 3.4), *HTTP POST Binding* [SAML-Bind(v2.0)] (Section 3.5) or *HTTP Artifact Binding* [SAML-Bind(v2.0)] (Section 3.6).
- **Enhanced Client or Proxy (ECP) Profile** [SAML-Prof(v2.0)] (Section 4.2)
  requires that the User Agent supports Web Service interfaces in which the SAML-messages are received using the *Reverse SOAP (PAOS) Binding* [SAML-Bind(v2.0)] (Section 3.3) and send using *SOAP Binding* [SAML-Bind(v2.0)] (Section 3.2).

- *Holder-of-Key Web Browser SSO Profile* [SAML-HoK]
  is a forthcoming SSO-profile, which – unlike the two profiles above which only support
  the less secure "Bearer" subject confirmation method according to [SAML-Prof(v2.0)]
  (Section 3.3) – uses the so called "Holder of Key" subject confirmation method according
  to [SAML-Prof(v2.0)] (Section 3.1) and hence a cryptographic binding between the User
  and her assertion.
- *PEPS-interface specification developed in STORK-project* [STORK-D.5.8.1b]
  defines a SAML-based interface between the Pan-European Proxy Service (PEPS) in the
  country of the Service Provider (S-PEPS) and the corresponding PEPS located in the citizen country (C-PEPS). Section 7 of [STORK-D.5.8.1b] specifies a set of STORK-specific
  attributes, which seem to be unrelated to other existing attribute profiles.

3 The Service Access Layer as interoperable smart card interface

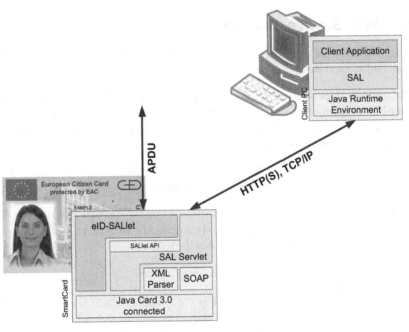

Figure 2: The SAL-on-card architecture

The SAL implementation can be realized on top of a Java Card 3.0 connected operating system
(see Figure 2). Hence, the SAL can be seen as a new interface to the smart card using well known
Internet protocols like TCP/IP and HTTP(S) for transport purposes. This approach highly increases the interoperability of the complete system. The communication is based on HTTP(S)
and the smart card offers a Servlet (SALServlet), which reacts on web service requests from the
outside world. The web service binding of the Service Access Layer is implemented according to
[CEN 15480] part 3.

Additionally, the SALlet concept (SALlet-API) allows an easy implementation and integration of new applets onto this platform.

4 New Authentication Concepts

ISO/IEC 24727-3 defines a set of generic authentication mechanisms. All these protocols assume the "classical" infrastructure, meaning that the smart card interface is APDU based and the middleware between the application and the smart card is responsible for translating high level Service Access Layer calls into APDU's. As a consequence, all these protocols assume after a successful protocol execution a channel protection by the means of secure messaging, which is only valid in terms of APDU's.

[CEN 15480] already contains a web service binding for some protocols. Additional web service bindings are available within [TR-03112(v1.1)]. In the following, we will investigate the web service binding of the Extended Access Control (EAC) protocol in an IP based smart card scenario.

4.1 EAC Web Service Binding

The web service binding defined in [CEN 15480] assumes a stack model, which is a combination of the Remote-loyal and Remote-ICC-stack.

In the ICC-resident stack scenario, the defined authentication data structures are not applicable. In the non-ICC-resident-stack scenario, the authentication protocol flow (PACE, Terminal Authentication and Chip Authentication) is coded in terms of APDU's and the APDU communication is encapsulated by the Service Access Layer.

In the case of the ICC-resident-stack the authentication protocol flow has to be encoded in XML-structures as input for a `DIDAuthenticate` command.

The necessary structures for the different `DIDAutenticate` calls are described in Figure 3, which are based – if possible – on the definitions provided in [TR-03112(v1.1)]. The protocol flow is according to the definitions in [TR-03110(V2.02)].

```
<complexType name="EAC_oncard_InputType_1">
        <complexContent>
                <restriction base="iso:DIDAuthenticationDataType">
                </restriction>
        </complexContent>
</complexType>


<complexType name="EAC_oncard_OutputType_1">
        <complexContent>
                <restriction base="iso:DIDAuthenticationDataType">
                        <sequence>
                                <element name="EncryptedNonce"
                                        type="hexBinary"
                                        maxOccurs="1" minOccurs="1" />
                        </sequence>
                </restriction>
```

```
                </complexContent>
        </complexType>


<complexType name="EAC_oncard_InputType_2">
        <complexContent>
                <restriction base="iso:DIDAuthenticationDataType">
                        <sequence>
                                <element name="DHPublicKey"
                                        type="hexBinary"
                                        maxOccurs="1" minOccurs="1" />
                        </sequence>
                </restriction>
        </complexContent>
</complexType>


<complexType name="EAC_oncard_OutputType_2">
        <complexContent>
                <restriction base="iso:DIDAuthenticationDataType">
                        <sequence>
                                <element name="DHPublicKey"
                                        type="hexBinary"
                                        maxOccurs="1" minOccurs="1" />
                        </sequence>
                </restriction>
        </complexContent>
</complexType>


<complexType name="EAC_oncard_InputType_3">
        <complexContent>
                <restriction base="iso:DIDAuthenticationDataType">
                        <sequence>
                                <element name="AuthToken"
                                        type="hexBinary"
                                        maxOccurs="1" minOccurs="0" />
                        </sequence>
                </restriction>
        </complexContent>
</complexType>


<complexType name="EAC_oncard_OutputType_3">
        <complexContent>
                <restriction base="iso:DIDAuthenticationDataType">
                        <sequence>
                                <element name="AuthToken"
                                        type="hexBinary"
                                        maxOccurs="1" minOccurs="0" />
                                <element name="RetryCounter"
                                        type="nonNegativeInteger"
                                        maxOccurs="1" minOccurs="0" />
                                <element name="EFCardAccess"
                                        type="hexBinary"
```

```xml
                                        maxOccurs="1" minOccurs="0" />
                            <element name="IDPICC"
                                    type="hexBinary"
                                    maxOccurs="1" minOccurs="0" />
                            <element name="Challenge"
                                    type="hexBinary"
                                    maxOccurs="1" minOccurs="0" />
                        </sequence>
                    </restriction>
                </complexContent>
        </complexType>


        <complexType name="EAC_oncard_InputType_4">
            <complexContent>
                <restriction base="iso:DIDAuthenticationDataType">
                    <sequence>
                        <sequence maxOccurs="unbounded"
                                minOccurs="0">
                            <element name="Certificate"
                                    type="hexBinary"
                                    maxOccurs="1"
                                    minOccurs="1" />
                        </sequence>
                        <element name="EphemeralPublicKey"
                                type="hexBinary"
                                maxOccurs="1" minOccurs="1" />

                        <element name="Signature"
                                type="hexBinary"
                                maxOccurs="1" minOccurs="1" />
                    </sequence>
                </restriction>
            </complexContent>
        </complexType>


        <complexType name="EAC_oncard_OutputType_4">
            <complexContent>
                <restriction base="iso:DIDAuthenticationDataType">
                    <sequence>
                        <element name="EFCardSecurity"
                                type="hexBinary" />
                        <element name="AuthenticationToken"
                                type="hexBinary" />
                        <element name="Nonce"
                                type="hexBinary" />
                    </sequence>
                </restriction>
            </complexContent>
        </complexType>


        <complexType name="EAC_oncard_AdditionalInputType">
```

```
<complexContent>
        <restriction base="iso:DIDAuthenticationDataType">
                <sequence>
                        <element name="Signature"
                        type="hexBinary"
                        maxOccurs="1" minOccurs="1" />

                </sequence>
        </restriction>
</complexContent>
</complexType>
```

Figure 3: Authentication Protocol Data Structures

4.2 Path Protection based on XML and WS Secure Conversation

In the case of the ICC-resident stack, the smart card interface is based on Web Services, which uses standard TCP/IP and HTTP as bearer. Hence the secure messaging mechanism has to be replaced by an analogous mechanism for web services. One possible solution is the usage of [XMLEnc] and [XMLSig] as in [WS-SecCon(v1.4)] for the protection of the communication channel. The session key generated within the authentication protocol execution of the EAC protocol can be used to derive the session keys used afterwards.

4.3 Path protection based on an EAC-TLS cipher suite

An alternative approach is the definition of a new TLS cipher suite, which re-uses the privacy concepts of the Extended Access Control protocol (EAC). This offers the benefit, that no additional binding of the different communication channels (TLS and SOAP) is necessary. The drawback is, that the existing XML-based SAL-API (e.g. `DIDAuthenticate`) is not applicable.

4.4 Integrating eID and SAML

Within this chapter we briefly discuss options for the integration of eID and SAML.

4.4.1 Naïve integration using Web Browser SSO Profile

An obvious integration approach is to use the SAML Web Browser SSO Profile [SAML-Prof(v2.0)] (Section 4.1) and only use the eID to perform the authentication. As the eID-specific part of the User Agent is activated by the Identity Provider in this case, the message flow is far from being optimal and especially susceptible to Man-in-the-Middle-attacks (cf. [EHS09]).

4.4.2 An ECP-based SAML-profile for eID integration

Because the eID-enabled User Agent already supports Web Service interfaces with SOAP and PAOS binding, it is more natural to use the Enhanced Client or Proxy (ECP) Profile defined in [SAML-Prof(v2.0)] (Section 4.2) and let the Service Provider activate the User Agent to avoid unnecessary and security critical redirects. For this purpose we define a few additional eID-specific elements, which may appear in the `<samlp:Extension>` element of `<AuthnRequest>` (cf. Section 4.4.2.1).

In order to avoid Man-in-the-Middle-attacks the proposed profile *may* be combined with the [SAML-HoK]-profile such that Man-in-the-Middle-attacks can even be avoided if there is no eID-specific CV-PKI, which allows the User Agent to recognize trustworthy TLS-certificates. If Man-in-the-Middle-attacks on TLS are already prevented by authentication protocol specific means, there is no need for using the mechanisms defined in [SAML-HoK].

Finally we propose to use the `<samlp:NameIdPolicy>`-element to indicate that a sector-specific identifier (cf. [STORK-D.5.8.1b], Table 25 and [LHP02], Section 3.2) is to be produced by combining some token specific "Source ID" with the `SPNameQualifier`-attribute provided by the Service Provider.

4.4.2.1 Authentication Request

As discussed above, it is beneficial to extend the `<AuthnRequest>` structure to minimize the communication overhead. In the following sub-sections we define extension elements, which may be placed within the `<samlp:Extension>` tag to allow an efficient SAML authentication process based on an eID token.

4.4.2.2 Requested Attributes

The following structure is somewhat similar to the `<AttributeQuery>`-element defined in [SAML(v2.0)] (Section 3.3.2.3) and simply contains a sequence of one or more `<Attribute>`-elements as defined in [SAML(v2.0)] (Section 2.7.3.1). Furthermore we propose to use an additional optional attribute `eid:Required` of `type="boolean"`, which may be present with a value of `true` in order to indicate that the requested attribute is required and that the User would need to cancel the entire authentication and identification process if it does not want to disclose this attribute.

```
<element name="RequestedAttributes" type="eid:RequestedAttributesType" />

<complexType name="RequestedAttributesType">
            <sequence>
                    <element ref="saml:Attribute" minOccurs="1"
                            maxOccurs="unbounded"/>
            </sequence>
</complexType>
```

This element is defined in [SAML(v2.0)] (Section 2.7.3.1) and specifies the requested attribute.

4.4.2.3 Authentication Protocol Data

The authentication protocol data structure may be used to include authentication protocol specific data in an `<AuthnRequest>`-element.

This element may contain arbitrary authentication protocol specific data and is specified as follows:

```
<element name="AuthenticationProtocolData"
        type="iso:DIDAuthenticationDataType" />
```

The type `DIDAuthenticationDataType` is defined in Part 3 of [CEN 15480] as abstract data type, which may contain arbitrary authentication protocol specific elements. This type is used as generic template for the specification of protocol specific data types such that it is possible to use `DIDAuthenticate` with arbitrary authentication protocols.

Once the User Agent receives an `<AuthnRequest>` containing an `AuthenticationProtocolData`-element it tries to find a matching token, which contains a DID with the required protocol and executes the protocol using the provided `AuthenticationProtocolData`. The result of this authentication step is then placed in the same element of the `<AuthnRequest>` structure, which is forwarded to the Identity Provider, which may reside on the smart card (cf. Section 4.5).

If additional protocol steps are necessary to complete the authentication protocol, the SOAP channel between the User Agent and the Identity Provider can be used to convey additional `DIDAuthenticate` commands directly. Note that in this case the User Agent must include appropriate Differential Identity Information in the `<samlp:Extension>` element as explained in Section 4.4.2.4.

Finally consider an example in which the Service Provider specifies that the EAC-protocol [TR-03110(V2.02)] must be used for authentication. Then the `AuthnRequest` from the Service Provider to the User Agent would contain an `AuthenticationProtocolData`-element of type `EAC1InputType` (see [TR-03112(v1.1)]), which would trigger the User Agent to obtain the user consent and perform the PACE-protocol with an appropriate eID. Furthermore the `AuthnRequest` message from the User Agent to the Identity Provider, which may reside on the smart card, would contain appropriate DID-information (cf. Section 4.4.2.4) and an `AuthenticationProtocolData`-element of type `EAC1_oncard_InputType` (see Figure 3), which triggers the execution of the local PACE protocol. Subsequent `DIDAuthenticate` requests are sent to the card to perform the remaining steps of the EAC protocol. Finally the requested attributes can be retrieved from the eID-token and an `Assertion` is produced, which is returned in the `Response`-element.

4.4.2.4 Differential Identity Information

If the Identity Provider needs to perform a complex authentication protocol and send additional `DIDAuthenticate` commands to the User Agent it requires corresponding Differential Identity Information, which may consist of the following elements, which are defined using types standardized in [CEN 15480]:

```
<element name="ConnectionHandle" type="iso:ConnectionHandleType" />

<element name="DIDName" type="iso:NameType" />

<element name="DIDScope" type="iso:DIDScopeType" />
```

`<ConnectionHandle>`
This element is of type `iso:ConnectionHandleType`, which is defined in [CEN 15480] and contains a handle for the connection to a card application. If the User Agent is able to recognize the type of a connected token and – possibly with assistance by the User – select an appropriate eID-token, which allows to perform the requested authentication protocol or fulfil the requested Identity Assurance Level, there may be a `ConnectionHandle`-element which should contain the `RecognitionInfo` child element when it is sent to an off-card Identity Provider.

`<DIDName>`
This element is of type `iso:NameType`, which is defined in [CEN 15480] and contains the name of a Differential Identity (DID) within the application addressed by the `<ConnectionHandle>`, which is to be used for performing (the remaining part of) a specific authentication protocol selected by the Service Provider or the User Agent.

`<DIDScope>`
This element is of type `iso:DIDScopeType`, which is defined in [CEN 15480] and may be used to remove ambiguities, if there are two DIDs (a local and a global) with the same name.

The `DIDName` and `DIDScope` element may only appear at most once in an `AuthnRequest`.

4.4.2.5 Response

In case of success the `Response`-element will contain an `Assertion`, which in turn contains an `AuthnStatement` and an `AttributeStatement`, which contains the requested attributes (cf. Section 4.1.2.1).

4.4.3 Identity Provider inside the eID-Token

Against the background of the novel concepts introduced above one may even envision a SAML-based Identity Provider, which is directly realized inside the eID-Token.

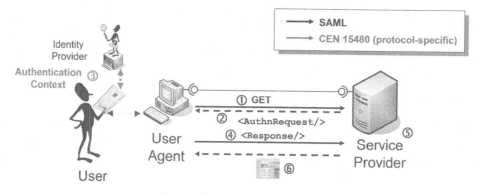

Figure 4: Scenario with IdP in eID

5 Conclusion

In this paper we have introduced a new smart card interface: The Web Service based Service Access Layer defined in [ISO/IEC 24727]. Since this interface builds upon existing well known and widely used Internet protocols it will facilitate a much better interoperability.

Using this as a basis, we have shown how the Extended Access Control Protocol can be implemented using this interface and how "secure messaging"-like trusted channels may be implemented in this case.

Additionally, we have discussed different options for the integration of current and future eID-tokens in SAML-infrastructures and in particular sketched a SAML-profile, which integrates the recent eID-standards [ISO/IEC 24727] and [CEN 15480], optimizes the message flow, avoids security problems and even allows the realisation of an Identity Provider directly on a smart card.

References

[BioP@ss] The BioP@ss homepage: www.biopass.eu

[CEN 15480] Comité européen de normalisation (CEN): Identification card systems — European Citizen Card — Part 1-4, Technical Standard (partly in preparation), 2010

[EHS09] J. Eichholz, D. Hühnlein, J. Schwenk: SAMLizing the European Citizen Card, in A. Brömme & al. (Ed.), Proceedings of BIOSIG 2009: Biometrics and Electronic Signatures, GI-Edition Lecture Notes in Informatics (LNI) 155, 2009, pp. 105-117, http://www.ecsec.de/pub/SAMLizing-ECC.pdf

[ISO/IEC 7816] ISO/IEC: Identification cards – Integrated Circuit Cards, Part 1-13 & 15, International Standard

[ISO/IEC 24727] ISO/IEC: Identification Cards — Integrated Circuit Cards Programming Interfaces — Part 1-6, International Standard (partly in preparation), 2010

[JC30] Java Card™ Platform, Version 3.0 Connected Edition, http://java.sun.com

[LHP02] H. Leitold, A. Hollosi, R. Posch: Security Architecture of the Austrian Citizen Card Concept, Proceedings of the 18th Annual Computer Security Applications Conference, IEEE Press, 2002, pp. 391-401

[SAML(v2.0)] S. Cantor, J. Kemp, R. Philpott, E. Maler: Assertions and Protocol for the OASIS Security Assertion Markup Language (SAML) V2.0, OASIS Standard, 15.03.2005, http://docs.oasis-open.org/security/saml/v2.0/saml-core-2.0-os.pdf, 2005

[SAML-Auth(v2.0)] J. Kemp, S. Cantor, P. Mishra, R. Philpott, E. Maler: Authentication Context for the OASIS Security Assertion Markup Language (SAML) V2.0, OASIS Standard, 15.03.2005. http://docs.oasis-open.org/security/saml/v2.0/saml-authn-context-2.0-os.pdf, 2005.

[SAML-Bind(v2.0)] S. Cantor, F. Hirsch, J. Kemp, R. Philpott, E. Maler: Bindings for the OASIS Security Assertion Markup Language (SAML) V2.0, OASIS Standard, 15.03.2005. http://docs.oasisopen.org/security/saml/v2.0/saml-bindings-2.0-os.pdf, 2005

[SAML-HoK] N. Klingenstein: SAML V2.0 Holder-of-Key Web Browser SSO Profile, OASIS Committee Draft 02, 05.07.2009. http://www.oasis-open.org/committees/download.php/33239/sstc-saml-holder-of-key-browser-sso-cd-02.pdf, 2009

[SAML-Prof(v2.0)] S. Cantor, J. Kemp, R. Philpott, E. Maler: Profiles for the OASIS Security Assertion Markup Language (SAML) V2.0, OASIS Standard, 15.03.2005. http://docs.oasis-open.org/security/saml/v2.0/saml-profiles-2.0-os.pdf , 2005.

[STORK] Secure idenTity acrOss boRders linKed (STORK) project website, http://www.eid-stork.eu, 2010

[STORK-D.5.8.1b] J. Alcalde-Moraño, J. L. Hernández-Ardieta, A. Johnston, D. Martinez, B. Zwattendorfer: STORK Deliverable D5.8.1b – Interface Specification, 08.09.2009, https://www.eid-stork.eu/ index.php?option=com_processes&Itemid=&act=streamDocument&did=960

[TR-03110(V2.02)] Federal Office for Information Security (Bundesamt für Sicherheit in der Informationstechnik, BSI): Advanced Security Mechanism for Machine Readable Travel Documents - Extended Access Control (EAC), Password Authenticated Connection Establishment (PACE), and Restricted Identification (RI), Technical Directive (BSI-TR-03110), Version 2.02, https://www.bsi.bund.de/cae/servlet/contentblob/532066/publicationFile/44802/TR-03110_v202_pdf.pdf , 2009.

[TR-03112(v1.1)] Federal Office for Information Security (Bundesamt für Sicherheit in der Informationstechnik, BSI): Technical Directive eCard-API-Framework, Version 1.1 of 15.07.2009, https:// www.bsi.bund.de/cln_156/sid_BFE35DE615DDE059B55587F30981D6BD/ContentBSI/Publikationen/TechnischeRichtlinien/tr03112/index_htm.html

[WS-SecCon(v1.4)] A. Nadalin, M. Goodner, M. Gudgin, A. Barbir, H. Granqvist: WS-SecureConversation 1.4, OASIS Standard http://docs.oasis-open.org/ws-sx/ws-secureconversation/v1.4/ws-secureconversation.pdf, 2009

[XMLEnc] XML Encryption Syntax and Processing, http://www.w3.org/TR/xmlenc-core/

[XMLSig] XML Signature Syntax and Processing, http://www.w3.org/TR/xmldsig-core/

A Simplified Approach for Classifying Applications

Lenka Fibikova · Roland Müller

Daimler Financial Services AG
{lenka.fibikova | roland.mueller}@daimler.com

Abstract

The following article focuses on the classification of information in applications. After a short introduction into classification, the readers will be confronted with the rationale for classifying information and media. Then the main components of a classification scheme, the process- and application-oriented approaches for classification and their advantages and disadvantages are discussed. Finally, a simplified approach for application classification is introduced and the experiences within a world-wide organization are demonstrated.

1 Introduction

Information classification, also known as information asset classification is quite an old practice of military and governmental organizations. These organizations usually dealt with information only intended for a restricted group of people and the disclosure of this information could cause damage to the respective country. For example, if a military operations plan would be revealed to the enemy then this could mean a loss of many people's life.

Merriam/Webster defines classification as a *"systematic arrangement in groups or categories according to established criteria"*. However, this definition does not provide a rationale for doing so.

In the military, classification was always tied to specific measures for protecting information. An important document needed to be locked away and only be transported to selected recipients in a guarded manner. The military only focused on confidentiality because the primary intend was to avoid disclosure to others. Categories in the military are Top Secret, Secret and Restricted and each of these levels of confidentiality meant different measures for protecting the information (e.g., methods of encryption). Non-classified information is considered to be accessible to everybody.

Information classification should cover the whole lifecycle of information starting with the creation of information, its processing and storage, its transmission and finally its destruction. For each of these stages appropriate handling measures are required.

Due to the fact that information per se is immaterial, the protection of information must concentrate on the respective representation or format of information which could be paper, electronic information in applications, verbal information and physical objects such as models or product samples.

2 Background

For an enterprise like Daimler or Daimler Financial there are important reasons for classifying their information:

1. It determines the level of protection that needs to be applied to information thus helping in two ways: On the one hand information which needs protection is adequately protected and on the other hand access to information not needing protection is not restricted by technical and costly means.

2. It helps to meet legal requirements for governance, risk and compliance and ensures that companies identify the information which falls under data protection and privacy legislation or specific industry regulations (banking secrecy).

3. It reduces operational costs because only the information which requires protection is protected by defined measures.

4. It enables access control mechanisms to function more effectively because access rights granted to groups of people can be easily implemented.

Therefore, information classification needs to be followed by two further steps:

1. How is information tagged to document its classification (so-called information labeling)?

2. Which measures and mechanisms have to be applied to ensure appropriate protection of the classified information (so-called information handling)?

These two topics will be left outside of the discussion.

3 Classification scheme

In order to be able to handle information in a standardized form, standardized classification schemes need to be used. A good classification scheme needs to satisfy two contradicting conditions:

1. It needs to be simple so that it can be understood by the information owners and user. Only if the users understand the scheme, the information can be classified and protected properly. And only if all users understand the classification scheme in the same way, the information can be handled properly by everyone.

2. The classification scheme must not be oversimplified; otherwise the protection measures will not be granular enough to achieve the economic advantages of the classification.

In the following we discuss a possible classification scheme considering three parameters: confidentiality, availability and integrity, which are the most commonly considered ones. Other parameters like reliability may be handled in a similar way.

3.1 Confidentiality

Probably everyone will agree that only a fraction of all information a company possesses is considered by the company to be available for the public. Figure 1 depicts this common understanding.

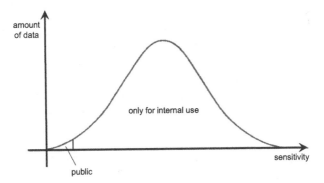

Figure 1: Classification scheme: Confidentiality - Step 1

This *public information* is easy to identify – it is all the information that can be found in the official company's brochures, on the official web sites, etc. Since each company has a specialized department, employees of which are the only authorized persons (or in small companies there is at least one such person) to release information for public use, it does not generally need to be handled in a special way.

The rest of the information needs a closer analysis. Figure 2 provides a possible characterization of the information (this is not yet a classification scheme):

- *Internal information that can be used unrestrictedly* within the company. This information may be found for example on the intranet, pin boards, in the employee mass mailings, etc. Similarly as for public information, there is only a limited number of persons that are authorized to "publish" information within the company.
- *Internal information with restricted use.* This is actually the most common type of information. It concerns information which employees use for their work. It is usually stored in various applications, on file servers, on exchange platforms (e.g., work boxes of Lotus Notes). This information should be available to the users only on a need-to-know basis, but there is no risk, if an unauthorized user gets access to fragments of the information (e.g., an individual print-out forgotten in the printer). Access to large amounts of such information should, however, be considered as a risk to the company.
- *Confidential information.* Information should be considered confidential if unauthorized access even to one piece of this information needs to be considered to be a risk. The reason might be legal requirements (e.g., protection of personal data) or internal interests of the company's management (e.g., plans for internal changes in an early stage). Since confidential information is created and used in various departments, it is very important that employees are aware that they are doing so.
- *Secret information.* This is information, unauthorized access to which could have damaging effects to the abilities of the company to run its business (e.g., business development plans in an early stage). This information is created in specialized departments, which are traditionally aware of the sensitivity of their information.

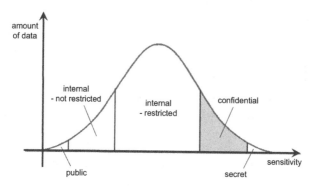

Figure 2: Classification scheme: Confidentiality - Step 2

The following table summarizes the above mentioned characteristics:

Type of information	Characteristic	Identification
Public	Released by specialized departments that are traditionally aware of they function	Easy: Internet, official communication, official brochures, etc., commonly carrying the logo of the company
Internal with unrestricted use	Released by specialized departments	Easy: intranet, pin boards, internal mailing lists
Internal with restricted use	Standard information	Easy: all other information with exception of specially identified (see confidential and secret)
Confidential	Created by various departments	Needs proper identification signs (labeling)
Secret	Created by specialized departments that traditionally are aware of their responsibilities	A standard user should not get in touch with such information – it should be handled individually

How to proceed:
- Ordinary information owners and users need to be aware only of two categories of information: internal with restricted use (usually named shortly internal) and confidential.
- Information users need to be repeatedly made aware of handling **confidential** information. Technical measures need to be defined and communicated to the information users.
- Protection of **internal** information may be handled by the standard technical measures. Information users should be requested not to forward any information to anyone outside of the standard processes and data flows without approval of their supervisor.
- With the other categories and protecting measures only the affected employees should be confronted.

3.2 Availability

Similarly as for confidentiality, we can analyze the protection needs also for availability (see also Figure 3):
- *Availability is not important at all.* This information is actually no more needed by the company and the company should consider removing this information in order to save the storage and processing capacities.

- *Standard availability needs.* Company's operation would be affected by their unavailability, but it would not have serious consequences.
- *Availability is important (sensitive).* Longer-lasting unavailability may have severe consequences to the company. This may have legal, contractual (information required for activities that have to be executed within a required time or at a particular time) or business reasons (information required within important business processes).
- *Availability is critical.* Any short interruption may have damaging consequences to the company and therefore adequate measures are required to prohibit business interruptions.

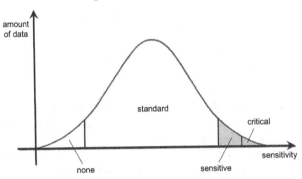

Figure 3: Classification scheme: Availability

How to proceed:
- Unnecessary information should be removed to save the storage and processing capacities.
- For availability-standard information, the standard technical measures should apply. Information users should be aware of which information they need to back up on their own.
- Information owners should be aware of their availability-sensitive and availability-critical information and initiate the respective controls. When availability is important (we deal with availability-sensitive information) then these controls must ensure that an outage does not exceed a defined period of time (so-called Recovery Time Objective or RTO) and that information is kept available for the respective application (Recovery Point Objective or RPO) with only restricted gaps. The technical measures must enable a fast recovery or avoid any downtime; however, the information owners should plan for alternatives when the IT is not available (business continuity planning). When availability is critical then we need to ensure that a system is available without any interruption and in those cases that an interruption comes up the business unit is prepared to overcome this interruption by other means.

3.3 Integrity

We can use the same approach also for integrity (see also Figure 4):
- *Integrity is not important at all.* This is the same unnecessary information as in case of availability.
- *Standard integrity needs.* Company's operation is affected, but it does not have serious consequences.
- *Integrity is critical.* This may be the case due to legal requirements (e.g., financial reporting for publicly traded companies) or due to internal requirements (e.g., internal policies)

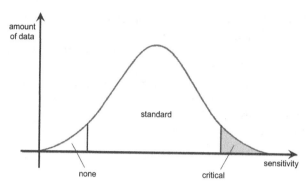

Figure 4: Classification scheme: Integrity

How to proceed:

- The same as for availability applies: Delete the unnecessary information.
- For integrity-standard information, the standard technical measures should apply. Logging of authorized changes is recommended.
- Information owners should be aware of their integrity-critical information. The technical measures must ensure that the unauthorized modification is not possible and all modifications are logged.

4 How to Classify Information

It is not easy to classify a piece of information on its own. The following questions arise when one tries to do so:

1. How small need the elements of information be that are going to be classified? Do we need to classify every piece of paper, every file, and every mail? Can information be grouped to reduce the amount of necessary classifications?

2. How to classify information that changes its classification? Information may be extremely valuable when it is newly created, for example when it is part of a new invention and it should not be revealed to the public. When this information is used for production then it is still of value but not anymore as much as before. And later, when the respective product is not produced anymore no protection is needed and its details are available to the public. How should this change within the information life-cycle be handled?

3. Where to document the individual classifications? How to identify the classification if the representation of the information does not allow for direct labeling (e.g., speech, binary outputs)?

The following sections introduce two approaches that enable to execute classification of all information in a smallest possible number of steps, respecting the life-cycle stage of the information, and in a way that enables reasonable documentation within existing inventories.

4.1 Process-oriented Approach

The second of the above-mentioned questions indicates that information classification needs to be classified within some context, which respects the life-cycle of the information. Business processes provide an ideal basis for specifying the life-cycle stage of the information. Moreover, processes not only reflect the time aspect, but also group information in a way, which is natural for the business people (in their role of the information owners) to understand.

Using the process-oriented approach, each business process is classified first. The information owners execute the following steps:

- Identify, which kind of information (information categories) is processed within the particular process. The input as well as generated information needs to be considered (e.g., personal data of the customer, credit information of the customer are the inputs and they are processed in the customer's credit rating, etc.).
- Classify each *information category* according to the confidentiality and integrity. As argued in Chapter 3, in a normal case the following classification categories need to be considered:
  - Confidentiality: internal, confidential
  - Integrity: standard, critical
  For both parameters, it must be ensured that the information does not change its classification within the process; otherwise a unique classification would not be possible. Consequently, changes in classification of information may only happen at the output of the process. If such a classification change is present, the particular process needs to be split in such a way that this condition is fulfilled.
- Identify importance of the particular process for the operation of the company. Here the following questions need to be answered? "If the process stops, after which time do serious consequences occur? Can stopping of this process get the company out of business?"
- Classify the *process* according to the availability as standard, sensitive or critical. For this, a company-wide policy should define the threshold, which downtimes are still considered as acceptable. All information for which its availability requirements exceed this threshold should be considered at least availability-sensitive. If its unavailability could get the company out of business, it is availability-critical.

After a process has been classified, all assets that support this process may inherit the classification (see Figure 5). For confidentiality and integrity only those information categories (and their classification) need to be considered that are actually stored or processed by the supporting assets. On the other hand, if a particular asset supports several processes, it should, of course, inherit the highest classification category for each of the three parameters – confidentiality, integrity and availability.

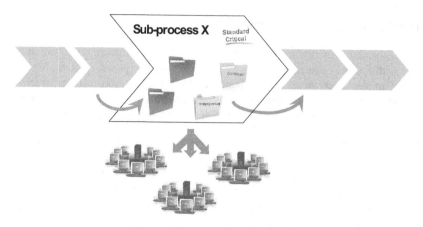

Figure 5: Process-oriented approach

At the beginning of the section we mentioned that the process-oriented approach provides answers to the first two questions – the grouping of assets and the time aspect. The third question still needs to be answered: With more and more companies operating in a process-oriented way, more and more companies create process handbooks describing the company-wide processes. The process handbook should be used to document the classification of the processes.

4.2 Application-oriented Approach

Companies that do not have process-oriented operation would need inconsiderable effort to identify all processes in order to be able to start with information classification. For those, the application-oriented approach will be a more appropriate one. This concentrates on business applications, since those are the source of almost all company's information.

Figure 6: Application-oriented approach

In the application-oriented approach (see Figure 6), the information classification is usually triggered by the application custodian (i.e. the IT department). The steps are similar to the process-oriented approach: The information owner needs to:

- Identify, which kind of information (information categories) is processed within the application. Again, the input as well as generated information needs to be considered.
- Classify each *information category* according to the confidentiality (internal, confidential) and integrity (standard, critical). The application inherits the highest classification category for each parameter.
- Identify processes that are supported by the application. The identification of the processes may be much more informal than in the process-oriented approach: The information owners need to answer the question, what consequences the unavailability of the application would have on their operations. Doing so, they need to consider also alternative methods, which may be used to keep their business processes working (e.g., using pen and paper), which may save resources necessary for creating sophisticated business continuity plans.
- Classify the *processes* according to the availability as standard, sensitive or critical. Again, the application inherits the highest classification category.

All outputs of the application inherit the classification of the included information categories. All assets that support running the application inherit the availability classification.

Documentation of the classification will take place in the application inventory.

5 Experiences

5.1 Application Classification

For five years Daimler Financial Services conducted application classification based on an application-oriented approach. The idea behind was to identify the potential monetary losses in cases where confidentiality, integrity or availability had been violated. The supporting media was a questionnaire consisting of three chapters for interviews on the three classification areas confidentiality, integrity and availability. The respective business owner was confronted with about 15 to 20 questions and was requested to estimate the potential monetary damage. In order to help him in judging the impact, a table with monetary thresholds for the different levels of confidentiality, integrity and availability was attached.

However, this approach led to endless discussions between business and IT about potential monetary impact. Any decision on the severity of an impact was based on estimation. For example, the impact that privacy-related customer data was revealed could cause a major damage and could as well be kept secret. And both results could be valid and there was no way to stop the struggle. These discussions made information classification activities a painful work. Therefore, only a small part of applications was successfully classified.

In the end, this approach which usually took at least half a day was rather a business impact analysis than an application classification.

We concluded out of this that we needed an approach which would avoid discussions but would provide results that are understood and therefore accepted.

5.2 Fast Lane Information Classification

In examining the application-oriented approach we decided that a good approach would be based on providing easy decisions for the people involved in the classification task. Therefore, we defined information categories and preset these categories with classification results on confidentiality and/or integrity. For availability we defined those business processes which have timely requirements related to availability

The only two tasks left to business and IT were to identify which information categories are processed or stored within a specific application and which business processes are supported by the respective application. Thus by selecting the information categories and business processes the preset values for confidentiality, integrity and availability could be determined.

5.3 The FLIC Tool

In order to support the information owners and application custodians in classifying their applications, ITF Information Security created an Excel-based classification tool called Fast Lane Information Classification (FLIC).

The FLIC tool has three features that significantly decrease the effort of application classification.

1. FLIC lists information categories and Daimler business processes which have specific classification requirements. The categories define the level of confidentiality and/or integrity and the processes the degree of importance with respect to availability.

2. The Daimler application inventory is used as the basis for information. This includes not only the identification information, but also supported processes for each application. The information is automatically filled into the tool.

3. The classification is calculated automatically. Since the calculation can reflect only the "normal" case, the information owners have the possibility to change the classification manually – however, they need to provide a reason for the change.

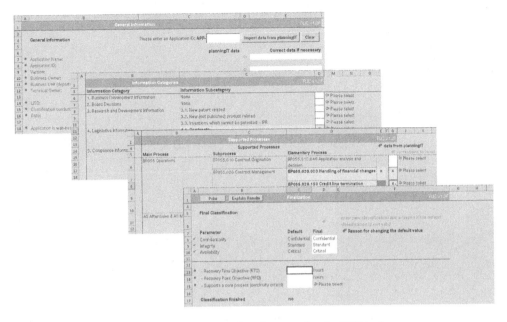

Figure 7: Information classification using the FLIC tool

Figure 7 shows the classification using the FLIC tool. It follows the process described in Section 4.2 in four steps:

1. *General information.* Identify the application and the persons involved in the classification (information owner, application custodian, local information security officer) – this information is partially prefilled from the application inventory.

2. *Information categories.* Identify information categories within the application that are confidential.

3. *Supported processes.* Identify availability-critical processes supported by the application.

4. *Finalization.* The default classification is calculated from the inputs of the step 2 and 3. Modification of the classification (if necessary) and approval by the information owner follow.

ITF, the IT organization for Daimler Finanancial Services, Sales & Marketing and Aftersales, has world-wide 2,500 applications. Within three months after the start of the classification project, more than 60% of all applications were classified. Since the information from the application inventory was automatically extracted and used for the classification, the project had a positive side effect of improvement of the application inventory data quality.

6 Conclusion

In summary we helped our business to fulfill a task which they had problems to achieve before. Within a short period of time (and by using a simple Excel tool), Daimler Sales & Marketing could classify its critical applications and document the respective results.

Technical and Economical Aspects of Cloud Security

Single Sign-on(SSO) to Cloud based Services and Legacy Applications "Hitting the IAM wall"

Marcus Lasance

Phillipssite 5, 3001 Leuven, Belgium
Verizon Business
marcus.lasance@verizonbusiness.com

Abstract

With the advent of the de-perimeterized organization and increased scepticism around 'Cloud Security' is SSO still a viable worthwhile goal for organisations?

Single Sign-On (SSO) projects are a special case of Identity and Access Management (IAM) projects. They are usually undertaken with the aim of increasing the user friendliness of Corporate IT systems' user log-on processes. This should result in abolishing the use of multiple username and password combinations the user has to remember and change at different intervals. The SSO aim should be achieved without jeopardizing information security in any way. Increasing user convenience in such a manner will increase user satisfaction with the IT department along with general productivity levels.

Cost control related to IT help desks resetting forgotten passwords should follow.

SSO can also help organizations address information security compliance requirements, through the central logging (and audit facilities) of all access attempts and authorization decisions granted in relation to the organization's restricted information resources. Sometimes compliance objectives are in fact the major business driver for SSO.

In the consumer space customer loyalty and retention rates are often cited as an important commercial driver for SSO projects.

With the advent of the de-perimeterized organization[1] and increased scepticism around 'Cloud Security' is SSO still a viable worthwhile goal for organisations?

This paper takes a closer look at special security issues arising when an organization attempts to create an Enterprise Single Sign-On (ESSO) solution that includes both legacy applications hosted within traditional organizational firewalls and a new breed of 'Cloud Based' solutions that are following the Software as Service (SaaS) model and therefore can be hosted with any number of Service Providers (SP) 'in the cloud'.

1 Examining the role of IAM as SSO enabler

When thinking about SSO and Information Security two conventional wisdoms often come to mind. The first is the concept of avoiding dependence on 'the weakest link' in your organizations defences. The second is the concept of not wanting to put all your eggs in one basket.

---

1 http://www.opengroup.org/jericho/deperim.htm

For the weakest link in protecting information assets read 'Username and Password' which, like no other authentication method, is highly vulnerable to social engineering attacks, malware key loggers and yellow 'post-it' notes left by lazy PC users for office cleaners to read.

In a homogenous single organization from an IT perspective the weakest link argument against SSO can be quickly countered by giving, as part of the project, all users a much stronger form of authentication. This usually means replacing 'Username and Password' with two factor authentication.

In other words, the bar is raised for everyone, without exception. This in itself can of course be a costly exercise, wiping out any potential cost savings of an SSO project.

Another question is: "Will all the business partners in a given federation be able to set the bar for information protection at the same high level?"

The question is not just related to the available budget in other parts of the federation, e.g. to purchase authentication tokens, but also a question of compatibility of security policies and audit capabilities between partners.

> *In the UK a 'fly on the wall' TV documentary recorded the unauthorized access of client financial records by call center employees from a marketing agency contracted by a well know high street bank. The call centre had a high staff turnover and was in fact 'recycling' a number of not individually assigned network access tokens to access client accounts. This is of course not the kind of federated SSO we want, as any audit log would prove absolutely nothing except that the bank was not really in control!*

The 'putting all your eggs in one basket' paradigm could be used to make a case against SSO, with the argument that if one individual computer system's security was to be breached at least the integrity of most other systems could be presumed still to be intact.

This is a very weak argument. How many users use the same username password combination for many of the corporate applications they access? For the simple reason they cannot begin to remember them all and writing them down is prohibited? The added protection provided by multiple sign-on(s) may be just an illusion!

2 No SSO without solid Identity Management!

As the example in the frame above illustrated, once SSO is enabled with a strong authentication form factor (RSA SecureID Token, PKI smartcard or OTP) it becomes of paramount importance to manage the users' entire life cycle with the organization. An ex-employee logging in with a token that was not decommissioned is still a security breach. This means, not only are we aiming to provide the right levels of access from day one with the organization and making the new employee immediately productive; we also need to ensure that access is removed the very instant an employee leaves the company, sometimes well before! The same applies to partner employees.

Based on our investigations, a number of data[2] breaches still originate from within the company, sometimes from disgruntled employees, sometimes unwittingly by current employees, who get tricked into downloading malware applets that log key strokes from passwords..

Role Based Access Control (RBAC) is an important mitigating factor of such risks. RBAC helps prevent the occurrence of 'role creep'. This is the often occurring situation, whereby during the course of their career within an organization employees tend to accumulate more and more access rights. This happens when access right for new roles are added to a user profile, but seldom removed when no longer needed.

The ability to introduce strict segregation of duties is a second benefit that should come from an RBAC project forming an integral part of any SSO or wider IAM project. Examples include purchasing managers not being able to approve their own purchase orders.

Looking more to IT roles, the person performing database back-ups does not require access to that database content as a user. So while he is allowed to make copies for safe keeping, he may not log into it and access sensitive data. In the context of IT, roles are also important in helping enterprises prevent default admin passwords on shipped devices to remain unchanged when such devices are deployed, as this class of credentials is especially prone to attack from malware. This area of IAM is often referred to as 'Privileged Account Management' and specialized vendor solutions exist that can be obtained from Verizon Business.

3 What makes Access Control 'in the Cloud' special?

The introduction of this paper already highlighted the fact that incompatible security policies between cloud partners can be an issue.

So can privacy issues. Will access to all event logs be given, when these are shared with other cloud customers and might reveal sensitive information about those other parties?

In this paper we limit ourselves to addressing technical issues like different communication protocols and encryption standards used.

A common term for these types of standards and the problems they try to solve is Federation.

Before we explain the concepts and standards around Federation it is useful to examine the situation organizations face when Federation is not required, because they have not truly begun the process of de-perimeterization. This state is sometimes called the 'moat and castle' model of the organization.

3.1 Conventional SSO Solutions

Until not very long ago, the bulk of SSO solutions on the market were designed to provide single sign-on to applications that on the whole reside within one and the same security domain.

SSO marketing terms like 'simple to install' and 'agent-less' are tell tale signs, that all such Web Access Control (WA) solutions do is examine the URL of the incoming browser request, look up

---

2 Verizon Business 2009 Data Breach Investigations Report

in a directory if a security policy is attached to it and execute the policy in the form of a simple 'grant' or 'deny' access decision.

A slightly more sophisticated form of access control uses session 'cookies' that are passed to agents that need to be installed on each web server of the organization, but does not require any client side software to be installed. Client side software plug-ins, often required to 'SSO enable' legacy applications, are usually a big turn-off for the IT department. This is due to the extra over-head this causes in desktop management, meaning locking down all work PCs to an approved specification and the right level of security patches like installed anti-virus software.

3.2 Access to non web based legacy applications

Of course not every business critical legacy application is necessarily web enabled. Because of the IT department's resistance to installing client-side software, to overcome this problem Citrix like terminal server solutions are dominating this end of the market. The user is in effect looking at a virtual desktop running on a server, which can be properly locked down and secured by the IT department, where a laptop might not.

3.3 Legacy Applications need user provisioning

Web Access Gateways providing SSO can be regarded as applications that escort users to the front door of an application. If it is a simple web page they want to look at, the user can see its contents, perhaps fill in a form, but not much more.

Most web-enabled corporate applications like ERM/CRM systems require further information to authenticate a user in a particular role. Some users have read-write access rights, but to only their own department's stored information. Others, like auditors, may search all departments but have read-only access. Legacy applications usually have information about all authorized users stored in specific user tables within an underlying Relational Data Base System (RDBMS). Users and their authorized roles do not appear out of nowhere. Traditionally they were created by a super-user, often someone in the IT helpdesk department. This is not good practice. It would be better to use an automated provisioning system in combination with a workflow tool and RBAC and put that responsibility back with the business where it belongs.

To allow the application to make its own authentication decisions, the Web Access solution can carry the necessary information attributes - like a unique username - in its HTML header. This header is formed when the Web Access gateway, which acts as a proxy for the real web server, redirects the user to their intended web application.

Note: Web Access Gateways generally do not create or delete users on target systems. This function is usually reserved for 'super users' in the business or administrative functions in the IT department. If user creation is automated, this is a function of provisioning systems and not generally considered to be part of an SSO project, but of a wider IAM project.

4 SSO to Web applications 'in the cloud' using federation

In our definition of cloud computing we will generally be talking about 'Private Clouds', that means outsourced IT applications where we have a business relation with the outsourcing provider and at a VPN like trusted connection to the Service Provider (SP). In the loosely coupled world of a Service Oriented Architecture (SOA) the problems we have seen connecting to trusted private clouds are only exacerbated.

A common factor between cloud applications is that they are generally well protected behind someone else's firewall. If the services were not provided by a reputable SP we would not want to do business with them in the first place! Thankfully some trust frameworks are emerging, so that we can start to form an objective opinion about the security policies and reputation of most public SPs.

Where we have some control over our own firewalls, we must assume that opening the necessary ports on other organization's firewalls - to allow automated user provisioning and deletions - will be severely restricted if not impossible.

As an IT industry this problem has long been acknowledged and standardized protocols have been created that allow the federation of Identities and access control policies. The relevant standards are:

- SAML
- XACML
- Liberty Alliance
- ADFS / WS-Security
- Information Cards/OpenID

It is important to remember that while the above industry initiatives provide a secure and standardized way to exchange user and role information, none of the above standards are designed to create a new user with the right access rights 'on the fly' at the target cloud system.

If we take the case of federation using the Security Assertion Mark-up Language (SAML), both the Service Provider (S)P and the Relying Party (RP) must install a Federation Server that supports the same version of SAML, which also has proven to be interoperable 'out of the box' in one of the leading Security Events' sand pits or interop demos.

Even after a new user has successfully been authenticated at the RP-end through a process of certificate exchange, the business partners will have to agree which other attributes can and need to be exchanged in the signed SAML header or subsequent back channel attribute requests over SSL. The privacy and other issues that need to be resolved before a successful federation can be set up must not be underestimated and can result in significant costs in the form of Professional Services (PS) charges.

When setting up a web of federated identity processes, each system or entity must establish trusted links with every other entity, creating a web of VPN connections. However, this complexity increases management overhead and limits the flexibility to leverage different specifications as new relationships are formed and dropped and cloud applications are added and removed from a portfolio of approved services.

Verizon Business PS has considerable experience in the setting up, testing and implementing of Federation Agreements between Business Partners.

By using Identity Managed Services – Web Access (IMS-WA), a completely outsourced IAM solution from Verizon, organizations can utilize the Verizon IdP as a single trusted link that all systems can leverage, much like a hub with spokes. Once a user is authenticated, the user can log in to any other federation-enabled service, including cloud applications like Salesforce.com and ADP.

5 SSO to Web applications 'in the cloud' using a User Centric Identity Management Framework (UCIF)

Verizon like many other global service providers has come to the realisation that for truly global web 2.0 types of clouds even the hub and spoke model of federation eventually will not offer a scalable or economical solution. This is often referred to as 'hitting the IAM wall'.

Verizon has joined forces with other global service providers to create the Open Identity Exchange (OIX). Along with the increasing acceptance of Information Cards and OpenID at social networking sites and services that are truly cloud based like GoogleDocs, comes the acceptance that, for some applications at least, there comes a limit to what can be achieved with a web of federation agreements and VPN tunnelling the cloud until it looks more like a bowl of spaghetti.

What is needed and what is emerging is a global identity meta system, where users are taking more and more responsibility for managing their own Identity affairs, including requesting access to the cloud applications they need to do their job. In doing this they will need to be backed up by a special kind of trust provider, also called an Identity Provider (IdP).

The ultimate aim should be that relying parties can stop hoarding silos of sensitive information about users, not essential for their core business processes. They now leave this for IdPs to worry about.

Protecting sensitive information is an expensive business for organizations and increasing regulation and audit requirements only adds to the burden.

From a macro economic and business perspective it makes sense to outsource this burden to a specialized IdP that can help enterprises collect and maintain the information which may be required for a full set of 'in house' identity and credentialing services, such as:
- Initial registration and verification of base identity data like name and address including the checking of government credentials like passports and e-Id cards
- Checking utilities (gas, water and electricity) provided to the individual's main place of residence
- Checking credit worthiness with credit agencies
- Checking where people geographically are and detecting anomalies in converging networks to help detect and prevent fraud.

- Checking professional qualifications with educational institutions and professional bodies to check an identity is licensed to practice in a restricted profession.
- Giving the user the ultimate control over what attributes of their identity are shared with Relying Parties.

Users that require access to cloud based services just present the SP with an Information Card containing signed claims and all the trusted attributes necessary to create a new account 'on the fly' or 'Just in Time'. Such claims could include role claims signed by an employer, professional claims like a license to practice signed by the professional body the user belongs to.

Identity Providers will also increasingly play a role in generating the audit logs for forensic investigations when things go wrong. For this purpose special audited Information Cards can be used. These can be compared with the event and access logs of the relying party in the cloud to extract relevant forensic data, while safeguarding the privacy of other cloud users.

The most successful SaaS providers in the cloud already are set up to consume Information Cards and OpenId as an alternative to SAML. All they need is a valid set of signed claims to give the user what they need and a commercial agreement (if not a 'free' service) about who will pay the bill!

The principle of 'minimum disclosure' means this could be as little as a verified claim the user is an adult, or a that a doctor is licensed to practice in a certain country.

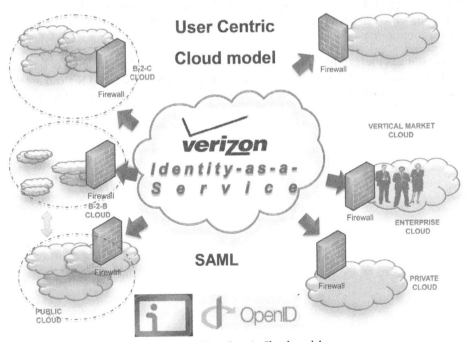

Figure 1: User Centric Cloud model

6 Conclusion

The complex account management and provisioning actions, necessary to achieve Single Sign-On (SSO) to an organisations' IT resources, were difficult enough to accomplish before the advent of 'Cloud Computing'. Easy availability of 'Software as a Service' means today entire departments are starting to use cloud computing resources, often without due consideration of cloud security concerns.

The access rights to privileged accounts, necessary to achieve Identity and Access Management by IT administrators, can often not be granted by cloud service providers who have to organise multi tenancy in their systems without jeopardizing security and privacy for their co-hosted customers.

The answer lies in the application of standards for user- and account provisioning, but also the realisation that in future identity must be seen as the central organizing principle for simplifying sign-on(s) in an increasingly complex digital world taking shape in the cloud.

Many experts believe privacy concerns can only be addressed by putting individuals back in charge of their own identities. This can mean 'just in time' provisioning and deprovisioning of accounts the user may have 'in the cloud' on the basis of proven identity claims supplied by trusted Identity Providers.

In the emerging global identity meta system, IdPs like Verizon Business will play a vital role in releasing the massive potential benefits for users and relying parties be they commercial organizations or governments.

By participating in the launch of OIX and the imminent issuance of different levels of assurance identities that can be used at an increasing number of Government and Social Networking sites, Verizon Business proves that also in this area of identity management for the cloud we intend to play a leading role.

Cloud & SOA
Application Security as a Service

Ulrich Lang

ObjectSecurity
Plug & Play Tech Center
530 University Ave, Palo Alto, CA 94301, USA

St John's Innovation Centre
Cowley Road, Cambridge CB4 0WS, UK
ulrich.lang@objectsecurity.com

Abstract

This paper introduces the concept of moving security and compliance policy automation for Cloud applications and mashups into the Cloud. This way, Cloud applications and mashups can be protected more seamlessly within the Cloud computing paradigm, and the secure software development lifecycle for Cloud applications is improved and simplified. The policy automation aspects covered in this paper include policy configuration, technical policy generation using model-driven security, application authorization management, and incident reporting. Policy configuration is provided as a subscription-based Cloud service to application development tools, and technical policy generation, enforcement and monitoring is embedded into Cloud application development and runtime platforms. OpenPMF Security & Compliance as a Service ("ScaaS"), a reference implementation using ObjectSecurity OpenPMF, is also presented. The paper argues that security and compliance policy management for agile distributed application landscapes such as Cloud mashups needs to be model-driven and automated in order to be agile, manageable, reliable, and scalable.

1 Cloud Computing

Cloud computing can be defined in simple terms as a style of computing where scalable and elastic IT capabilities are provided as a service to multiple customers using internet technologies [Gart09a]. NIST defines and categorizes Cloud computing in more detail (see [MeGr09]) Cloud computing is still a rapidly evolving landscape and there is considerable provider investment and hype around cloud computing, as many business models and ideas are rapidly emerging. It is becoming clearer that not all enterprise computing will move to the Cloud due to various constraints and requirements, but that suitable Cloud services will emerge that will replace the need for a number of in-house IT services. In the consumer world, this trend towards Cloud services is currently complemented by the uptake of thin client devices (e.g. tablets, netbooks, and smartphones). An important Cloud concept is that multiple Cloud services can also be integrated using so-called Cloud mashups. In simplest terms, a mashup is a way to obtain data from multiple sources and combine it in new ways to create a new solution. For example, using a mashup, internal company data of nearly any type can be combined and integrated with Web services, feeds, and just about any other outside information. A Cloud mashup shares many of the characteristics of SOA and web applications, with the exception that Cloud services integrated using mashups are per definition always hosted as a Cloud service. Mashup tools are application and data integration platforms that allow users to create such mashups using numerous data sources and has a graphical user interface used to simplify integration. Cloud computing promises many benefits, including reduced cost, increased storage, high degree of automation, flexibility, mobility, and less need to deal with IT 'plumbing'. As a general rule, it needs to be assessed for each case whether the benefits of Cloud computing are significant enough to outweigh the current shortcomings. There is a general observation that the return on investment grows with increasing scale of the Cloud and decreasing migration time. Also, security and compliance will play a critical role for government Cloud adoption.

2 Cloud Security & Compliance

Security is currently often stated as an inhibitor for Cloud adoption. According to Forrester [Forr10], in Q3/2009, around half of all IT managers in North America and Europe decided against the use of Cloud services due to security concerns. But in general, Cloud computing does not necessarily have to be any more or less secure than most other current environments; as with many new technologies, it creates new opportunities, but also new risks. The Cloud provider argument that security is inherently better because the provider will have more pooled resources and expertise to do security better than the user organization could is as skewed as the argument that Cloud security is inherently unachievable – the truth is probably somewhere in the middle and depends on the particular use case [LaSc10]. The Cloud Security Alliance (CSA) has produced a publication [CSA09] that details various governance and operational aspects of Cloud security, and an alternative categorization can be found in [Gart08a].

A number of general observations can be made related to Cloud security: As far as the responsibilities for security and compliance are concerned, the lower down the stack the Cloud service provider stops (e.g. PaaS or IaaS), the more security is the consumers responsibility. Also, Cloud mashups have significant security implications because information flows and resource usage need to be controlled across logical and geographical boundaries. And multi-tenancy (i.e. several users sharing common resources) implies a need for policy-driven enforcement, segmentation, isolation, governance, service levels, and chargeback/billing models for different consumer constituencies. Compliance reporting will also be a necessary Cloud feature.

3 Cloud Application Security & Compliance

Just as with traditional application security, Cloud applications need to be secured. The CSA identified the a number major Cloud application security aspects [CSA09], which are in line with many identified security concerns associated with web apps and SOA [LaSc08a]: In particular, Cloud computing and security affect the complete Software Development Life Cycle (SDLC), for example because the SDLC security must support Cloud application dependencies and agility. Also, Cloud SDLC must support the complex ownership, provisioning and responsibility of tools and services used to develop, test, and manage Cloud applications. Identity and Access Management (IAM) also play an important role for Cloud application security, and includes identity provisioning, authentication, federation, and authorization management. And compliance, which is often critical for Cloud, affects the SDLC, applications, data, platforms, and processes. A particularly challenging application security area (conceptually related to SOA) are Cloud mashups.

In the following, this paper specifically focuses on application policy automation, including the following aspects: policy configuration, technical policy generation using model-driven security, application authorization management, incident reporting, and automatic updates.

3.1 Authorization Management

The resulting high cost and complexity of maintaining a secure IT environment – and reliably updating when the agile IT environment changes – is frequently voiced as an adoption hurdle for Cloud (and also SOA) applications [Davi08, LaSc08a].

Authorization management, which is nowadays often categorized as part of Identity & Access Management (IAM), is a solution approach that involves the management and enforcement of access policies for all protected resources. Standards such as eXtensible Access Control Markup Language (XACML) [Oasi05] have emerged. XACML is a declarative access control policy language implemented in XML and a processing model, describing how to interpret the policies. The technical architecture components to implement this functionality are referred to as Policy Access Points (PAPs), Policy Decision Points (PDPs), Policy Enforcement Points (PEPs), and Policy Information Points (PIPs).

Authorization management plays a critical part of Cloud application security, and even more so for Cloud mashups, because different actors (e.g. users or Cloud applications) should only be able to invoke each others' services if they are authorized to do so in a specific situation based on security policies.

Authorization management becomes a challenge, especially when systems and participants get numerous, when interconnected applications evolve dynamically ("agility"), and when policies become feature-rich, fine-grained and contextual. In order to support agile application environments such as Cloud and SOA, authorization management itself needs to be at least equally agile, and also automated, manageable, fine-grained, contextual.

While conventional authorization management tools and approaches are a good enforcement mechanism, they do not sufficiently support agility, manageability, and scalability for agile Cloud and SOA applications. It is too time-consuming and error-prone to implement business-centric compliance requirements happen across agile, large, and interconnected applications in a cost-effective way. There are simply too many, too complex technical security rules to manage, so that authorization policies can become unspecifiable or unmanageable, and the confidence in the enforced policy can be undermined. In addition, traditional and well understood security policy concepts – in particular boundary and separation security concepts like firewalls and VPNs and traditional access control models – are not able to support today's increasingly complex and contextual security policies [KaHD09]. They are therefore unsuitable for the protection of business assets and information flow in today's interconnected, dynamic, multi-organizational, service-chained application scenarios with multiple stakeholders and only partial mutual trust. Data-centricity and process-centricity add additional complexity [LaSc09a].

3.2 Model Driven Security Policy Automation & Reporting

To tackle the described policy management challenges, the authors have advocated the use of model-driven security (MDS) since 2002 [Lang10, LaSc02]. In some respects, MDS applies the reasoning behind model-driven software development approaches [OMG06, OMG03] to security and compliance policy management. The view is supported by various scientist and IT analyst [Gart08b] groups, and e.g. by U.S. Navy SPAWAR [Davi08], which advocates four essential security implementation aspects, including the need for agile policy management: "an enterprise, top-down dynamic digital policy execution schema that can be widely implemented" is considered a critical component of future mission-critical Information Assurance (IA) architectures.

This paper's reference implementation is based on ObjectSecurity OpenPMF [ObSe10a], the only full-fledged MDS product in the market today. It is available as a customized deployment and as a packaged development tool add-on for Eclipse and Intalio BPMS IDEs, and for a wide range of runtime application platforms. A number of high-profile end users and vendors are working or have worked with the authors around OpenPMF and MDS because they see the significance of model-driven security for their projects, including US Navy, US Air Force, UK Ministry of Defence, BAA Heathrow Airport, a large German enterprise software vendor, and others. OpenPMF is currently going into production for US Navy. It is also used in the development of a crisis management system as part of the EU FP7 project CRISIS, and was used for a secure air traffic management systems (ATM) prototype as part of the EU FP6 project AD4, for a prototype of a secure System Wide Information Management (SWIM) system. OpenPMF is used for the Cloud security reference implementation in this paper.

As a basis for the Cloud application policy automation reference implementation presented in this paper, Intalio's Cloud hosted open source Business Process Management System (BPMS) [Inta10] was used as a SaaS application. It allows to graphically model business processes as well as to execute these processes, and can be connected to outside systems using Web services and Cloud mashups.

Model-Driven Security (MDS) [LaSc09] is defined as follows: In essence, MDS makes agile policy management possible and manageable through automation. MDS is a tool supported process based on modelling security requirements at a high level of abstraction, and on using other information sources available about the system, especially the applications' functional models (produced by other stakeholders), to automatically generate fine-grained, contextual technical authorization (and other) rules.

The model-driven security process can be broken down [Lang10] in the following steps: Policy modelling, automatic policy generation, policy enforcement, policy reporting, and automatic update.

1) Policy Modelling: In the first step of model-driven security and compliance requirements are modelled by MDS experts as a high-level security policy model in a model-driven security tool (these can be simply selected as a Cloud policy feed or pre-built templates by the customer). Such policy models are expressed at a high level of abstraction in Domain Specific Languages (DSL), using generic modelling languages (e.g. UML) or Enterprise Architecture Frameworks (e.g. DODAF [DOD07], MODAF [MOD08], NAF). Security professionals can either simply selecting appropriate out-of-the-box best-practice security policies (default or custom-made), or model their own policy models in the Eclipse open source IDE & modelling platform (and related

products. A typical example of a default policy would be "only allow the execution of the BPM workflow ordering; block everything else and raise an alert". A typical example of a tailor-made policy would be "doctors are only allowed to access the patient record of the patient they are currently treating, and only if they have a need to know according to the process workflow" (this could be part of HIPAA compliant Cloud platform).

2) Policy Auto-Generation: These inputs are then automatically transformed into machine enforceable, technical, low-level, fine-grained, contextual security policies using model transformation techniques. Conceptually, the high-level security policy model is applied to the functional models of constituent software systems by mapping security policy model actors to system actors and constraining the behaviour of those system actors in accordance with the security policy model. Examples of generated technical policy rules include access control rules, logging rules or configuration of crypto systems. Application developers can easily generate technical security and compliance policies for their applications by simply selecting a pull-down menu item within their development tool (e.g. Eclipse and Intalio BPMS). There is no need to be a security specialist. OpenPMF's model-driven security policy auto-generation then automatically generates the corresponding applications and process specific fine-grained technical policy rules from the chosen general security requirements at the click of a button. After that, the generated technical security policy rules can then be deployed into the runtime infrastructure by selecting another pull-down menu. OpenPMF generates fine-grained technical authorization and logging rules for in OpenPMF's Policy Definition Language (PDL) or in an exportable standard XACML notation.

3) Policy Enforcement: The deployed technical policies are then enforced across Cloud or SOA applications by local enforcement points integrated into the runtime application platform (or at a domain boundary). In OpenPMF, the OpenPMF runtime policy repository loads the generated policy rules at deployment time, and distributes them to the various OpenPMF policy decision / enforcement points (PDP/PEPs) on each protected application runtime platform. This policy update is asynchronous and can happen at application start-up or whenever security rules change (without the need to restart the protected end-system). Note that OpenPMF's enforcement points do not need to query a centralized PDP for decisions. This greatly enhances performance and robustness.

4) Policy Monitoring: The local enforcement points also deal with the monitoring of security compliance relevant incidents, which are centrally collected and analysed. OpenPMF's local policy enforcement points pass security relevant events (e.g. policy incidents) back up to the central runtime security manager at runtime, which itself passes aggregated events up to the plug-in monitoring GUI inside Eclipse (depicted in the figure below). This way, a seamless user experience within Eclipse is achieved. Incidents can also be exported to third party Intrusion Detection Systems (IDS) in the standard Syslog format. In the authors' current work with Promia for U.S. Navy, the compliance monitoring and reporting functionality is itself also a Cloud service (based on Promia's Raven product with OpenPMF application security monitoring).

5) Automatic Update: MDS uniquely ensures that application agility is not hindered by "security stovepipes": whenever the applications (or their interaction configurations) change, model-driven security can automatically update security enforcement and monitoring. Without MDS, administrators would need to manually administer, implement, and continually update a large number of complex security configurations in overlapping, decentralized and siloed ways, which would be time-consuming, costly, error-prone, and inefficient. In OpenPMF, policy updates can

automatically be pushed from the policy generator to the OpenPMF plug-ins (PDPs / PEPs) whenever the application changes (in particular interconnections between services). This way, the security rules are automatically kept 'in synchronization' with agile application workflows and information flows.

When employed effectively, MDS has a number of benefits:

1. Reduces manual administration overheads and saves cost/time through automation.

2. Reduces security risks and increases assurance by minimizing human error potential,

3. Ensures that the security implementation is always in line with the functional behaviour of the system, improving both security and safety of the system,

4. Unites policy across security silos (e.g. different application runtime platforms),

5. Enables IT agility by supporting automatic updates and policy generation,

6. Helps to align business requirements and IT implementation,

7. Forms part of a more automated model-driven approach to agile accreditation.

Model-driven security adoption sometimes still gets challenged because of its dependence on system / workflow specifications (i.e. models) – however, modelling aspects of the interconnected system (esp. interactions) is an important part of state-of-the-art Cloud PaaS and mashups, and is also part of robust systems design. Also, modelling systems does not actually add to the total cost of policy management. This is because if security administrators have to manually specify detailed technical security rules because their tools do not support MDS, they are effectively specifying the security related aspects of the application specification within their policy administration tool. In practice, this is impossible for non-trivial systems, esp. over the whole system life cycle. Model-driven security simply re-uses this information (which often make up the greater part of security policy rules) from models specified by specialists (and / or tools) who understand applications and workflows better anyway (i.e. application developers / integrators, and process modellers). This argument supports the authors' practical experience that, even after only a short while in operation, MDS can greatly reduce costs of effort of protecting the system and improve security and safety compared to traditional, manual policy definition and management.

4 OpenPMF SCaaS: Security & Compliance as a Service

With the emergence of Cloud PaaS, it was only logical to also make the various parts of MDS available on demand as a cloud service. The author's work presented in this paper therefore extends their prior work [RSLa06, LaSc09a] by moving MDS into the Cloud and using it to protect and audit Cloud applications and mashups. This includes two particular complementary aspects:

1. Provide application security and compliance policies as a Cloud service to application development and deployment tools (i.e. policy as a subscription)

2. Embed application security and compliance policy automation into Cloud application deployment and runtime platforms (i.e. automated policy generation, enforcement, monitoring).

This differs from local non-Cloud deployments, where MDS is conventionally installed within or alongside a locally installed development tool (e.g. Eclipse, Intalio BPMS), to protect applications on a number of local runtime application platforms (e.g. various web application servers, JavaEE, DDS, CORBA/CCM) and to support local monitoring and reporting.

While it is only natural to question the trustworthiness and reliability of a Cloud based authorization policy management service (especially for mission-critical environments), the implications of such a deployment scenario need to be seen in relation to the inherent level of trustworthiness and reliability of the protected Cloud applications. If the protected Cloud services themselves are simply accessed over the internet, then many attacks on the policy management service (e.g. denial-of-service) could also directed at the protected services themselves – in this case the Cloud based policy manager does not add to the risk. If more trustworthiness and reliability are required, then for example a private Cloud with Quality of Service (QoS) enabled, hardened infrastructure would be required for both the policy manager and the protected services. In summary, Cloud based security policy management will be the right choice for some services provisioned to some organizations, but not for others.

The following sections below discuss moving various parts of the model-driven application security & compliance policy automation architecture into the Cloud. Different deployment scenarios are possible, e.g. the security features in the development tools and application platform are all hosted in the same Cloud service as part of a PaaS provisioning, or where some security features are hosted separately (esp. policy configuration and monitoring).

4.1 Policy Configuration in the Cloud (Policy as a Service)

One of the central concepts of this paper is that policy configurations are provided as subscription-based Cloud service to application development tools. Offering specification, maintenance, and update of policy models as a Cloud service to application developers and security experts has significant benefits:

- Instead of having to specify (or buy and install) and maintain the policy models used for model-driven security on an on-going basis, application developers and security specialists can now simply subscribe to the kinds of policy feeds they require without the need to know the details of the models. The policy model Cloud service provider (e.g. Object-Security for OpenPMF SCaaS) takes care of policy modelling, maintenance, and update.
- The user organization does not need to be a security and compliance expert because the up-to-date policy models will be provided as a feed to them on an on-going basis.
- The upfront cost hurdle is minimized thanks to the subscription model.
- There is no need by the end user organization to continually monitor regulations and best practices for changes.

For more complex policies, some simple set-up and some potential tagging of security relevant information may be necessary, e.g. for a PCI DSS policy model subscription, payment information related interfaces may need to be tagged alongside the application mashup models.

In general, the described outsourcing model is not new. It has been successfully used for years for other aspects of security, e.g. antivirus and antispyware. Users simply subscribe to a policy feed from the antivirus provider and let the antivirus software client automatically enforce that policy (but in contrast to antivirus, this paper discusses the outsourcing model applied to Cloud application security).

The OpenPMF reference implementation includes an early-stage test project (hosted at cloud.openpmf.com) that delivers policy update feeds as a Cloud based subscription service to Eclipse based development and mashup tools (both Cloud hosted and local).

4.2 Automatic Technical Policy Generation in the Cloud

The automatic policy generation feature of MDS is integrated into the development, deployment, and mashup tools (to get access to functional application information). It consumes the policy feed described in the previous section.

Platform as a Service (PaaS) sometimes includes both Cloud hosted development and mashup tools and a Cloud hosted runtime application platform. In this case, automatic technical policy generation using model-driven security (MDS) can also be moved into the Cloud, so that technical security policies can be automatically be generated for the application during the Cloud hosted development, deployment and/or mashup process. This is in particular the case for mashup tools, because those tools are more likely to be Cloud hosted, are often graphical and/or model-driven, and are concerned with interactions and information flows between Cloud services.

If the development tools are not hosted on the PaaS Cloud, then the MDS technical policy auto-generation feature needs to be integrated into the local development tools.

The OpenPMF SCaaS reference implementation has been built using Cloud hosted Intalio BPMS with some default security and reporting policy templates. OpenPMF currently supports Eclipse based development tools (and integration work with other development tools is on-going).

4.3 Automatic Security Policy Enforcement in the Cloud

Another central concept of this paper is that technical policy enforcement and monitoring is embedded into Cloud application runtime platforms.

Policy enforcement should naturally be integrated into the PaaS application platform so that the generated technical policies are automatically enforced whenever Cloud services are accessed. As described in the previous section, policies are either generated within Cloud using hosted MDS and PaaS development tools, or are uploaded from local MDS and development tools.

How policy enforcement points are built into the PaaS application platform depends on whether the PaaS application platform (1) allows the installation of a policy enforcement point (e.g. various open source PaaS platforms, including Intalio Cloud), (2) supports a standards based policy enforcement point (e.g. OASIS XACML), or (3) supports a proprietary policy enforcement point (e.g. Amazon Web Services).

In the reference implementation, OpenPMF's policy enforcement points have been installed into the Axis2/Tomcat web services which are used as the application runtime platform for Cloud hosted Intalio BPMS.

4.4 Automatic Policy Monitoring into the Cloud

Policy enforcement points typically raise security related runtime alerts, especially about incidents related to invocations that have been blocked. The collection, analysis and visual representation of those alerts can also be moved into the Cloud. This has numerous benefits:

1. Incidents can be centrally analysed for multiple Cloud services together with other information (e.g. network intrusion detection),

2. An integrated visual representation of the security posture across multiple Cloud services can be provided,

3. Integrated incident information can be stored for auditing purposes, (4) Compliance related decision support tools can be offered as a Cloud service.

In the on-going reference implementation, OpenPMF's policy monitoring points can send information to a Cloud based Promia Raven monitoring & compliance service, which can analyse and visualize OpenPMF's application layer incidents with its own network incidents (and other information), and can provide concrete audit related decision support based on the current monitoring security posture.

5 Related Work

Some security tools are available as Cloud services, e.g. for Web application testing. However, most are unrelated to model-driven security based authorization management as a Cloud service, which has – to the knowledge of the authors – not been implemented before, mainly due to the slow adoption of standards, especially for PEPs. ObjectSecurity avoided this problem for the OpenPMF reference implementation by directly collaborating with the Cloud provider – this way, suitable integration points could be developed into their infrastructure.

The authors' previously presented Model Driven Security Accreditation (MDSA) [LaSc09c, LaSc09d] concept and prototype implementation is related to the work described in this paper. MDSA applies model-driven security approaches to the automation of assurance evaluation (e.g. [CoCr06]) and compliance. MDSA automates analysis and documentation for well specified (e.g. model-driven) applications such as the ones described in this paper. This work has shown the viability of using model-driven approaches to automate some of the compliance analysis, documentation, evaluation, certification, and accreditation, because there is traceable correspondence between security requirements and actual IT security, and there is reliable documentation. However, MDSA is not the main focus of this paper.

6 Conclusion

This paper presented the concept of moving security and compliance policy automation for Cloud applications and mashups into the Cloud, to protect Cloud applications and mashups more seamlessly within the Cloud computing paradigm, and to improve and simplify the secure software development lifecycle for Cloud applications. The policy automation aspects covered in this paper include policy configuration, technical policy generation using model-driven security, application authorization management, and incident reporting. The presented work extends prior work by two core concepts: Firstly, policy configuration is provided as a subscription-based

Cloud service to application development tools; secondly, technical policy generation, enforcement and monitoring is embedded into Cloud application development and runtime platforms. The reference implementation called OpenPMF Security & Compliance as a Service ("ScaaS") is based on ObjectSecurity OpenPMF, Intalio BPMS, and Promia Raven. In conclusion, the paper argues that security and compliance policy management for agile distributed application landscapes such as Cloud mashups needs to be model-driven and automated in order to be agile, manageable, reliable, and scalable.

Acknowledgements

The author would like to thank his colleague Rudolf Schreiner (ObjectSecurity), John Mullen from Promia, Inc. and Michael H. Davis (US Navy SPAWAR) for providing valuable discussions, comments and suggestions.

References

[AlMo09]   Alford, Ted and Morton, Gwen. The Economics of Cloud Computing: Addressing the Benefits of Infrastructure in the Cloud, Booz Allen Hamilton, 2009

[Bern09]   Bernard Golden, The Case Against Cloud Computing, January 2009, http://www.cio.com/article/print/477473

[CoCr06]   CCRA, Common Criteria v3., 2006. www.commoncriteriaportal.org

[CSA09]   Cloud Security Alliance. Security Guidance for Critical areas of Focus in Cloud Computing V2.1, December 2009

[Davi08]   Davis, M. et al. SOA Information Assurance Concerns (presentation), ISSA / The Security Network. 2008. http://www.sdissa.org/, ISSA/SecurityNetwork Cyber Security Collaboration Summit (www.igouge.com)

[DOD07]   US Department of Defense. Department of Defense Architecture Framework (DoDAF). 2007. www.architectureframework.com/dodaf

[Forr09]   Forrester Research, Enterprise And SMB Hardware Survey, North America And Europe, Q3 2009

[Gart08a] Heiser, Jay and Nicolett, Mark. Assessing the Security Risks of Cloud Computing, Gartner, June 2008, (ID: G00157782)

[Gart08b] Wagner, R. et al. (Gartner, Inc.). Cool Vendors in Application Security and Authentication, 2008" (G00156005). 2008. www.gartner.com

[Gart09a] Plummer, Daryl and Bittman, Thomas, et al. Cloud Computing: Defining and Describing an Emerging Phenomenon. 17 June 2008 (ID: G00156220)

[Inta10]   Intalio, Intalio Website, www.intalio.com, 2010

[KaHD09]   Karp, Alan H.; Haury, Harry; Davis, Michael H. From ABAC to ZBAC: The Evolution of Access Control Models. 2009. (HPL-2009-30)

[Lang10]   ObjectSecurity. Model Driven Security blog, www.modeldrivensecurity.org

[LaSc02]   Lang, Ulrich and Schreiner, Rudolf. Developing Secure Distributed Systems with CORBA. Artech House, 288 pages, February 2002, ISBN 1-58053-295-0

[LaSc08a] Lang, Ulrich and Schreiner, Rudolf. SOA Security Concerns and Recommendations, (PDF eBook v2.0), December 2008 (based on the Secure SOA project secure-soa.info)

[LaSc09a] Lang, Ulrich and Schreiner, Rudolf. Security Policy Management with Model Driven Security - A new security management approach applied to SOA (PDF eBook v2.0), November 2009

[LaSc09c]   Lang, Ulrich and Schreiner, Rudolf. Model Driven Security Accreditation (MDSA) For Agile, Interconnected IT Landscapes. The 1st ACM Workshop on Information Security Governance, November 13, 2009, Hyatt Regency Chicago, Chicago, USA

[LaSc09d]   Lang, Ulrich and Schreiner, Rudolf. Model Driven Security Accreditation (MDSA) For Agile, Interconnected IT Landscape (PDF eBook), June 2009

[LaSc10]   Lang, Ulrich and Schreiner, Rudolf. Cloud Application Security, January 2010, (PDF eBook)

[MeGr09]   The NIST Definition of Cloud Computing Authors: Peter Mell and Tim Grance Version 15, 10-7-09 National Institute of Standards and Technology, Information Technology Laboratory, http://www.csrc.nist.gov/groups/SNS/cloud-computing/index.html

[MOD08]   UK Ministry of Defence. The MOD Architecture Framework Version 1.2. 2008. www.modaf. com

[Oasi05]   OASIS Consortium (editor: Moses, Tim). eXtensible Access Control Markup Language (XAC-ML) Version 2.0. 1 Feb 2005 (ID: oasis-access_control-xacml-2.0-core-spec-os)

[ObSe10a]   ObjectSecurity. ObjectSecurity OpenPMF website, www.openpmf.com

[OMG03]   Watson, A., and al. Object Management Group Overview and guide to OMG's architecture, 2003. www.omg.org/mda, document omg/03-06-01 (MDA Guide V1.0.1)

[OpCr10]   Open Crowd, Cloud Computing Taxonomy, 2010 (http://www.opencrowd.com/ views/cloud. php)

[RSLa06]   Ritter, Tom, and Schreiner, Rudolf, and Lang, Ulrich. Integrating Security Policies via Container Portable Interceptors in IEEE Distributed Systems Online, vol. 7, no. 7, 2006, art. no. 0607-o7001 (Best Paper Award, ARM2005).

[UKGo10]   UK Government, Government ICT Strategy, Smarter, cheaper, greener (p23ff), 2010, (http://www.cabinetoffice.gov.uk/media/317444/ict_strategy4.pdf)

Authentication and Trust: Turning the Cloud inside out

Christian Brindley

Regional Technical Manager, EMEA – VeriSign Europe
2nd Floor, Chancellors Road, London W6 9RU, United Kingdom
cbrindley@verisign.com

Abstract

There is no doubt that enterprises of all sizes are moving more of their critical business applications into the cloud, relying on services such as SalesForce.com, Google Apps and Amazon Web Services to organise and protect their core business data.

It is also true to say that very few enterprises base their entire infrastructure in the cloud. There is almost always a part of the IT core which is managed and protected in house, leading to a hybrid approach to cloud computing.

In any given enterprise, the split between in house and in cloud infrastructure speaks volumes about that organisation's perception of the cloud. Often, the single part of the enterprise IT infrastructure to be retained in house is the authentication and identity management system.

This paper puts forward the argument that authentication and identity management should in fact be the first element of an enterprise infrastructure to be moved into the cloud. Only then will the cloud model realise its full potential of zero footprint in house, finally setting organisations free to focus on their core business.

1 Introduction: Shaking things up

Cloud computing is a disruptive technology: it falls nicely into Gartner's definition of "causing a major change in the accepted way of doing things" [CECL08]. In fact, back in 2008, Gartner included cloud computing as one of the top ten disruptive technologies for 2008-2012 [CECL08], and few would disagree that this position holds fast today.

Disruption brings with it the opportunity to apply new approaches to old problems. This is particularly true of the opportunity offered by cloud computing to rethink our approach to security.

Unfortunately, security is often perceived as a barrier rather than a driver for adoption of the cloud model. There are a number of surveys run by various organisations to test CIO/CSO appetite for the cloud: each survey takes a different approach and has different motivations, but a common slant is to present security as a negative.

As a typical example, one survey [RELI08] asks participants to choose from the following reasons to use the cloud:
- Performance

- Cost Savings
- Rapid Deployment
- Uptime/High Availability
- Consumption-Based Pricing
- Scalability
- Capacity

And from the following reasons not to use the cloud:
- Security
- Support
- Integration With Existing Systems
- Vendor Lock-In/Portability
- Consumption Pricing
- Performance/Availability Concerns
- Speed to Activate
- Regulatory/Compliance Concerns

This is a common approach. Various surveys swap reasons from one list to the other, but the majority put security in the list of potential barriers to cloud services.

Of course, security is always going to be at the forefront of an executive's considerations when moving to the cloud. However security should be seen as a benefit of the cloud rather than a drawback.

According to NIST, the benefits of cost and agility determine **why** to migrate to the cloud, and the issues of security determine **how**. The argument presented here is that security should determine **both how and why**.

2 What do we mean by Security in the Cloud?

The phrase "Security in the Cloud" introduces two vast topics: both security and the cloud are broad and subjective terms, which need to be limited in scope for the purposes of any meaningful analysis.

2.1 The Cloud

NIST [MEGR09] define cloud computing as

> "a model for enabling convenient, on-demand network access to a shared pool of configurable computing resources (e.g., networks, servers, storage, applications, and services) that can be rapidly provisioned and released with minimal management effort or service provider interaction".

Note that this does not dictate whether the cloud services are located within the enterprise, or with a third party. Well known provisioning models for cloud computing include:
- **Private Cloud**
  This is an architectural model where services are compartmentalised and usually virtual-

ised, but still operated in house within the corporate data centre, and available to no one else but the owning organisation.

- **Community Cloud**
  This is an infrastructure which is shared within a closed community of organisations which have similar requirements and policies, usually within a particular industry vertical or service type.
- **Public Cloud**
  This is the model where hosted services are operated by third party providers on behalf of anyone who will pay for them. This is what most people see as "the" cloud.

The private cloud is a compelling model, placing the enterprise on a good footing for future migration of services to third party providers. The community cloud can also be interesting for closely related organisations which have very particular needs, and want to share costs and resources. However, the greatest benefits of cloud computing are to be found in the public cloud: this model is the most agile and economically beneficial of the three.

2.2 Security

Security of cloud services is of course a core consideration when building a corporate IT strategy. Security of the cloud and security in the cloud are related but different topics: this discussion focuses largely on the latter, exploring security related services offered in the cloud.

Such services include core functions such as Authentication, Identity Management and Access Control, but also extend to services for wider security considerations such as DDOS Mitigation, Intrusion Detection and so on. For the sake of this discussion, we will be focusing mainly on authentication services in the cloud.

3 Why start with security?

The classic advice on how to eat an elephant is "one bite at a time". Moving the entire IT infrastructure into the cloud is an elephantine task, so we need to break the strategy down into manageable bites.

There are a number of ways to categorise cloud services. We could approach the cloud by asset type (data or application), or by model (software as a service, platform as a service, infrastructure as a service). A more fine grained approach is to break down infrastructure by function – e.g.

- Storage
- Database
- Information
- Process
- Application
- Platform
- Integration
- Security
- Management/governance
- Testing
- Infrastructure

Having identified the bites, the question is then where to start. Human nature is to start with the challenge we fear least. For each asset, the Cloud Security Alliance [CSASG09] encourages us to consider the following

1. How would we be harmed if the asset became widely public and widely distributed?
2. How would we be harmed if an employee of our cloud provider accessed the asset?
3. How would we be harmed if the process or function were manipulated by an outsider?
4. How would we be harmed if the process or function failed to provide expected results?
5. How would we be harmed if the information/data were unexpectedly changed?
6. How would we be harmed if the asset were unavailable for a period of time?

At first glance, it would seem from these considerations that a cloud based security infrastructure is our worst nightmare. The natural instinct therefore is to locate our security services within our direct control and push everything else to the cloud. Direct control implies a traditional in-house strategy, or at least a private cloud.

However, control does not equate to security: if we are in control of something which is not within our core competence, the results may be acceptable but are not always ideal. The cloud offers the best of breed technology for securing access, provided by established experts in their field. The agility of deploying in the cloud means that security services can be maintained and updated regularly, either by the existing provider, or by switching to a new provider.

Having made the decision to push our security services into the cloud, it makes perfect sense to use such services as the starting point for our cloud strategy. This establishes the trust anchor for our cloud policy, and drives the provider selection process for the remaining services we are pushing to the cloud.

4 Breaking things down further

There are a number of security service offerings in the cloud. A good starting point is identity and authentication, which are often grouped together but in fact have different roles to play in the cloud.

As a simple illustration of identity, George Bush is an old friend of mine. We used to work together as programmers in a small software house in the UK. If he had turned up at the White House during the Bush Administration, he would have been able to prove that he is George Bush by presenting his passport, fingerprints and iris scan, but since he's not "that" George Bush, he would not have gained access. Identity only has meaning in context, and the only way to anchor identity to a context is by authentication.

Once this anchor is established, the authentication process itself is anonymous: for example, if we know that a user has a secure credential such as a one time password generator, then we can validate the credential without examining the identity of the user him/herself. This makes authentication an ideal first step for moving into the cloud, because we can expose only an anonymous credential.

Within the enterprise, we organise identity by unique identifiers. The identifiers we choose usually contain information about the underlying identity: for example, my unique identifier within

VeriSign is cbrindley. If we choose anonymous identifiers, then this removes another barrier for moving to the cloud. For convenience, we could transform identifiers before they are exposed to the cloud, for example through the use of aliases or better still by a one way hash. In this way, we can comfortably move deeper into the cloud.

Once the authentication process is in the cloud, this opens up a number of possibilities. By treating user authentication as a black box, we have abstracted the process to the point where we can be completely flexible on the underlying mechanisms. For example, the cloud service could determine the most appropriate way to authenticate the user – via one time password, PKI certificate, voice call, risk profile or any combination of these approaches. We are not directly involved in this process, but we can be sure that at the end of the process we have an authentic identity which forms the basis of our decision making process.

This demonstrates how we can divide the most sensitive aspects of our corporate infrastructure into separate boxes, and hand each one of those boxes to different providers in the cloud. Identity is meaningless without authentication, and authentication is meaningless without identity, so we can safely delegate both to separate entities.

5 The technical opportunity

There is now a comprehensive range of standards and policies to support the movement of security services into the cloud.

From the technical point of view, we have all of the standards required to build secure interoperable ID management services, such as SPML and SAML, underpinned by established security standards such as OATH HOTP, PKI etc.

From the practices point of view, there are numerous standards emerging for secure and auditable operation of cloud security services, such as the Trusted Cloud Initiative from the Cloud Security Alliance [CSAN10].

This allows the provision of completely fungible security services in the cloud – i.e. portable building blocks which can be moved between providers and deployment models with ease.

Given the technical opportunity, and the known strategic benefits of the cloud, what is holding us back?

6 The cultural barriers

Information Technology has generated an explosion of new terminology in a very short space of time. As humans, we tend to understand concepts through the use of analogy, and no more so than in the field of computing, where everything from a file to a virus is named after something from the physical world with which we are familiar.

Often, the choice of analogy can have side effects. This is the case for cloud computing. In the physical world, clouds are shifting and opaque, bringing unsettled weather patterns and troubled times. This creates a negative filter through which we view outsourced services when considering where to park our critical business applications and data.

When first approaching the cloud environment, we start from a position of distrust: questions arise around the safety of our systems, of service downtime, loss of data and unauthorised access. This means that we tend to look over our shoulder at the threats behind us rather than the opportunities ahead.

On the other hand, looking at the growing trend among enterprises to move into the cloud, we are overcoming these objections as we gain trust in the outsourced model and the organisations that underpin it. This is driven in the large part by the undeniable economic benefits of cloud computing.

However, we still have some way to go before the cloud is seen as the most secure option for our business systems. According to the Cloud Security Alliance [CSATT10], the top threats we see in the cloud are

- Abuse and Nefarious Use of Cloud Computing
- Insecure Application Programming Interfaces
- Malicious Insiders
- Shared Technology Vulnerabilities
- Data Loss/Leakage
- Account, Service & Traffic Hijacking
- Unknown Risk Profile

Interestingly, all of these threats are present within the in-house environment of any large enterprise network: in this case, it is the job of the enterprise security team to mitigate these threats.

Moving the threats to the cloud has a number of advantages. Firstly, the threats are managed by a team whose core business is providing secure environments. Secondly, scrutiny of an external provider may well be deeper and broader than is the case for in house provisioning. Enterprises will demand evidence of secure practices and technology, along with references from other customers to build confidence in the offering.

7 Case Study: TriCipher security for Google Apps

TriCipher, Inc. provides Internet identity services to protect web and enterprise portals, the people that use them and the business processes that flow through them against fraud and identity theft.

The TriCipher myOneLogin solution offers single sign on for various third party Software as a Service products, including Google Apps, and includes a choice of authentication mechanisms, including

1. A user-selected security image and message
2. Browser-based second factor
3. One Time Password authentication

Looking at myOneLogin with Google Apps, the entire solution is in the cloud: Google provide the application platform, TriCipher offer identity services and first factor authentication, and VeriSign provide One Time Password authentication. Each service is entirely compartmentalised and interoperable through SAML federation technology.

This is a fairly specific use case, but demonstrates how application cloud services may already be secured by peering between cloud providers. Having established the starting point for cloud based security – i.e. SAML federation in the cloud, this allows the enterprise to progress into the cloud with other SAML enabled services.

8 Conclusion

What is the enterprise trying to achieve through cloud computing?

Cost reduction is the obvious factor, but migration to the cloud is driven by more than pure cost: for example, a cloud provider may be brought on board as experts in their field, and true partners in running the infrastructure. Agility is also a key benefit of the cloud, allowing the enterprise to reshape and reorder their infrastructure with ease.

Can the intermediate aims of moving in house services to the cloud be boiled down to a single overall goal, common to all cloud migration strategies?

There are many cloud services which we use unthinkingly, but are still critical to our online businesses. For example, the public DNS infrastructure is vital to all applications and services running on the Internet today: core DNS services are run and managed entirely in the cloud, and the low visibility of top level DNS is a testament to its success as a reliable cloud service. Likewise, public PKI validation services are essential for online ecommerce, and are hosted entirely in the cloud, beyond the firewalls of the relying enterprises and consumers.

The ultimate goal of cloud computing is for all of our business systems to be in this category of services we rely on but do not think about. Ideally, we would have no IT infrastructure inside the firewall. Ideally, we wouldn't even have a firewall. Some would challenge this vision, but few would completely dismiss it.

The enabler for any level of cloud based computing is trust. If we are to place our entire infrastructure in the cloud, the enabler is complete trust.

The cloud isn't going away: as a model, the cloud is flexible, rapid to deploy, cheap to run, and provisioned by experts in their fields. Enterprises already feel confident that their data is secure, to the extent where they are putting their most sensitive sales and marketing data out with third parties such as SalesForce.com.

However, enterprises still feel the need to hold on to the last piece of control, by keeping the authentication systems close to their people, inside the firewall.

The inverse of this approach is to use the cloud for authentication first and foremost. Outsourced authentication then becomes the bedrock for all future migration into the cloud, ensuring a consistent and proven methodology for securing access to all cloud based services.

Authentication is one of the few parts of the infrastructure which spans all applications and services: if left till last, this part can be much harder to swallow than if tackled at the outset of an organisation's cloud strategy.

Organisations can pick and choose each layer of the managed authentication system, resulting in the best of breed technology for each aspect of authentication. An enterprise has an open market from which to choose the strongest authentication devices, combined with the most flexible single sign on systems, and the most effective user experience.

There are well defined protocols for interoperability of cloud based identity and authentication, and emerging standards for high assurance security practices. This means that services are highly flexible, allowing enterprises to swap between providers with ease, with or without altering their overall strategy.

With the security features available in the cloud, we should extend NIST's definition of cloud computing to be

> *"a model for enabling convenient, on-demand network access to a* [secure] *shared pool of configurable computing resources (e.g., networks, servers, storage, applications, and services) that can be rapidly provisioned and released with minimal management effort or service provider interaction".*

Once we adjust our perception of the cloud, focusing on the security benefits available from the public cloud model, this removes our dependency on in house IT infrastructure, thereby unlocking the cloud's full potential for agile, secure and cost effective solutions for all our information system requirements.

References

[CSASG09] Security Guidance for Critical Areas of Focus in Cloud Computing V2.1, Cloud Security Alliance, 2009

[CSATT10] Top Threats to Cloud Computing v1.0, Cloud Security Alliance, 2010

[MEGR09] The NIST Definition of Cloud Computing v15, NIST 2009

[CECL08] Top Ten disruptive technologies for 2008 to 2012, Gartner 2008

[RELI08] Survey Finds Businesses Have Big Plans for Cloud Computing, Version 1.0, ReliaCloud/Evalueserve 2010

[CSAN10] Cloud Security Alliance and Novell deliver first vendor-neutral Trusted Security Certification program to spur mainstream cloud adoption, CSA Press Release 2010

[TRIC09] TriCipher to Offer Triple-Strength Protection With VeriSign for Google Apps Accounts , TriCipher Press Release 2009

User Risk Management Strategies and Models – Adaption for Cloud Computing

Eberhard von Faber [1(+2)] · Michael Pauly [1]

[1] T-Systems
{Eberhard.Faber | Michael.Pauly}@t-systems.com

[2] Brandenburg University of Applied Science
Eberhard.vonFaber@fh-brandenburg.de

Abstract

Third party services are an alternative to in-house ICT production and widely engaged. But the use of such industrialized and standardized ICT services, especially cloud computing, seems to conflict with underlying principles of risk management and security. A schema for the classification of service delivery models is introduced to realize the situation. Sourcing is a rather linear sequence of actions, whereas risk management is highly recurring and iterative. In an adapted process user organisations will not decode every specific security control since that is no longer appropriate in industrialised ICT production markets. Users will concentrate on rating the vendor ("who") and assessing the service ("what"). Then special issues ("how") are considered. Detailed guidance is given for these three steps. In this paper an adapted approach to user risk management is described. By this means users can get the most out of novel ICT provisioning models.

1 Introduction

Development of information and telecommunication technology (ICT) is characterised by changes in architecture and provisioning. Cloud computing is seen as the cutting-edge. Novel service delivery or provisioning models can help corporations to master some of their current challenges – for example, cost and market pressures that call for increased productivity. While conventional outsourcing can help enterprises cut costs, it cannot deliver the flexibility often being required. When it comes to selecting a sourcing model, cost and flexibility are only two of the many factors that have to be taken into account. Further important aspects are data privacy, security, compliance with applicable legislation, and quality of service. Security and governance are essential criteria when preparing and taking sourcing decisions.

In chapter 2 it is described that common notion of security does not match with consequences from development of provisioning models. The security dilemma, especially with cloud computing, gives rise to reconsider established risk management strategies and models.

In chapter 3 a classification of the service models is presented which helps to identify the origin of uncertainty and risk and therefore to select an appropriate service delivery model.

Users can buy several ICT service, but they can not outsource the risk. The ICT service provider is responsible for the security, but the user organisation must manage the risks. This new situation has radical impact as discussed in chapter 4. It becomes more complicated since established risk management processes are highly iterative and circular. But purchasing ICT services is a rather linear.

In chapter 5 a risk management process is described which is adapted for using third party ICT services. User organisations will concentrate on rating the vendor ("who"), assessing the service ("what"), and then consider remaining special issues ("how"). For the vendor rating a trust model is sketched and sources of information being required are identified. The service model rating is performed using the service delivery classification model. In addition, public and private cloud services are compared. Remaining special issues can be discussed utilizing a further landscape security model being presented.

Enterprise risk management may undergo further radical changes. One reason is finally addressed in chapter 6. Self-service especially in public clouds and consumerization will cause security managers to make more changes. A summary is given in chapter 7.

2 The Cloud Dilemma, Facts and Benefits

Risk management requires transparency and knowledge of implementation details. Security requires the ability to make changes and to directly control and check (refer to Fig. 1). Cloud computing is a specific model for the provisioning of ICT services built to be more efficient than other models. The advantages are generated through the economies of scale. This in turn requires a distinct division of labour (between user organisation and service provider), standardisation and automation of production as well as a sole service delivery. ICT services are delivered to the user, nothing else.

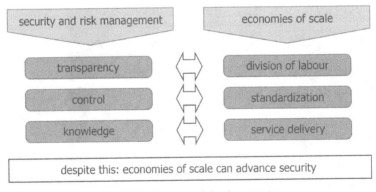

Fig. 1: The dilemma of cloud computing

Fig. 1 visualises that the two approaches directly contradict. Clouds are inherently non-transparent for the user organisation. Any effort spent to provide information for more transparency would, strictly speaking, limit the degree of division of labour and therefore decrease the economic benefits. Raising transparency and control would suspend division of labour and therefore neutralize economies of scale. Also, the ability to influence and control what the user is utilizing is very limited in cloud computing. Little control is often associated with a situation which is insecure and risky. But standardisation (at the vendor site) results in less control by the user. The dilemma becomes apparent if one assumes to be a standard user without any inside knowledge who only conceives the service and the interface it is provided on. A security or risk analysis needs to check the existence of security measures and look for vulnerabilities. But users don't have the required information. They only get the ICT service with performance indicators and a lot more. But users don't see how the ICT service is produced. The cloud is opaque.

However, the provider's service may have a high level of security. There are economies of scale (or economies of benefit) which support and improve information security. Security aspects know that

- the availability of resources and people,
- the maturity of processes as well as
- the existence of expert skill and experience

are essential to accomplish and maintain an adequate level of security. In addition, security tasks such as patch management and other security support can be simplified and performed in a more efficient way. This can significantly improve the level of security and mitigate risks.

3 Classification of Service Models and Origin of Risks

Less transparency and control are not specific to cloud computing. The more tasks are outsourced and the more technology is at the providers' side, the more the users lack ad-hock knowledge and direct control. This can be shown by looking at the evolution of division of labour and the related service models in ICT.

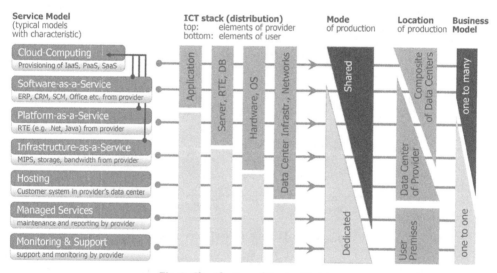

Fig. 2: Classification of Service Models

Fig. 2 shows a model which classifies the different types of ICT service delivery using three major characteristics [vFab2009]. It will be used to show origins of risk and cloud computing is not a totally new situation. On the left hand side of Fig. 2, there is a list of seven (typical) service delivery models (from monitoring & support at the bottom to cloud computing at the top).

The *ICT stack* is depicted in the center of Fig. 2, divided into *Data Center Infrastructure & Networks* (right), *Hardware & Operating System, Server/Run Time Environment/Data Base* and *Application* (left). Each service delivery model utilizes the whole ICT stack (column).

Monitoring & Support: All elements of the ICT stack are owned by the user. There are no other users. As a result the systems are *Dedicated Systems* (specific to the user, refer to characteristic *Mode of Production* in Fig. 2). Technology is situated in the user's data center (refer to characteristic *Location of Production* in Fig. 2). The service provider only monitors the systems providing reports about performance and incidents. The provider is typically also responsible for ICT support. – *Managed Services*: This service model comprises all services from the first model. But the service provider actively manages the user's systems. Examples are software updates and perhaps also configuration.

Hosting: Starting with this third model the technology is located in the data center of the service provider (refer to characteristic *Location of Production* in Fig. 2). But most elements of the IT stack are still dedicated to a specific user. Different users only share the Data Center Infrastructure & Networks.

Infrastructure-as-a-Service: More and more elements of the ICT stack are now shared by different users: In this model (formerly also „utility-computing") users share computer systems. – *Platform-as-a-Service*: In this model only *Applications* are user specific („dedicated"). All other elements of the ICT stack are used by more users simultaneously („shared"). – *Software-as-a-Service*: Here many users are provided with one software. In fact, there are different versions (not shown in the figure) depending on the realisation of access, software construction and data management. *Cloud Computing* provides ICT "as-a-service" (refer to Fig. 2) where potentially all elements are shared and the production is located in the users data center or a compound of them.

This classification model serves to discuss specific security concerns and the origin of real threats and risks. It becomes apparent that cloud computing is not a totally new situation for security. Five issues continuously varied through the evolvement of service delivery models (Fig. 2):
- division of labour (between user organisation and service provider),
- different ownership or possession of ICT (see distribution of ICT stack),
- shared use of ICT (from networks, data centers, up the stack),
- other location of production,
- business model of the service provider (important for service management and contract).

Cloud Computing is just the cutting-edge, but a cause to reconsider risk management.

4 Demand for an Adapted Approach

4.1 Perceived Security and Business Risk

For user organisations it is essential to distinguish between their perceived situation with less transparency and direct control on the one hand and security or risk exposure on the other. The *confidence model* in Fig. 3 shall visualise the situation. There are two types of security valuation ((a) and (b) in the figure) which rather supplement than contradict. Fig. 3a: Security is perceived as much stronger if the user has direct control requiring possession or at least free access to the ICT. Thorough knowledge (perhaps provided by an independent evaluation facility as result of a well-defined process) gives assurance. Less confidence is obtained if the user can only measure the performance by monitoring the ICT solution and its security behaviour. Predictability shall represent the situation where there is no detailed information about the ICT solution and its security behaviour. Instead the user can measure the ICT operator (service provider if external). If the measurement is more a judgement, the term credit is used here.

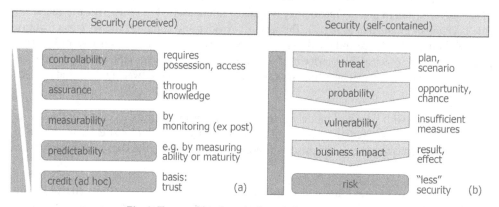

Fig. 3: Two worlds - Security has six flavours (at least)

Locking into security literature [SP800-30] one can find other descriptions of security (Fig. 3b). Security is the absence of unaccepted risks: A risk is generated if a threat can - with a given probability - utilize a vulnerability (absence or imperfection of appropriate security measures) to cause a business impact.

User organisations shall not thoroughly adhere to factors in Fig. 3a. The definition of risk (Fig. 3b) reminds the following:

- Threats and probability are also determined by the service model (the way ICT is produced and used).
- It is up to the ICT service provider if there are vulnerabilities or not.
- The business impact can only be estimated by the user (and not by the service provider).

As a result the risk management process affects activities of both the user and the provider. The interaction and reciprocity of both workspaces is a complicated issue and needs to be arranged.

4.2 Standard Risk Management versus Ultimate Purchase

In the next years enterprises will continue to intensify the use of third party ICT services and reduce internal legacy production. Though ICT Services and ICT can almost completely be taken over by ICT service providers, the risks associated with this can not. IT risks are business risks. Those risks can not be "outsourced". User organisations can buy the design, integration and operation of ICT from specialised service providers, but they are still responsible for information security. That means that users have to have the ability and the resources for corporate ICT risk management. They have to define their general security and compliance requirements and need to make the comparison with the ICT services provided from the external. The ICT service provider is responsible for the security, but the user organisation must manage the risks. This new situation has radical impact. Existing risk management models and processes are not appropriate and need to be adapted.

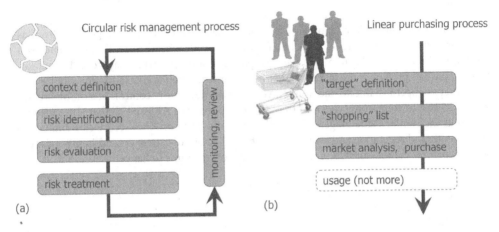

Fig. 4: Two worlds – risk management and purchasing process

Risk management is defined in the international standard ISO/IEC 27005 (refer to Fig. 4a and [ISO27005]). The process is as follows: After having established the context, risks are identified, then estimated and evaluated followed by the so called risk treatment, where actions are taken. Typically security controls are implemented in this stage. Finally, the residual risk is considered in order to take a decision if the situation can be accepted or not. The main thing here is that this process is highly iterative. It is a closed loop with the demand of fast feed-back within the internal cycle.

The purchase of third party services is rather linear and consists of the two stages "requirements definition" and "purchase and use" (refer to Fig. 4b). Both are decoupled, especially if predefined, highly standardized products or services are to be acquired. Corporate risk management processes need to be adapted for this.

5 Risk Management for Third Party ICT Services

5.1 General Model of Adaption

An adapted risk management process has a clear focus on a linear sequence of non-recurring actions (refer to Fig. 4b). Most is conducted before any ICT service is received from a third party. This section is sketched in the following. In the usage phase (after purchase) risk management can be circular.

The first part ("requirements definition") shall comprise context definition, risk identification, risk estimation and evaluation for an *anticipated situation*, and finally the elaboration of a security target (as a "purchase list"). New elements are the anticipated assessment and an explicit "irrevocable" security target. The second part ("purchase and use") use the target as major input, and comprise the investigation of the market, negotiations and contracting as well as use and control. Note that typically no changes can be made after having signed the contract. User organisations have to live with the "security" they have purchased. This will become more common as ICT production is industrialized.

In addition to a more "linear" approach, user organisations must prepare to go away from assessing specific security controls ("realization") towards rating what they get ("service" and "vendor"). Especially the cloud is non-transparent, opaque. Confidence will come from "the market". An example can provide more clarity. Going by car or using public transportation can be risky and perhaps dangerous. But no one would investigate all the security controls of a car before purchasing it. The customer only checks if the car is equipped with ABS and all that. The customer also ranks the vendor ("due diligence"). Vendors invest a lot to produce secure cars and to care about their brand reputation and avoid failure. That behaviour of customers and suppliers is typical for a mature market. For ICT services one can expect the same to happen.

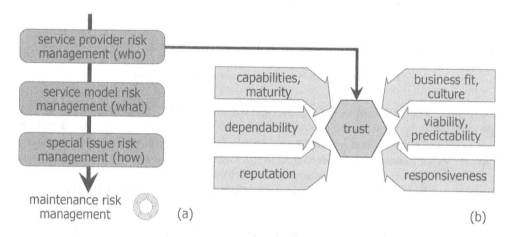

Fig. 5: Elements of risk management process (a), vendor rating (b)

User organisations will concentrate on rating the vendor ("who") and assessing the service ("what") as shown in Fig. 5a (i.e., left). A purchase decision may require more clarity. Hence special issues ("how") are also considered.

5.2 Managing Vendor Risks

A major source of security problems is the service provider or the insufficient performance of the provider, respectively. Hence, user organisation must set-up a *service provider risk management* in order to mitigate the risks associated with the selection of a service provider.

There is a huge amount of information which can be used in this process. Areas are shown in Fig. 5b. Sources of information are, for example, (i) quality and coverage of vendor portfolio, (ii) vendor statements in white papers etc., (iii) analyst ratings and market surveys, (iv) third party certifications of the vendor's processes and practices, (v) reference projects, (vi) information of peers having experience with the vendor, (vii) general brand image, (viii) business model, strategy, go-to market and partnering, (ix) size, financial viability, market presence and power, (x) research activities and innovations, (xi) contracting and service, (xii) availability and responsiveness. Such information needs to be analysed with respect to security and risk management relevant issues before choosing the service provider.

5.3 Choosing the Service Model

Another source of uncertainty and risk is the service model (Fig. 2) and the way ICT services are provided. Development of a sourcing strategy is tightly linked with the overall risk management. Users may decide not to have any data outside their own control. Or, have a multi-vendor strategy to divide risks. One example which is intensively discussed today is the selection of the cloud model. This example is analysed in the following without rating a vendor nor a product, i.e., following the approach described above.

Public and private clouds are significantly different with respect to security. An unbiased consideration however must be independent from vendor and service, that is, with a look onto the opaque cloud. Fig. 6 shows a general risk analysis performed along seven aspects. For each aspect the threat level or potential risks is rated. That reveals the differences of the cloud types. The rating considers tendencies and typical conditions. It does not look at specific implementations, vendors or products.

Security or risk relevant issue	rating of threat level / potential risk	
	Public cloud	Private cloud
Identity theft and misuse (number of users and assumed level of control)	High	Low
Attack exposure, likelihood of being attacked (knowledge and accessibility of interface, motivation)	High	Medium
Security at users' site (assumed security level and related effort)	High	Low
High-tech security first in special markets and later in mass-markets (e.g. DLP, specific encryption)	Medium	Low
Custom security requirements cannot be met (degree to which provider can meet those, if any)	High	Low
Security issues during migration or change of provider (e.g. loss of data due to a lack of standard interfaces)	High	Medium
Gaps in overall security level, limitations in liability (more likely e.g. in case of multi-tier production)	Medium	Low

Fig. 6: Public vs. private cloud – a comparison of threat level or potential risk (neither vendor nor product rating; tendency and typical conditions are considered instead)

This shows that even the provisioning model makes a big difference.

5.4 Managing Specific Issues

In most cases user organisations can not expect that vendor rating (see section 5.2) and the selection of the service delivery model (see section 5.3) can answer all security concerns. So, it is advantageous to have some sort of check list to identify specific issues which need to be addressed in addition [vFab2010]. Fig. 7 shows twelve security areas or aspects relevant specifically for cloud computing. Such a sketch can be useful for the "due diligence" during the purchasing and contracting process. Note that the user organisation must elaborate a "security target" definition beforehand (see section 5.1) which enables to perform a comparison. Security assessments conducted by independent security evaluation facilities can be a powerful means to provide assurance.

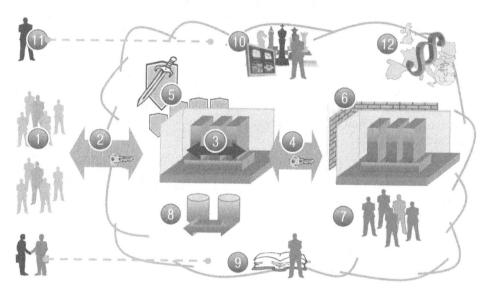

Fig. 7: Landscape security model - security areas or aspects for cloud computing

The twelve areas or aspects chosen in Fig. 7 are: (1) access control, management of digital identities including roles and rights, security level and controls at the users' side, (2) secure communication into the cloud, (3) separation of data and applications of different users (multi-tenancy), (4) secure communication within the cloud, (5) protection of IT systems, applications, platforms etc., (6) environmental and physical security (data center security), (7) personal security and security organisation (resources, qualification, check-up), (8) Business Continuity Management, backup und disaster recovery, (9) contracting, SLA, service management, reporting, integration into user infrastructure and business processes, data transfer and transition phase, vendor capabilities, (10) security management, policies, and organisation of the vendor, (11) incident management (ICT service provider and user organisation), change management, (12) requirements management, compliance, data privacy.

6 Outlook

But enterprise risk management may undergo other radical changes. One threat is described in the remaining of this contribution. There is a new challenge for enterprise security management. Products and even services that originate and develop in the consumer space are very easy to deploy. Work and private life overlap. Employees like to use what they know and like best. With cloud computing even complex applications and ICT services are easy to deploy. Self-service in public clouds allow use of application which traditionally are provided by the internal IT department and rolled out throughout the company in a defined manner using established processes and practices. Employees will start to use their own equipment. Business units will start to buy ICT services from the clouds and put company data on those and Web 2.0 platforms. The internal IT department may be ignored. The problem is that self provisioned servers or systems are hard to find and to monitor by the internal IT department. Such kind of "guerrilla" systems does also not match with any security policies or guidelines. This trend of the consumerization of IT will require further adaption of enterprise risk management.

7 Conclusion

Risk management is seen to require transparency and knowledge of implementation details. Security requires the ability to make changes and to directly control and check. But clouds are inherently non-transparent for the user organisation. Users will not see how the ICT service is produced. This constitutes the security dilemma with cloud computing giving rise to reconsider established risk management strategies and models. Note that the economies of scale associated with cloud computing can also significantly support and improve security.

Less transparency and control are not specific to cloud computing. The more tasks are outsourced and the more technology is at the providers' side, the more the users lack ad-hock knowledge and direct control. A classification of the service models is presented which shows that. The model also helps to identify the origin of uncertainty and risk and therefore to select an appropriate service delivery model.

Considering different flavours or meanings of security (confidence model) it turns out that some aspects are not appropriate, others are not practical, and risk analysis and mitigation processes must properly being split between user and provider organisation while taking into account the conditions explained earlier. The interaction and reciprocity of both workspaces is a complicated issue and needs to be arranged. Users can buy several ICT service, but they can not outsource the risk. The ICT service provider is responsible for the security, but the user organisation must manage the risks. This new situation has radical impact. It becomes more complicated since established risk management processes are highly iterative and circular. But purchasing ICT services is rather linear with a conclusive result.

An adapted risk management process must therefore have a clear focus on a linear sequence of non-recurring actions. New elements are the evaluation for an anticipated situation and an explicit "irrevocable" security target. The major steps of this part of the overall process are described in the remaining of the paper. In the usage phase (after purchase) risk management can be circular.

The linear sequence of non-recurring actions consists of a three major steps. User organisations will concentrate on rating the vendor ("who") and assessing the service ("what"). Then special issues ("how") are considered. For the vendor rating a trust model is sketched and sources of information being required are identified. The service model rating is performed using the service delivery classification model. In addition, public cloud services and private cloud services are compared with respect to threat level and potential risks. Special issues can be discussed utilizing a further landscape security model being presented.

With such an adapted approach to user risk management user organisations prepare to go away from assessing specific security controls ("realization") towards rating what they get ("service" and "vendor"). Assessing every specific control is no longer appropriate in industrialised ICT production markets. Especially the cloud is opaque for users. Otherwise users will not get the most out of novel ICT provisioning models.

All figures are illustrative.

References

[SP800-30] Gary Stoneburner, Alice Goguen, Alexis Feringa: Risk Management Guide for Information Technology Systems; NIST Special Publications 800-30

[ISO27005] ISO/IEC 27005 – Information technology – Security techniques – Information security risk management

[vFab2009] Eberhard von Faber: Auslagerung von IT-Services: Klassifikation und Risikomodell, Leitlinien für Anwender im "global sourcing"; BSM Anwender 201, Schriftenreihe: The Bulleting Security Management, ISSN 1869-2125, Herausgeber: Eberhard von Faber und Friedrich-L. Holl, Bezug: www.security-management.de

[vFab2010] Eberhard von Faber: Cloud-Computing - Die Sicherheit im Fokus; it-management 4/2010, ISSN 0945-9650, S. 60-64

Security and Compliance in Clouds[1]

Kristian Beckers[1] · Jan Jürjens[1,2]

[1] Project Group APEX, Fraunhofer ISST, Dortmund, Germany
kristian.beckers@isst.fraunhofer.de

[2] Software Engineering (LS 14), Fak. Informatics, TU Dortmund, Germany
http://jan.jurjens.de

Abstract

The use of cloud computing services is an attractive opportunity for companies to improve IT Services and to achieve almost unlimited scalability of the IT infrastructure, and all of this at a significantly reduced cost than this is possible with internal resources. However, the use of a cloud service requires a company to trust the vendor to deal with the company's secret data. In order to check the compliance demands for the required security level, the business processes of the cloud vendor have to be inspected thoroughly. This is a time consuming and expensive task which has to be repeated continuously. Furthermore, company data is increasingly subject to compliance checks for legal regulations that differ in each geographical location, for instance the Sarbanes-Oxley Act (SOX) or the HIPPAA Act in the health domain in the U.S., or Basel II, Solvency II in Europe. We report on ongoing research about an automated compliance analysis method specifically for the analysis of the business processes of a cloud service provider. Nowadays, customers of cloud services can only inquire the existence of single security features like a firewall. The review of the entire security concept on a process level is seldom possible.

1 Introduction

"Cloud computing is a model for enabling convenient, on-demand network access to a shared pool of configurable computing resources (e.g., networks, servers, storage, applications, and services) that can be rapidly provisioned and released with minimal management effort or service provider interaction." according to the US National Institute of Standards and Technology (NIST).

The economical attraction of cloud computing is the ability to purchase computer resources without any upfront commitment and to pay only for the used amount of resources. This ability offers a number of new possibilities in the business world. Thus, companies are not limited to activities that their current resource pool can accomplish anymore. Cloud computing offers them almost unlimited scalability of IT resources. Furthermore, Return on Investment (RoI) calculations can be done faster, due to the fact that cloud computing has in many cases no fixed cost [JaSc10].

The usage of cloud computing services is an attractive opportunity for companies to improve IT-Services, achieve almost unlimited scalability of the IT infrastructure and all of this at a significantly reduced cost than this is possible with internal resources. However, the usage of a cloud

---

1 This work was supported through the Fraunhofer-Attract project "Architectures for Auditable Business Process Execution (APEX)"

service requires a company to trust the vendor explicitly with companies' secrets. One way to ensure the trust is satisfied is to maintain a strong security supervision of the cloud service. In order to check the compliance demands for the required security level, the business processes of the cloud vendor, at least the ones regarding the security of the cloud service, have to be inspected thoroughly.

This is a time consuming task that can only be executed by experts in the field and thus an expensive task. Furthermore, this effort has to be repeated constantly in order to verify the security level is maintained. While single technical methods exist in a cloud, e.g. network security, holistic automatic compliance checks on the basis of business processes are rather limited [StRu09]. An automated compliance analysis method specifically for the analysis of the business processes of a cloud service provider is a solution to this problem. This will provide a verifiable trust relationship between cloud vendors and customers at a low cost. Nowadays, customers of cloud services can only inquire the existing of single security features like a firewall. The review of the entire security concept on a process level is seldom possible.

Furthermore, company data e.g. in the form of business processes are increasingly subject to compliance checks for legal regulations, for instance the Sarbanes-Oxley Act (SOX) or the Health and Human Services Health Insurance Probability and Accountability Act (HIPPAA) in the U.S[AFG+09][CSA10]. This in particular relevant to cloud computing since a number of cloud vendors are based in the U.S., making customers data from all over the world subject to these compliance checks. However, legal regulations for risk management are not solely relevant in the U.S., for instance in Europe the Basel II and Solvency II accords aim also towards this goal.

A tool-supported method specifically designed for the evaluation of business process against legal and security compliance requirements making use of current model-driven and generative techniques such as the Eclipse Modelling Frameworks to achieve these goals in a process that includes cost-effective adherence to compliance regulations can improve the current situation. Furthermore, these techniques provide workflow monitoring capabilities for dynamic compliance checks.

Cloud computing business will grow at an accelerated rate then conventional enterprises. "It used to take years to grow a business to several million customers – now it can happen in months." according to Berkeley Armbrust et. al. [AFG+09]. This requires security systems to scale with an increased frequency as well. Moreover, businesses providing a service in the cloud want to interact with numerous business partners that use different technologies for security. Solutions for Cloud Federation Management is required that enables e.g. the authorization of users between the different security technologies of the business partners.

2 Security Issues in Cloud Computing

"Cloud computing is a model for enabling convenient, on-demand network access to a shared pool of configurable computing resources (e.g., networks, servers, storage, applications, and services) that can be rapidly provisioned and released with minimal management effort or service provider interaction." [MeGr09]. A study from the IDC in 2009 points out that the security of cloud services presents a significant barrier for the acceptance of cloud computing systems in companies [IDC09]. The cause is a poor support of security techniques [StRu09], the significant requirements on scalability and elasticity of cloud computing systems [MeGr09], for which specific security techniques are just in development.

The security issues in the cloud computing area have resulted in the founding of user alliances, for instance the Cloud Security Alliance (CSA), which supports companies with the security evaluation of cloud systems [CSA10]. Confidentiality in cloud computing systems is a significant problem. There are possibilities today to transfer data to and from the cloud encrypted, also data can be stored encrypted. However, the processing of encrypted data is still a problem of research. Thus, data in today's cloud systems have to be decrypted to be processed [MaKuL10]. Moreover, authentication of cloud users in numerous systems is solely based upon the verification of credit card data [MaKuL10]. This is the reason for a rising number of attacks from within the cloud [Esso09][Bar09][MeGr09][CASa10].

An unresolved legal issue is the storage of data in a foreign country. Which law is applied in this case? The law from the country the data originates or the law from the country where the data is actually stored? Can the government of the country where the data is stored access the data? Can the customer choose a law? [BIE09]. The availability of cloud systems is not without interruptions, e.g. Amazon's Cloud System had already multiple outages. In Juli 2008 the systems was down for 8 hours [MaKuL10]. Moreover, attacks on the availability of clouds are becoming more frequent, for instance Distributed Denial of Service (DDoS) attacks [Esso09][AFG+09]. Solutions for these problems are topics of ongoing research. Data integrity checks in cloud systems cannot be executed in most cases by cloud users. These have to rely on the services of the cloud vendors [MaKuL10][StRu09]. Further research investigates message-, configuration-, and software integrity of cloud computing systems [StRu09].

3 Privacy regulations on a global scale

Personal data of German companies cannot be stored in a so-called unsecure third country e.g. India or the USA, due to legal reasons. However, there are data protection contracts, for instance the safe harbor agreement for the USA, which enables cooperation with a company in an unsecure third country. However, until today no international agreement on the usage of cloud computing has been devised and each cloud computing endeavour has to be prepared and checked individually [Cav08][BIE09].

Business transactions in a cloud computing system demand a unique assignment of a transaction to a user. Electronic certificates can be used to proof these transactions. However, the verification of the certificates should be provided by an independent third party. Furthermore, there are conflicting goals of accountability and data privacy in a cloud in a cloud computing system [StRu09].

"However, these systems have to consider privacy constraints, which make the job even harder. Information in digital form facilitates the collection and sharing of large amounts of data. The simple approach only to "collect as little information from individuals as possible" [HaScC08] is not practical, due to identity-risk-analysis procedures. For instance, in order to establish that an identity in a financial transaction is not forged or stolen a significant amount of data has to be checked. In the case of fraud detection based upon unusual usage of a credit card e.g. purchases in countries where it was never used before, user profiles are necessary that require lots of data. Moreover, in order to categorize information into security levels in order to determine which data needs more or less protection, the data has to be present [HaScC08].

A number of guidelines for privacy are available, the most widely accepted [HaScC08] are the *Fair Information Practice principles (FIPs)*, which state that a persons informed consent is required for the data that is collected, collection should be limited for the task it is required for and erased as soon as this is not the case anymore. The collector of the data shall keep the data secure and shall be held accountable for any violation of these principles. In the European Union the *EU Data Protection Directive* doesn't permit processing personal data at all, except when a specific legal basis explicitly allows it or when the individuals concerned consented prior to the data processing [HaScC08]. The US has no central data protection law, but separate privacy laws for e.g. the *Gramm-Leach-Bliley Act* financial information, the *Health Insurance Portability and Accountability Act* for medical information, and the *Children's Online Privacy Protection Act* for data related to children [HaScC08].

In the computing world two further major informational privacy concerns are eavesdropping of data and the linking of an individual to a set of data. The eavesdropping issue can be addressed via encryption of data and the linking issue requires different pseudonyms for different contexts. Workflows over different domains should be "delinked", for instance in an online shop the shop itself needs to know the goods that are purchased, the delivery service requires only the shipping address and the payment service requires only the financial information. All of them should use a different pseudonym to prevent user profiling [HaScC08]. Identity management systems that support multilateral security and privacy requirements exist in most cases isolated. The SSONET architectures combine the existing parts [ClKö01]. The BBAE federated identity management protocol offers enhanced security and privacy, due to the absence of single points of control [PfWa03].

The research question how much information is required in what scenario is been addresses as so-called *contextual integrity* and how can this be automated [BDMN]. In addition, ongoing research proposes to "stick" policies by cryptographic means to data, to ensure the data is only used for the purpose the user gave an informed consent [MoPeB03]. Bertino et. al. identified also confidentiality of business relations among various Cloud Services Providers (CSP) as a requirement for cloud computing identity management [BPFS09].

4 Compliance in clouds

The service level of a cloud vendor is defined in so-called *Service Level Agreements (SLAs)*, which often cannot be negotiated. Instead a customer has to accept the SLAs presented by the vendor. Moreover, automatic audit tools to verify the presented SLAs are fulfilled are missing [MaKuL10].

Relevant security standards for cloud computing are the Statement on Auditing Standards (SAS) Number 70 Type II and the ISO certificate 27001. SAS 70 II confirms a cloud vendor from an external party that monitoring activities for IT technologies and processes are present and documented. The ISO certification demands a management concept for IT security, which e.g. evaluates security measures in Plan-Do-Check-Act cycles on a permanent bases [MaKuL10]. One result of an SAS 70 II certification is a security report, which is filed under the individual standards of the evaluated organisation. It is not a certificate with a predefined set of terms [StRu09]. A further type of compliance in the cloud area are so-called Trust Audit Frameworks, e.g. SysTrust or WebTrust. These frameworks focus on internal controls in a company based upon financial systems. These systems were developed for ecommerce applications [StRu09].

Cloud computing offers elasticity, services can be added or deleted on demand by a customer. Thus, any part of the cloud computing system has to support this scalability. In Fig.1 we present several areas of Governance, Risk and Compliance that has to be modified or even reinvented to achieve a viability for cloud computing. In Governances policies have to be written that accommodate the permanent change of a system. Today's policies are written for comparable stable systems and are tightly focused on them. This will not suffice for a cloud computing system, because of the elasticity. Furthermore, a detailed classification of data is required. Data in a closed company network needs to be protected and the responsible personal in a company has full control of the infrastructure. In a cloud computing scenario data will be given to a cloud provider and the customer has to trust on the security capabilities of the vendor. Thus, for instance highly sensible data or processes that are vital for a company should not enter the cloud. Moreover, multiple customers or even cloud vendors might be involved in a business process that involves cloud usage. In these cases the trust of each partner has to be taken into account of security considerations.

Risk management requires a strategy that includes every possibility of security failures with a cloud computing integration. This becomes increasingly difficult due to the almost infinitive number of possible scenarios, because of the change of the companies structure when cloud computing is used in a part of it. In addition, possible impacts of cloud computing on the effectiveness and efficiency of business processes of a company has to be evaluated on a similar scale. Numerous new threats and vulnerabilities of cloud computing have to be analysed and the risk analysis itself for each cloud scenario has to be verified continuously.

Compliance also becomes more difficult, due to the fact that companies rely on cloud vendors for security policy enforcement, the adherence to regulations e.g. SOX or Solvency II. Furthermore, companies have to find ways to gain control of specific scenarios. For instance, in case highly classified data made it into the cloud by accident an emergency procedure should exist that erases the data completely from the clouds systems.

GRC in Clouds

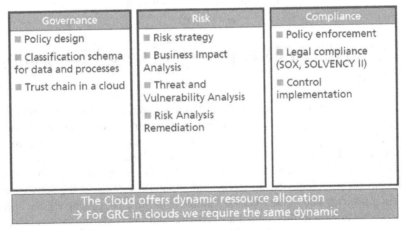

Fig. 1: Governance, Risk and Control (GRC) in cloud computing systems

In Fig. 2 we are presenting examples for GRC related standards that can help to evaluate a cloud computing scenario. However, there are almost no specific standards for cloud computing. On an economic level the integration of cloud and company has to result in effective and efficient business processes. This can be verified, for instance with the ISO 9001, the Gartner BPM Maturity Model, and the EDEN Maturity Model for Business Processes. Cobit and Coso offer models for documenting, analysing and creating internal control systems. Relevant security standards are the BSI Grundschutzhandbuch and the Common Criteria. A topic specifically relevant for cloud computing is transparency. In many cases customers of cloud computing offers have to trust the vendor that the GRC demands are met. However, several standards evaluate the capabilities of the cloud system, like ISO 27001, SAS 70 Type II, and Truste. Further agreements for instance safe harbor ensure that certain privacy demands are met.

Cloud GRC Related Standards

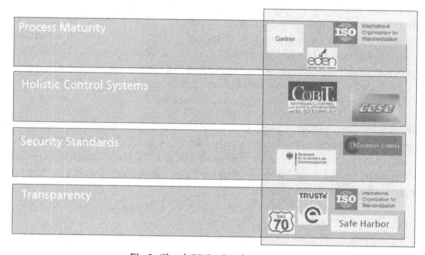

Fig 2: Cloud GRC related standards

5 Applying the APEX approach to Cloud Computing Systems

The Fraunhofer-Attract project Architectures for Auditable Business Process Execution (APEX) develops a software tool for the insurance domain that eases the effort of implementing the increasing number of compliance frameworks, laws and regulations in the insurance domain (in particular Solvency II) into their processes and into the IT landscape. Numerous requirements arise from these compliance regulations. This poses demands at the software that is developed for and used in the insurance domain in two ways: One the one hand, the Software must be developed in a way that allows the software vendors to make a convincing argument that it is sufficiently reliable to support the sophisticated requirements derived from the compliance regulations (such as security requirements), which today often is not the case. On the other hand, it creates a demand for special purpose software whose function it is to monitor and enforce compliance of the company's business processes while they are executed over the IT infrastructure. Developing these kinds of systems efficiently while meeting compliance demands with minimal cost overhead is a goal which reveals a severe gap in current software engineering methods and tools. Current approaches and technologies neither support the seamless analysis and management of compliance risks and requirements during the software life-cycle nor their systematic enforcement in the context of service-oriented architectures.

We are currently investigating how to adapt the APEX approach for an application to cloud computing systems. In the following we present an approach for improving cloud security based upon the APEX work. Enterprise cloud software platforms also have to deal with inherent compliance problems. On the one hand, customers should be able to check if their security requirements are met with a specific cloud computing offer. On the other hand, customers require the ability to verify that the cloud offer satisfies legal compliance regulations. Compliance monitoring software is required as well in clouds, together with an approach to machine-interpretable and enforceable policies that map to the business level extend the pursued approach towards the achievement of compliance in the presence of dynamically created adaptive business processes and value chains in open service architectures. These challenges demand an extension of the APEX method to take the elasticity of cloud computing into account.

A compliance repository is designed in the APEX project to be functionality directly in line with customer demands and current development efforts. For the area of compliance management in legal and security requirements, there is no ready-to-use solution on the market today. State-of-the-art is to express these as additional requirements in Word or RE-tools with very poor semantics and traceability or assurance mechanisms. We are currently investigating how to adapt the APEX approach for an application to cloud computing systems. Even though the elasticity in the clouds demands a more frequent compliance checks, the rules, laws and regulations do change rarely. Moreover it will still take some time before regulations and laws appear in significant numbers,

We are currently investigating how to adapt the APEX approach for an application to cloud computing systems.

We aim to close the semantic gap between business processes and security/legal requirements. A repository maps these requirements to specific tasks within a business process in order to simplify the implementation and maintenance of compliance checks. The repository will provide an ontology that leads for instance from the security requirement confidentiality to the specific encryption functions in a business process. In addition, we provide methods and tools for model-driven development and adaptation of compliant service-oriented enterprise systems the eclipse modelling framework will be extended to support input from different business process modelling tools. Furthermore, proven model checking software will be integrated into the framework to execute the actual compliance checks.

Moreover, we enable compliance monitoring workflow engines to support compliance monitoring and reporting of the business process execution. Moreover, we aim to integrate all project results into a compliance-engineering framework for developers, business analysts and auditors.

A tool support offers the required scalability of security analysis in a cloud computing in a cost effective manor. Human security experts will no doubt still be required, however numerous analyses can be executed when e.g. the cloud system scales and provide information for security specialists. This approaches the cloud security and compliance problem on a holistic level from compliance regulations and business process to the technical level of soft- and hardware. This tool will present the technical realization of a semantic repository (to be linked to the processes and ontologies of a given company) that will allow reference to compliance demands at different levels of abstraction as well as integration of compliance artefacts in a traceable fashion.

Furthermore a business process modelling language that spans all development stages and technical layers for enterprise cloud business applications. It integrates compliance-relevant artifacts and related security/legal properties as a requisite part of the language. It can be used to specify which data is needed, which process steps need to be executed, and which constraints have to be satisfied within a given business process. A set of model transformations from business process models to model checking tools for the automatic compliance checks derived from security policies and legal resolutions to enforce these policies at all layers of the application. These solutions include Role-based Access Control, separation of duty, rights delegation, network, and middleware layer protection, legal aspects of SOX, Basel II and Solvency II. This leads to a business process modelling framework specific for the cloud environment that is tightly integrated into the Eclipse tool platform. This allows the combination of existing Eclipse solutions for development, debugging, versioning, validation etc. with the modelling tool. Our framework will allow the differing stakeholders in the cloud usage process, who do not (and simply can not) possess all the required compliance, security and risk expertise, to verify quickly the requirements, as well as design, develop, test, deploy and audit the cloud software integration of the business software solutions that fully take compliance-driven aspects into account. The needs of the different stakeholders that will later adopt the Secure-Clouds approach are an important factor for its success. As basic roles interacting with the Secure-Clouds methods and tools we identified the following actors: The auditor is in charge of checking the system with regard to the fulfilment of compliance requirements. The auditor requires aggregated information on business level. He/she will use the compliance repository. The business analyst is an expert of the business domain with a focus on analysing security risks and compliance constraints at business level. He/she will use the Secure-Clouds compliance repository, as well as the Secure-Clouds modelling language. The deployer develops the services configurations in the runtime environment. The deployer works at the levels of the Technical Architecture and Code and Runtime Environment and uses Secure-Clouds techniques of model-driven software development. The test engineer is responsible for developing, executing and analysing system tests. In the process the test engineer focuses on security and compliance aspects and uses model-based techniques for test specification and execution. He/she uses the Secure-Clouds modelling language and model-driven development tools. Our research will provide assurance for the compliance of the currently almost exponentially increasing amount of cloud business operations is expected to become unmanageable. Our work ensures security and legal compliance by design and will allow its users to quickly assess, evaluate and trace the necessary requirements when integrating, deploying and maintaining cloud business operations.

Our research profits from previous work in the field of secure software engineering. There has been a significant amount of work towards Model-based Security Engineering: [Jur02,Jur05] presents a verification framework for UML models enriched with security properties through a UML profile called UMLsec. Supporting tools perform automated analysis on the UMLsec models for security and compliance properties [HöJü08]. Also relevant are approaches for Model-Driven Security for Role-Based Access Control such as [LoBaD02] or the SECTET-Framework presented in [HaAlB06].

There is virtually no work towards engineering enterprise cloud software platforms given a set of compliance regulations. Also relevant are standardization efforts such as the OMG's Regulatory Compliance Alliance. Furthermore the Cloud Security Alliance has done significant work in identifying security threats in enterprise cloud environments [CSA10]. We will also investigate methods for assessing the effectiveness of security investments in the cloud computing context using ideas such as presented in [HGF+05].

6 Conclusion

Today the security and compliance of cloud computing systems is evaluated on different levels of granularity. For instance the BSI showed possible attacks on a detailed level [Esso09], while the Cloud Security Alliance focused on more general attacks [Cav08]. A detailed analysis of the topic is presented in [MaKuL10] and [StRu09], which both describe the possibility to increase security technique due to improved compliance. Documentation, monitoring and control of security measures are vital sales arguments for cloud computing offers. Moreover, a research initiative already exists for automated audits of cloud systems [CAA10]. Specific concepts for identity management and data privacy in cloud computing are topics of ongoing research [Cav08] [BPSF09].

Another fundamental approach to the security issues is the transparency of security. Customers have to accept clouds as a black box solution, which they have to trust. Security certification and automated audits are technical possibilities and increase the trust of customers. This is an important possibility for distinction in the cloud market.

Several cloud security approaches focus on possible attacks. However, there is virtually no work towards engineering enterprise cloud software platforms given a set of compliance regulations. Our research aims to fill this gap.

References

[AFG+09] Armbrust, M.; Fox, A.; Griffith, R.; Joseph, A.D.; Katz, R.H.; Konwinski, A.; Lee, G.; Patterson, D.A.; Rabkin, Ariel; Stoica, Ion; Zaharia, M.: Above the Clouds: A Berkeley View of Cloud Computing, technical report, UCB/EECS-2009-28, EECS Department University of California, Berkeley, 2009

[Bar09] Bartsch, M.: Cloud Security, TüV Informationstechnik GmbH, Unternehmensgruppe TÜV NORD, Präsentation, 2009

[BeBaS08] Beres, Y.; Baldwin, A.; Shiu, S.: Model-Based Assurance of Security Controls, technical report HPL-2008, HP Labs Bristol, 2008.

[BDMN] Barth, A.; Datta, A.; Mitchell, J. C.; Nissenbaum, H.: Privacy and Contextual Integrity: Framework and Applications SP ,06: Proceedings of the 2006 IEEE Symposium on Security and Privacy, IEEE Computer Society, 2006, 184-198

[BPFS09] Bertino, E.; Paci, F.; Ferrini, R.; Shang, N.: Privacy-preserving Digital Identity Management for Cloud Computing. IEEE Data Eng. Bull., 2009, 32, 21-27

[BIE09] Bierekoven, C.; Rödl & Partner: Die Herausforderung für die Daten- und Rechtssicherheit, GI Workshop „Cloud-Computing", 2009

[BPSF09] Bertino, E.; Paci, F.; Shang, N.; Ferrini, R.: Privacy-preserving Digital Identity Management for Cloud Computing, IEEE Data Eng, Bull, 32(1), 21--27, 2009

[CAA10] The Cloud Audit A6, http://www.cloudaudit.org/page3/page3.html, 2010

[CSA10]   The Cloud Security Alliance: Security Guidance for Critical Areas of Focus in Cloud Comput-
            ing, homepage,http://www.cloudsecurityalliance.org/, 2010

[CASa10]   The Cloud Security Alliance: Top Threats to Cloud Computing, homepage,http://
            www.cloudsecurityalliance.org/, 2010

[Cav08]   Cavoukian, A.: Privacy in the clouds, Identity Journal Limited, Springer, 2008

[ClKö01]   Clauss, S.; Köhntopp, M.: Identity management and its support of multilateral security Comp.
            Netw., Elsevier North-Holland, Inc., 2001, 37, 205-219

[Esso09]   Essoh, A.D.: IT-Grundschutz und Cloud Computing, SECMGT Workshop, BSI, 2009

[HaAlB06]   Hafner, M., Alam, M. & Breu, R. (2006) Towards a MOF/QVT-based Domain Architecture for
            Model Driven Security. Proceedings of the 9th International Conference on Model Driven En-
            gineering Languages and Systems (Models 2006). Geneva, Italy.

[HaScC08]   Hansen, M.; Schwartz, A.; Cooper, A.: Privacy and Identity Management IEEE Security and
            Privacy, IEEE Educational Activities Department, 2008, 6, 38-45

[HGF+05]   Houmb,S.H.; Georg, G.; France, R.; Bieman, J.; Jürjens, J.: Cost-Benefit Trade-Off Analysis using
            BBN for Aspect-Oriented Risk-Driven Development, ICECCS 2005, IEEE Computer Society,
            pp 195-204

[HöJü08]   Höhn, S.; Jürjens, J.: Rubacon: automated support for model-based compliance engineering,
            30th International Conference on Software Engineering (ICSE 2008), ACM 2008, pp. 875-878

[IDC09]   IDC-Study: Cloud Computing in Deutschland ist noch nicht angekommen http://www.idc.
            com/germany/press/presse_cloudcomp.jsp, 2009

[JaScl0]   Jaeger, T.; Schiffman, J.: Outlook: Cloudy with a Chance of Security Challenges and Improve-
            ments IEEE Security and Privacy, IEEE Computer Society, 2010, 8, 77-80

[Jur02]   Jürjens, J.: Principles for Secure Systems Design, PhD thesis, 2002, Oxford University

[Jur05]   Jürjens, J., Secure Systems Development with UML, Springer Academic Publishers, 2005.

[LoBaD02]   Lodderstedt, T., Basin, D.; Doser, J.: SecureUML: A UML-Based Modeling Language for Model-
            Driven Security. IN JÉZÉQUEL, J.-M., HUSSMANN, H. & COOK, S. (Eds.) 5th International
            Conference on the Unified Modeling Language. Springer, 2002

[MaKuL10]   Mather, T.; Kumaraswamy, S.; Latif, S.: Cloud Security and Privacy, O'Reilly, 2009

[MeGr09]   Mell, P.: Grance, T.: Effectively and Securely Using the Cloud Computing Paradigm, NIST, Pres-
            entation, 2009

[MoPeB03]   Mont, M. C.; Pearson, S.; Bramhall, P.: Towards Accountable Management of Identity and Pri-
            vacy: Sticky Policies and Enforceable Tracing Services DEXA ,03: Proceedings of the 14th In-
            ternational Workshop on Database and Expert Systems Applications, IEEE Computer Society,
            2003, 377

[PfWa03]   Pfitzmann, B. & Waidner, M.: Federated Identity-Management Protocols - Where User Authen-
            tication Protocols May Go-In 11th Cambridge International Workshop on Security Protocols,
            Springer-Verlag, 2003, 153-174

[StRu09]   Streitberger, W.; Ruppel, A.: Cloud Computing Sicherheit – Schutzziele.Taxonomie.Marktüber-
            sicht, Fraunhofer Institute for Secure Information Technology SIT, 2009

Applying BMIS to Cloud Security

Rolf von Rössing

ISACA / SCM Ltd
rvr@scmltd.com

Abstract

Recent developments in information technology operations have shown two distinct trends. Firstly, products and services have become increasingly commoditised, thus leading to successive waves of outsourcing and offshoring. Secondly, the introduction of intelligent end-point devices and direct accessibility of web-based services has blurred the boundaries of traditional companies and their perimeter. As a result, the "cloud computing" paradigm creates new challenges for security management, including the business value and cost-benefit considerations.

Traditional security models often fail to address this new universe, inasmuch as they are based upon the axiomatic idea of a "closed" corporate IT environment. Practical difficulties in outsourcing or third-party situations are therefore, at best, treated as a business issue that is addressed at the contractual or legal level. In many instances, this causes legal and technical problems, as service level agreements and contracts are flawed instruments for describing a fully de-perimeterised IT environment and its practical requirements. This in turn increases the risk of systemic failures, operational damage, and legal ramifications.

The ISACA Business Model for Information Security (BMIS) provides a systemic foundation for managing cloud-based products and services in terms of their security aspects. The paper shows how the general model is applied and how the use of BMIS enhances the overall security level. It is further shown how aspects of governance, risk and compliance (GRC) may be included in order to align operational information security management with business requirements. The paper addresses practical steps towards securing a heavily clouded environment using recognised frameworks such as COBIT or the ISO 27000 series. Recommendations are given to enable direct use of the BMIS in day-to-day security management.

1 Changes in the Security Universe

In recent years, many IT resources and devices have been decentralised to what has become known as the "cloud". Corporate entities and other organisations no longer operate primarily in-house, and business requirements indicate that further decentralisation and outsourcing of non-critical IT components will continue. In terms of structural change, this has led to a significant expansion of the security universe:

- Outward shift of the security perimeter / de-perimeterisation
- Disconnect between application and infrastructure layers
- Multi-stage outsourcing, multiple contracts with third parties, unknown third parties
- Emergence of intelligent end-point devices
- Outsourcing / out-tasking of critical data storage and critical services to public providers

Typical "cloudy" setups such as SaaS, PaaS or IaaS tend to blur the distinction between what is internal to the corporate entity and what is external. The physical perspective on IT components and services is unreliable, in that services may be executed from within the firm but physically located in a third-party environment. The example of remote configuration management and remote helpdesk functionality highlights how security (both in terms of activity and responsibility) are clearly situated beyond the corporate perimeter. In terms of information security, the de-perimeterised environment blurs responsibility and accountability, particularly when security breaches or attacks occur.

As an indirect consequence, the application layer and the infrastructure layer as seen from the corporate security management perspective have separated. Business-facing applications are operated by cloud providers, whereas infrastructure may be provided by an entirely different set of third parties. In conjunction with the somewhat blurred responsibilities, this disconnect offers new (indirect) attack vectors and increases the risk of undetected security incidents.

Following the technical separation of IT components and services, the relationship between the firm itself and external providers is controlled by a growing number of contractual agreements. Business and cost pressures have created multi-tier outsourcing situations that the principal may not be aware of, for instance in a SaaS scenario with second degree outsourcing to a hosting provider, and third degree outsourcing to a housing provider.

Simultaneously, computing power and complexity have moved from a centralist (mainframe) paradigm to a multitude of intelligent end-point devices. While convenience to the consumer and a growing number of business-critical mobile services often supersede any security concerns, modern mobile devices can easily emulate or surpass the functionality of internal computers. This in turn creates a considerable risk of attacks and security breaches at the periphery rather than within the centre.

In line with the above-mentioned developments, social patterns in IT have changed drastically as a result of the availability and convenience of cloud computing. Individuals have embraced social networks and free services, such as cloud-based data storage and cloud-based social applets. This effectively rules out any "closed" sets of rules and controls that information security managers have operated in the past. New approaches to security management will have to acknowledge the users´ willingness (or indifference to) openly sharing what is seen as critical data.

Summarily, the shift towards cloudy environments presents a formidable challenge to information security. No longer can the security universe be managed by "closed" paradigms and related instruments. Traditional security models fail to address the cloud-based risks, and traditional management structures have little control over the outlying entities that operate critical parts of the company´s IT environment.

2 Reviewing Contractual Instruments

From a business perspective, cloudy IT environments tend to separate components and services in terms of providers and their tasks. IT management in general has moved from performing technical activities to transacting business with third parties. Much of what used to be the responsibility of internal information security is now governed by contractual relationships and defined service levels only. This creates interesting challenges [DLAP10, ISAC09b] that reach far beyond traditional contract design and internal service level definition:

- Multiple parties to agreements
- Weaknesses in service description, metrics and measurements

- Fragmentation in corporate relationships, dispersal, subcontractor relationships
- Gaps in contractual coverage, information security problems outside the contract

In a homogeneous corporate entity, or set of entities, multiple parties delivering or receiving a service are by definition part of the same legal entity or its affiliated entities. For services related to information security, overall protection is a shared interest for all actors, at least to a degree. In a cloudy environment, shared interest cannot be assumed with reasonable certainty, as the parties to any agreement are restricted to viewing their area of activity. This leads to a non-linear increase in the number of contracts or agreements required to manage a heterogeneous and cloudy set of actors. Furthermore, the inherent complexity of agreements increases if there are multiple parties: responsibility, accountability, consultancy and information (RACI) are highly differentiated in a legal sense.

Services and cloud-based products require a more precise definition than services and products that are managed internally. The latter are often implemented and operated with a tacit understanding amongst specialists whose experience acts as a catalyst, whereas the former are typically delivered by individuals who are unfamiliar with both the environment and the corporate culture of the principal company. Contracts and service level agreements are generally normative, and less descriptive in nature. This is due to the fact that they are instruments for managing a relationship. The description of the subject-matter is often deferred and set aside in annexes or schedules to the contract. In practice, service descriptions are often flawed or insufficient to exhaustively define a cloud-based deliverable. There is a further lack of available and recognised metrics and measurements, particularly in fields that are central to the cloud[1].

Cloudy environments introduce fragmentation of corporate relationships, inasmuch as products or services formerly managed from the inside of a corporate entity are now subject to any number of relationships between parties. Additional dispersal – mostly in the geographic sense – arises from the cloud itself, as the exact physical location and jurisdiction of a product or service can no longer be predicted with any degree of certainty. Likewise, cloudy products and services may be subject to unknown subcontractor relationships that form part of an indirect contractual landscape. In practice, the fragmentation and the growth in the number of parties involved in delivering the product or service are likely to create significant security risks.

By definition, the content of any contract is confined to the legal and technical context. Even in intra-firm agreements, it is often difficult to convey both the corporate culture and the mutual expectation levels. In cloudy environments, contracts inevitably show significant gaps that relate to unwritten rules, behavioural items, and other intangibles that are part of the principal´s corporate fabric. Information security is however often based on exactly these assumptions, particularly in those firms where senior management propagates a "culture of trust" or "openness". As a result, any information security provisions agreed between multiple parties require more than a legal or contractual definition. It is not enough to establish elaborate systems of policies or controls, as witnessed by numerous security incidents in cloudy environments.

In summary, the move towards the cloud as the dominant paradigm has effectively obviated the traditional, linear model of contracts between a distinct number of known parties. Products and services in the cloud require a new approach towards governing and regulating design, deliv-

---

1 As an example, metrics and measurements for network availability have existed for some time, but related resilience metrics are still being developed.

ery and management. For information security purposes, reality and operational security in the cloud are difficult or impossible to translate into contractual provisions, unless there is a wider model that includes a common understanding of information security across the cloud, and shared interest in all participating actors.

3 Systemic Risks and Crises

The growing number of cloud-based applications, products and services has created a number of significant systemic risks, including several new risk categories. Information as such forms both the purpose and the justification for cloudy environments, and hence, information security is rapidly becoming a primary area of focus. [CSA09, ISAC09b], among others, define the intrinsic risks of cloudy arrangements, whereas [CSA10] identifies the top ten practical threats. The CSA has further defined several key areas of focus, or domains, that have been recognised in day-to-day practice [CSA09]:

- Governance and Enterprise Risk Management (including legal and contractual issues)
- Legal and Electronic Discovery
- Compliance and Audit
- Information Lifecycle Management
- Portability and Interoperability (including exit strategies)
- Traditional Security, Business Continuity and Disaster Recovery
- Data Center Operations
- Incident Response, Notification and Remediation
- Application Security
- Encryption and Key Management
- Identity and Access Management
- Virtualization

Systemic risks and crises are difficult to quantify, but some foundational approaches have been suggested [Fara10]. Not surprisingly, the general perception of risks and the categorisation of operational impact have not changed significantly with the advent of the cloud, as shown by very early work [Slov78, FSLR+78, JoTv84] integrated by [Fara10].

When applying standardised methods of business impact analysis (BIA), risks are deconstructed according to their immediate and secondary consequences on the business as such, or the mission-critical activities of any organisation. For information security in cloudy environments, this yields:

Table 1: Risks [ISAC09b] and Impact

Risk or Risk Category	Impact
Provider / contract risk	operational, contractual, reputational
Information handling (by providers), availability, sustainability	operational, legal / regulatory, reputational
Location of information	legal / regulatory, reputational
Third party access	operational, legal / regulatory, reputational
Public clouds, co-location of information assets	operational, legal / regulatory, contractual, reputational
Business continuity / disaster recovery	operational

For information security purposes, [CSA10] defines the immediate security concerns and their mapping towards the cloud reference architecture and service types, providing a useful basis for the practical case of applying any security model:

Table 2: Threats [CSA10], Domains and Cloud Service Types

Threat	Focus Areas / Domains	Cloud Service Types
Abuse and Nefarious Use of Cloud Computing	Data Center Operations Incident Response, Notification and Remediation	IaaS, PaaS
Insecure Interfaces and APIs	Application Security	IaaS, PaaS, SaaS
Malicious Insiders	Governance and Enterprise Risk Management Traditional Security, Business Continuity and Disaster Recovery	IaaS, PaaS, SaaS
Shared Technology Issues	Data Center Operations Virtualization	IaaS
Data Loss or Leakage	Information Lifecycle Management Encryption and Key Management Identity and Access Management	IaaS, PaaS, SaaS
Account or Service Hijacking	Governance and Enterprise Risk Management Incident Response, Notification and Remediation Identity and Access Management	IaaS, PaaS, SaaS

[CSA10] further introduces an "unknown risk profile" which covers any unforeseen or new types of risks arising from the cloud paradigm. Other works [Rava10] underpin the necessity to be prepared for new and unknown cloud risks that may arise in due course.

Summarily, the risks brought about by the cloud itself have been defined and categorised, allowing the application of security models and methods. However, existing models fail to cover the full range of risks, particularly from a business perspective [Roes09]. Given the specific nature of risks, threats and foreseeable impacts, the overall likelihood of systemic crises and massive operational impact arising from cloud computing has increased significantly, as compared to in-house or traditional models. This is emphasised even further by the general reluctance observed in field studies [ISAC10b, ISAC10c, ISAC10d] – the majority of companies still appear to be pondering the risks of moving towards the cloud.

4 Applying the BMIS

As an overarching model, BMIS a shown in figure 1 is designed to both integrate and improve information security in the context of risks and threats. Specifically, the model addresses the interdependencies between the business and IT, as well as the multiple relationships arising from moving products and services towards cloudy environments. In practical terms, introducing BMIS encompasses several initial steps that lead to an iterative cycle of managing security. It is noted [ISAC09, ISAC10a] that the decisive influence is the core business of the organisation, or its mission-critical activities.

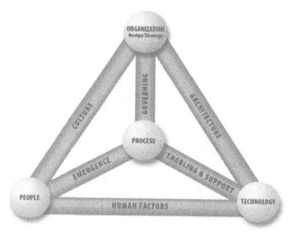

Figure 1: BMIS Overview Diagram

The systemic approach taken requires alignment of existing security arrangements as well as regulations and standards. In the cloud, these tasks may lead to an initially high effort. However, the upfront investment in aligning BMIS with the existing business priorities and corresponding security arrangements reduces cost in the long run.

4.1 Taking Stock – What is There in Terms of Security

Considering the new information security environment, the "Jericho Cube" [Jeri09] offers a high-level visualisation of cloudy IT in its widest sense. Figure 2 shows the cube which is used as a basis for organising and structuring the overall information security system and its subsystems.

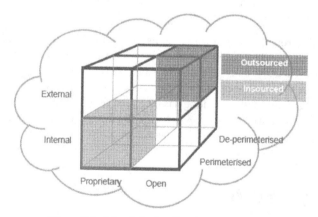

Figure 2: Jericho Cube for Cloud Representation

As a lateral layer, the stock-taking exercise should include a number of business areas closely related to information security [ISAC10b]:

- Laws and regulations
- Enterprise governance / corporate governance

- Security compliance within the context of general compliance
- Other security components, e. g. policies and standards, BCM, health and safety etc.

While this may appear to be a rather pedestrian approach towards systemic security, collecting the information will often clarify existing security-related subsystems. By mapping them to the cube representation, the overall business universe is segmented and allows systematic treatment of individual security problems.

The mapping is then completed by analysing the contents of each category as described above, and provisionally assigning them to the elements and dynamic interconnections of the model. As an example, policies and standards might be assigned to the organisation element as well as the culture or governing dynamic interconnection, depending on the corporate environment and information security design.

Having thus completed the stock-taking within the firm, the BMIS should be applied across the cloud, using the cube model. This will in turn lead to security arrangements that are managed directly (i.e. internally), and others that reside in the cloud or form part of contractual relationships. It is then straightforward to apply the model, via the instrument of contractual provisions, to third party relationships or interfaces.

4.2 Cloud Requirements and Internalising Them to the BMIS

Following the stock-taking exercise and having noted any gaps that may exist at the practical level, the model is aligned to existing standards such as ISO 27001 or BS 25777. [ISAC10a] recommends the use of the COBIT model [ISAC08] as a "common language" that links information security to general enterprise IT governance and compliance. Figure 3 outlines the process of assigning elements of recognised standards with the elements and dynamic interconnections, whereas Figure 4 shows a drill-down of contents.

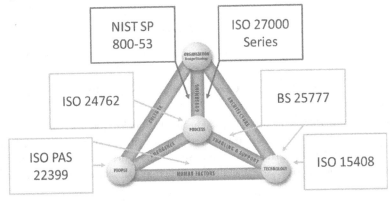

Figure 3: Alignment of Common Standards With BMIS Components

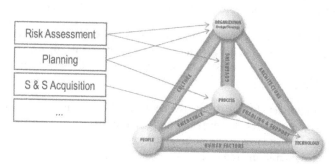

Figure 4: Common Standards and BMIS - Aligning Contents (Example: NIST SP 800-53)

In addition to the immediate information security standards that are used in day-to-day practice, wider frameworks for information management and IT infrastructure are mapped to the model in a similar manner. The COBIT framework provides a number of generic mappings for this purpose. Figure 5 shows the integration process at a high level. The detailed alignment steps are described in [ISAC10a] and within the COBIT mapping documentation.

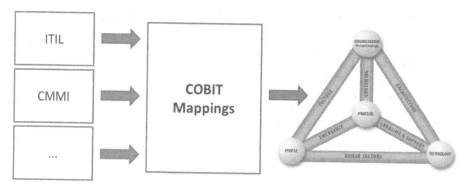

Figure 5: Mapping Generic IT Frameworks to the BMIS

In order to adequately address the new situation brought about by cloudy IT environments, static security arrangements and models are transposed into a dynamic format, creating subsystems that respond to internal and external influence, as shown in Figure 6. These subsystems underpin the changing nature of security, as well as the fundamentally different approach represented by the BMIS.

In any given subsystem, external and internal actors influence systemic behaviour, as do existing risks. In the example of Figure 6 below, the decisive elements are "attractiveness" and "total attacks", and the actors influencing these are depicted in Figure 7.

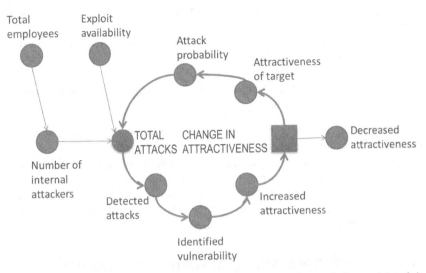

Figure 6: Systemic Representation of Information Security (Example: Internal Attacks)

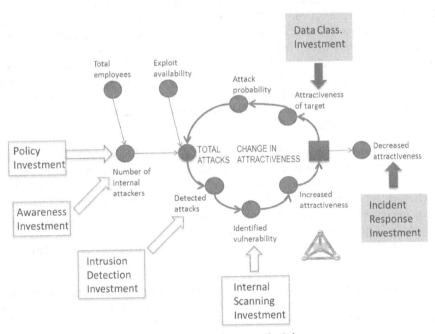

Figure 7: Actors Influencing the Subsystem

Specific requirements for information security in cloudy environments thus link to multiple dimensions within the BMIS, as do the risks and threats listed in tables 1 and 2:

- Cube model – location and management approach, organisational models etc.
- Risk and threat mappings to cloud security focus areas

- Alignment of existing security arrangements to the BMIS (elements and dynamic interconnections)
- Alignment of existing security arrangements to common standards (usually in place or partially in place, depending on the company being reviewed)
- Risk and threat mappings to security subsystems
- Alignment of existing security arrangements to the nodes of security subsystems (for instance through specific investments)

In a setting with multiple companies and business relationships, each business partner may use the BMIS to address these dimensions. The sum of all models across multiple suppliers, platforms and locations allows tracking and tracing of security measures across multiple BMIS instances. For instance, an awareness programme may be initiated in the "Organisation" element and the "Culture" dynamic interconnection in one firm, and continued in a service provider firm through the "Governing" dynamic interconnection, particularly if the outsourcing organisation stipulates awareness campaigns as one of the contractual requirements.

4.3 Introducing and Measuring Systemic Improvements

The BMIS is supported by a number of existing frameworks and incidental guidance, most notably [ISAC08, ISAC09c, ISAC09d, ISAC09e, ISAC09f]. These provide a comprehensive set of metrics, measurements and maturity models that are easily applied to cloud security. In using the BMIS to approach information (and cloud) security from a systemic perspective, these tools of the trade are applied repetitively, and in an iterative manner. In this sense, they provide sustainable data for measuring and comparing the "before and after" of any change applied to the security arrangements across the cloud. In practice, at least the COBIT framework has gained international recognition and may serve as a common language for auditors, compliance officers and security practitioners alike.

It is noted that systemic improvements are introduced at the level of security subsystems, and then consolidated at the level of BMIS elements and dynamic interconnections. The multiple dependencies of any subsystem (see Figures 6 and 7) require a walk-through analysis of any planned changes. When seen as a "flat" table, such targeted security measures and investments may appear unconnected, or even disjointed. It is however the systemic view that provides the logic behind single steps towards improving information security across the cloud. This is even more important where cloudy environments consist of multiple actors, contractual relationships and locations.

Once the internal logic of the cloud security system as a whole is known, applying improvements to individual subsystems, companies or platforms is straightforward. The results then lend themselves to more traditional models of analysis, such as maturity levels or key performance indicators.

5 Conclusion

The de-perimeterised security universe created by cloudy processes and environments clearly highlights the need for new approaches in information security. Given the traditional security models and governance frameworks currently in place, the outbound and inbound relationships have acquired more than contractual significance, and "unwritten" content and rules. It is concluded from empirical developments in major global clouds that both contract design and the degree of specification in documents cannot match the level of complexity that is rapidly growing on and between the cloud layers.

In terms of matching the speed of these developments, it is further concluded that traditional and static security models cannot adequately address ever-changing requirements, mainly due to their linear view and their bias towards isolated security measures and activities. In contrast, the BMIS introduces a dynamic and systemic view of conceptual and day-to-day security. As a result of reviewing existing cloud security approaches, it follows that the BMIS is capable of integrating these components and dynamicising them.

While works like [ISAC10a] are contributing to the detail and practical implementation of the model, further research is in progress to fully integrate it with internationally recognised frameworks such as COBIT. This step will be imperative for practical use and acceptance in the information security community. Forthcoming work, for instance COBIT Security[2], will use the BMIS as a basis for designing and maintaining cloud security.

References

[CSA09]   Cloud Security Alliance. Security Guidance for Critical Areas of Focus in Cloud Computing v2.1. [www.cloudsecurityalliance.org/guidance/csaguide.v2.1.pdf] accessed 2010-07-19.

[CSA10]   Cloud Security Alliance. Top Threats to Cloud Computing v1.0. [http://www.cloudsecurityalliance. org/topthreats/csathreats.v1.0.pdf] accessed 2010-07-19.

[DLAP10] DLA Piper [Peter van Eecke]. Cloud Computing Legal Risks. Presentation. [http://www. isaca.org/Groups/Professional-English/cloud-computing/GroupDocuments/DLA_ Cloud%20computing%20legal%20issues.pdf] accessed 2010-07-19.

[Fara10] Farahmand, F. Risk Perception and Trust in Cloud. ISACA Journal vol. 4 (2010).

[FSLR+78] Fischoff, B.; P. Slovic; S. Lichtenstein; S. Read; B. Combs; "How Safe Is Safe Enough? A Psychometric Study of Attitudes Towards Technological Risks and Benefits," Policy Sciences, 9(2), 1978, p. 127-152.

[ISAC08] ISACA. COBIT 4.1. Rolling Meadows, IL: ISACA, 2008.

[ISAC09a] ISACA. An Introduction to the Business Model for Information Security. Rolling Meadows, IL: ISACA, 2009.

[ISAC09b] ISACA. Cloud Computing: Business Benefits with Security, Governance and Assurance Perspectives. Rolling Meadows, IL: ISACA, 2009.

[ISAC09c] ISACA. Enterprise Value: Governance of IT Investments – The ValIT Framework 2.0. Rolling Meadows, IL: ISACA, 2009.

[ISAC09d] ISACA. Mapping of ValIT 2.0 to MSP, PRINCE2 and ITIL v3. Rolling Meadows, IL: ISACA, 2009.

---

2   This module, and others, will form part of the major new release COBIT 5 that is to replace COBIT 4.1 in due course. The planned publication date is not yet final, but expected for 2011.

[ISAC09e] ISACA. The Risk IT Framework. Rolling Meadows, IL: ISACA, 2009.

[ISAC09f] ISACA. The Risk IT Practitioner Guide. Rolling Meadows, IL: ISACA, 2009.

[ISAC10a] ISACA. Business Model for Information Security. Rolling Meadows, IL: ISACA, 2010 (forth-coming).

[ISAC10b] ISACA. 2010 ISACA Risk / Reward Barometer, US Edition. Rolling Meadows, IL: ISACA, 2010 (March).

[ISAC10c] ISACA. 2010 ISACA Risk / Reward Barometer, Latin American Edition. Rolling Meadows, IL: ISACA, 2010 (April).

[ISAC10d] ISACA, 2010 ISACA Risk / Reward Barometer, Oceania Edition. Rolling Meadows, IL: ISACA, 2010 (July).

[Jeri09]   Jericho Forum. Cloud Cube Model: Selecting Cloud Formations for Secure Collaboration. [https://www.opengroup.org/jericho/cloud_cube_model_v1.0.pdf] accessed 2007-07-19.

[JoTv84]   Johnson, E. J.; A. Tversky; "Representations of Perceptions of Risks," Journal of Experimental Psychology, General, vol. 113, no. 1, 1984, p. 55-70.

[Rava10]   Raval, V. Risk Landscape of Cloud Computing. ISACA Journal vol. 4 (2010).

[Roes09]   Roessing, R. v. The ISACA Business Model for Information Security: An Integrative and Innovative Approach. Proceedings of ISSE 2009.

[Slov78]   Slovic, P.; "Perceptions of Risk," Science, 236, 1978, p. 280-285.

Security Services
and Large Scale
Public Applications

Critical Infrastructure in Finance PARSIFAL Recommendations

Bernhard M. Hämmerli[1] · Henning H. Arendt[2]

[1]Acris GmbH & HSLU
bmhaemmerli@acris.ch

[2]@bc*
henning.arendt@atbc.de

Abstract

The PARSIFAL projekt (Protection and Trust in Financial Infrastructures) project is a Coordination Action funded within the FP7 European Research Programme Joint Call for Information and Communications Technologies and Critical Infrastructure Protection. Project Coordinator is ATOS Origin Sae/Spain, partners are ACRIS GmbH/Switzerland, @bc. - Arendt Business Consulting/Germany, Avoco Secure Ltd,(UK, EDGE International BV/Netherlands, Waterford Institute of Technology/Ireland. This article summarizes the recommendations for future research how to better protect Critical Financial Infrastructures (CFI) in Europe. It should be a valuable guidance to initiate projects that address these stakeholders' recommendations.

1 PARSIFAL – An Overview

The European Programme for Critical Infrastructure Protection (EPCIP) [2] lists 11 sectors of critical infrastructure including the Critical Financial Infrastructure. The PARSIFAL (Protection and Trust in Financial Infrastructures) project is a Coordination Action funded within the European Research Programme Joint Call for Information and Communications Technologies and Critical Infrastructure Protection. Project Coordinator is ATOS Origin Sae/Spain, Partners are ACRIS GmbH/Switzerland, @bc. - Arendt Business Consulting/Germany, Avoco Secure Ltd,(UK, EDGE International BV/Netherlands, Waterford Institute of Technology/Ireland. Cooperation partners of PARSIFAL are the European Finance Forum and another FP7 project Communication Middleware for monitoring Financial Critical Infrastructure (CoMiFin). The duration of the project was 18 months. It started September 2008 with the following project objectives

- Bringing together CFI research stakeholders
- Contributing to the understanding of CFI challenges
- Developing longer term visions, research roadmaps, CFI scenarios and best practice guides
- Coordinating the relevant research work, knowledge and experiences

This summary serves for both: for executives of the finance industry to initiate projects that address the stakeholders' recommendations, and for the research community to address the topic and find partners in the financial sector. The methodology (section 2) describes the process which led to the mapping of challenges to scenarios (section 3) and the eight overall recommendations (section 4). The dependencies and interrelation of the eight recommendations are analysed (section 5) in order to generate a consecutive order of projects. The prioritization process of the eight recommendations (section 6) is discussed and the three key documents with background and detail level information created by the project partners are presented (section 7). Finally conclusions are taken.

2 PARSIFAL Methodology

PARSIFAL strengthened engagement between the European Commission and the Financial Services Industry in terms of trust, security and dependability. For Critical ICT infrastructures, directions for future research programmes were elaborated.

PARSIFAL established an Experts Stakeholders Group (ESG) to align research in this area to the needs of the Financial Services Industry. The ESG includes key actors in the CFI protection with sub-groups representing the financial industry, academia and government. ESG topics covered financial, IT, R&D, 'Trust, Security and Dependability' (TSD), and service providers' perspectives. Members include high level decision-makers as well as managers and experts related to the topics. PARSIFAL engaged closely with other R&D projects in the ICT/CIP/CFI domains, most specifically the CoMiFin project funded in the same call. The activities of the project centred on two ESG workshops, where stakeholders exchanged their views directly and discussed future scenarios and challenges from various perspectives in a first workshop in which the research challenges of the financial sector were discussed in the following three topics related expert groups:

1. Controlling Instant On Demand Business in CFI: Authentication, identity management, resilience and denial of service;
2. Entitlement Management and Securing Content in the Perimeterless Financial Environment: Identity, policy, privacy and audit;
3. Business Continuity and Control in an Interconnected and Interdependent Service Landscape: Compliance, protecting critical processes.

The three stakeholder working groups used written exercises and discussion to define future scenarios and challenges in CFI protection.

The discussions in the groups were twofold. First, the future scenarios were discussed, which need a change in security or more attention. The scenarios are the justification of why something could be more important in the future. Second, expected technology developments, technology related innovations, and research challenges were discussed. Finally, a mapping of the challenges to the scenario helped to eliminate technology visions without any clear relation to improvements in the financial infrastructure.

3 Mapping CFI Challenges to Scenarios

As a result of their first workshop, PARSIFAL mapped challenges in CFI protection to appropriate scenarios. This action compared and clarified the challenges of securing CFI.

Figure 1 is a condensed re-presentation of a 30 scenarios by 30 challenges matrix that shows the main areas of concern, as directly expressed by the stakeholders.

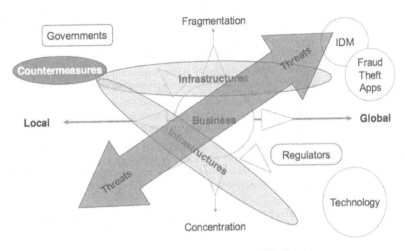

Fig. 1: Mapping Scenarios and Challenges

The **key ideas** and **paradigms** in this diagram are:
- Infrastructure - technology platforms, increasing complexity
- Infrastructure - business practises and working patterns, increasing complexity
- Infrastructure - data security methodology, highly distributed networks and borderless environments
- Countermeasures - robust Identity Management (IDM), new threat/ fraud recognition methods
- Systems - identity mechanisms and identity management
- Compliance - highly distributed networks and borderless environments, data security in highly distributed networks
- Global threats versus local measures

4 PARSIFAL Recommendations and Research Directions

The project results in the form of recommendations for future research are results from preparation papers of the project team, the presentations at the workshops, the written work done at the workshop and the post processing in the research team.

As a result of the discussions on CFI challenges and scenarios, PARSIFAL formulated eight recommendations for future research in the area of CFI protection:

Table 1: Work-Streams and Recommendations

Stream 1: Instant on Demand Business	1. Classification of identity attributes for wired on-line and mobile users of financial services should be defined and well understood by providers of these services and their customers.
	2. Trust indicators need to be developed, which allow for the various gradients of trust any entity might achieve when using specific financial services.
	3. Support platforms are needed for the management of multiple identities to allow consumers to authenticate themselves with various professional and private identity attributes.
Stream 2: Entitlement Management	4. Digital identities are required that are highly standardised across the financial services sector, with the introduction of mandatory IDs for all financial institutions, cross border interoperability and a "single/global" identity issuing authority.
	5. Data Security measures are required, such that (1) a digital identity links directly with a security policy to a data object, (2) data is secured as encapsulated entities, and (3) with flexible security policies that are based on individual access rights plus Digital Rights Management (DRM) for enterprise content to allow for flexible security policies and geographic boundary control.
	6. New Computing Paradigms need to be analysed, which allow for de-perimeterization of the organisation, e.g. Cloud Computing, supported by any new security focus. Predictive models need to be created to understand security risks. Cross border legal issues need to be resolved.
Stream 3: Business Continuity	7. Design and implementation of secure platforms and applications should be researched, such that an alternative and secure communication system/infrastructure will be available, including an adequate coordination response team(s) at a national and international level.
	8. Testing, design and implementation of such secure platforms should be elaborated as well as applications- and infrastructures- test through trustworthy multilateral exercises between CIP-sectors and governments. Models for business continuity need to be extended to (1) sharing risks and (2) end-to-end communication between trade participants, as well as to (3) the volume and the complexity of specific financial markets. These models should be "crash" tested, regularly evaluated and updated.

The target population of our recommendations can be divided into four groups:

1. The European Comission.
2. Providers of financial services and operators of financial infrastructures.
3. EU Member States Governmental agencies and regulators.
4. IT security experts and researchers.

5 Dependencies between the Recommendations

In a complex process with consideration of the stream and sense of urgency figure 2 was developed showing the timeline (starting with recommendation six), the dependencies and interrelation of the recommendations.

The eight recommendations are dependent, time- and content-wise. These dependencies should be considered in more detail when deciding which area of research to emphasize. Figure 2 takes into account these dependencies and outlines the research program which might result from the recommendations, where each recommendation could be a 2-3 year Specific Targeted Research Project (STREP).

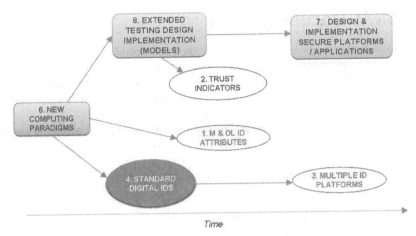

Fig. 2: Timescale for the 8 Recommendations

6 Stakeholders' Voting on the Recommendations

Experts from the stakeholder group and many other experts were invited to vote on the eight recommendations. The following options were available for voting: Absolutely urgent, Urgent, Must be addressed, Not urgent. Although the results are apart from each other, the results points clearly out, that the recommendations have found agreement in the community and which one have highest priority.

The figure below shows the voting results on the recommendations presented during the 2nd PARSIFAL workshop. Votes were cast in terms of urgency in which the recommendation should be looked at with a view to a resolution of the issue. The PARSIFAL project team received nearly 200 votes primarily from stakeholder in the financial industry, but also some votes from related scientists.

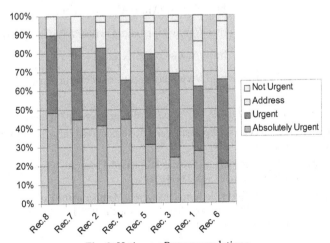

Fig. 3: Voting on Recommendations

7 PARSIFAL Documentation

Valuable information to define and support future research is provided with the PARSIFAL deliverables. Besides the reports about stakeholders and workshops three key documents were created:

- **Ontology of financial risks and dependencies within and outside the financial sector:** introduces the reader to the idea of using ontologies and glossaries to better understand the risks within the CFI and the key concepts as used in the project.
- **Trusted sharing of confidential information in CI:** covers the most recent research in the area of securing data within a CI and current developments in data security including digital identity.
- **Gap analysis and future needs report:** defines the general background, the strategies and the requirements for future research.

All deliverables can be found on the PARSIFAL website under the section "Documentation": http://www.PARSIFAL-project.eu/

For additional information you can also check our Wikipedia article PARSIFAL Project_EU at: http://en.wikipedia.org/wiki/PARSIFAL_Project_EU

8 Conclusion

The PARSIFAL stakeholders clearly indicated that future research is needed in all eight recommended areas. Research organisations and finance institutions/service providers should team up to address these challenges to better protect Europe's financial infrastructure in the future. The project documentation is a valuable source of information. Specifically the ontology of financial risks and dependencies should be useful for experts dealing with the CIP topic in the financial industry.

References

Project Website: http://www.PARSIFAL-project.eu/

Wikipedia: http://en.wikipedia.org/wiki/PARSIFAL_Project_EU

CoMiFin Website: http://www.comifin.eu/

European Finance Forum website: http://www.europeanfinanceforum.org

[1]   European Commission CORDIS FP7 http://cordis.europa.eu/fp7/understand_en.html

[2]   EPCIP http://europa.eu/rapid/pressReleasesAction.do?reference=MEMO/06/477&format= HTML&aged=0&language=EN

[3]   Challenges for the Protection of Critical ICT-Based Financial Infrastructures http://www. springerlink.com/content/n321540q23411034/

[4]   European Central Bank Gertrude Tumpel-Gugerell, Member of the Executive Board of the ECB, opening speech of a PARSIFAL-workshop 16-17 March 2009 http://www.ecb.europa.eu/press/ key/date/2009/html/sp090316.en.html

[5]   2nd PARSIFAL Workshop "Securing the Future Critical Financial ICT-Infrastructure", 1 December 2009 http://www.europeanfinanceforum.org/Securing-CFI-12-2009.163.0.html?&ftu=a12e170569

[6]   1st PARSIFAL Workshop "Securing the Future Critical Financial ICT-Infrastructure", 16-17 March 2009   http://www.europeanfinanceforum.org/Securing-CFI-2009.156.8.html?&ftu=a12e170569

[7]   PARSIFAL Project Summary, May 2010 http://www.PARSIFAL-project.eu/images/documents/PARSIFAL_Marketing%20Document.pdf

[8]   FC10 Financial Cryptography and Data Security '10, Fourteenth International Conference, 25-28 January 2010 http://fc10.ifca.ai/Program.htm

[9]   La Universidad de La Laguna celebra el XIV Congreso de Criptografía financiera, el primero que se celebra en Europa Europa Press, 24 January 2010 (in Spanish) http://www.europapress.es/islas-canarias/noticia-universidad-laguna-celebra-xiv-congreso-criptografia-financiera-primero-celebra-europa-20100124074547.html

[10]   Protection and Trust in Financial Infrastructures (PARSIFAL) Project Summary and Recommendations European Finance Forum (in German) http://europeanfinanceforum.org/Meeting.45.0.html?&no_cache=1&eventanchor=1974&location=&cHash=c597458d20&ftu=47efd15071

The SPOCS Interoperability Framework: Interoperability of eDocuments and eDelivery Systems taken as Example

Thomas Rössler · Arne Tauber

E-Government Innovation Center (EGIZ)
Inffeldgasse 16a, A-8010 Graz, Austria
{thomas.roessler | arne.tauber}@egiz.gv.at

Abstract

The European Services Directive demands interoperability between European eGovernment services and infrastructures in order to support European Service Providers as good as possible. This requirement leads to many challenges in various areas like electronic documents, electronic delivery, electronic identification etc.

This paper introduces an approach to these challenges: The EU Large Scale Pilot SPOCS. This large scale pilot aims to develop interoperability frameworks to link various existing eGovernment solutions of EU Member States resulting in a seamless landscape of eServices relating to the Services Directive.

Two important areas which are tackled by SPOCS are the interoperability of electronic documents and interoperability of electronic delivery systems. Both areas strongly relate to existing infrastructures of Member States and are involved in nearly every eGovernment procedure. This paper introduces SPOCS' interoperability frameworks regarding electronic delivery and electronic documents as two examples representing the overall interoperability framework delivered by SPOCS mid of 2012.

1 Introduction

The current national implementations of the EU Services Directive are first but important steps ahead. However, in order to bring a real benefit to European Service Providers, a better electronic support is needed. This would help to strengthen European businesses and to strengthen the business location Europe tremendously.

Consequently, the Services Directive (SD) demands to build up on existing eGovernment infrastructure as the Service Providers' domestic eGovernment elements, e.g. its eIdentity tokens, eDelivery accounts etc., should work abroad as well. Therefore, an advanced interoperability concept is needed to bridge the various national eGovernment elements, like eDelivery channels, eDocument sources etc.

While the cross border use of eIdentities is already tackled by the EU Large Scale Pilot Project (LSP) STORK[1], the interoperability in other areas of eGovernment is not well developed yet. The

---

1 STORK: secure identities across borders linked; see http://www.eid-stork.eu

new EU LSP SPOCS[2] takes up this challenge and will provide an interoperability framework for those eGovernmental areas which are required to conduct typical Services Directive related processes fully electronically.

In this paper, we sketch the given situation regarding the implementation of the Services Directive by discussing the situation we found in partner countries of SPOCS. Next we discuss the vision of SPOCS and SPOCS' main principles. Finally, this paper highlights as an example of the SPOCS interoperability framework two interoperability approaches, e.g. the envisaged interoperability framework for eDelivery and eDocuments. At the end, conclusions are drawn.

2 The given situation

Every Member State has its own eGovernment infrastructure in place. Although the existing eGovernment infrastructure bases usually on existing standards and stat-of-the-art technologies, it is often quite proprietary on the application level. Taking eDocuments as an example, many national eGovernment applications and services make use of XML for information exchange. Although national XML specifications base on existing international XML schemes, e.g. specifications/standards from UN/CEFACT or OASIS etc., the resulting instance documents can be neither automatically processed nor automatically interpreted by any third party (i.e. a party that is not aware about the scheme of the particular instance document). Furthermore, a receiving third party is not even aware that the document in question has been issued by a public authority of a foreign country (in this example we assume a typical SPOCS scenario: a European Service Provider provides a national eDocument to a public authority of a foreign country).

On the other hand, it is very unlikely that existing national solutions or schemes will be replaced be new ones in the near future. Especially in this time of financial challenges public authorities reduce investments to a minimum so that the protection of investment gains importance. In addition to this, the replacement of existing national schemes would take an inappropriate amount of time.

As a consequence, any interoperability framework that is planned to be introduced in the near future has to accept the national infrastructure as a given and should built on top of it. An international interoperability infrastructure has to bridge existing domestic services by introducing a common interoperability layer. This interoperability layer bridges the various national systems by introducing a common interoperability protocol. From this perspective, the principles introduced by EIF/PEGS seems being suitable. Only in a long term perspective the change of national infrastructure seems to be feasible.

Based on these observations, the following principles for an interoperability framework—for the SPOCS framework in particular—can be defined:

1. Accept national infrastructure as a given
2. Bridge by introducing an international interoperability protocol/layer

In the next section we briefly show how we are going to introduce an interoperability framework by addressing the aforementioned principles in the course of the LSP SPOCS.

---

2 SPOCS: simple procedures online for cross-border services; see http://www.eu-spocs.eu

3 The Vision of SPOCS

Considering a real cross-border eGovernment application, many aspects are touched, for example the cross-border use of eIdentities, eDocuments, eDelivery systems or eSafe applications. In order to foster the interoperability of national eGovernment services and infrastructures, the European Commission has launched several Large Scale Pilot Projects in the past. Usually, each Large Scale Pilot (LSP) addresses specific aspects and use-cases. For example, the LSP STORK aims to create an interoperability framework for the cross-border use of national eIdentity tokens (concerning the eIdentities of physical persons) and the LSP PEPPOL aims to create a European infrastructure for improving online procedures for tendering.

Unlike the other LSPs the new LSP SPOCS has a much broader scope. The scope of SPOCS is to develop the infrastructure for future Point of Single Contacts (PSC) in accordance with the EU Services Directive. In other words, SPOCS aims to prepare a framework which enables Service Providers (i.e. the users in terms of the EU Services Directive) to use their national eGovernment infrastructure and elements, such as their eIdentity tokens, eDelivery portals, eSafe applications, eDocuments etc., in front of foreign eServices provided by foreign PSCs. Thus, SPOCS' results will support Member States to "…ensure that all procedures and formalities relating to access to a service activity and to the exercise thereof may be easily completed, at a distance and by electronic means, through the relevant point of single contact and with the relevant competent authorities." (article 8, EU Services Directive [Euro06]).

Although the Services Directive focuses on foreign Service Providers—considered from the point of view of the country offering eServices—the resulting interoperability framework should be applicable to other areas as well. Especially the private sector could and should benefit from the solutions developed by SPOCS. Solutions and especially interoperability frameworks can only achieve impact on the market if they are used by a critical mass.

Moreover, the LSP SPOCS intends to adopt and adapt (if necessary) interoperability solutions provided by other interoperability projects wherever possible. For instance, the interoperability framework provided by the LSP STORK for authenticating physical persons is going to be used in SPOCS scenarios as well. On the other hand, the SPOCS interoperability framework for eDocuments will base on results provided by the PEPPOL. From this perspective SPOCS is the most integrative LSP of all.

The primitive principles of the SPOCS vision can be briefly summarised as follows:

1. Provide access to all foreign services by electronic means.
2. Enable Service Providers to use their existing domestic eGovernment infrastructure in connection with services abroad.
3. The solutions to be developed should be versatile and open for other sectors as well (e.g. private sector)
4. Adopt or adapt existing interoperability solutions.

In the following sections we briefly highlight two areas where SPOCS is going to develop concrete interoperability frameworks. These two examples demonstrate perfectly how the chosen interoperability approaches following the primitive principles stated before help to achieve the vision of SPOCS.

4 Example: eDocuments

One area where SPOCS is going to improve interoperability is the area of eDocuments. Connecting to the motivation given in the introduction, the interoperability framework we are going to deliver supports receivers and creators of eDocuments in:

1. processing of received documents automatically

2. verifying electronic signatures on documents

3. interpreting the semantic of a document

4. identifying the issuer of a document

In order to address these requirements, we have constituted four basic principles for the interoperability framework concerning eDocuments: the interoperability framework for the exchange of eDocuments…

- should introduce a multi-layered framework for cross border exchange of (existing) eDocuments – the documents should be given as payload elements
- should not be restricted to support only selected eDocument formats/technologies as payload
- should introduce optional layers for supporting semantic interoperability
- should provide an optional authentication layer in addition to the authentication mechanisms provided within the payload documents.

In other words, these requirements imply a logical scheme introducing further layers for holding additional information—e.g. meta-data, authentication data, etc.—in addition to an existing electronic document. This approach ensures that nearly every existing eDocument can be wrapped by applying the SPOCS eDocument framework in order to support cross-border exchange.

The proposal developed within SPOCS has been created after 6 month of assessment (assessment result and a summary of related work are provided in [RoSp10a]). During our assessment phase the given situation regarding eDocuments in the participating countries have been analysed. Furthermore, our proposal has been reflected against existing studies and projects in this field, e.g. Siemens-Timelex study [GrMa09] or the results provided by PEPPOL. Especially the collaboration with PEPPOL assured us to follow our approach since the eDocument container format developed by PEPPOL follows similar principles. Our interoperability solution—to be introduced in the full version of our paper— can be finally seen as a more generic and versatile form of PEPPOL's Virtual Company Dossier (VCD) [Pepp09a][Pepp09b]. In contrast to the VCD, our eDocument interoperability framework is a flexible scheme for creating multi-layered eDocument containers. Furthermore, the SPOCS container can be realised through various technologies (e.g. ZIP-based or PDF-based container).

4.1 Layers of an OCD

Figure 1 provides an overview about the defined layers of an OCD container. The current OCD specification defines [RoSp10b]:

- **Payload Layer:**
  The Payload Layer is the only required layer of an OCD container. It holds one or many electronic documents. The payload layer is not restricted to hold files and documents of specific formats; instead, it is able to hold any kind of electronic data. Furthermore, the payload layer is able to hold references to external files as well.

It is important to mention that the documents given in the payload layer are not going to be modified or changed. The payload layer holds files and documents as they have been issued by the issuing party (e.g. public authority). Assuming that a document has been issued by a public authority the document might be electronically signed. The signature on the document is the only one which has per se a legal meaning according to the policies and laws of the issuing authority. The OCD payload layer does not affect signatures given on original e-documents held at the payload layer.

- **Metadata Layer (optional):**

The Metadata Layer is an optional layer although it is strongly recommended to have Metadata in every OCD container. In fact, the current OCD specification introduces two different levels of Metadata. Metadata of the base level just describe the structure and the content of an OCD. These basic Metadata must be given in every OCD. In addition to that, further Metadata regarding the payload documents given in the Payload Layer of an OCD should exist. These additional Metadata give information, for instance, about the issuer of the document, the owner of the document, whether a document of the payload layer is electronically signed—and if so how and where to verify it—document type, a unified description of the content of the document, etc.

The Metadata are given as XML data following a unified structure (structure is basically defined in the OCD specification). However, which elements of the Metadata are used depends on the use case and the given documents. In the worst case, just a type identifier might be available; in the best case, the Metadata layer represents or summarises even the content of a given e-document. In order to achieve this flexibility, also the OCD Metadata structure is very flexible and extendable. For the future, we hope to have OCD containers with Metadata layers containing all the data given in the payload document. In this high-end scenario, the attached payload document would only be used as an additional proof. However, this scenario requires an adequate organisational and also legal framework.

- **Common Authentication Layer (optional):**

In addition to the electronic signature given on the payload document, the entire OCD container might be electronically signed as well. Currently, the issuer of an OCD container can sign it twice: either by signing the Metadata layer and/or by signing the binary file representing the OCD (e.g. the ZIP file or PDF file). Since the Metadata layer holds references to all payload documents (by the use of optional Hash-values), a signature over the Metadata would implicitly sign the payload documents as well. On the other hand, a signature over the OCD file results obviously in an electronic signature covering all elements of an OCD container.

As mentioned in the discussion of the payload layer, this additional signature does not necessarily have a legal meaning. In fact and according to the OCD specification, this additional signature is just a technical signature following well established electronic signature formats/standards (e.g. X/P/C-AdES BES). However, if the issuer of the OCD container is a public authority this signature might get an additional legal meaning depending on the organisational and legal policies of the issuer.

Additionally, other layers might be useful. For instance, a payment order or an official translation could be added to an OCD container in form of additional layers. The current OCD specification is open for adding additional layers, although, the current specification does not foresee having concrete additional layers. This is an option for a future extension of the OCD specification.

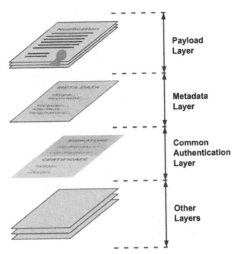

Figure 1: Layers of an OCD container

4.2 Use of OCD in the SPOCS context

Figure 2 is the so called "SPOCS Big-Picture". It illustrates the three main transactions of a SPOCS enabled procedure (seen from the point of view of the Service Provider):

1. Service Provider of Member State B contacts the Point of Single Contact (PSC) of Member State A; the Service Provider accesses information, provides data, fills-in a form etc.

2. Occasionally, the PSC might ask the Service Provider to provide some additional documents or certificates (e.g. a certificate of educational competence); SPOCS assumes that such a certificate could be stored in the private eSafe account of the Service Provider. Therefore the Service Provider initiates her eSafe portal (generally denoted as "Source of Authentic Documents") to provide a particular certificate or document to the PSC or the Competent Authority of Member State A.

3. Finally, the PSC or the Competent Authority of Member State A is going to send a document, e.g. a notification etc., to the Service Provider. In the context of SPOCS, eDelivery is going to be used for this kind of reliable communication.

This description is of course very simplified. However, along all these transactions, eDocuments play an important role. Therefore, the OCD container is going to be introduced in all transactions in order to transport information which is available in form of eDocuments. Therefore, OCD based eDocuments are used, for instance:

- .. for transmitting attachments from and to the Service Provider
- .. for providing documents which are held in the Source of Authentic Documents (e.g. eSafe, registers etc.) to the PSC or Competent Authority
- .. to delivery notification or certificates issued by PSCs/Competent Authorities to Service Providers.

Technically speaking, OCD containers are the envelope of information which is transmitted in the course transactions required by SPOCS processes.

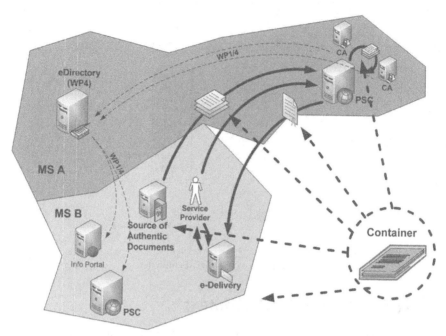

Figure 2: Usage of OCD in the context of SPOCS

5 Example: eDelivery

EDelivery is a second exemplary area where SPOCS is going to provide a framework for inter-connecting the various existing national solutions. From the usability perspective it is important to give users (i.e. Service Providers) the possibility to receive documents send by foreign public authorities through their existing national eDelivery portals. On the other hand, also for public authorities sending documents to receivers abroad it is vital having a messaging system which ensures that the receiver gets her document and might be requested to provide a proof of receipt if needed.

In contrast to simple e-mail based systems, various national eDelivery systems (certified mailing systems), like the Austrian eDelivery Services, the German DE-Mail or OSCI-based portals, the Italian registered e-mail etc., serve a certain level of quality and provide:
- tracking of communication
- a qualified end-to-end communication between all involved entities, e.g. the sender, the receiver and a eDelivery service provider
- a qualified proof of receipt, i.e. the receiver itself or her eDelivery service provide acting on her behalf sends a proof of receipt to the sender in the time the receiver picks up the mail

Also with respect to eDelivery we are able to build on preliminary results provided by other LSPs. The eDelivery pilot work-package of the LSP STORK demonstrates how the results of STORK can be used to realise cross-border eDelivery. Although the scope of STORK's eDelivery pilot has been put on identification issues, the interoperability model applied will influence the eDelivery interoperability framework to be developed by SPOCS. Following the EIF/PEGS approach, by introducing national eDelivery gateways we are able to couple existing national eDelivery systems with an intermediary interoperability layer. The intermediary interoperability layer is used to route a message from one eDelivery domain to another one, or in other words, from one country to another country. However, all national specialities and complexities remain in the national eDelivery domain.

5.1 Cross-Border eDelivery Framework

Figure 3 illustrates the basic idea of the cross-border interoperability framework which has been initially developed by STORK and is currently going to be further developed by SPOCS.

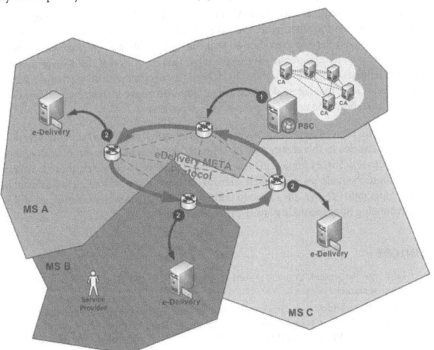

Figure 3: Cross-Border eDelivery framework of SPOCS

The cross-border interoperability framework requires having a unified interoperability layer—the so called eDelivery Meta Protocol—which couples the eDelivery systems (or generally speaking eDelivery domains) of different Member States. For accessing the unified cross-border eDelivery layer, so called eDelivery gateways are introduced. A gateway acts as:

- … legitimate receiver from the point of view of the sender's eDelivery domain/MS
- … legitimate sender from the point of view of the receiver's eDelivery domain/MS

and vice versa.

From a technical perspective, the gateway is an adaptor bridging two different technical protocols. A detailed description of the eDelivery gateway can be found in [RoTa09] and [ApSp10].

5.2 Usage of Cross-Border eDelivery in SPOCS

Referring to the big picture given in Figure 2, eDelivery is planned to be used for sending official documents, e.g. notifications, certificates, etc., from a Competent Authority (or PSC) to the Service Provider abroad. Ideally, these documents are sent to the domestic eDelivery provider of the Service Provider so that she is not required to register with a new or foreign eDelivery provider in another country.

6 Conclusions

EU Member States developed their national eGovernment infrastructure focusing to address their national needs. On the other hand, the EU Services Directive imposes countries to provide their services to foreign Service Providers so that they can easily and electronically make their applications in front of foreign public administrations. This requires that the eGovernment infrastructure and elements of one country need to be brought together with eGovernment services of other countries. At least messages, like eDocuments, and primitive infrastructural elements, like eDelivery services, should be usable in cross-border scenarios.

The EU Large Scale Pilot Project SPOCS aims to provide solutions by introducing several interoperability frameworks. In this abstract we have briefly sketched how we aim to address interoperability by discussing two examples: eDocuments and eDelivery. However, these two examples perfectly highlight the main principle of all interoperability frameworks going to be developed by SPOCS: interoperability frameworks have to build on existing national solutions and will bridge them by introducing interoperability layers/protocols.

References

[Euro06]   European Parliament, Council: Directive 2006/123/EC of 12 December 2006 on services in the internal market.

[GrMa09]   Graux, Hans and Majava, Jarkko: eDocuments and e-Delivery in the context of the services directive - Analysis & impact assessment report. Internal Market and Services DG, European Commission. Version 1.1, 30 January 2009.

[Pepp09a]   PEPPOL Consortium, WP2; Deliverable D2.1: Functional and non-functional requirements specification for the VCD, including critical synthesis, comparison and assessment of national vs. pan-European needs; Version 1.1

[Pepp09b]   PEPPOL Consortium, WP2; Peppol WP2 - Virtual Company Dossier: Vision, Objectives and Potential Scenario; http://www.peppol.eu/Download/final-public-documents-and-presentations/pdf-description-of-wps/peppol-wp2-virtual-company-dossier-vision-objectives-and-potential-scenario/view (as seen on 28 November 2009).

[RoSp10a]   Rössler, Thomas (editor) and SPOCS WP2: Inventory of standard documents and relations to open specifications (D2.1), version 1.0, 10 February 2010.

[RoSp10b]   Rössler, Thomas (editor) and SPOCS WP2: Standard Document and Validation Common Specifications (D2.2), version 0.8, 25 May 2010.

[RoTa09]   Rössler, Thomas and Tauber, Arne: Interoperability - Coupling Of E-Delivery Domains. In: proceedings of the International Conference on E-Government: EGOV200, 2009.

[ApSp10]   Apitzsch, Jörg (editor) and SPOCS WP3: Specifications for interoperable access to eDelivery and eSafe systems (D3.2), version 0.8, 26 May 2010.

STORK: Architecture, Implementation and Pilots

Herbert Leitold[1] · Bernd Zwattendorfer[2]

[1] Secure Information Technology Center - Austria, A-SIT
Herbert.Leitold@a-sit.at

[2] Graz University of Technology, E-Government Innovation Center, EGIZ
Bernd.Zwattendorfer@egiz.gv.at

Abstract

Who one is on the Internet turns out essential once sensitive information is exchanged or transactions of value are carried out. Electronic identification and identity management provide the solutions. Governments are important players in the area, having a tradition of providing qualified means of identification of their citizens. However, migration to electronic identities often developed as national islands that are based on one country's domestic legal, administrative and socio-cultural tradition. Once the citizens are crossing borders electronically, these islands need to get connected and interoperability becomes an issue.

The project STORK is an EU Large Scale Pilot driven by 17 EU/EEA Member States and the European Commission. The project promises to bridge national eID islands by developing and testing common specifications for electronic identity interoperability. Taking the existing national infrastructures as a basis, models have been developed for the cross-border interoperability framework. The framework is tested in six real-world pilot applications.

This paper describes the project STORK. It discusses the interoperability models that have been developed. These are the "proxy model" that introduces national identity gateways and the "middleware model" that is limited to a client to service provider relationship. Rationales for selecting a particular model are given and the principle architecture of STORK is discussed.

1 Introduction

Electronic identity (eID) is understood as key-enabler for a variety of services on the Internet. Once the identity of communicating entities is established with a level of certainty matching the value associated with the service, the communication partners can gain the confidence and trust needed for concluding the transaction. Such transactions can range from social networks to get in touch with friends, to buying a book at an online shop, to have a look at one's stock deposit and to trade a few shares, to file a tax declaration, or to access one's medical data in an electronic health record. In each case authentication is involved, i.e. claiming an identity and proving it true. As the examples also show, value associated with a transaction can be pecuniary in case of e-commerce, legal duties in case of e-government, or can touch fundamental data protection questions when in e-health sensitive data is involved.

The more we get active on the Internet and the more value transactions get carried out, the higher the importance of high levels of assurance by secure means of authentication linked to qualified identities gets. E-government is such an area where high assurance in the citizen's identity may be needed. Several states therefore as early as in the late 1990's started to plan and to develop electronic identity systems and beginning of the 2000's started to deploy them.

Examples of early developments are the Austrian Citizen Card, the Belgian BelPIC, the Estonian eID card, the Italian CIE and CNS cards, or the Finnish FineiD. Other countries followed with mass roll-outs such as Portugal and Spain. A study that has been carried out by the European Commission under IDABC and that recently has been amended shows that that 13 out of 32 surveyed countries issue eID cards – as the smartcard examples just given [GrMM09]. Other countries provide eID via authentication portals using username passwords such as the UK Government Gateway or DigiD (that may be complemented with SMS transaction codes) in The Netherlands. Further countries rely on PKI software certificates and/or base their eID on banking authentication systems such as the Swedish BankID. Some deploy mobile solutions as in Austria and Estonia and several countries have combinations of these methods.

Given this diversity of technologies and given that solutions that have been deployed about a decade ago and are still in operation it is not too hard to guess that interoperability is a concern. Solutions evolved in their national environment under its legal and administrative constraints, thus carrying national specifics. The EU recognised early that this can hamper the Common Market in an Information Society. In 2005 the Manchester Ministerial Declaration gave a political message by stating that *"By 2010 European citizens and businesses shall be able to benefit from secure means of electronic identification that maximise user convenience while respecting data protection regulations. Such means shall be made available under the responsibility of the Member States but recognised across the EU"* [Manc05].

Note, that the Manchester Declaration does not put technology in its epicentre, but emphasises user convenience, security, and data protection and points to the need of mutual recognition. Cross-border eID interoperability is a complex and multi-disciplinary issue covering legal, operational and technical aspects. A vehicle to clear the bar of the Manchester Declaration and to get hands-on experience with the issues involved is to test concepts in real world applications on a large-enough scale. This has been initiated by the European Commission by co-funding an eID Large Scale Pilot under the Competitiveness and Innovations Framework Programme, ICT Policy Support Programme (CIP, ICT-PSP). STORK – which stands for *Secure identiTy acrOss boRders linKed* – is the eID Large Scale Pilot that origins from this initiative.

STORK is introduced in the remainder of this paper. In section 2 the project objectives are discussed. These are to develop common specifications for an interoperability framework and – as the prime objective – to test its implementation in six concrete cross-border applications. These pilot applications are also briefly described in this section. Section 3 sketches the legal and operational aspects that had to be tackled. In the main part of the paper – section 4 – the interoperability models that have been developed are described. These are the "proxy model", the "middleware model", and its combinations. The architecture of STORK is described in section 5 and, finally, conclusions are drawn.

2 Goals of STORK

STORK brought together fourteen EU/EEA Member States in 2008 which then has been enhanced by three further Member States in 2010[1]. The aim of the consortium has been to take their national eID systems as a basis and to develop and build an interoperability framework on top of it. The underlying assumption of STORK is that the national electronic identity systems remain unchanged – note the huge investments that would be at stake if an infrastructure rolled out nation-wide and integrated in many of service providers would need to be changed.

In a three year journey, the goals of STORK are to get clarity on how the legal and operational issues (discussed in the next section 3) can be addressed. This comprised the first phase of the project. A major goal was to develop the technical specifications to enable cross-border interoperability (discussed in section 4) and to implement these (section 5). This phase covered the second project year.

The proof of the pudding is in its eating. The main and final phase of the STORK project is to deploy its interoperability framework to six real-world applications. This phase shall establish the lessons learned, to see where the concepts are successful, or where we might got stuck, respectively. The pilots shall run for one year in the period from mid 2010 to mid 2011. The six pilots are:

1. The first pilot *Cross-Border Authentication Platform for Electronic Services* aims at integrating the STORK framework to e-government portals, thus allowing citizens to authenticate using their electronic eID. The portals can range from sector-specific portals such as the Belgian "Limosa" application for migrant workers to regional portals serving various sectors such as the Baden-Württemberg "service-bw" portal or national portals as the Austrian "myhelp.gv" for personalised e-government services.

2. In the *Safer Chat* pilot juveniles shall communicate between themselves safely. The pilot will be carried out between several schools. The specific requirement is that in the authentication process the age group delivered by the eID is evaluated to grant access. Unique identification that is the basis of the other pilots is less important.

3. *Student Mobility* supports exchange of university students, e.g. under the Erasmus exchange program. As many universities nowadays have electronic campus management systems giving services to their students, STORK shall be used to allow foreign students to enrol from abroad using their eID and to access the campus management system's services during their stay, respectively. The prime requirement is authentication, as in the first pilot on cross-border authentication.

4. The fourth pilot *Electronic Delivery* objective is cross-border qualified delivery, replacing registered letters. On the one hand, delivering cross-border requires protocol conversions between the national delivery standards. On the other hand, qualified delivery usually asks for signed proof of receipts. The latter – signed proof of receipts – is the specific requirement in this pilot. This enables cross-border tests of signature-functions that most smart-card based eIDs have.

5. To facilitate moving house across borders, the pilot *Change of Address* has been defined. In addition to authentication, the pilot has transfer of attributes, i.e. the address, as a requirement.

---

1 Austria, Belgium, Estonia, France, Germany, Iceland, Italy, Luxemburg, Portugal, Slovenia, Spain, Sweden, The Netherlands, and United Kingdom; later extended by Finland, Lithuania, Norway, and Slovak Republic.

6. The *European Commission Authentication Service* (ECAS) is an authentication platform that serves an ecosystem of applications that are operated by the European Commission. Member States use these services to communicate among themselves and with the European Commission. Piloting administration-to-administration (A2A) services with national eIDs is an STORK objective. The pilot A2A Services and ECAS integration serves this objective by linking up STORK to ECAS.

3 Legal and operational aspects

An initial activity of STORK was taking stocks of the legal and operational eID environment. Major findings can be summarised by three categories: Firstly, the use of national identifiers. Secondly, data protection and legitimacy of cross-border processing of electronic identity and, finally, the security and assurance levels associated with eID tokens. These three aspects are summarised in this section.

Personal identifiers are the basis of identity management. Some countries use unique citizen identifiers across sectors, such as citizen register numbers in Belgium or Estonia or the tax number (codici fiscale) in Italy. Austria derives sector-specific identifiers from a unique source taken from the residents register. Germany uses service-provider-specific identifiers, unique identifiers are however not provided, as it would be unconstitutional to have such persistent citizen identification. Regulations on the use of national identifiers exist in most countries and restrict their use. These restrictions can lead to situations where using the identifiers is only possible in the country of origin, cross-border use is prohibited in several cases. A solution proposed by STORK is to apply one-way functions to the base identifiers and thus to derive identifiers that can be used abroad. Whether such a scheme is used is on the discretion of the country: In STORK e.g. Austria and Belgium apply a cryptographic transformation of national identifiers.

Data protection is key to enable cross-border eID. The EU Data Protection Directive – and thus national laws implementing it – gives several options to make processing of personal data legitimate. These include situations where the processing is necessary to perform a contract to which the data subjects is party, or where the processing is necessary to perform a legal obligation of the data controller. The legal analysis by STORK however argued it unlikely that such situations exist in all situations STORK aims to cover. Therefore, STORK relies on consent of the citizen as the basis for legitimacy of the data processing. Personal data that are to be transferred as well as the receiver of these data are shown to the user. The user has to give explicit consent prior to personal data being communicated.

The national eIDs in STORK can range from username-password schemes, via software certificates to smart cards and qualified certificates. To categorise these, STORK has developed a Quality Authenticator Assurance (QAA) consisting of four levels. These levels range from low assurance (QAA level 1) to high assurance (QAA level 4), the latter e.g. given with qualified certificates. The idea followed is that the Service Provider requests a certain QAA level needed for the particular service. Service is granted, if the citizen's eID token matches or exceeds the requested level.

4 Interoperability Framework

The project is based on two lines of thoughts on how an interoperability framework can be build: (1) In the first approach, the service provider integrates all foreign eID tokens using a middleware. We refer to this approach as "*middleware model*". (2) In the second approach, cross-border eID transactions are delegated to a national gateway – a proxy – that hides the specifics of national eID tokens and infrastructure from other countries. We refer to this as "*proxy model*".

The advantage of the middleware model is that a clear user-to-service provider relationship is given from a data protection and from a liability perspective: No intermediaries are involved that liability might be shifted to, or that the personal data is transferred to. End-to-end security between the citizen domain and the service provider domain can be technically granted, as the middleware can make use of the eID token's security functions. A drawback however is that maintaining the middleware needs support of the eID issuers, as each eID needs to be integrated and modifications are needed once generations change or new token types get into use. Such changes in the middleware need to be rolled out to service providers.

The advantage of the proxy model is that the proxy serves just its national eID tokens and its national service providers. In the cross-border case the communication is leveraged to a common proxy-to-proxy protocol. This advantage however comes with a situation where the proxy steps into the citizen to service provider relationship. This can lead to a liability shift. From a data protection perspective, the proxy becomes a data processor or data controller. The trust-relationship is established between two proxies, and between a proxy and an end-entity (citizen or service provider). Thus, an entity asserts a fact (such as the authentication of a citizen) towards its direct neighbour (e.g., one proxy to another proxy, but in that case not to the end entity). This leads to point-to-point trust relationships asking for properly securing the intermediaries, as a compromised proxy might intercept data or impersonate users.

The following sub-sections discuss the two models and its combinations in detail.

4.1 Conceptual Models

The national eID solutions deployed in their domestic infrastructure, such as citizen cards or central authentication portals, are based on different models or frameworks. This sub-section bases on the general interoperability concepts discussed above and describes the two models Pan-European Proxy Service (PEPS) and Middleware (MW) in a cross-border context. This also builds the basis for interoperability within the STORK architecture. [EJL+10]

4.1.1 PEPS Model

The PEPS bundles several services required for a cross-border eID solution and hides the complexity and specifics of national solutions from other countries. The services provided by a PEPS include the identification and authentication at identity providers, the additional retrieval of identity attributes, or the secure transfer of the identity information to service providers (SP) [MaGr07]. **Fig. 1** illustrates the PEPS Model in a logical view.

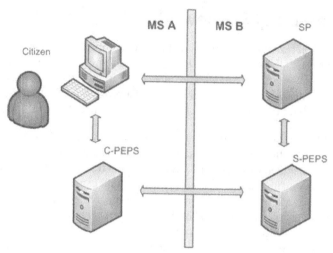

Fig. 1: PEPS Model

In the scenario shown in the figure, MS A as well as MS B host its own PEPS server. The PEPS server defines a central and single[2] instance responsible for the communication with identity providers and attribute providers and for the transfer of identity information across borders. Additionally, a connection and trust relationship between the PEPS and its own country service providers exists. In this model the PEPS asserts the SP that a citizen presenting the requested identity information has been successfully authenticated at a needed authentication level. Since there are several parties involved where data can be transformed, trust relationships and security are established on a point-to-point basis.

A PEPS can act as so-called S-PEPS (PEPS in the Service Provider's country) or C-PEPS (PEPS in the citizen's origin country). The S-PEPS communicates with the SP requesting authentication and the C-PEPS, thus acting as intermediary between SP and C-PEPS. The C-PEPS retrieves requests from a calling S-PEPS and triggers the identification and authentication for a citizen at an identity and/or attribute provider.

4.1.2 MW model

In the MW (Middleware) model a citizen directly authenticates at a service provider. The citizen remains the owner of the data and the service provider is the data controller. Identity data is usually stored on a secure token, e.g. smart cards, and will only be released if the user gives his consent to do so, e.g. by entering a PIN. No intermediary is in the path between the citizen and the service provider. **Fig. 2** illustrates the MW model.

---

2 Considering scalability, the load of this instance can be shared and balanced among a couple servers.

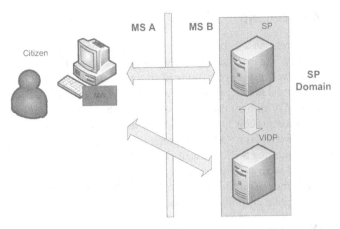

Fig. 2: MW Model

The MW model consists of two pieces of software, one running on the user's PC (referred to as client-middleware) and one running on the service provider's system (server-side middleware – referred to as virtual identity provider VIDP). Generally, the client-middleware handles the communication with the secure token and the server-side middleware. The server-side middleware is responsible for transmitting the identity information retrieved from the token to the SP application. The MW model can ensure end-to-end security.

4.2 Interoperability Scenarios

The conceptual interoperability model of the STORK project combines the PEPS and the MW model. The aim of STORK has been the design and development of a common architecture and framework to enable citizens' of PEPS and MW countries secure cross-border authentication. The Security Assertion Markup Language [SAML] has been chosen for transferring eID and authentication data between the models. The message exchange format has been specified in Deliverable D5.8.1b [ALJ+09]. By combining both models, four different cross-border scenarios can be distinguished that are discussed in the following subsections.

4.2.1 PEPS – PEPS Scenario

In this scenario, a citizen from a PEPS country wants to authenticate at a service provider in another PEPS country. The SP delegates the authentication process to its S-PEPS which in turn forwards the request to the citizen's origin C-PEPS. The C-PEPS triggers the actual authentication process with the user by invoking the appropriate identity and attribute provider. If authentication was successful, the C-PEPS assembles a so-called SAML assertion containing the requested identity data, wraps it into a SAML Response message and returns it to the S-PEPS. The S-PEPS verifies the assertion and forwards the citizen to the SP that grants or denies access to the requested resource. Following the point-to-point trust relationship, the messages are validated at each receiver, re-signed and forwarded to the next hop.

4.2.2 PEPS – MW Scenario

In this interoperability scenario a citizen from a MW country wants to use services from a SP located in a PEPS country. The first steps (SP forwarding the request to the S-PEPS) are equal to the scenario above. However, instead of transferring the request to the C-PEPS the citizen is redirected to the so-called virtual identity provider (VIDP) which is installed in the S-PEPS domain and which manages the MW authentication. Depending on the citizen's home country, the VIDP delegates the authentication process to the national server-side middleware. After successful authentication, the VIDP assembles a SAML Response according to the common STORK format and transfers it to the requesting S-PEPS. Again, the S-PEPS forwards the response information to the SP. The end-to-end security assumption of the MW model terminates at the VIDP as if it was a service provider in the pure middleware model. The VIDP to S-PEPS and the S-PEPS to SP communication follow a point-to-point trust relationship.

4.2.3 MW – MW Scenario

A citizen from a MW country wants to authenticate at a SP located in another MW country. In this case, the VIDP is directly located in the SP domain. As in the previous scenario, the VIDP calls the appropriate server-side middleware for actual citizen authentication. As in the two other scenarios, the VIDP assembles an SAML Response message to be returned to the SP.

4.2.4 MW – PEPS Scenario

In the last of the four combinations a citizen from a PEPS country wants to authenticate at a SP in a MW country. The VIDP in the SP domain assembles an appropriate STORK request and transmits the authentication request to the C-PEPS of the citizen's country. Equal to the PEPS-PEPS scenario, the C-PEPS invokes the identity and attribute provider. Having successfully authenticated the citizen, the C-PEPS returns the response containing the authentication data to the requesting VIDP. The VIDP verifies the response message and redirects the user back to the SP.

5 Implementation Architecture

Besides the design of a conceptual architecture another aim of the STORK project's common specifications has been the implementation of the interoperability framework. The implemented components are used in the pilots acting as enabler for cross-border identification and authentication.

5.1 PEPS Architecture

Fig. 3 illustrates the basic architecture of a PEPS server, including the functionality for authentication (*AuthenticationPEPS*) and validation (*ValidationPEPS*).

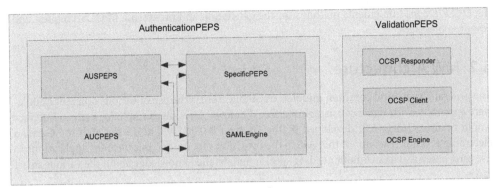

Fig. 3: PEPS Architecture

Both functionalities, S-PEPS and C-PEPS, are implemented in the same component. That means, a PEPS can either act as S-PEPS or C-PEPS or can support both functionalities. Details on the PEPS architecture can be found in Deliverable D5.8.1c of the STORK project [BAL+09].

5.1.1 Authentication PEPS

The *AuthenticationPEPS* consists of four main components – the *AUSPEPS*, the *AUSCPEPS*, the *SpecificPEPS*, and the *SAMLEngine*.

The *AUSPEPS* Component manages the authentication process between a SP and a S-PEPS. Authentication requests from a service provider are received at this component whereas authentication responses are returned to the calling SP.

The *AUCPEPS* component reflects the inbound functionality of a C-PEPS. Authentication request messages sent from a S-PEPS are received and handled by this component. Furthermore, responses containing either citizen's identity and authentication data or an error message are returned to the requesting S-PEPS.

The *SpecificPEPS* component covers country specific functionality and must be implemented by each PEPS country. The Specific PEPS component is in charge of communicating with national identity providers and attribute providers and the translation of the identity information and national protocol into the common STORK format.

The *SAMLEngine* component encapsulates all SAML related functionality necessary for STORK processing. This engine supports methods for the generation and validation of SAML AuthnRequest and SAML Response messages as well as methods for digitally signing or verifying them.

5.1.2 Validation PEPS

The *ValidationPEPS* implements the business logic for digital certificate validation. The main subcomponents include an online certificate status protocol (OCSP) engine as well as an OCSP client and responder. The *OCSP responder* is in charge of handling OCSP requests either sent from a SP or a partner PEPS. Additionally, the responder generates OCSP responses to be returned to the requesting entity. The *OCSP Client* component is responsible for generating OCSP requests for certificate validation to be sent to a partner PEPS. Similar to the SAMLEngine component the *OCSP Engine* implements methods for the generation and processing of OCSP request and response messages.

5.2 MW Architecture

The general idea behind common middleware architecture is the use of various different middleware approaches through a consistent interface. On lower level, an example for such an interface would be the eCARD-API developed by the German BSI [BSI09] and used with the German electronic ID card. The aim of this API is the provision of a unique interface for applications to use card-based services without needing specific and detailed knowledge about the various smart cards.

The MW architecture developed within STORK tracks the same aim but on a higher level. **Fig. 4** illustrates this modular architecture.

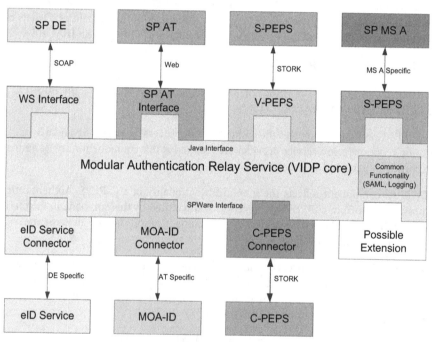

Fig. 4: MW Architecture "MARS"

The VIDP core – Modular Authentication Relay Service (MARS) – provides common functionality such as logging, configuration or SAML message generation. The components on the top of the VIDP core define so-called "Plug-Ons". They are responsible for mapping various authentication requests from service providers or S-PEPSs from different countries to a common Java interface. The Plug-Ons can either be Web Service-based (SOAP) or a Web server component. The components shown at the bottom of the VIDP core are so-called "Plug-Ins" that process the connection to different national server-side middleware components or to a C-PEPS in case MW-PEPS authentication is desired.

The current implementation of this architecture provides the following components:

- WS Interface: This interface is used by German service providers and is SOAP-based.
- SP AT interface: Web interface for supporting Austrian legacy service providers.
- V-PEPS: This component receives SAML AuthnRequest messages from a S-PEPS and forwards the message to the VIDP.
- eIDService Connector: This Plug-In handles the communication with the German eID service.
- MOA-ID Connector: This connector delegates an authentication request to the Austrian server-side middleware MOA-ID.
- C-PEPS Connector: With this module citizens of PEPS countries can be authenticated at service providers relying on a MW model.

The modular design of this architecture also allows the realization of an S-PEPS or C-PEPS. For this, the Plug-On covering the S-PEPS functionality must be implemented. Details on the MW architecture can be found in Deliverable D5.8.1a [BJA+09].

6 Conclusion

STORK is a Large Scale Pilot aiming at cross-border interoperability of eID. The basic assumption is to build a technological infrastructure on top of existing national eID infrastructure. Two models are followed by countries in STORK – proxy and middleware. The decision of which model to follow depends on the country. It may be based on weighing liability, scalability, data protection and end-to-end security considerations.

The technical infrastructure has been developed and deployed to six pilot applications. At time of writing this paper, the pilots just launched. Thus, no lessons learned can be derived at this early stage. What is known is that pilots operate proving the technology feasible. The main issue to be tackled for a sustainable cross-border eID ecosystem is mutual recognition. This is in particular the case if no community basis for mutual recognition can be relied on, such as the Signature Directive for the recognition of qualified certificates.

Actually, STORK is not the end of a journey, rather a first leap: By demonstrating core elements of the Manchester Declaration [Manc05] STORK has contributed to this challenging objective. The lessons learned from STORK and its pilots can serve as valuable basis for Key Action 16 of the Digital Agenda where the Commission aims to *"propose by 2012 a Council and Parliament Decision to ensure mutual recognition of e-identification and e-authentication across the EU based on online 'authentication services' to be offered in all Member States (which may use the most appropriate official citizen documents – issued by the public or the private sector)"* [Comm10].

References

[ALJ+09]   Alcalde-Morano, Joaquín; López Hernández-Ardieta, Jorge; Johnston, Adrian; Martinez, Dan-iel; Zwattendorfer, Bernd; Stern, Marc: D5.8.1b Interface Specification, STORK Deliverable, 2009

[BAL+09]   Berbecaru, Diana; Alcalde-Morano, Joaquín; López Hernández-Ardieta, Jorge; Portela, Renato; Ferreira, Ricardo: D5.8.1c Software Design. STORK Deliverable, 2009

[BJA+09]   Berbecaru, Diana; Jorquera, Eva; Alcalde-Morano, Joaquín; Portela, Renato; Bauer, Wolfgang; Zwattendorfer, Bernd; Eichholz, Jan; Schneider, Tim: D5.8.1a Software Architecture Design. STORK Deliverable, 2009

[BSI09]   Bundesamt für Sicherheit in der Informationstechnik (BSI): Das eCard-API-Framework (BSI TR-03112), 2009

[Comm10]   European Commission: A Digital Agenda for Europe, COM(2010) 245, 2010

[EJL+10]   Eichholz, Jan; Johnston, Adrian; Leitold, Herbert; Stern, Marc; Heppe, John: D5.1 Evaluation and assessment of existing reference models and common specs, STORK Deliverable, 2010

[GrMM09]   Graux Hans, Majava Jarkko, Meyvis Eric: Analysis & assessment report. In: Study on eID In-teroperability for PEGS: Update of Country Profiles. IDABC European eGovernment Services, European Commission, 2009

[MaGr07]   Majava, Jarkko; Graux, Hans: Common specifications for eID interoperability in the eGovern-ment context. In: eID Interoperability for PEGS. Editor: IDABC European eGovernment Ser-vices, European Commission, 2007, p. 25.

[Manc05]   Ministerial Declaration approved unanimously on 24 November 2005, Manchester, United Kingdom Presidency of the EU, 2005

[SAML]   Security Assertion Markup Language (SAML), OASIS Security Services (SAML) TC, http://www.oasis-open.org/committees/tc_home.php?wg_abbrev= security

Secure Networking is the Key to German Public e-Health Solution: Migration Towards an Integrated e-Health Infrastructure

Bernhard Weiss

secunet Security Networks AG
Government - eHealth
bernhard.weiss@secunet.com

Abstract

All around the world headlines warn about the exploding costs of healthcare as advanced medicines and technology are boosting life expectancy. Something needs to be done to contain these costs. An efficient and economic solution demands an electronic healthcare card system based on an integrated communication network which has been designed in Germany to help reduce costs.

This system has been designed to meet the requirements of the healthcare modernization legislation passed by German Parliament in 2003. Its deployment is among other reasons challenged by networks and applications already in use by e-health professionals. These parallel infrastructures have been setup over the past years and already enable e.g. physicians to exchange information online and optimise their processes by accessing a centralised infrastructure. But these systems do not provide the level of interoperability required. Thus limiting use to regional groups only. This leads in consequence to different sectoral but not interoperable networks.

This paper will discuss the success factors for a secure, flexible and interoperable e-health infrastructure solution capable of integrating existing applications and services. It will outline that only an integrated e-health infrastructure can enforce data privacy protection at multiple levels as legally required.

1 Introduction

All around the world headlines warn about the exploding costs of healthcare. Advanced medicines and technology are boosting life expectancy. This has the side effect of driving up healthcare costs significantly. Something needs to be done to contain these costs. A number of countries have implemented conventional measures aimed at saving money like spending caps which limit the amount of coverage offered. But further steps are needed.

An efficient and economic solution for transport, usage and storage of healthcare data like prescriptions, emergency data, health records or master data of an insured person demands an electronic healthcare card system based on an integrated communication network.

This infrastructure must guarantee the unambiguous identification of all participants to reduce fraud and streamline administration. It must also improve communication by providing mechanisms for secure exchange and storage of sensitive information and the use of centralised services. It must also ensure that connected systems, used by a healthcare professional to interact with the infrastructure, are protected against external - network based - threads.

Furthermore all technological and organisational security mechanisms must be embedded in a framework defined by legal requirements, particularly those demanding data privacy protection. Be it that for example certain data and information about a physician may only be used anonymised or that records of an insured person must be pseudonymised before being stored or used by centralised services.

Based on these requirements a nationwide e-health solution utilising electronic healthcare cards and an integrated communication network has been designed in Germany which can help reduce costs remarkably.

But despite all efforts its deployment is still challenged by conflicting interests, recurring delays due to the high complexity of the system and also by networks and applications already in use by e-health professionals.

This paper will discuss the success factors for a secure, flexible and interoperable e-health infrastructure solution capable of integrating existing applications and services.

The first part illustrates the current situation of Germany's e-health systems. This will then be compared with the identified success factors of selected international e-health infrastructure projects.

The second part then details and discusses the migration towards an integrated e-health infrastructure which addresses the needs of all stakeholders.

2 The current state of German e-health infrastructure systems

In 2003, the German Parliament passed healthcare modernization legislation that required the introduction of electronic Healthcare Cards (eHC) for patient data and Health Professional Cards (HPC) utilising an integrated communication network with centralised services [SGBV291a].

Development and deployment of Germany's eHealth infrastructure project was handed to and still is being managed primarily by a commercial enterprise established by leading healthcare organizations [SGBV291b].

Since then Germany's new public e-health infrastructure has been under development. Its design led to a high security system which can reduce fraud considerably, thanks to the inclusion of a photo and online verification of the card's validity. It is also able to improve communication and information sharing by eliminating media discontinuity in prescriptions and discharge letters. In addition it allows for annual-savings by regularly verifying and automatically updating master data of an insured person like for example copayment status information.

It furthermore is based on standardised interfaces and protocols. Interoperability will be tried and tested on network and application layer during homologation.

After years of development, conflicting interests and regularly recurring delays due to the high complexity of the system have amplified criticism to a point where a critical inventory became necessary.

As part of the critical inventory, initiated by the federal government and ended on 04/19/2010, the framework for the realignment of the telematic infrastructure was defined [gema10].

The objective of this realignment is to contribute to the requirements of increased efficiency, shorter implementation period and a reduction of complexity by defining a timely and secure viable stage.

Subsequently the project had been refocused onto these primary applications:
- Management and update of master data of an insured person,
- storage of emergency data and
- direct communication between healthcare professionals using e-Mail.

Details will be worked out until end of 2010. Public tenders are expected in 2011 with first deployments in 2012.

Beside this comprehensive nationwide card based e-health network, parallel infrastructures like KV-S@feNet [KBV09] and GP centered provisioning solutions [SGBV73b] have been setup over the past years. These networks already enable physicians to exchange information, send invoices online for clearance and optimize their processes by accessing a centralised infrastructure. Even Internet access is possible by either using the infrastructure or an additional provider.

The main disadvantage of these infrastructures is the different set of specifications they are based on so that interoperability among these systems and in particular with the newly defined e-health infrastructure is mostly not given. Furthermore most of these solutions are only open to regional groups. This leads in consequence to different sectoral but not interoperable networks. Additionally compliance to legal requirements, IT regulations and standards has not been independently tested.

Up to now we did only discuss the scenario of different incompatible communication infrastructures which are to be replaced by a comprehensive nationwide card based e-health network.

But there might be more options available:
1. Wouldn't it make sense to migrate these sectoral infrastructures towards an integrated e-health infrastructure?
2. Wouldn't it make sense to use them in parallel?

This will be discussed in the next chapter.

3 Parallel vs. integrated e-health infrastructures

Whether one integrated e-health infrastructure as shown below or various parallel networks with separate communication paths should be preferred is to be discussed.

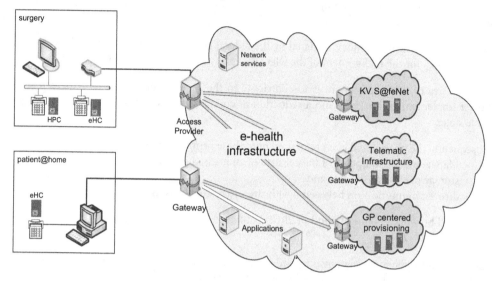

Figure 1: Example for an integrated e-health network

Physicians for example might already use sectoral networks like KV-S@feNet for information exchange (e.g. discharge letters, online invoices, etc.) or Internet access. This can be migrated towards an integrated infrastructure if similar services are provided. Managed Internet service may be the catch-word to be used by the network access provider.

For pharmacies this may not be the case as they often already use virtual private networks (VPN) to connect to their purchasing association. This VPN service also includes Internet access in many cases.

It even poses a larger challenge to address the communication needs of a hospital. Other stakeholders may have further needs.

Most requirements can be separated by the fact if an e-health card is needed or not. This can be further divided whether an application of the telematic infrastructure is used or another service.

As a result the matrix below, listing the communication paths of the stakeholders, is drafted.

Table 1: Communication needs of different stakeholders

eHC	Telematic infrastructure (TI)	Application	physicians	dentists	pharmacies	hospitals
eHC required	Application of TI	Verification and update of master data	X	X	X	X
		Emergency data	X	X	X	X
		Prescriptions (future use)	X	X	X	X
		Patient health records (future use)	X	X	X	X
	Not an application of the TI	Payment (eHC used as ID card)	X	X	X	X
eHC not required	Application of TI	Direct communication (discharge letter)	X	X		X
	Not an application of the TI	KV-S@feNet	X			
		Purchasing		X Dental Laboratory	X Wholesale	X Wholesale
		Company applications			X	X

Before going into details, it is necessary to review the latest changes to healthcare legislation.

In June 2010, German Parliament prepared amendments to healthcare legislation in such a way that online access to the telematic infrastructure will become mandatory [17/2170]. Physicians, dentists and medical facilities will be required to verify the obligation of the health insurance company to provide indemnification on a quarterly base. This will be done by verifying and if necessary updating the master data stored on an eHC of an insured person.

It is a special feature of this legislation, that online access to the telematic infrastructure is not required for the practice management system. The verification and update process can be established independently from the practice management system.

Therefore access to the telematic infrastructure adds to the communication needs of all stakeholders as shown in Table 1. They now have to choose between managing multiple communication paths on separate network or application layers. Whereas managing separate network connections may prove difficult, due to the lack of interoperability among those.

It therefore would be beneficial for all participants if any service could be accessed seamlessly through one unified network connection as shown in Figure 1. This would significantly lower the barrier for future services offerings of accredited suppliers.

Because of its high security standard, its standardised interfaces and tried and tested interoperability on network and application layer the newly defined nationwide e-health infrastructure could be the solution.

Before looking at the migration towards an integrated public e-health infrastructure it could help to find out about the key success factors in international e-Health infrastructure projects.

4 Comparison to international e-Health infrastructure projects

The following chapters will highlight the key success factors of e-Health infrastructure projects in Austria and Taiwan.

4.1 Austria

In 2005, the Main Association of the Austrian Social Insurance Institutions [SVC10] introduced a healthcare smart card dubbed the ecard [WikiEC10]. Initially 8 million patient data cards for the insured and 30,000 Health Professional Cards were rolled out within a period of 6 months.

Unlike Germany's forthcoming health card, the Austrian ecard was designed as a key card. That means it only contains administrative data and signature applications. Initially, it will serve as a health insurance certificate that gives cardholders access to medical care. The ecard can also store electronic signatures and be used as citizen ID card.

The card isn't currently being used to store medical data due to data privacy protection concerns. However, its design will make it easy to upload applications in the field later on. Enhancements, such as the integration of hospitals and pharmacies (eprescriptions), are in the pipeline.

The e-card solution is an online system through which insurance claims can be verified immediately. In the event that an online connection to the centralized data center can not be established, an offline usage is possible. Any insurance-related information can be stored during an off-line session (e.g. doctor visits) and transferred later after the connection is restored.

The key success factors were:
- Used as a key card containing only administrative data and signature applications.
- Avoidance to store medical data due to data privacy protection concerns.
- Prepared for uploads of applications later in the field.
- Online system which allows insurance claims to be verified immediately.

4.2 Taiwan

Before the smartcard was introduced, paper cards were used to audit patient information. Based on these information's service providers were then reimbursed monthly. Even though the system was well maintained, it faced identity fraud, false insurance premium claims from health care institutions, complex program vouchers, waste of resources due to high frequency of paper card replacement, and high losses due to discontinuity of insured applicants. To solve these problems, in 2003, Taiwan became the first country to introduce a nationwide card based eHealth network

So far, 22 million patient data cards and 345,000 Health Professional Cards have been issued [SmCd05] by the Bureau of National Health Insurance (BNHI). The entire project spanned only 28 months, with the production rollout taking place in the final 12 months. The Taiwanese card stores personal data, insurance details, medication, and information on treatment and costs [WikiTW10].

This project required multiple stages which included among others:
- Design and facilitate the execution of security policies.

- Design, manufacture, and distribute approximately 22.3 million smartcards and 300,000 reader security access module cards.
- Design and develop a comprehensive computing network between BNHI headquarters and its branches and a medical virtual private network.

It resulted in significant savings. Mainly thanks to streamlined administration and avoided fraud. In addition, the technology can provide physicians with significantly better information, leading to an increase in healthcare quality. The system combines online (e.g. for backup or validation) and offline services, but the cards themselves are self-sufficient in offline operations, allowing medical data to be accessed in emergencies or environmental disasters. The Taiwan health card also contains a photo and is sometimes used as a national ID card.

The key success factors were:
- A comprehensive system security plan to guard the cardholder privacy.
- A comprehensive plan for the entire information system structure.
- A marketing project plan.
- Integration testing and acceptance procedures.

5 Migration towards an integrated public e-health infrastructure

By combining the results of the analysis done in the previous chapters with the requirements for an effective protection of systems, used by a healthcare professional to interact with the infrastructure, against external - network based - threads and for data protection during transport it becomes clear, that only a single communication link as shown in Figure 1 can address the identified risks.

Furthermore one unified communication link allows seamless access to all accredited services. This in addition provides a convenient way for use of services that are added in the future.

Due to its high security standard, its standardised interfaces and tried and tested interoperability the newly defined nationwide e-health infrastructure is the only suitable solution which can address all requirements. It can guarantee the unambiguous identification of all participants hence reducing fraud and streamlining administration. It can also improve communication by providing mechanisms for secure exchange and storage of sensitive information and the use of centralised services. Furthermore it adheres to the framework defined by legal requirements, particularly those demanding data privacy protection.

In adherence to the requirements of the amendments to the healthcare legislation from June 2010 a migration towards an integrated e-health infrastructure requires the inital setup of secure communication network infrastructure. The timeframe postulated after the critical inventory will allow for all participants to prepare for the migration.

From the perspective of physicians and dentists all services would then be offered by the integrated public e-health infrastructure. This may also include Internet access.

Any necessary equipment for accessing the services may be offered by the network access provider, as he is the only contractual partner of the e-health professional beside the provider of the medical information system. Hence interoperability and reliability can be guaranteed.

For pharmacies and hospitals access to the integrated infrastructure is necessary but only for services defined in the new amendments to the healthcare legislation. Other services are still accessed using different communication paths.

The achieved compliance to the key success factors of assimilable e-health infrastructure projects identified in chapter 4 could also foster acceptance by all stakeholders.

6 Conclusion

An integrated public e-health infrastructure accepted by a majority of its stakeholders has to take into account not only the legal requirements but also the practical experiences an e-health professional gained while using any of the already available solutions and applications.

Acceptance can be increased by taking the different needs of the stakeholder into account during the implementation process by offering migration possibilities to ensure a seamless transition.

Only by offering a flexible solution challenges faced by existent networks and applications can be addressed.

It can finally be concluded that only an integrated e-health infrastructure can besides any organisational security mechanisms enforce data privacy protection at multiple levels as legally required.

References

[gema09]   gematik – Gesellschaft für Telematikanwendungen der Gesundheitskarte mbH: Release 4.0.0 - R2A. Specifications, gematik – www.gematik.de, 2009.

[gema10]   gematik – Gesellschaft für Telematikanwendungen der Gesundheitskarte mbH: 20.04.2010 - Bestandsaufnahme abgeschlossen. Press release, gematik – gematik.de/cms/de/header_navigation /presse/pressemitteilungen/pressemitteilungen_1.jsp#, 2010.

[KBV09]   KBV – Kassenärztliche Bundesvereinigung: Das KV-SafeNet. Information, KBV – www.kbv.de /12164.html, 2009.

[SGBV291a] Sozialgesetzbuch (SGB) Fünftes Buch (V) - Gesetzliche Krankenversicherung: § 291a. Legislation, juris – www.gesetze-im-internet.de/sgb_5/__291a.html.

[SGBV291b] Sozialgesetzbuch (SGB) Fünftes Buch (V) - Gesetzliche Krankenversicherung: § 291b. Legislation, juris – www.gesetze-im-internet.de/sgb_5/__291b.html.

[SGBV73b] Sozialgesetzbuch (SGB) Fünftes Buch (V) - Gesetzliche Krankenversicherung: § 73b. Legislation, juris – www.gesetze-im-internet.de/sgb_5/__73b.html.

[SmCd05]   Smart Card Alliance: The Taiwan Health Care SmartCard Project. Leaflet, Smart Card Alliance Secure Personal Identification Task Force, Smart Card Alliance, 2005.

[SVC10]   SVC: Willkommen bei der e-card. Webportal, Sozialversicherungs-Chipkarten Betriebs- und Errichtungsgesellschaft m.b.H. - SVC, www.chipkarte.at/, 2010.

[WikiEC10] Wikipedia: e-card (Chipkarte). Encyclopaedia, Wikipedia, de.wikipedia.org/wiki/E-card_%28 Chipkarte%29, 2010.

[WikiTW10] Wikipedia: Healthcare in Taiwan. Encyclopaedia, Wikipedia, en.wikipedia.org/wiki/Healthcare _in_Taiwan, 2010.

[17/2170] Deutscher Bundestag – Drucksache 17/2170: Änderung des Fünften Buches Sozialgesetzbuch. Legislation, 50. Sitzung des Deutschen Bundestages am 18. Juni 2010 - dip21.bundestag.de/ dip21/btd/17/021/1702170.pdf.

Advanced Security Service cERTificate for SOA: Certified Services go Digital!

J-C. Pazzaglia[1] · V. Lotz[1] · V. Campos Cerda[1] · E. Damiani[2]
C. Ardagna[2] · S. Gürgens[3] · A. Maña[4] · C. Pandolfo[5]
G. Spanoudakis[6] · F. Guida[7] · R. Menicocci[7]

[1]SAP Research, France
Jean-christophe.pazzaglia@sap.com

[2]Università degli Studi di Milano, SESAR Lab, Italy

[3]Fraunhofer Institute for Secure Information Technology, Germany

[4]Universidad de Malaga, Spain

[5]Engineering Ingegneria Informatica, Italy

[6]City University of London, UK

[7]Fondazione Ugo Bordoni, Italy

Abstract

Service-oriented architectures (SOA) constitute a major architectural style for large-scale infrastructures and applications built from loosely-coupled services and subject to dynamic configuration, operation and evolution. They are the structuring principle of a multitude of applications and the enabling technology for recent software paradigms like Mashup or SaaS.

Assessing the trustworthiness of such complex and continuously evolving systems is a challenging task since a) methodologies – mainly based on certification processes – developed for assessing conventional static systems can hardly handle the dynamicity and variety of SOA based systems, b) few artifacts can be used to support and automate the assessment of the trustworthiness of a stand-alone service, and no means exist to assess the trustworthiness of composite applications, c) there is no mechanism to express and confront claimed security properties.

To address these issues and to realize our vision of bringing Certification-based Assurance to Service-based Systems, ASSERT4SOA has 3 main objectives: 1) to develop methods and tools to support certification of SOA based software by providing abstract models for these systems that capture their peculiarities and the security properties they satisfy ; 2) to develop schemes for expressing certification claims in the SOA lifecycle and mechanisms for handling them; 3) to provide mechanisms and tools enabling to reason about ASSERTs (Advanced Security Service cERTificates) in order to assess the trustworthiness of service based systems at runtime.

ASSERTs, to be issued by trusted authorities, will contain the specification of security properties and of other information relevant for assessing a service's trustworthyness. ASSERTs will be bound to the service to ensure their own trustworthiness. They will enable service consumers to assure application level security properties during service orchestration and to achieve composite application certification.

1 Concept and Objectives

Service-oriented architectures (SOAs) constitute a major architectural style for large-scale infrastructures and applications that are built from loosely-coupled well-separated services and that are subject to dynamic configuration, operation and evolution. Nowadays, SOAs are the structuring principle of a multitude of commercial infrastructures and applications and the enabling technology for new software paradigms such as Software-as-a-Service (SaaS), Mashup or Social Network applications. The execution of this new type of software eventually spans a number of different organizations, and may involve powerful servers as well as resource-constrained devices (e.g., mobile devices).

Today, most business oriented SOA applications are what we could call "closed SOAs", in which all components have been developed, are controlled, maintained and executed by the same entity. Yet to achieve all its benefits, we have to look at "open SOAs" in which not all services are developed, maintained, controlled and executed in-house. Many companies are faced with the challenge of moving their current applications into the service world, but find it difficult because this has to be done without adding new security risks. Unfortunately, from a security point of view, the implementation of even a closed SOA can be extremely complex [SEI08], taking into account the business-critical applications that developers want to expose as Web services. In the case of open SOAs, the fact that trust becomes an essential element has motivated that, opposed to closed SOAs, the number of open SOAs that run critical or security sensitive applications is still minimal [CCR].

Assessing the trustworthiness of such complex and continuously evolving software ecosystems is a challenging task [DAI08] for businesses and citizens since:

1. The methodologies – mainly based on certification processes – have been developed for assessing conventional static systems and components and thus have difficulty in dealing with the dynamicity and variety of SOA based systems.

2. Few artifacts[1] can be used to support and automate the assessment of the trustworthiness of a stand-alone service.

3. No mechanism exists to specify certification requirements at design time and to use them at run time for assessing the fit of services with required assurance level.

4. No means exist to assess the trustworthiness of composite applications, from an end-user or an auditor perspective.

5. No automated procedure has been proposed to challenge the effectiveness of security properties after the certification phase.

To address these drawbacks, the project ASSERT4SOA (FP7-ICT-2009-5 - Grant agreement no 257351) propose to develop an infrastructure that will:

---

1 mainly the server identity and its associated reputation

1. develop enhanced methods for the certification of complex and continuously evolving SOA–based software systems and services and make use of existing certification processes within the SOA context (where possible),

2. develop mechanisms and tools for the assessment of SOA–based systems' and services' trustworthiness, both at design time and runtime, based on systems and service certification,

3. integrate the methods, mechanisms and tools of (i)–(ii) into the SOA lifecycle.

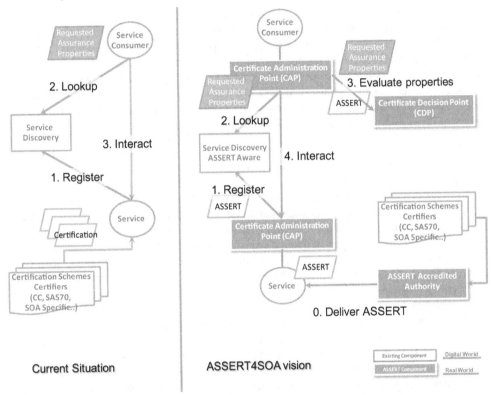

Figure 1: Current situation vs. the ASSERT4SOA Vision

Figure 1 shows how the first sketch of our infrastructure will take into account the security properties certified by existing certification schemes. These properties will be encapsulated into Advanced Security Service cERTificates (i.e., a specific type of certificate shortly referred to as "ASSERT" henceforth) by trusted authorities (AAA). ASSERTs will then be bound to services to enable service consumers to find and assess services. More specifically, ASSERTs will enable users to assess the trustworthiness of a (standalone) service, choose between two different services, replace a service taking into account the runtime context, assure application level security properties and, ultimately, achieve composite application certification by relying on the certification of the individual application components, assessed by accredited software certification agencies. In the following section, we will describe the main drawbacks of certification scheme that prohibit their usage in an open and dynamic SOA environment.

2 Certification Drawbacks

Certification is a well–established approach for the provision of assertions on security properties of entities (products, systems, services). People using or any entity interacting with certified
entities can rely on the asserted properties, provided that the process of certification is known to
produce sufficient evidence for the validity of the property for the certified entity. Today's certification processes typically include a thorough examination by experts following pre–defined
and publicly accepted criteria. However, the evidence itself is not typically part of the awarded
certificate. Thus, the relying party needs to trust the certificate, the experts, and the certification
scheme. This trust is established by the scheme being run by accredited authorities, the accreditation of the experts themselves, and the certificate being officially approved. While this applies to
product and system certification (as, for instance, with the Common Criteria [CEM04]), if the
scope of the examination is the system itself, we need an even higher level of trust in the case of
process certification (as, for instance, with ISO 9001). In cases where the scope is the process that
has been used to produce a system, the relying party also needs to assume and accept that certain
process qualities are likely to result in certain different system qualities.

Clearly, although well established and successful for the assessment of individual and static systems and components, this approach of providing certificate–based assurance of security does
not scale well to service–based systems that are characterized by dynamic service discovery and
binding, high degree of distribution, and ever–changing environments. This is because:

- Current schemes produce certificates and explanations that are intended for human users
  and aiming to support them in deciding whether to use/buy the system or not. Thus, current certificates are formulated in natural language and address a high abstraction level.
- The asserted properties are not explicitly mentioned in the certificate. They are either part
  of the scheme (like in BSI Grundschutz) or expressed in a separate document (like the Security Target in a CC evaluation). In CC, for example, security requirements are expressed
  in natural language and the structure given by the related methodology (CEM).
- Currently, certificates refer to a particular version of the product or system. In general,
  changes in the system structure require re–certification. Though CC contains an assurance class on flaw remediation, it is rarely used and does not provide methodological support for analyzing the security impact of system changes.
- The system that is subject of certification is considered to be monolithic. In CC, the system
  borders are explicitly defined, and security assumptions on the environment can be expressed. CC v3.1 allows to deal with composite systems (i.e., derive a system certification
  from certificates of its components), but requires a perfect match between assumptions
  and component guarantees.
- Existing certification schemes do not provide support for dynamic changes of components
  (i.e., at run–time). Even in CC v3.1, changing components would require new evaluator/
  expert interaction and repetition of (parts of) the evaluation and certification.
- The next section will now analyze the market trends related to SaaS and Security certification to evaluate the potential benefits brought by the ASSERT4SOA vision.

3 Market Trends and Potential Impact

3.1 SaaS Technology

An IDC study [IDC09] a states that: i) by the end of 2009, 76% of U.S. organizations will use at least one SaaS–delivered application for business use; ii) the rate of U.S. companies that spent at least 25% of their IT budgets on SaaS applications in 2008 will increase to nearly 45% in 2010; iii) the market's growth will accelerate the shift to SaaS for the whole value chain; iv) customers in Europe, Middle East, Africa (EMEA) and Asia/Pacific (excluding Japan) will grow, and is expected by the end of 2009 that nearly 35% of worldwide revenue will be generated outside of the U.S.

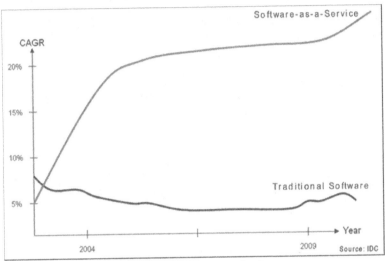

Figure 2: Growth of SaaS Technology

"With a broad slowdown across IT sectors, businesses are increasingly bearish about their short–term ability to invest, whether for stability, growth, or cost savings down the road," said Robert Mahowald, director, On–Demand and SaaS research at IDC. "But SaaS services have benefited by the perception that they are tactical fixes which allow for relatively easy expansion during hard times, and several key vendors finished the year very strong, reporting stable financials and inroads into new customer–sets."

In Figure 2, IDC shows the predicted trend of growth of SaaS that will continue at least for all 2009. In particular, IDC shows that starting from $4.2 billion spent for SaaS worldwide in 2004 (39 percent more than 2003), the growth has been continuous in the following years and will reach $10.7 billion in 2009.

Another survey by Gartner [GAR09] foresees that the demand for software–as–a–service (SaaS) will increase reaching $9.6 billion in 2009, a 21.9% increase from 2008 revenue of $6.6 billion (see Table 1).

Also they foresee a consistent growth through 2013 with SaaS revenue of $16 billion for the enterprise application markets. As stated in the introduction, SOA is the enabling technology of the development of complex applications delivered via SaaS.

3.2 Limitation of Security Certification

In parallel, in the security area, a recent survey from Gartner shows a 2.74 percent of increase in budgets (from 2009 – 2010) for security services including security assessment and certifications. This figure should be considered strong for a mature market and given the negative figures from other IT services after IT budget adjustments due to the current economic slowdown.

Future results from ASSERT4SOA can therefore build upon two strong markets and impact a steadily growing market in the field of IT Security Services.

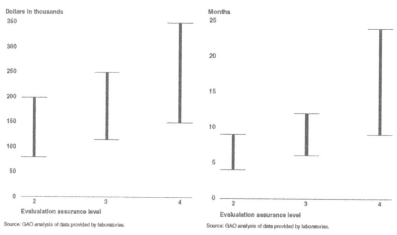

Figure 3: Costs and schedules for CC evaluations performed (EAL2 through EAL4)
[GAO06]

The impact in costs for companies exceeds the $100,000 USD for an in–depth assessment (for example, a SAS 70 type 2). Besides, if an application security assessment is required, from 10,000 to $40,000 USD will be a minimum extra cost per application. Considering the complexity of the current global environment, assessments overseas are often necessary and the total costs might reach the $150,000 USD. In 2006, the US Government Accountability Office published a report on Common Criteria evaluations that summarized a range of costs and schedules reported for evaluations performed at levels EAL2 through EAL4. The Figure 3[GAO06] shows that an evaluation based on the Common Criteria framework was estimated to cost from $100,000 to $170,000 USD for the Evaluation Assurance Level 2 (the minimum level of security) and takes four to six months. On the other hand, an evaluation with the highest level of security (EAL 4) costs from $300,000 to $750,000 and takes one to two years.

Additional findings from another Gartner survey regarding "Third–Party Security Controls" strengthen our vision about the expected impact of ASSERT4SOA in the market. The lack of certifications that specify security and privacy controls to the degree of granularity that most companies require is clearly stated. Thus, companies need to use a combination of methodologies for security assessment practices such as (by order of preference):

1. Questionnaires (62%)
2. Go on–site (54%)
3. Attestations or certifications (52%)
4. Third–party provider (37%)

Certification is then considered a competitive market based on the previous data without forgetting the business meaning it represents in terms of new incomes for certified products. The estimated market spending in 2006 only for Common Criteria, reached the $9 billion USD worldwide. Thus, it is foreseen that certified products would be mandatory as a prerequisite for contract agreements, especially for insurance companies, banks and supervisory authorities.

The benefits of ASSERT4SOA are clearly attempting to be beyond economic figures. The new methods for certification proposed by ASSERT4SOA will not only provide a real business opportunity but certainly multiple the benefits in terms of trust reliability along the service chain. The following sections highlight how ASSERT4SOA will trigger these changes.

4 Bringing Certification–based Assurance to Service–based Systems

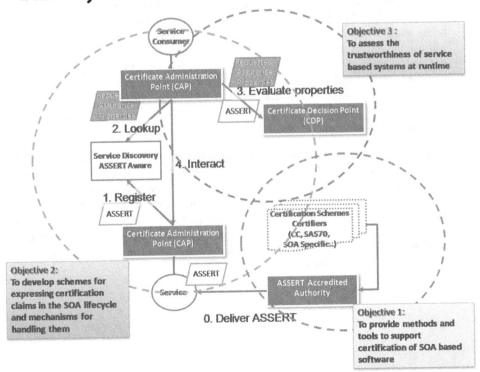

Figure 4: The ASSERT4SOA Objectives

Towards overcoming the above stated shortcomings and realizing its vision, ASSERT4SOA has 3 main objectives.

1. **To provide methods and tools to support certification of SOA based software:**
   ASSERT4SOA will provide methodological guidelines to support accredited software certification agencies to assess service based applications and systems. This will be done by identifying peculiarities of SOA based applications and providing abstract models for these systems (architecture, building components, deployment model, etc) and for the security properties they provide. These abstractions may be used by the agencies in the definitions of security targets and profiles used during the certification process.

2. **To develop schemes for expressing certification claims in the SOA lifecycle and mechanisms for handling them:**
   ASSERT4SOA will propose a format to express all the necessary information for assessing the adequateness of a service with respect to security properties that need to be provided. This includes the certified properties and information about the validation and testing that have been performed during their certification process. These properties will be encapsulated into ASSERTs by trusted authorities. The project will further develop an infrastructure (components, protocols and mechanisms) for reasoning and managing certification claims during the life cycle of service based systems (design, deployment, lookup, service call, service composition, etc). The information contained in ASSERTs will enable to match the certificate's compliance with respect to an assurance level or policy involving a set of desired security properties.

3. **To assess the trustworthiness of service based systems at runtime:**
   ASSERT4SOA will provide new mechanisms enabling to reason about certificates and hence assess the trustworthiness of service based systems at runtime. These mechanisms will use the information provided by ASSERTs (security properties, verification methods applied and results, models) in order to identify the impact that the incorporation of particular services with certified properties (or the absence of the same) will have on the composite application. These mechanisms will also support determining whether, when and how services can be replaced at runtime and whether single service discovery or adaptations of the existing composition should be attempted.

The mapping of the above objectives onto the ASSERT4SOA vision is depicted in Figure 4. They are complementary and aims at the provision of a service–based certification process and deployment that will enable users – end-users, customers, auditors, service developer – to assess the security of critical services (banking & finance, government, infrastructure, etc) based on proved methodologies. To achieve these objectives, the consortium brings together 7 partners from 4 Member States of the European Union with a proved expertise and experience in the research area of ASSERT4SOA including service based systems development, security engineering, test and model based checking and software certification.

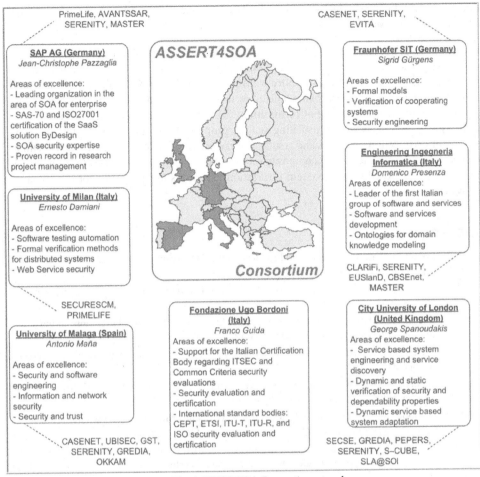

Figure 5: The ASSERT4SOA Consortium at a glance

5 Conclusion

Security certification represents a big challenge for both evaluation bodies and users. Initial problems are encountered from the definition/standardization of the evaluation criteria. Critics mostly refer to a predominant protection of the operators' interest over those of the users.

Although the most recent criteria editions such as Common Criteria and ISO ECITS have addressed important weaknesses of previous standards (ITSEC, CTCPEC), important aspects still remain unsatisfactory. These include: (i) the lack of flexibility of governmental agencies supervising certification resulting in long–time certification process that hinders wide deployment of certification, particularly in the SOA context, (ii) poor meaning and usefulness of the results; a high evaluation level does not necessarily mean a general high degree of security (an EAL4 level for example may be achieved only under very restrictive assumptions on the product's environment, such as operating with no connection to the internet, while an EAL2 level can be achieved under more realistic conditions); (iii) high certification costs which very often exceed expected revenues from the product.

The ASSERT4SOA framework will introduce mechanisms to clearly counteract these problems by providing a new system infrastructure within the SOA context that will allow more flexibility of authority bodies. This infrastructure will integrate new methods, mechanisms and tools that will (I) offer guidelines to provide holistic security enforcement along the service lifecycle, enabling a more flexible handling of certification, (ii) simplify assessment methods and enable comparison of certificates by encapsulating security properties and other important information relevant for certification processes and results, (iii) reduce certification costs and time consumption by supporting certification of composite service based systems through certification of their components as opposed to static system verification that needs to be repeated for every change in a system.

References

[CCR]   Common Criteria Evaluated Products, http://www.commoncriteriaportal.org/products_ STAT.html, accessed October 2009

[CE05]   "Economic Assessment of the Barriers for the Internal Market for Services", Copenhagen Economics, 2005.

[CEM04]   Common Methodology for Information Technology Security Evaluation. http://www. commoncriteriaportal.org/files/ccfiles/cemv2.4r256.pdf

[DAI08]   E. Damiani, C.A. Ardagna, and N. El Ioini, "Open Source Security Certification". Springer, December 2008.

[GAO06]   Report GAO-06-392. United States Government Accountability Office. http://www.gao.gov/ new.items/d06392.pdf. Retrieved 2006-07-10.

[GAR09]   J.J. Robinson, Demand for software-as-a-service still growing, http://www.idc.com/getdoc. jsp?containerId=prUS21641409, May 2009. accessed October 2009

[IDC09]   Software as a Service Market Will Expand Rather than Contract Despite the Economic Crisis, IDC Finds, http://www.idc.com/getdoc.jsp?containerId=prUS21641409, accessed October 2009

[SEI08]   Securing Web Services for Army SOA.http://www.sei.cmu.edu/solutions/softwaredev/securing-web-services.cfm

Privacy and
Data Protection

Data Protection and Data Security Issues Related to Cloud Computing in the EU

Paolo Balboni

Via Mascheroni 2, 20122, Milan, Italy, Avv. Dr. Paolo Balboni Law Firm
European Privacy Association, Italian Institute for Privacy, Tilburg University
paolo.balboni@paolobalboni.eu

Abstract

We are in the midst of a revolution within computing. It goes under the name of cloud computing. Analysts estimate that in 2012, the size of the enterprise cloud-computing business may reach $60 billion to $80 billion – or about 10% of the global IT-service and enterprise-software market [DeSa09]. Such inevitable revolution brings about a lot of benefits but also several legal concerns. It has emerged from a recent study that security, privacy and legal matters represent the main obstacles that are encountered when implementing cloud computing, because the market provides only marginal assurance. This paper briefly describes the main legal issues related to cloud computing and then focuses on data protection and data security, which are by far the biggest concerns for both cloud service providers (CSPs) and (potential) customers. I build on the work done last year as contributor to the European Networks and Information Security Agency (ENISA) 'Cloud Computing Risk Assessment' to further analyse data protection and data security issues. It is worth clarifying that the present paper analyses cloud computing services offered by CSPs to businesses (as opposed to consumers), i.e., B2B cloud computing.

1 Introduction

We are in the midst of a revolution in computing . It goes under the name of cloud computing. In a nutshell, cloud computing is "a model for enabling convenient, on-demand network access to a shared pool of configurable computing resources (e.g., networks, servers, storage, applications, and services) that can be rapidly provisioned and released with minimal management effort or services provider interaction." [MeGr09] Analysts estimate that in 2012, the size of the enterprise cloud-computing business may reach $60 billion to $80 billion – or about 10% of the global IT-service and enterprise-software market [DeSa09]. Such inevitable revolution brings about a lot of benefits but also several legal concerns.

It has emerged from a recent study that security, privacy, and legal matters represent the main obstacles that are encountered when implementing cloud computing, because the market provides only marginal assurance[1]. [ChHe10]

---

1 In this respect, it is worth pointing out the project: 'Common Assurance Maturity Model' (CAMM) http://common-assurance.com, which aims at serving as the new business barometer to assess, measure, and qualify the security profiles of selected Cloud Service Providers. CAMM's objective is to provide business users, and security professionals with granular articulations of the level of security associated with a particular cloud provision. Culminating with assured and tested information which may then be leveraged to gain insight as to how a Cloud Providers profiles meet with (potential) customers' overall organisation security, governance, and compliance expectations.

This paper briefly describes the main legal issues related to cloud computing (Section 2) and then focuses on data protection and data security (Section 3), which are by far the biggest concerns for both cloud service providers (CSPs) and (potential) customers. I build on the work done last year as contributor to the European Networks and Information Security Agency (ENISA) 'Cloud Computing Risk Assessment' [BaMS09] to further analyse data protection and data security issues.

The following specific questions will be addressed:

a. When does Directive 95/46/EC apply (Subsection 3.1)?

b. How are data protection roles (i.e., data controller and data processor) distributed in the cloud environment, and thus the related duties, obligations, and possible liabilities (Subsection 3.2)?

c. Which data security measures need to be applied (Subsection 3.3)?

d. What are the possible ways to lawfully transfer personal data to countries outside the European Economic Area (EEA) (Subsection 3.4)?

e. How can data subject rights be guaranteed (Subsection 3.5)?

Section 4 hosts the conclusions.

It is worth clarifying that this paper analyses cloud computing services offered by CSPs to businesses (as opposed to consumers), i.e., B2B cloud computing (as opposed to B2C). For an analysis of data protection issues related to B2C cloud computing services I recommend reading the paper entitled "Cloud Computing and Its Implications on Data Protection" drafted for the Council of Europe by a group of researchers leaded by Yves Poullet of the Research Centre on IT and Law (CRID). [PGG+10] Whereas, for an analysis of technical and legal issues related to the use of cloud computing services by Governments, a dedicated ENISA study "Security and resilience in Gov clouds" will be published by the end of 2010.[2]

2 Main Legal Issues Relate to Cloud Computing

Cloud computing can be defined as the ultimate expression of outsourcing. Whereby the customer contracts out to the CSP computing resources (e.g., networks, servers, storage, applications, and services), which are fundamental to run customer's business. Inevitably, the stability and the results of customer's business become very dependent from the CSP correct performance. Moreover, considering that the services provided by CSP are mainly e-mail, messaging, desktops, account and finance, payroll, customers' billing, project management, CRM, sales management, and custom application development, a significant number of customer's critical information and personal data may circulate in the cloud and thus be managed/processed by the CSP.

The cloud model is strongly based on the concept of 'location independence'. Fundamentally, "the provider's computing resources are pooled to serve multiple consumers using a multi-tenant model, with different physical and virtual resources dynamically assigned and reassigned according to consumer demand." [MeGr09] Information and personal data are rapidly transferred from one datacenter to another and the customer invariably has no control or knowledge over the exact location of the provided resources. Exceptionally, the customer may be able to specify the

---

2   Keep an eye on the ENISA website: www.enisa.europa.eu.

location, but only at a high level of abstraction (e.g., country, state or datacenter) and at additional cost.

The main legal concerns related to the cloud model are related to data protection and data security; confidentiality of the information and intellectual property; law enforcement access; CSP professional negligence; subcontracting of cloud services and CSP change of control; and 'vendor lock in'. [BaMS09]

Data protection and data security issues will be dealt with in Section 3.

Secret information, 'know-how', copyrighted work, and patented inventions may circulate in the cloud. An information security breach in the cloud may directly threaten the customer, and may never be fully restored in subsequent legal proceedings. Therefore, such issues should be addressed in dedicated contractual clauses, i.e., 'Confidentiality/Non Disclosure Clause' and 'Intellectual Property Clause'. Whereby the boundaries of parties' responsibility and related liabilities should be clarified. Service Level Agreements (SLAs) and Technical Annexes may be particularly suitable for specifying technical means of transferring, conservating, processing, accessing, and safeguarding customer's business-sensitive information. [BaMS09] [PGG+10]

As already pointed out, computing resources are usually offered to customers from different locations at different times; information and data related to their businesses can easily and quickly be transferred from one datacenter to another one in an entirely different country . Customers should be aware that requirements and restrictions concerning law enforcement access to data may significantly vary from one country to another. In fact, datacenters can be established in countries that provide little or no protection to personal data in the framework of law enforcement activities. Moreover, exactly "[t]he development of datacenters might provide great opportunities to public authorities to access to a great amount of information pertaining to its citizens or to foreign citizens. Even considering democratic countries, the United States of America constitute a problematic example due to the very controversy third party data issue in the limited scope of the Fourth Amendment protection". [PGG+10] Therefore, if particularly business-sensitive information/data are to be processed in the cloud, customers should consider whether to specify the location (e.g., country, state, or datacenter) where their information/data will be processed. Customers, that request such customization of cloud-computing services, have to be prepared to bear additional costs. Moreover, it will be advisable for the parties to specify in a clause "how a law enforcement entity may be given access and what type of notice will be given to the parties if this occurs." [BaMS09]

By contracting out to the CSP fundamental computing resources, customer's business becomes very dependent from the CSP's correct performance. CSP failures or shortfalls in the provision of the cloud services may significantly impact on customer business and customer ability to meet its own duties and obligations towards clients and employees; potentially exposing the customer to actions for damage in contract or tort. On the other hand, customers' negligence in using cloud-computing services may lead to loss and damage for the CSP. SLAs and "Liability" and "Indemnity" clauses will play a fundamental role in this matter. Detailed SLAs, in which CSP levels of performance are accurately spelled out, coupled with contractual clauses that clearly allocate, on the one side, general parties duties and obligations, and, on the other side, parties' liabilities and responsibilities will be crucial for a fruitful relationship.

Given the high dependability that customer business may have from the chosen CSP, it is likely that customers will carefully select the CSP on the basis of its reputation, professionalism, the conditions it offers or its technical skills. Thus, customers may be reluctant to see the CSP sub-contracting the relevant services to a third party unknown by the customers – which may not offer the same, e.g., professional or technical guarantees. Moreover, the control of the CSP can also change. This may, as well, impact on CSP reputation, professionalism, technical skills and, sometimes, also terms and conditions of the services. Guarantees and warranties on the sub-contractors should be issued by the CSP to customers. Changes of control should be promptly notified by the CSP to the customer, who may want to negotiate the right to terminate the contract in case such an event occurs. [BaMS09] [PGG+10]

Last but not least, cloud solutions should be interoperable; enabling customers to migrate cloud services from one CSP to another without technical or contractual restrictions or substantial switching costs. It is extremely important to avoid 'vendor lock-in' in order to prevent barriers to market entry, fully benefit from increasing variety of cloud services and models, and foster competition in this emerging market. Contracts that do not contemplate procedures to migrate from the selected CSP to another and/or impose restrictions on this matter should be avoided.

3 Focus on Data Protection and Data Security Issues

Personal data[3] are usually processed[4] in the cloud. In Europe, processing of personal data is mainly regulated by the Directive 95/46/EC, which is currently under revision. The Directive imposes quite stringent duties and obligations on the actors of such processing, mainly on the 'Controller'[5] but also on the 'Processor'[6]). Given the above, the fact that personal data can be rapidly transferred by the CSP from one datacenter to another and customer has usually no control or knowledge over the exact location of the provided resources (the 'location independence' concept), understandably stimulate customers' concerns on data protection and data security compliance.

3.1 When Does the Directive 95/46/EC Apply?

Article 4 of the Directive 95/46/EC sets forth that: "1. Each Member State shall apply the national provisions it adopts pursuant to this Directive to the processing of personal data where: (a) the processing is carried out in the context of the activities of an establishment of the controller on the territory of the Member State; when the same controller is established on the territory of sev-

---

3 'Personal data' shall mean any information relating to an identified or identifiable natural person ('data subject'); an identifiable person is one who can be identified, directly or indirectly, in particular by reference to an identification number or to one or more factors specific to his physical, physiological, mental, economic, cultural or social identity. Article 2 (a) Directive 95/46/EC of the European Parliament and of the Council of 24 October 1995 on the protection of individuals with regard to the processing of personal data and on the free movement of such data (Directive 95/46/EC).
4 'Processing of personal data' ('processing') shall mean any operation or set of operations which is performed upon personal data, whether or not by automatic means, such as collection, recording, organization, storage, adaptation or alteration, retrieval, consultation, use, disclosure by transmission, dissemination or otherwise making available, alignment or combination, blocking, erasure or destruction. Article 2 (b) Directive 95/46/EC.
5 'Controller' shall mean the natural or legal person, public authority, agency or any other body which alone or jointly with others determines the purposes and means of the processing of personal data; where the purposes and means of processing are determined by national or Community laws or regulations, the controller or the specific criteria for his nomination may be designated by national or Community law. Article 2 (d) Directive 95/46/EC.
6 'Processor' shall mean a natural or legal person, public authority, agency or any other body which processes personal data on behalf of the controller. Article 2 (e) Directive 95/46/EC.

eral member States, he must take the necessary measures to ensure that each of these establishments complies with the obligations laid down by the national law applicable; (b) the controller is not established on the member State's territory, but in place where its national law applies by virtue of international public law; (c) the controller is not established on Community territory and, for purposes of processing personal data makes use of equipment, automated or otherwise, situated on the territory of the said member State, unless such equipment is used only for purposes of transit through the territory of the Community. 2. (...)."

Literally, the Directive applies both if the Controller is established in the EU and if the Controller is not established in the EU but uses equipment located in the EU for processing personal data (e.g., datacenters, servers, etc.). However, it is particularly interesting to mention the extensive interpretation given by the European Data Protection Supervisor, Peter Hustinx, in his recent speech on "Data Protection and Cloud Computing under EU Law", in which he stated that:

- "A cloud provider established in the EU – or acting as processor for a controller established in the EU – will in principle be 'caught' by the EU law.
- A cloud provider which uses equipment (such as servers) in an EU Member State – or acting as a processor for a controller using such equipment – will also be caught.
- A cloud provider in other cases – even if it mainly and mostly targets European citizens – would not be caught by EU law." [Hust10]
- He then continued saying that, given that the Directive is in the process of being reviewed[7], amendments directed to ensure that CSPs that target EU citizens "do not escape the application of EU law" [Hust10] may be considered.[8]

3.2 Data Controller or Data Processor?

It is necessary to identify the Controller, the Processor and their interaction in order to determine "who is responsible for compliance with data protection rules, how data subjects can exercise their rights, which is the applicable national law and how effective Data Protection Authorities can operate." [Arti10a]

The Directive 95/46/EC imposes, in fact, the main duties and obligations concerning personal data processing upon the Controller. More precisely, these are:

a. processing the personal data according to the principles of fairness, lawfulness, finality, adequacy, proportionality, necessity, and data minimisation (Article 6);

b. processing the personal data after having obtained the data subjects unambiguous consent, unless one of the causes of exclusion of the consent is met (Article 7);

c. processing the personal data after having provided the data subject with the necessary information (Article 10);

---

7 Vice-President Reding has recently announced that the Commission would take a little bit more time for the revision process than previously envisaged. It will present a Communication on data protection in the autumn of this year, followed by a legislative proposal in the first half of 2011. European Data Protection Supervisor (EDPS) Newsletter, N° 25, July 2010, available at: http://www.edpsweb.europa.eu/EDPSWEB/webdav/site/mySite/shared/Documents/EDPS/Press-News/Newsletters/Newsletter_25_EN.pdf.

8 For further guidance on the issue of establishment and use of equipment relevant for the applicability of the Data Protection Directive see Article 29 Data Protection Working Party's opinions on online social networking and search engines – respectively Opinion 5/2009 on online social networking; Opinion 1/2008 on data protection issues related to search engines; available at: http://ec.europa.eu/justice_home/fsj/privacy/workinggroup/wpdocs/2009_en.htm.

d. guaranteeing the data subject the rights laid down in Article 12 - e.g., to obtain confirmation as to whether or not data relating to the data subject is being processed, to obtain information on the purposes of the processing, the categories of data concerned, the recipient or categories of the recipients to whom the data are disclosed; to rectify, erase or block the data processed in a way which is not compliant with the provision of the Directive; etc. – (Article 12);

e. implementing appropriate technical and organizational security measures to protect personal data against accidental loss, alteration, unauthorised disclosure or access, and against all other unlawful forms of processing (Article 17);

f. choosing a Processor that provides sufficient guarantees with respect to the technical security measures and organisational measures governing the processing to be carried out, and ensuring compliance with those measures (Article 17);

g. transferring of personal data to 'third countries which do not ensure an adequate level of protection within the meaning of Article 25 (2) only in case the data subject has given the previous consent unambiguously to the proposed transfer or under the condition that other procedures are in place as per Article 26 (e.g., 'Model Contracts for the transfer of personal data to third countries', 'Safe Harbor Principles' – if the data are transferred to the United States or 'Binding Corporate Rules'). [BaMS09]

According to the definitions of the Directive, the distinction between Controller and Processor is fairly clear. The Controller is the one who determines purposes and means of the processing of personal data. The Processor is the one who processes personal data on behalf of the Controller. Applying such definitions to the cloud-computing environment is quite challenging. At first sight one may say that the customer is the Controller and the CSP the Processor. [BaMS09] Nevertheless, CSPs often determine the means and sometimes also the purposes of the processing – falling thus under the definition of Controller.[9] On 16 February this year, the Article 29 Data Protection Working Party adopted an opinion specifically on the concepts of Controller and Processor, whereby the Working Party has tried to provide some guidance to interpret such definitions in complex environments. [Arti10a] However, in a cloud-computing environment it remains quite unclear and such roles still need to be determined on a case-by-case basis, in the view of the nature of the cloud services. This has actually been confirmed by the European Data Protection Supervisor, Peter Hustinx, in his speech on "Data Protection and Cloud Computing under EU Law" on 13 April 2010, where he called for further guidance from the Working Party on the matter. [Hust10][10] In this respect, it is noticeable that cloud computing is on the Working Party agenda in 2010 and 2011. [Arti10b] Anyway, CSPs and customers should carefully evaluate their data protection roles, respective duties and obligations and relevant liabilities before entering into a contractual relationship.

---

9   E.g., the CSP "of an Infrastructure as a Service (IaaS), caring about the efficiency of its service, could automatically allocate processing and stocking capabilities between various facilities located worldwide. For instance, at a time "t", the most efficient could be to use a data center and processing capabilities located in Germany. But, due to the increasingly use of these facilities at a time "t+1", it could be more effective to have recourse to facilities located elsewhere in the world, for instance in India, in providing the service – which could involve a duplication of data, etc. In this respect, the technology at stake would automatically imply a transborder data flow the controller of whose is not necessarily easy to determine." [PGG+10]

10 It is worth pointing out that on 18 June 2010 the Data Protection Authority of the German Region Schleswig-Holstein issued a legal opinion on Cloud Computing that, among other topics, addressed also the legal basis for cloud computing and related processor and controller issues. [Unab10]

Failure to comply with the Directive 95/46/EC may lead to administrative, civil and also criminal sanctions, which varies from country to country, for the Controller. Such sanctions are mainly detailed in the relevant statutory instruments by which the Directive has been implemented in the various EU Member States.

3.3 Data Security Measures

Data integrity and data availability are two extremely important elements in the provision of cloud-computing services. [ChHe10] However, one has to keep in mind that there is an inevitable trade-off here: more data security is likely to lead to reduce availability, in other words, too much security kills performance. [BaMS09] [PGG+10]

Article 17 of the Directive 95/46/EC states that:

1. "Member States shall provide that the controller must implement appropriate technical and organizational measures to protect personal data against accidental or unlawful destruction or accidental loss, alteration, unauthorized disclosure or access, in particular where the processing involves the transmission of data over a network, and against all other unlawful forms of processing. Having regard to the state of the art and the cost of their implementation, such measures shall ensure a level of security appropriate to the risks represented by the processing and the nature of the data to be protected.

2. The Member States shall provide that the controller must, where processing is carried out on his behalf, choose a processor providing sufficient guarantees in respect of the technical security measures and organizational measures governing the processing to be carried out, and must ensure compliance with those measures.

3. The carrying out of processing by way of a processor must be governed by a contract or legal act binding the processor to the controller and stipulating in particular that:
   - the processor shall act only on instructions from the controller,
   - the obligations set out in paragraph 1, as defined by the law of the Member State in which the processor is established, shall also be incumbent on the processor.

4. For the purposes of keeping proof, the parts of the contract or the legal act relating to data protection and the requirements relating to the measures referred to in paragraph 1 shall be in writing or in another equivalent form."

Pursuant to Article 17, appropriate security measures have to be implemented by the Controller or by its Processor. Most of the Member States laid down very stringent mandatory data security measures. [BaMS09] Regardless of whether the CSP is to be considered a Controller or a Processor, the customer will have to ensure that the CSP has appropriate security measures in place. It is worth stressing that, according to Article 17 (3) second indent, in case of a Processor established in a Member State, the applicable law for security of processing shall be the national law of the Member State where the Processor is established. [Arti10a] However, my experience as an ICT business lawyer tells me that such a provision is quite difficult for customers to accept. In fact, customers tend to require CSP to comply with their relevant data protection law. This happens mainly for two reasons: a) customers internal security procedures are mainly based on the implementation of security measures mandated by their national data protection law; b) they are afraid that if the CSP do not comply with customers' national data protection law, as far as security measures are concerned, this will expose them to possible sanctions by their local Data Protection Authority.

Data security mandatory requirements are definitely one of the fields of regulation in which consistency at least in Europe must be achieved; and possibly at global level. In the absence of relevant uniform regulation, CSPs quite often implement widely recognised technical standards, e.g., ISO 27001, to reassure customers on the fact that they have in place high data security measures.[11]

3.4 Data Transfer to Countries Outside the EEA

Cloud models entail that customer information and data are often transferred by the CSP from one datacenter to another that can be located anywhere in the world. However, the Directive 95/46/EC prohibits transfers of personal data to countries which do not ensure an adequate level of protection within the meaning of Article 25 (2). Unless the data subject has given the previous consent unambiguously to the proposed transfer or under the condition that other procedures are in place as per Article 26 (e.g., 'Model Contracts for the transfer of personal data to third countries', 'Safe Harbor Principles' – if the data are transferred to the United States, or 'Binding Corporate Rules').[12]

It is not very convenient to base the transfer on data subject's consent because the same data subject can withdraw it at any time. 'Model Contracts for the transfer of personal data to third countries' seem to present some advantage over data subject's consent, however, these are rules that rely on a definition of data transfer from 'point to point'. A contract is required for each transfer to a country where the legal framework is not adequate. The same goes for 'Safe Harbor Principles', which apply to data transferred to the United States. Such legal framework for transferring of data seems inadequate in the cloud-computing environment where data flows often concern numerous countries (and possible several companies). 'Binding Corporate Rules' (BCRs) adopted by large multinational companies offering cloud-computing services seem to be a workable solution, at least when the transferring of data take place within the same companies or corporations. [PGG+10]

The European Data Protection Supervisor, Peter Hustinx, in his recent speech on "Data Protection and Cloud Computing under EU Law" maintained on this point that "the solution should [...] be found in the context of the review of Directive, in particular in the rules on international transfers. For example, streamlining the rules on BCR or introducing an extended responsibility for controllers with respect to data transfers." [Hust10].

Customers and CSPs have to make sure that an appropriate framework to lawfully transfer the data is in place.

---

11   ISO 27001 standards meet, e.g., minimum security measures mandated by the Italian data protection law.
12   The Directive 95/46/EC allows personal data to be transferred outside the EEA only when the third country provide an 'adequate level of protection' for the data (Article 25) or when the Controller adduces adequate safeguards with respect to the protection of privacy (Article 26). BCRs are one of the ways in which such adequate safeguards (Article 26) may be demonstrated by a group of companies in respect of intra group transfers although the BCRs are not a tool expressly listed and set forth in the Directive. See: Article 29 Data Protection Working Party Opinions: 74, 133, 153, 154, 155; all available at: http://ec.europa.eu/justice_home/fsj/privacy/workinggroup/wpdocs.

3.5 Data Subject Rights

We have already pointed out that the Controller has the obligation of guaranteeing the data subject the rights laid down in Article 12 – e.g., to obtain confirmation as to whether or not data relating to the data subject is being processed, to obtain information on the purposes of the processing, the categories of data concerned, the recipient or categories of the recipients to whom the data are disclosed; to rectify, erase or block the data processed in a way which is not compliant with the provision of the Directive; etc. – (Article 12).

Especially when the CSP falls under the definition of Processor, it is extremely important that the CSP engages in a very close cooperation with their customers to ensure that the latter, in their quality of Controllers, are in the position to fulfil their data protection obligations towards the data subjects. It is advisable to specify the terms of such cooperation between the parties in the relevant contract.

4 Conclusions

Cloud computing seems an unavoidable fast-pace revolution. [DeSa09] The present analysis has showed that cloud-computing services are bringing quite a number of legal concerns together with unquestionable economic benefits. Special attention has been dedicated to data protection and data security matters, by far the biggest issues for CSPs and (potential) customers. [ChHe10]

Bad news:

- There is uncertainty regarding the fundamental elements of data protection regulations within a cloud-computing service scenario. For example, difficulties in assigning the roles of Controller and Processor undermine unambiguous allocations of duties, obligations, and relevant liabilities upon CSPs and customers (see Subsection 3.2). Furthermore, the 'tools' provided by the Directive 95/46/EC to lawfully transfer personal data outside the EEA (with the partial exception of BCRs) seem unsuitable to adequately support cloud-computing services (see Subsection 3.4).
- Mandatory data security measures differ not only outside the EU but also among Member States. This makes it quite challenging both for CSPs to comply with them, but also for (potential) customers to rely on CSPs' data security measures. Uniform regulations concerning appropriate mandatory data security measures are needed (see Subsection 3.3).

Good news:

- The Directive 95/46/EC is currently under revision and we expect improvements as to its applicability to the cloud-computing environment. The European Commission will present a Communication on data protection in the autumn of this year, followed by a legislative proposal in the first half of 2011.
- Cloud computing has been included in the Article 29 Working Party Programme 2010-2011. Further guidance from the Working Party in this context will be very helpful.
- The European Networks and Information Security Agency (ENISA) is working on a study which deals with security and legal/compliance issues related to the use of cloud computing services by Governments. The provisional title is "Security and Resilience in Gov Clouds" and it will be published by the end of 2010.

- An international projects – named 'Common Assurance Maturity Model' (CAMM) (http://common-assurance.com) backed by ENISA, the Cloud Security Alliance, and a large number of global Organisations from both Private, and Public Sectors – will deliver at the beginning of 2011 a new business barometer to assess, measure, and qualify the security profiles of selected CSPs. More precisely, CAMM's objective is to provide business users, and security professionals with granular articulations of the level of security associated with a particular cloud provision. Culminating with assured and tested information which may then be leveraged to gain insight as to how a Cloud Providers profiles meet with (potential) customers' overall organisation security, governance, and compliance expectations.

In the meantime, until regulations and/or case law address data protection and data security concerns specific to cloud computing, customers and CSPs should try to address the legal issues in the terms of their contracts, following the suggestions provided in the present analysis.

References

[MeGr09]   Mell, Peter & Grace, Tim: The NIST Definition of Cloud Computing. National Institute of Standards and Technology, 2009, available at: http://csrc.nist.gov/groups/SNS/cloud-computing/cloud-def-v15.doc.

[DeSa09]   Dean, David & Saleh, Tamim: Capturing the Value of Cloud Computing. How Enterprises Can Chart Their Course to the Next Level. The Boston Consulting Group, 2009, p. 1, available at: www.bcg.com/documents/file34246.pdf.

[ChHe10]   Chung, Mike & Hermans, John: From Hype to Future. KPMG's 2010 Cloud Computing Survey. KPMG, 2010, pp. 8 and 28, available at: www.kpmg.nl/Docs/Corporate_Site/Publicaties/From_Hype_to_Future.pdf.

[BaMS09]   Balboni, Paolo, Mccorry, Kieran & Snead, David: Cloud Computing – Key Legal Issues. In: Cloud Computing Risk Assessment. European Networks and Information Security Agency (ENISA), 2009, p. 97 – 111, available at: http://www.enisa.europa.eu/act/rm/files/deliverables/cloud-computing-risk-assessment/at_download/fullReport.

[PGG+10]   Poullet, Yves, Van Gyseghem, Jean-Marc, Gérard, Jacques, Gayrel, Claire & Moiny, Jean-Philippe: Cloud Computing and Its Implications on Data Protection. Council of Europe, 2010, available at: http://www.coe.int/t/dghl/cooperation/economiccrime/cybercrime/Documents/Reports-Presentations/2079_reps_IF10_yvespoullet1b.pdf.

[Hust10]   Hustinx, Peter: Data Protection and Cloud Computing under EU Law. European Data Protection Supervisor, Third European Cyber Security Awareness Day, BSA, European Parliament, 13 April 2010, available at: http://www.edps.europa.eu/EDPSWEB/webdav/site/mySite/shared/Documents/EDPS/Publications/Speeches/2010/10-0413_Speech_Cloud_Computing_EN.pdf.

[Arti10a] Article 29 Data Protection Working Party: Opinion 1/2010 on the Concepts of "Controller" and "Processor". Article 29 Data Protection Working Party, 2010, available at: http://ec.europa.eu/justice_home/fsj/privacy/docs/wpdocs/2010/wp169_en.pdf.

[Arti10b] Article 29 Data Protection Working Party: Work programme 2010 – 2011. Article 29 Data Protection Working Party, 2010, available at: ec.europa.eu/justice_home/fsj/privacy/docs/wp-docs/2010/wp170_en.pdf.

[Unab10]   Unabhängiges Landeszentrum für Datenschutz Schleswig-Holstein: Cloud Computing und Datenschutz. Unabhängiges Landeszentrum für Datenschutz Schleswig-Holstein, 2010, available at: https://www.datenschutzzentrum.de/cloud-computing.

The Mask of the Honorable Citizen

Johannes Wiele

Johannes@wiele.com

Abstract

This article explores a very old concept of anonymity in private and business life: The Venetian Bauta mask and disguise which was mainly used during the 18th century. The mask was standardized and its use was regulated by government to give Venetian citizens the freedom to do business, to pursue interests on their own and to take part in political activities without being identified while still being recognized and respected as legitimate and honorable members of the Venetian society. I'd like to find out if this concept could be a paradigm for internet identity management and anonymity concepts. This piece of writing presents work in progress. Research will go on and can be followed on www.licence-to-mask.com.

1 Anonymity under Suspicion
1.1 Real World Anonymity

In modern democratic nation states human beings acting anonymously often raise suspicion. In many countries it is forbidden to wear a mask when taking part in public demonstrations. Democracy itself is understood as a political achievement which allows citizens to speak freely and to stand by their opinion without risking repression. Therefore, a person hiding his or her identity in public puts himself or herself in the position of a potentially dangerous outsider or risks being treated as a malicious coward [Kaba98, p. 17]. In most modern Western societies, the interchange of identification is understood as a gesture of goodwill which reduces the scope for dishonesty and as an enabler of communication [Kaba98]. Any refusal to comply with this practice raises strong feelings and provokes emotional reactions. In 2009 and 2010, these phenomenon added even more contentious issues to the already heated discussion about Muslim women wearing the Burka in public.

In the economic system, the reciprocally revealed identity of contractors is the fundament of accountability and payment. Paying cash while staying an anonymous customer is still widely accepted for smaller transactions, but as using debit and credit cards gets more common day by day there are even first approaches coming up to ban cash to reduce crime. At least the head of the Swedish Work Environment Authority (Arbetsmiljöverket) has already raised the prospect of such a ban on cash to help tackle the problem of robbery in Sweden's retail stores (see http://www.thelocal.se/26072/20100414/). The idea gets strong support by parts of the Swedish police. In general, the common "I have nothing to hide, so why should I care about surveillance?" argument still makes it easy to enforce measures against anonymity and privacy practices in most countries of the world [Solo07]. Worldwide, privacy rights are under pressure.

1.2 Internet Anonymity

On the internet, the situation is a little bit different and much more complicated. The internet is an international, multicultural environment with a very heterogeneous population. Especially many of the older inhabitants and many of the politically active "netizens" think of anonymity in cyberspace as the only real warrantor of privacy and freedom of speech. Internet power users are aware of the fact that surveillance within the modern communication networks is extremely easy to execute as long as the user does not prevent it by the deliberate use of encryption and anonymizing tools and habits. Even members of the youngest user generation, the "digital natives", who for quite a while did not seem to care at all for privacy, start to change their habits of freely providing personal information to anyone after having experienced first bad encounters with different flavors of customer or user profiling on the internet.

So privacy activists, data protection officers and many savvy users today stand united to defend the right to anonymity in the virtual world. On the other side, electronic commerce companies and service providers, copyright advocates, federal prosecutors, members of well-known three letter agencies and the police of many countries strongly argue against anonymity on the internet. From their point of view, anonymity fosters internet-based crime to an extent that already requires countermeasures. Actually there are many types of crime and deception which only work because hiding their identity can be easy for skillful cyber criminals. From personal harassment to industrial espionage und sabotage to robbery, money-laundry and kidnapping [Kaba98, p. 16], the range of internet-based atrocities alleviated by methods of forging the actor's identity covers nearly any type of crime [see also Kaba98, Introduction]. Today child pornography is the worst example, in fact so horrible that today nearly any kind of resistance against measures reducing privacy rights can be broken by just mentioning it.

But does all this really justify any steps to take away of the right to surf the web anonymously? An approach like that would misalign the balance of power on the net as respectable web users would have to give up any chance of avoiding profiling, tracing, targeted advertising and even dragnet investigation done by any business, individual, country, or even criminal organization around the globe. Security measures which discriminate against the honest majority of the internet population may not only interfere with human rights, they also may raise reactance effects strong enough to undermine any regulating influence on internet community in the future.

This article is meant to show that there is an alternative. Unfortunately this alternative does not exist as a simple project outline or set of simple measures. It would require a cultural change, but it is proven by a famous European civilization of the past.

2 Anonymity in Ancient Venice

In old Venice citizens for centuries were used to wear masks in everyday life, not only during carnival times. The reason was simple: This vibrant, international and multicultural business town was crowded and comparatively small [see Karb95, p. 359]. As an island, it was not so easy to leave it. To get somewhere, you had to walk narrow streets or use small boats floating through narrow channels. Most of the noble citizens knew each other. Because of that, it was nearly impossible for them to go to a business meeting, to a friend, to a lover or to the casino without being seen.

2.1 The Invention of the Bauta Device

To solve the problem, inspired by the carnival tradition the use of masks and disguises in daily life came up. This practice was acknowledged and regulated by the government. The mask itself was standardized to be suitable for official political events when all citizens were required to act anonymously as peers. Only citizens belonging to the nobility class of Venice had the right to use it.

It was forbidden to wear weapons along with the mask, and police had the right to enforce this ruling. Venetians trapped wearing mask and weapons lost the right to wear the Bauta and were forced to deliver it to the police. Furthermore, they had to pay a penalty and sometimes were sent to prison. The degree of penalty was frequently modified in Venetian history [Tosc70, p. 85]. The result of this practice was that whenever in Venice someone met someone else wearing the mask, he or she could be reasonably sure that the other person was a legitimate citizen of Venice with some accountability and that this person was unarmed.

The name of this very special "society mask" [Tosc70] was "Bauta". The name is ambigous: Sometimes it means the face mask, the "larva", sometimes a complete disguise. On old Venetian paintings, this small white mask leaving the mouth part of the face open for talking, eating and drinking can often be seen. It was usually accompanied by a black cape and a tricorn. Regulation required that all Bautas in Venice had to be made of the same basic materials. It was not allowed to use expensive fabric or jewelry. The mask was meant to hide the financial status of its bearer.

Fig. 1 shows how the Bauta looked like.

Fig. 1: Wearing a Bauta in Second Life

By the way: Of course this is a photograph taken in a virtual world. To take this picture, I went into Second Life, bought a virtual Bauta, got dressed and placed myself on the beautiful stairway of the virtual Bavarian State Library.

Myself? Psychologists may be able to explain why in Second Life there is a virtual market for virtual masks. Why do the inhabitants of this phantasy world buy masks for avatars they use? Isn't the avatar itself already a mask? If an avatar like the ones in Second Life or in multi-user games like World of Warcraft is more like a second identity than a disguise, the presence of virtual masks in a virtual world simply shows that it is a basic human need to wear a mask from time to time.

2.2 Hedonistic and Unethical?

Research on the Venetian society mask is rare. In former times, most observers from other countries ignored the phenomenon, because they did not understand the implications of the underlying anonymity concept.

Additionally, over the centuries Venetian lifestyle has been stigmatized as hedonistic and unethical. For strangers, especially carnival and the fact that so many citizens wore masks gave reason for suspicion. Someone who wears a mask has something to hide, they thought, and what else would a person want to hide than something felonious or unethical?

Mario Belloni today finds a way to say it more friendly [Bell, p. 14], but the basic rating of Venetian culture still is the same:

"They were merchants and adventurers who risked their riches, and often their own lives, on a daily basis on the ships which sailed for the mysterious East. Pirates, storms, attacks by enemy fleets, strange lands: mystery and adventure! These people couldn't let up even in Venice, in their own city. Adventure for them was a way of life. They therefore created a city which offered all types of adventure, in every sense of the world! Carnival and masks everywhere represent absence of rule and freedom of action. You can do everything you want when you hide behind them, and adventure is possible again, even in the city, among the offices of the institutions, regardless of the laws and the vetoes of morality, however severe they may be. And so carnival breaks its boundaries and masks enter the realm of everyday life. In some places they were actually compulsory by law! Games of chance (a good example of adventure in the city), were a bit like the 'national sport' of Venice, but in the state casino (the "Ridotto") you could only play if you were masked."

Of course there's truth in this explanation. Just visit Cologne in Germany today when the carnival season arrives, and you will certainly find out that this kind of feast is an event to do things you would not do at other times. But Belloni's explanation of why masks were worn in daily Venetian life may be at least partly wrong. Belloni does not differentiate between the Carnival use of masks and the role of the Bauta as a society mask.

Karbe [Karb05] and Toscani [Tosc70] have collected a choice of references and arguments suggesting that the use of the Bauta had a serious and sophisticated social and political background. According to these two authors, the Venetians had a deep understanding of what anonymity was good for. And, what's most important, a citizen wearing a mask in Venice did not escape law and order. Of course he or she could do things which were not meant to be attributed to him or her by others, but his or her behavior still had to comply with certain expectations and laws. Venetians wearing Bauta and Volto were not up to antisocial behavior.

Today, for older generations the internet life perhaps looks as suspicious as the Venetian life may have looked like from the perspective of other cultures in the past. In 2009 for example, even a judge at the German constitutional court, Udo Di Fabio, unintentionally emphasized this kind of digital divide when in a speech he compared the practice of publishing anonymously on Wikipedia to wearing the Burka in public. From his point of view anonymous publication is a danger to the freedom of the press and to democracy itself [Difa09]. Di Fabio unfortunately missed that Wikipedia has an effective anonymous peer review process in place.

Looking at ancient Venice and the intent, in both cases critics misunderstand social cultures in which the inhabitants know about the merits of anonymity and how to live with it. To drill a little bit deeper into this topic, I'd like to refer to the discussion of advantages and disadvantages of anonymity in cyberspace.

3 Social Disadvantages and Advantages of Anonymity

Social psychologists have suggested that people acting anonymously introduce severe problems and risks to a society. The theory of deindividuation (see references in [Kaba98], [Pavl05, p. 18]) led to fears that anonymity on the internet may foster antisociality, especially "reduced inhibitions, reduced reliance on internet standards that normally qualify their behavior, and little self-awareness" [Kaba98, p. 8]. Technology is often understood as an additional factor, as internet users mostly act isolated sitting alone in front of PC lacking personal social response and benign mutual control. This setting makes it easy to ignore taboos and other inhibitions.

Technology like email and especially instant messaging also speeds up information exchange and discussions tempting users to react fast and emotional without thinking first. For the same reasons, aggression and dishonesty are boosted by the very special situation of computer-based anonymous interaction, and the self-awareness of the users gets partly lost. The impact of all these aspects is even more dramatic if the actor is not an average internet user but a criminal mind.

On the other hand, anonymity sometimes paves the way for pro-social behavior [Kaba98, p. 11]. Today, this can be experienced when taking part in internet image boards like 4chan (ww.4chan. org, see fig. 2) and krautchan (www.krautchan.net). Seen from the outside, these communication platforms with their political incorrect, rude and sexually explicit language and picture exchange may look like a perfect example of how social interaction may degenerate when anonymity rules, but from time to time the boards facilitate altruistic reciprocal help. Users try to help other users who have anonymously posted personal problems with an impressive amount of patience.

The most important advantage of anonymity on the internet is the fact that acting anonymously allows to "combat the compilation and analysis of personal profile data" [A.M. Froomkin, see Kaba98, p. 16]. Without being able to hide themselves, activities like buying goods of any kind, doing research on diseases or following a politician's blog inevitably would be subject to profiling activities of institutions the user does not even know about. In fact, the imbalance of power on the net often undermines real mutual identification, too, as the average internet user has no chance to learn about who is analyzing his or her habits when he or she is surfing the web or communicating with others.

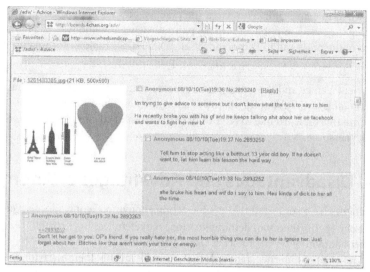

Fig. 2: Anonymous help on 4chan

4 Venetian Practice – Staying Honest while Wearing a Mask

4.1 The Ethical and Political Framework

As already mentioned, the use of the Bauta mask and disguise was not only accepted by the Venetian citizens, but also regulated by the government. Some of the details of the mask-related laws show the political and social importance of the Bauta as an "anonymizer" device. For example, every Bauta had to look more or less the same. No expensive fabric or jewelry was tolerated [for example see Tosc70, p. 96]. The reason for this ruling was that during official gatherings of political institutions, the financial and social status of a single noble Bauta bearer had to stay hidden. Because of this, each argument uttered by any of the citizens could stand for itself. It was common practice to whisper or to speak with an altered falsetto voice to make it even more difficult to identify the speaker. This practice made it easier to address difficult and controversial topics [Tosc70, p 171].

Therefore, within the Venetian communicative political culture, the use of the Bauta had a background comparable to the methods used to guarantee election secrecy in modern countries. By wearing the mask, citizens explicitly accepted [Tosc70, p. 170] their political person (which, by the way, is the old Latin word for mask) and explicitly assumed responsibility for the welfare of the Venetian society.

Lars Cassio Karbe points out that in return to these responsibilities the Venetian citizen had the advantage of being able to initiate negotiations with potentially dangerous foreign traders without revealing their real identities early [Karb95, p. 359]. From the point of view of the foreigners the Bauta itself provided solid evidence that the potential business partner wearing a mask was in fact a noble citizen of Venice and therefore to be taken serious. In this context, the Venetian government licensing the Bauta use to its citizens acted as some kind of identity service provider and escrow holder.

4.2 The Role of Playing a Predefined Role

The Bauta not only unfolded its effects when noble citizens officially met for political decision making. The society mask was an element deeply interwoven with the Venetian culture. When running into each other accidentally in the streets, the greeting procedure between bearers of the Bauta and between other persons and a mask followed rules which could be called a ritual. A person wearing a mask was called "signora maschera", "Mrs. Mask", without specifying the sex. The salutation was informal: "Maschera, ve saludo!" – "All hail, mask!", associated with some elegant gestures [Tosc70, p. 170]. Bauta bearers always had to prove by their behavior that they were respectable citizens. The Bauta itself only was acknowledged if the conduct of its owner went with it. Any failure to meet expectations would have resulted in exclusion from society-related activities. Misconducts resulting in official attempts to remove the mask would at least have meant a substantial loss of reputation.

Perhaps this makes it easier to understand why the Bauta at the same time was capable of being the Mask of the responsible political citizen's identity and the mask of the individual joining a game in the Venetian casino or paying a visit to his or her lover. Wearing the Bauta meant accepting the predefined role of a free Venetian citizen. The limits and the liberties associated with this role were known and accepted by all members of the Venetian society. All citizens adhered to the ceremonies and the dramaturgy of this very special role [Karb95, p. 359]. Venetians were used to live a "second life" within reality, not outside it. Venice successfully managed to create a social and ethical framework of anonymity which at the same allowed personal freedom and reduced the risks of misuse.

4.3 Living twice without deindividuation

The fact that weapons were not allowed to be worn with the mask indicates that the Venetian society already knew about the risks of deindividuation. Ignation Toscani [Tosc70] provides evidence that this part of the ruling beginning in the 15th century was discussed again and again during Venetian history, simply because from time to time despite all efforts of ruling and police work Bauta masks were misused to commit crime. But the problem apparently never grew big enough to force the Venetian society to abandon the use of the Bauta in public. The use of the Bauta did not end because of a failure of the concept. It was only abandoned when Venice was conquered by the Austrians who imposed their very own culture on the realm of the city on the seas.

5 The Impact of Psychological Contracts

Today studies about white-collar criminality have proven that the existence of an ethical framework accepted by a person significantly reduces the risk that this person will ever commit a crime, because human beings simply hate to disobey rules set and accepted by their own community [see Pric07]. The responsibility and honor associated with the Bauta may have had a similar effect on those who were allowed to wear it.

Only at first sight it seems to be a miracle why this concept apparently worked. Of course the means to enforce mask ruling were fragile. There was no "number plate" helping to identify someone having committed a crime while wearing a mask by evaluation of witness account. There was no trusted identity provider who, like in modern concepts of anonymous payment, could help to realign identity information with a certain person if the situation required the removal of the mask. Any approach to identify someone wearing a Bauta had to rely on direct physical interaction.

It was the strength of the psychological components of the Bauta model which compensated for these problems. The Venetian anonymity concept simply worked because the psychological contract a Venetian citizen virtually signed by putting on the Bauta disguise was extremely strong as every noble citizen shared it. The advantages of being able to live parts of their lives anonymously were directly bound to staying within predefined limits of good conduct. The political role of the Bauta added a feeling of social importance and responsibility as every Bauta also represented the dignity of the Venetian nation. Shared ethics, incentives and the acceptance of the Bauta combined to a cultural fundament of anonymity which neutralized its risks.

When I presented some preliminary thoughts on the implication of the Bauta on a conference in Munich in May 2010 and asked the question if the concept behind it could be a suitable model for anonymity on the internet, participants raised the objection that the Bauta concept would only work in a closed community. They assumed that ancient Venice was one and the internet was not. I am not quite sure about that. Of course Venice in the 18th century was geographically an island and therefore more "closed" than other communities, but as a city of international commerce it was also multicultural and heterogeneous. The "closed community" of the noble citizens with their habits, their way of executing democracy and their cultural preferences was formed not only by the marine boundaries of the city on the sea, it was also formed by historic experience and social agreement. From my point of view, the internet can be seen as a similar place of social interaction, and the Venetian strategies at least could contribute to a reduction of anonymity-related risks.

6 Acceptance as the Key Factor

In his article on anonymity and pseudonymity on the internet, M. E. Kabay comes to the conclusion that direct government approaches to govern cyberspace will always be subject to failure [Kaba98, p. 35]. He favors allowing anonymous and pseudonymous interactions, but also points out the benefits of making identification traceable to a fight crime and misuse. Besides that, he suggests concentrating on efforts to implement an ethical framework tailored for the internet world. Parents should "integrate cyberspace into the moral universe of the children", and "corporations and other organizations ought to integrate ethical decision-making into their management procedures [Kaba98, p. 35].

From my point of view, the introduction of traceable information should be limited to the world of financial transactions where it is necessary to prevent commercial damages and betrayal. In the area of web-based communication, research and entertainment, where a ban of anonymity would be unfair, explicit acceptance of anonymity on the net is the key to the success of any effort to implement an ethical framework for anonymous internet-based communication. As long as society tends to see anonymous users primarily as potential criminals or traitors and as long as anonymity is understood as a second-choice exception from responsible social life, wearing a virtual mask to internet users will always mean stepping out of the limits of civilization. So paradoxically the devaluation of anonymity on the net does not help to reduce the risks related to it, but increases them, as it forces anonymous users to act outside the boundaries of society where the threshold which normally lets human beings hesitate to misbehave is lowered.

Only by really integrating an anonymity mode of living into their culture, ancient Venice managed to implement an amount of social control effectively reducing the danger of misuse. Defining a role model of anonymous internet use and putting an end to the infamous "I have nothing to hide" argument [See Solo07] along with the development of simple guidelines and agreeing to them could be the most important step to preserve the advantages of allowing anonymity while still reducing the disadvantages. Unfortunately, this step cannot be forced by governments or other institutions. It can only be brought forward by society itself. Analyzing the Venetian model, I bet that if anonymity on the net would be consequently handled as human right and means of preserving democracy and personal privacy, the development of practices of acceptable anonymous internet use would start to flourish immediately and begin its own long-term evolution process. At the end, society could end up with agreeing on standards regulating under what circumstances acting and communicating anonymously is acceptable and under what circumstances revealing a person's identity is obligatory.

On the technical side, the success of the Venetian model suggests that more attention should be paid to strategies to allow immediate reactions to misbehavior of anonymous users on the net. Reflecting the Venetian ban of wearing weapons along with masks it would be interesting to focus on technologies reducing the potential damage an anonymous internet user could cause – for example by only allowing fully identified users to send program files to other users or systems. Behavior-based security measures are already part of the security technology of the financial industry, and more and more antivirus scanners come with components analyzing the actual behavior of programs. On communication platforms allowing anonymous discussions, allowing users to rate contributions may be a suitable method to introduce a gentle kind of social control and strong incentives to stay within accepted limits of behavior.

References

[Bell]   Belloni, Mario; "Maschere a Venezia, History and Technique", Venice

[Difa09]   Di Fabio, Udo, "Ohne freie Presse gibt es keine Demokratie", speech held in Solingen at the 200 year anniversary of the Solinger Tageblatt (http://www.solinger-tageblatt.de/Home/Solingen/Ohne-freie-Presse-gibt-es-keine-Demokratie-d1a2b4a0-ed9d-46ed-a2dd-b80186f14187-ds)

[Kaba98]   Kabay, M. E.; „Anonymity and Pseudonymity in Cyberspace: Deindividuation, Incivility and Lawlessness Versus Freedom and Privacy", Munich 1998 (Paper presented at the Annual Conference of the European Institute for Computer Anti-virus Research EICAR (http://www.mekabay.com/overviews/anonpseudo.pdf)

[Karb95]   Karbe, Lars Cassio; "Venedig oder Die Macht der Phantasie", München 1995

[Pavl05]   Pavlíček, Antonin; "Anonymity in the internet and its influence on the communication process", Prague 2005 (Diss. Charles University, http://sorry.vse.cz/~pavlant/sources/Dissertation-Pavlicek-Anonymity.pdf)

[Pric07]   Pricewaterhouse Coopers; „Wirtschaftskriminalität 2007. Sicherheitslage der deutschen Wirtschaft" (http://www.pwc.de/fileserver/RepositoryItem/studie_wikri_2007.pdf?itemId=3169192)

[Solo06]   Solove, Daniel J.; "A Taxonomy of Privacy", 154 U. Pennsylvania Law Review 477 2006

[Solo07]   Solove, Daniel J.; "'I've Got Nothing to Hide' and Other Misunderstandings of Privacy", 44 San Diego Law Review 745 2007 (http://papers.ssrn.com/sol3/papers.cfm?abstract_id=998565I)

[Tosc70]   Toscani, Ignazio; "Die venezianische Gesellschaftsmaske", Saarbrücken 1970 (Diss. Universität des Saarlands)

Towards Future-Proof Privacy-Respecting Identity Management Systems

Marit Hansen

Unabhängiges Landeszentrum für Datenschutz Schleswig-Holstein
Holstenstr. 98, 24103 Kiel, Germany
marit.hansen@datenschutzzentrum.de

Abstract

Privacy-respecting identity management systems take into account the user's choices and may help her in her decisions. They have the potential of being the user's gateway and guardian to the digital world. However, if these systems should play an important role throughout the user's life, concepts for long-term privacy protection combined with identity management are sought. The text identifies five major challenges of lifelong privacy-respecting identity management systems and sketches how developers of identity management systems could tackle them. Still, it is not an easy task that may be solved by each identity management system on its own, but policy makers will have to provide support, e.g., in building common infrastructures or integrating national eID solutions.

1 Introduction

Today most identity management systems that have been developed address the user's privacy to a certain extent. By those systems, users can become better aware of personal data they disclose and may restrict the access by other parties to some or all data. It is debatable whether many of today's identity management systems are really privacy-enhancing and whether they fulfil all the provisions of the applying data protection regulations, but at least numerous systems support the principles of notice and choice: Users are informed on the disclosure of their data and may decide upon this information whether they want to use a service or not, whether they give consent to the processing of their data, and whether they opt out. Some even help users in accessing their rights to get access to their personal data, in withdrawing previously given consent or in requesting correcting or erasure of their data. And some support users in choosing and managing various pseudonyms and proving their authorisations by private credentials that can prevent context-spanning linkage of user activities [HaCS08].

The relevance of privacy and identity management for an individual does not terminate after a few years, but it continues as a minimum throughout the individual's life. This is true for the offline and for the online world. Thus, privacy-respecting identity management systems should be designed in a way that they support their users over multiple decades or at least provide migration options to shift the privacy and identity management functionality to others of the users' identity management systems. This is even more the case because identity management systems will become important technologies that act as the user's communicational gateway and guardian to the digital world [HaBe03].

The text is organised as follows: After this introduction, chapter 2 identifies five main challenges for designing privacy-respecting identity management systems that cover a longer period of time. Chapter 3 takes up these challenges and gives advice how to tackle them, yielding in future-proof identity management systems. Chapter 4 summarises the findings in a conclusion and gives an outlook.

2 Challenges for designing long-term privacy-respecting identity management systems

Although a few computer scientists such as Paul Baran as long ago as 1965 already discussed the risks of lifelong data trails for the privacy of individuals [Bara1965], long-term effects of data processing have rarely dealt with on a large scale. The velocity of technological progress in this area makes it hard to reliably predict future consequences, especially societal effects that were not foreseen by technology developers. Egbert Dommering even states: "When a technology reaches a vast diffusion, it affects society in a way which was not part of the design" [Domm06].

Designing privacy-respecting identity management systems that can be used for a long time bears various challenges, as shown in the following sections.

2.1 Keeping pace with progressing technologies

An identity management system is not isolated, but intertwined with other technologies – its design, maintenance and further development has to consider in particular the available hardware, operating systems, application software, protocols and interfaces for data transfer. Technological progress requires also adaption of the identity management system, simply for continuing operative readiness.

2.2 Preventing erosion of the IT security level

Identity management systems have to provide security safeguards for the managed information and the handled communication processes. Without further development of these safeguards and extensions in response to upcoming risks, the level of security will quickly erode [Schn00]. However, long-term security is not easy to achieve, e.g., nobody knows how long today's cryptographic implementations will be considered safe enough for usage in an identity management system [CGHN97], [BuMV06]. Today's security assumptions may be proven false all of a sudden, and if core elements of our IT systems are concerned, this may affect the entire concept of information society that bases on the technologies in use.

2.3 Coping with various areas of life

Fig. 1 visualises that personal data of an individual are increasingly disclosed over lifetime in different areas of life, involving a variety of data controllers. As these data sets consist of parts of the individual's personal data that form her identity, they are called "partial identities" [PfHa10]. For instance, shortly after birth the data processing of an individual regularly begins with entering the name, date and place of birth of the newborn as well as information on the parents in a governmental data base. Also, specific personal data – and thereby partial identities – are needed in the health care system, for insurances, when attending a school or university, in an employment relationship, for membership in clubs etc.

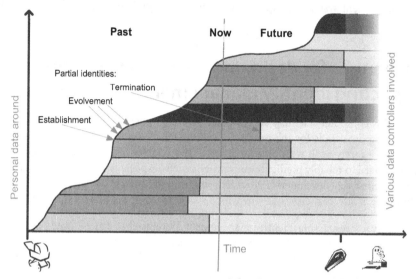

Fig. 1: Increasing disclosure of personal data during an individual's lifetime

Not all of these partial identities should and need to last the full lifespan. Still the data disclosed do not vanish immediately, but often have to be kept at least for some time due to legal obligations (e.g., for tax reasons). Or they exist even longer than legally allowed because data controllers forget to erase the data or ignore their obligations according to data protection law that personal data that are not necessary for a given purpose must not be stored and processed.

2.4 Avoiding future risks for the individuals' privacy

The legal conditions of the setting for using the identity management system may vary over time, e.g., by changes in law. Similar dynamics may occur in political or societal contexts. Although privacy protection of individuals is a fundamental right, there may be situations in which all former legal guarantees become void. It is not predictable how people in a leading role will interpret today's personal data or which policies will apply in the future, e.g., in case of totalitarian regimes [SeAn08]. Because of the amount of personal data that an individual discloses over lifetime (cf. Fig. 1) – often without any guarantee that the data will stop to exist at a certain point in time – the risk of misuse, e.g., by taking them out of context and using them for unforeseen purposes, is apparent.

2.5 Handling different stages of life

Choice by individuals in the matter of privacy and identity management requires that they sufficiently understand privacy- and security-relevant aspects concerning their private spheres, have the ability to make informed decisions and can communicate them in a suitable way. However, each individual undergoes stages of her life in which she cannot fully act on her own concerning her privacy and identity management (cf. Fig. 2, [CHP+09]). Some of these phases of incapacity usually last only a short period of time, e.g., phases of illnesses or blackouts in case of accidents. Others presumably persist for the rest of the life, e.g., progressing dementia of a person. Still other phases are characterised by growing autonomy, e.g., the evolvement from a newborn child to a young adult – here more and more decisions can be transferred to the adolescent who has to learn to gradually take over responsibility for the own life [Art+09].

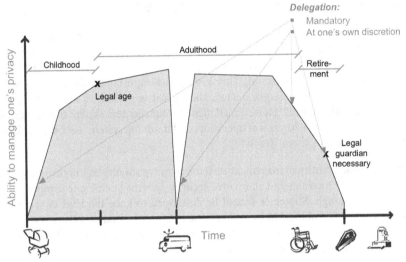

Fig. 2: Example of an individual's ability to manage her privacy in different stages of life

3 How to future-proof privacy-respecting identity management systems?

"Future-proofing" denotes the process of trying to anticipate further developments so that action can be taken to minimise possible negative consequences and to seize opportunities. Surely, nobody can predict technological (and related: societal) progress in the next 50 years. Extrapolating from the past with a boost of technological advancement does not yield reliably exploitable information that may give a glimpse to the next decades. Yet, it is clear that privacy-respecting identity management systems should apply technological and organisational mechanisms to anticipate future development that is relevant for the individuals or at least to avoid unnecessary risks that may or may not occur during an individual's lifetime [StHR09]. The following sections discuss possible measures to tackle the challenges outlined in chapter 2.

3.1 Keeping pace with progressing technologies

In case data formats, storage devices or readers change, a migration to new formats or storage devices is necessary if reading and correctly interpreting the data should still be feasible [HaPS08]. This is also mandatory if the privacy-respecting identity management system should be enabled to cover nearly all areas of life (cf. section 2.3). Here the provision of interfaces to related IT systems that are not part of the user's identity management system can be helpful, e.g., handling of authorisation tokens, SIM cards, national eID cards, health cards, or third party services that support users in assessing privacy and security risks when communicating with others or performing transactions. It is not clear, yet, how identity management systems will work together with RFIDs (they at least could act as displays for enhancing the transparency for interested users), with surveillance systems, with implants or other upcoming technologies.

3.2 Preventing erosion of the IT security level

An identity management system that is assumed to be secure at a specific point in time may be at risk after some time if no additional precautions have been taken. Maintenance of a sufficient level of IT security needs establishing processes to react immediately to known risks and upcoming attacks [Schn00]. In the long-term setting, this is of utmost importance. Note that calculations of profitability consider about five years by default, and legislative periods as well as planning terms usually don't go beyond that time. However, an identity management system that should be used over lifetime needs more than 70 years of operation, and if not the system itself, then at least some parts of the data handled by them [HaTh10].

The robustness of the identity management system's security should be improved by providing redundancy of security modules and alternative security systems in case one component cannot be considered safe enough. Strategies should be developed to keep the level of security if one security system has to be substituted by another one to prevent its failure. Of course it has to be ensured that an adversary cannot disable security modules himself and substitute them by, e.g., Trojans or by components with flaws that the adversary could take advantage of.

The full lifecycle of data and each partial identity has to be taken into account when managing them over a longer period of time. This means that before personal data are collected for a specific purpose, it has to be clear when and how they will be erased at a later point in time. In addition, reliable processes to handle security incidents or emerging risks have to be installed. Depending on the applicable legislation on security breach notification and the specific case it may be mandatory or at least appropriate to inform supervisory authorities and/or the users themselves about actual or possible privacy and security threats.

This comprises the hard- and software of identity management systems, but also eID tokens such as national electronic identity cards with a lifetime of, say, ten years that are part of governmental identity management systems. This long time period requires possibilities and processes for updating the eID cards or even call back those tokens to be implemented in due time.

Of course the design of the identity management system has to support checkability so that checks, risk analysis and adaption of the system to counter possible risks are regularly conducted. These processes have to be documented so that the whole system including its maintenance is audit-proof.

3.3 Coping with various areas of life

Privacy-respecting identity management system will have to face the challenge of giving the user a comprehensive overview on her partial identities and their evolvement over time, e.g., what data has been disclosed to whom under what conditions. Such an identity management system would have to integrate the data and the related communication from governmental eIDs, health cards or SIMs of mobile phones. It would provide storage space for school reports or diploma certificates, and it also should inform users on who is allowed to request or demand access to those documents and how sensitive those data are [HaPS08].

The identity management system should also offer ways to archive data in a secure way, to use back-up and restore systems, and to hide parts of the data in case others demand access without being authorised.

3.4 Avoiding future risks for the individuals' privacy

Today's data protection regulation contains many topics that aim at risk minimisation also for long-term settings, e.g., from the European privacy-related directives the principles of data minimisation, purpose binding, proportionality, separation of different data bases, special treatment of sensitive data, transparency and the individuals' privacy rights to access, rectification or erasure of their data . These principles could help a lot – if they were taken seriously. However, the current IT world does not implement the data minimisation principle by default – quite the opposite: There is no guarantee that personal data will be erased when they are not needed anymore, in many cases context-spanning linkage is possible because the users have to give their names or other personal data or they unwittingly leave informative data trails by each action on the Internet. The plea of Viktor Mayer-Schönberger [Maye09] to delete data and teach the Internet how to forget by clever implementation is legitimate, but probably unrealistic in the IT world that is dominated by players who store almost all data they can get.

Another feature is demanded by Martin Rost and Andreas Pfitzmann in their presentation of an extension of the classical protection goals [RoPf09]: In addition to the classical protection goal "integrity" they point out that various settings do not need "integrity" in the sense of ensured correctness of data, but a kind of opposite guarantee, namely that the data is somewhat fuzzy or in some range falsified. They propose to add some noise to data where it is appropriate to reduce the risk of misuse, both of interpreting the data as being true and exact as well as employing them for undesired linkage.

Risk minimisation means also to minimise irrevocable consequences. Here individuals are usually not informed well enough about what will happen with their personal data. For instance, if they later decide that they do not want to continue their (contractual) relationship with another party and request erasure of their personal data, it may turn out that those data have been transferred to various other parties who may use them, e.g., for marketing purposes. Related is the problem of giving consent once which currently is sufficient for years and years of data processing. Risk reduction would mean to remind individuals of their given consent in regular intervals, or even better having expiring consent, e.g., after one year so that the individual does not have to actively withdraw her consent for some data processing [StHR09].

The given examples seem to primarily address policy makers instead of application designers who want to future-proof their systems. But surely fair data processing is characterised by the mentioned features, and if this statement is not convincing, it should be noted that misuse of personal data that is caused or at least supported to a certain extent by an identity management system may make a bad impression among the user community. Thus, privacy-respecting identity management systems should help individuals to master the risks that occur because of data processing, and allow them to manage their privacy according to their desires [CHP+09].

3.5 Handling different stages of life

To support individuals in their various stages of life, delegates can be appointed who can help them or act on their behalf. The mandate of authority is issued by the delegator. This may be the person concerned herself, but there are also cases where other entities explicitly decide on the delegation (e.g., in the case of incapacitation of a person the guardianship court rules on delegation) or where the delegation is foreseen in law (e.g., when parents are the default delegates of their young children).

By now, the involvement of delegates is not foreseen in many online applications. Simply transferring the individuals' authorisation credentials to their delegates is not an acceptable solution as this cannot be distinguished from undesired impersonation or identity theft. Instead, delegates should be issued their own credentials. The processes to issue, change, or revoke a mandate have to be defined. For guidance on decisions in accordance with the presumed will of the individual, delegates should get instructions or even (machine-readable) preferences and conditions beforehand if possible. These may be derived from the individual's identity management system; delegates may import them into their identity management systems, probably in distinct parts of their systems. The information shall only become accessible by others in the case of explicit clearance by the person concerned. Further, delegates should document their actions in an auditable way which also should be reflected in the used identity management systems.

The design of identity management systems should consider all these aspects of the involving delegates. This is not only demanded because of an ageing population where the need for support in many areas of life increases. Also delegation in the working life, like representing a company or covering for a colleague, should be reflected in privacy-respecting identity management systems.

Similarly to preparations for the case of absence, individuals should be offered a way to express their will concerning the use of data that are managed by the identity management system [HRSZ10].

As soon as delegation processes are in place, another feature of lifelong privacy-respecting identity management systems will come to life: Children could get own identity management systems that at first are handled by their parents who are in charge of managing their kids' privacy until they can make the relevant decisions on their own. The identity management system for a child would contain the documentation of all privacy-relevant transactions the parents have done on behalf of their son or daughter. Later, when a child has gained more and more insight into privacy issues and is able to manage them in a responsible and self-determined way, the identity management system can be partially or entirely taken over by the grown up young adult.

Technically, this could be solved by identity management systems that support different data bases that can be quite easily separated at a later point in time. Children may also have some kind of restricted identity management system that provides already the possibility for own decisions in a certain range so that later a smooth transition of the power of decision from the parents to the grown child is enabled. In other cases, parents could issue credentials expressing their decision that their child can show via the own restricted identity management system.

4 Conclusion and outlook

The development and design of privacy-respecting identity management systems that cover an individual's lifetime or at least decades of her life poses several challenges for application developers as well as policy makers. Because no identity management system exists in vacuo, but is intertwined with many other IT systems or organisational processes, the mutual dependencies have to be taken into account which means updates or even migration of the system. Similarly, long-term security issues have to be countered by professional security and privacy management.

Another challenge lies in providing a comprehensive overview of a big number of areas of life so that users can get a consistent picture on their privacy and identity management. The involvement of many partial identities, various data controllers and huge amounts of disclosed personal data over lifetime call for methods to minimise the risk of misuse. Finally, identity management throughout life would mean to support users also in stages of their lives when they cannot handle their identity management on their own, in particular by choosing delegates who (presumably) act on their behalf.

Future-proofing identity management systems would mean to consider at least all those sketched challenges and foresee measures and processes to tackle them in an appropriate way. In a world where many companies don't know whether they will survive the next few years, long-term-proof development and maintenance are by no means standard. The brevity of time periods in most economic models, e.g., for the Return of Investment, the difficulty in assessing possible future effects, and presumably increasing costs when providing for a use of an identity management system throughout lifetime, are obstacles that probably will only be overcome with the help of government and policy makers. At least when building governmental eID infrastructures, their developers should be well aware of the challenges concerning lifelong identity management. Here policy makers come into play to support the integration of eID systems into other identity management systems, provide for regulatory clarity and foster standardisation on formats and semantics where appropriate. However, the research on this topic is in its infancy, judging on today's level of implementation. At any rate, most of the identified challenges have to be tackled if the idea of an information society should work, and concepts for delegation will be demanded in two areas as a minimum: firstly in the working context where co-workers have to act on behalf of absent colleagues and secondly by the ageing society where people want to stay autonomous as long as possible and get the specific help they need – also in privacy and identity management.

Acknowledgement

The author is thankful for being part of the European project "PrimeLife – Privacy and Identity Management in Europe for Life"[1] that devotes part of its resources on the topic of lifelong privacy and identity management.

---

1 The research leading to these results has received funding from the European Community's Seventh Framework Programme (FP7/2007-2013) under grant agreement n° 216483. The information in this document is provided "as is", and no guarantee or warranty is given that the information is fit for any particular purpose. The above referenced consortium members shall have no liability for damages of any kind including without limitation direct, special, indirect, or consequential damages that may result from the use of these materials subject to any liability which is mandatory due to applicable law.

References

[Art+09]   Art. 29 Data Protection Working Party: Opinion 2/2009 on the protection of children's personal data (General Guidelines and the special case of schools). WP 160, 398/09/EN, adopted on 11 February, 2009, http://ec.europa.eu/justice_home/fsj/privacy/docs/wpdocs/2009/wp160_en.pdf.

[Bara65]   Baran, Paul: Communications, computers and people. Proc. of the AFIPS Joint Computer Conferences, Part II: Computers: Their Impact on Society, ACM, 1965, pp. 45-49.

[BuMV06]   Buchmann, Johannes / May, Alexander / Vollmer, Ulrich: Perspectives for cryptographic long-term security. Communications of the ACM, Vol. 49, No. 9, 2006, pp. 50-55.

[CGHN97]   Canetti, Ran / Gennaro, Rosario / Herzberg, Amir / Naor, Dalit: Proactive Security: Long-term Protection against Break-ins. RSA Laboratories' CryptoBytes, Vol. 3, No. 1, 1997, pp. 1-8.

[CHP+09]   Clauß, Sebastian / Hansen, Marit / Pfitzmann, Andreas / Raguse, Maren / Steinbrecher, Sandra: Tackling the challenge of lifelong privacy. In: Cunningham, Paul / Cunningham, Miriam (Eds.): Proceedings of eChallenges 2009, 2009.

[Domm06]   Dommering, Egbert J.: Regulating technology: code is not law. In: Dommering, Egbert J. / Asscher, Lodewijk F. (Eds.), Coding Regulation: Essays on the Normative Role of Information Technology, The Hague, 2006, pp. 1-17, http://www.ivir.nl/publications/dommering/Regulating_technology.pdf.

[HaBe03]   Hansen, Marit / Berlich, Peter: Identity Management Systems: Gateway and Guardian for Virtual Residences. Accepted paper for the EMTEL Conference April 23-26, 2003, London, http://www.lse.ac.uk/collections/EMTEL/Conference/papers/hansen_berlich.pdf.

[HaCS08]   Hansen, Marit / Cooper, Alissa / Schwartz, Ari: Privacy and Identity Management. In: IEEE Security & Privacy; Vol. 6, No. 2, 2008, pp. 38-45.

[HaPS08]   Hansen, Marit / Pfitzmann, Andreas / Steinbrecher, Sandra: Identity Management throughout one's whole life. In: Information Security Technical Report (ISTR) Vol. 13, No. 2, Elsevier Advanced Technology, Oxford (UK), 2008, pp. 83-94, doi:10.1016/j.istr.2008.06.003.

[HaTh10]   Hansen, Marit / Thomsen, Sven: Lebenslanger Datenschutz – Anforderungen an vertrauenswürdige Infrastrukturen. In: Datenschutz und Datensicherheit (DuD) Vol. 34, No. 5, 2010, pp. 283-288.

[HRSZ10]   Hansen, Marit / Raguse, Maren / Storf, Katalin / Zwingelberg, Harald: Delegation for Privacy Management from Womb to Tomb – A European Perspective. In: Bezzi, M. et al. (Eds.), Privacy and Identity Management for Life, IFIP AICT 320, Springer, Berlin, Heidelberg, New York, 2010, pp. 18-33

[Maye09]   Mayer-Schönberger, Viktor: Delete: The Virtue of Forgetting in the Digital Age. Princeton University Press, 2009.

[PfHa10]   Pfitzmann, Andreas / Hansen, Marit: A terminology for talking about privacy by data minimization: Anonymity, Unlinkability, Undetectability, Unobservability, Pseudonymity, and Identity Management. Working document, v0.34, 2010, http://dud.inf.tu-dresden.de/Anon_Terminology.shtml.

[RoPf09]   Rost, Martin / Pfitzmann, Andreas: Datenschutz-Schutzziele – revisited. In: Datenschutz und Datensicherheit (DuD), Vol. 33, No. 6, 2009, pp. 353-358.

[Schn00]   Schneier, Bruce: Secrets and Lies: Digital Security in a Networked World. John Wiley & Sons, 2000.

[SeAn08]   Seltzer, William / Anderson, Margo: Using population data systems to target vulnerable population subgroups and individuals: issues and incidents. In: Asher, Jana / Banks David / Scheuren, Fritz J. (Eds.): Statistical methods for human rights, Springer, 2008, pp. 273-328.

[StHR09]   Storf, Katalin / Hansen, Marit / Raguse, Maren (Eds.): Requirements and concepts for identity management throughout life. PrimeLife Deliverable H1.3.5, Kiel/Zürich, November 2009, http://www.primelife.eu/images/stories/deliverables/h1.3.5-requirements_and_concepts_for_idm_throughout_life-public.pdf.

Privacy Compliant Internal Fraud Screening

Ulrich Flegel

SAP AG, SAP Research CEC Karlsruhe
Vincenz-Prießnitz-Str. 1, 76131 Karlsruhe, Germany
ulrich.flegel@sap.com

Abstract

In the year 2009 several data privacy scandals have hit the headlines where major corporations had a legitimate need for detecting fraud conducted by their own employees, but chose inappropriate measures for data screening. This contribution presents architectures and pseudonymization technology for privacy compliant fraud screening or fraud detection, in order to reduce the number of undiscovered fraud cases and to reduce the time to discovery.

1 Introduction

During the first quarter of the year 2009 two major German corporations hit the headlines with large scale privacy law violations. Telekom conducted fraud screening by comparing employee account numbers and supplier account numbers to discover shell companies [Wel09]. Deutsche Bahn also compared employee telephone numbers and addresses with those of its suppliers [Wel09]. Shortly after, Airbus had to admit having conducted similar screenings [Reu09]. As a reaction to these scandals the German privacy law has been concretized, clarifying the scope of legal fraud detection measures. The scandals and the amendment of privacy law have created a demand for technology allowing for effective fraud screening in compliance with pertinent privacy law. This article presents architectures and pseudonymization technology allowing for automated fraud screening on pseudonymized data in compliance with privacy law in order to reduce the number of undiscovered fraud cases and to reduce the time to discovery.

Section 2 sets the scene by introducing a process that is prone to fraud and highlights fraud potential. Section 3 describes the state of the art process for detecting fraud in ERP systems and this fraud detection process is briefly assessed w.r.t. privacy law in Section 4, while Section 5 explicates the reconciliation of conflicting interests during this process. In Section 6 we propose an architecture for fraud screening on pseudonymized data, state the requirements for pseudonymization in this architecture and introduce a technical approach meeting the requirements. After assessing the improvement over the state of the art we conclude in Section 7.

2 Example Scenario

Private sector enterprises manage their business processes using *Enterprise Resource Planning* (ERP) systems. Business processes are implemented in an ERP system while accounting for internal controls, such as the principle of *Segregation of Duties* (SoD). Internal controls aim at avoiding occupational fraud done by employees of the company. Major pain points for fraud are the purchasing and sales departments in a company. Therefore we use a purchasing business process as a running example. We restrict our description to the details that are necessary for understanding the remainder of this text.

2.1 Example Purchasing Process

When an employee needs to purchase an article for his business activity, she creates a respective *purchase requisition* (PR) in the ERP system (see Figure 1). Before approval by the employee's manager the purchase requisition is *blocked*, approval changes it into a *posted* PR. According to the posted PR the purchasing department determines a suitable supplier and creates a *purchase order* (PO) from the posted PR. Suppliers or vendors are entered, i.e. created, by a manager of the purchasing department into the ERP system.

Upon reception of the ordered article the employee of the company creates a respective *goods receipt* in the ERP system, such that the associated invoice may be approved. When an invoicing clerk of the company receives the aforementioned invoice from the supplier, he creates an appropriate *blocked invoice* document in the ERP system. If the invoiced amount exceeds a specified threshold a manager of the purchasing department checks the invoice against the PO and the goods receipt and approves the invoice, which is then converted into a *posted invoice*. Posted invoices are paid during the next *payment run*, which periodically occurs in an automated fashion.

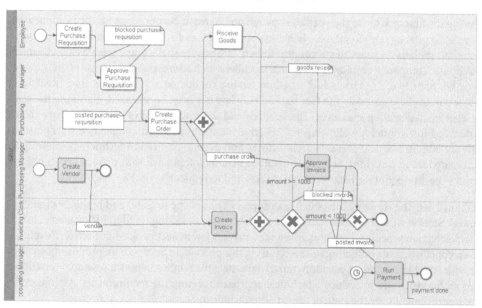

Figure 1: Simplified Purchasing Business Process in BPMN notation [GDW09]

This example process demonstrates the segregation of duties between different departments and roles for effective enforcement of internal controls. The involved employees use the same ERP system during runtime (see Figure 2), which is hosted by the (internal) IT service provider of the company.

2.2 Example Fraud Scenarios

The internal controls arranged for in the business process implemented in the ERP impede possible fraud, but they cannot avoid fraud altogether. This results from the activity margin necessary to complete business process instances during daily business, and from the incompleteness of the process implementation. For example the business activity of external actors, i.e. suppliers, are usually only partially covered by the local ERP system of the purchasing company. Hence, in order to detect collusion between purchasing agents and suppliers there exist some indirect evidence, but the actual agreements are not documented in the ERP system. Examples for such indirect evidence are buyer-supplier pairs with higher than average early or advance payment of invoices.

3 Fraud Detection in ERP Systems

Evidence for fraud may be collected by inspecting the business transactions performed in an ERP system. ERP systems usually exhibit at least one *audit component* interface (see Figure 2) that allows for case-based extraction of business data from the ERP databank management system(s) (DBMS) for auditing purposes. This data necessarily is collected or generated during the course of the normal business activity within the ERP system. The audit component merely filters this data and exports it for the purpose of detecting fraud. Figure 2 depicts the state of the art architecture for detecting fraud in internal ERP systems.[1]

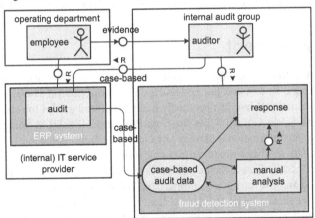

Figure 2: Conventional Realization of manual fraud detection

The fraud detection process within large enterprises works (with some variations) as described in the following. A member of the company's internal audit group receives some confidential clue or evidence from some operating department employee ("*whistleblower*"), which justifies case-based extraction and analysis of audit data from the ERP system. The case-based analysis of

---

1 In this article IT systems are modeled using *Fundamental Modeling Concepts* (FMC) [KGT06].

the extracted audit data aims at refuting or corroborating the suspicion implied by the initial evidence and is performed by internal auditors today mainly manually with some basic tool support [FVB10]. In addition to the extracted data the auditors leverage system-external information, e.g. from employee interrogation. In the case of a substantiated fraud a response is initiated, possibly comprising sanctions and criminal investigation. The actual response is out of the scope of this article.

3.1 Example Audit Data

The audit data extracted based on a specific case allows for comprehending the related business activity in its actual temporal order, including information on relevant documents, their owners and approvers. Documents relevant in the example purchasing process are *Purchase Requisitions, Purchase Requisition Approvals, Purchase Orders, Purchase Order Confirmations, Financial Documents, Invoices, Vendor Master Data*. The document field or attribute data extracted in the audit data is illustrated using purchase requisitions (PR) and the corresponding approvals as an example (fields/attributes with sensitive data w. r. t. privacy or business are underlined):

Purchase Requisition: *PR Number* (id), *PR Item* (id), *Material* (id), *Short text* (string), *Requisition Tracking number* (id), *Quantity* (integer), *Unit* (integer), *Delivery Date* (date), *Material Group* (id), *Plant* (id), *Store Location* (id), *Pgr Requisnr.* (user id), *Fixed Vendor* (id), *Total Value* (real), *Currency* (string), *Unloading point* (string), *CoCode* (id), *Recipient* (id), *Cost Center* (id), *Profit Center* (id), *Name* (string), *Street* (string), *House number* (string), *Postal Code* (integer), *City* (string), *Country* (string)

Purchase Requisition Approvals: *PR Number* (id), *WF Instance* (id), *Approval Date 1(-7)* (date), *Approval Time 1(-7)* (time), *Approval Action 1(-7)* (string), *Approver 1(-7)* (string)

4 Legal Assessment

A legal assessment of the implications of a given technical system is usually only possible for a given and specific legal system and law or regulation. A more general assessment across different legal systems or national laws is necessarily fuzzy and more geared towards general principles, such as Bizer's Seven Golden Rules for Data Protection [Biz07]. A comprehensive, more general assessment for international privacy law compliant fraud detection is bound to appear [FKM+10]. A detailed, legal assessment of fraud detection within the context of German privacy law has been published by Flegel, Raabe and Wacker [FRW09]. In the following that legal subsumption is omitted and the results are summarized. While the results are based on German law, the general mind set should be transferable at least to national privacy law in European Union (EU) member countries, where directive 95/46/EC [95/95] harmonizes member country national privacy law.

ERP systems lawfully collect and store data for the purpose of executing the regular business processes of a company. Privacy law is involved when audit data is extracted by the ERP audit component and sent to the internal audit group for fraud detection. Privacy law already covers the case of investigating on a case-by-case basis for given clues for a criminal offense. However, this exemption does not cover a continuous extraction of audit data and screening for fraud evidence. The rationale of the lawmaker is to be understood in analogy to pertinent law about video surveillance, where continuous surveillance for the purpose of exposing clues for criminal offenses would affect the employees of a company. As such, privacy law protects employees from a technical measure that continuously extracts clear text audit data from ERP systems for fraud screening.

5 Organizational Reconciliation of Conflicting Interests

Since fraud screening on continuously extracted audit data is prohibited by privacy law (cf. Section 4), a legal fraud detection facility needs to avoid audit data retention and rather focus on cases for which evidence justifies the suspicion that fraudulent activity is taking place. Hence, some piece of evidence is necessary and needs to be examined by the internal audit group, the works council and the responsible data protection officer in order to asses, if the given evidence justifies a fraud suspicion (refer to Section 3 for a description of the fraud detection process). Such evidence usually stems from whistle blowing or regular financial audits. As a result, the number of undiscovered fraud activity can be assumed to be high. The organizational reconciliation of the conflicting interests between employee privacy and fraud detection as described in Section 3 avoids a continuous surveillance. However, the control function of the internal audit group is restricted and leads to unreported fraud cases. Also does the organizational reconciliation not allow for timely results and response. In fact, even if a company employs measures for reducing fraud, the actual time before detection is 15 months (median) [oCFE06].

6 Towards Automated Fraud Screening

Both pain points, the long time before detecting a fraud and the possibly high number of undetected frauds could be mitigated, if business transactions could be continuously and comprehensively screened for fraud evidence in near real time. In such a system the internal audit group would not primarily rely on whistle blowing (cf. evidence arrow from operating department employee to internal audit group audit in Figure 2). Rather, audit data is continuously extracted from the ERP and automatically screened for fraud (see *analysis of evidence* at the IT service provider in Figure 3). Also the audit data in such a system may be analyzed for fraud evidence on the discretion of the internal audit group, i.e. not only for given fraud suspicions. Clearly, such a system would not be legal, if no additional measures are taken to comply with privacy law.

Compliance with privacy law can in this case be established by pseudonymizing the audit data that is continuously extracted and only making the pseudonymized audit data available for automated and/or manual analysis (see *pseudonymizer* in Figure 3). If this screening has produced a fraud suspicion based on the pseudonymized audit data, additional audit data may be needed to be analyzed for corroborating or refuting the suspicion. Since now a suspicion is given, the scope of the additional audit data is determined for the given case and may be extracted in clear text (see *case-based audit data* in Figure 3). As described in Section 3 the additional audit data extracted for the case must be relevant for the case, the scope must not be defined unnecessarily large. It may be necessary to disclose some pseudonyms in the pseudonymized audit data for the given suspicion in order to determine the exact scope for extracting clear text audit data. The technical realization of the pseudonymizer and the organizational processes must ensure that the original data behind pseudonyms can only be disclosed for audit data that leads to a fraud suspicion (see Section 6.1).

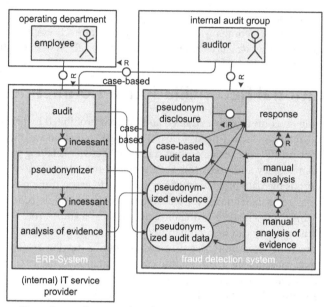

Figure 3: pseudonymized evidence screening for fraud detection

The proposed pseudonymization complements the rather random approaches to discovering fraud by whistle blowing and infrequent financial audits. Pseudonymization enables a comprehensive screening of all business transactions while respecting the confidentiality of sensitive data, such as personal data. This architecture design also allows for outsourcing of the fraud screening to a specialized external service provider, if we ensure that the service provider cannot disclose the pseudonyms.

6.1 Requirements for Audit Data Pseudonymization for Fraud Screening

Pseudonymization is a suitable measure to achieve privacy law compliance of continuous fraud screening, if the technical implementation meets several requirements:

1. **Confidentiality:** Pseudonymization is used to keep sensitive, e.g. personal, data confidential. This data must not be stored in a way that allows relating it to a natural person, which would allow bypassing the pseudonymization.

2. **Linkability:** Analyzing pseudonymized audit data for fraud suspicions, i.e. fraud screening, must be possible as effectively as for the unpseudonymized audit data. Technically the relationships between audit data features that are relevant for fraud screening need to be retained during pseudonymization.

3. **Technical purpose binding:** For fraud scenarios known in advance, the circumstances of pseudonym disclosure should also be agreed in advance and technically enforced. This allows for timely response to detected fraud evidence and avoids time-consuming decisions on the organizational level.

4. **Organizational purpose binding:** For fraud scenarios that are not known in advance, agreements for a technical purpose binding cannot be found in advance. Nevertheless,

it should be possible to disclose pseudonyms for new fraud scenarios subject to organizational purpose binding. The system must technically enforce the participation of the relevant stakeholders [Gem97], such as works council and/or data protection officer.

5. **Confidentiality of pseudonym mapping:** The mapping that relates the generated pseudonyms to the original data must be keep confidential.

6.2 Example Approach

In the following we assume that there is a process agreed by the works council and the data protection official according to which the internal audit group has identified and agreed collaboratively with the works council and with the data protection official, which audit data attributes are sensitive and/or personal data and need to be treated confidentially. In our running example the following attributes have been identified:

Purchase Requisition: *PR Number, PR Item, Short text, Requisition Tracking number, Fixed Vendor, Unloading point, Recipient, Name, Street, House number*

Purchase Requisition Approvals: *PR Number, WF Instance, Approver 1(-7)*

Accordingly the pseudonymizer (see architecture in Figure 3) shall replace these attributes with suitable pseudonyms, while respecting the requirements from Section 6.1. In the following we briefly demonstrate for the architecture described in Section 6 how a suitable technical approach for pseudonymization [Fle07] meets the requirements from Section 6.1.

6.2.1 Confidentiality and Linkability

Firstly the pseudonymizer replaces all sensitive and/or personal data attributes with pseudonyms and symmetrically encrypts each original data attribute with a randomly chosen key k of suitable length and unknown to a possible attacker[2]. This ensures confidentiality of the original data. Whenever during pseudonymization the linkability of data attributes needs to be retained, the same pseudonym is chosen for identical original data attribute values.

6.2.2 Technical Purpose Binding

Technical purpose binding aims at restricting pseudonym disclosure to the detection of a fraud suspicion. This requires that fraud suspicions be technically specified in advance. The activity of defining fraud suspicions needs to participate the works council and the data protection officer to ensure that the definitions actually comply with the definition of fraud suspicion given in privacy law.

A known fraud suspicion be technically characterized by n occurrences of specific types of business activity that are manifested in the audit data. From the key k that can be used to decrypt the encrypted original data then n or more shares are computed using an information theoretically secure secret sharing threshold scheme [Sha79]. The threshold scheme ensures that k may only be computed efficiently, if at least n shares have been generated. Each generated share is related to exactly one occurrence of aforementioned activities. Each time when an activity of a known fraud scenario is executed, the internal audit group receives the related share of key k. As soon as

---

2 In the current context we consider as attacker an entity that aims at disclosing the original data replaced by the pseudonyms.

the fraud suspicion has been completely substantiated, n shares have been generated and allow for efficient computation of key k. Using k the original data may be decrypted, i.e. disclosed. As a result, pseudonym disclosure is technically bound to the occurrence of fraud activity.

6.2.3 Organizational Purpose Binding

A similar approach is taken for organizational purpose binding of pseudonym disclosure. In advance the group of persons that need to participate in pseudonym disclosure decisions is determined, e.g. members of the internal audit group, of the works council and a data protection officer. Then a random key g is chosen secretly, and for each member of the decision group is generated a distinct share of g that is confidentially distributed to that member.

During runtime the random keys k are encrypted using g in a threshold cryptosystem [Gem97]. If for a new fraud scheme occurrence the group decides to disclose the pseudonyms, each group member uses her personal share of g to compute some share of k from the encrypted k. Combining the shares of k computed by the group members allows for recovering k and then to decrypt the original data.[3]

6.2.4 Confidentiality of Pseudonym Mapping

The extracted audit data must be pseudonymized before it is stored in secondary memory. Then the original data can only be accessed after pseudonym disclosure subject to technical or organizational purpose binding. Audit data extraction and pseudonymization are performed under the control of the IT service provider and out of the access reach of the internal audit group. The keys k are generated and stored in the primary memory of the pseudonymizer machine. Hence, pseudonymization can only be controlled via access to the primary memory of that machine or by modifying the configuration files of the pseudonymizer. State of the art technology cannot prevent both attacks, if conducted by administrators with system privileges. The group of system administrators for the pseudonymizer machine can be kept small, such that organizational controls are effective.

6.3 Revisited Assessment with Pseudonymization

The architecture depicted in Figure 3 together with the pseudonymization approach introduced in Section 6.2 implements the demarcation stipulated in pertinent privacy law insofar a comprehensive screening of clear text audit data is technically made infeasible and strongly hindered organizationally. A rededication for other purposes than fraud screening, e.g. behavior or performance monitoring, would require the collusion of the persons participating in organizational purpose binding and would create significant effort for disclosing all relevant pseudonyms. The data subject, i.e. the employee, can rely on the confidentiality of his personal data as long as she does not engage in fraudulent activity.

7 Conclusion

Enterprises rightfully collect and store data for the execution of their business processes. The recent fraud screening scandals were concerned with the fact that personal data of a large percent-

---

3 Note that the group does not recover g, but the individual k's. Hence, g is not disclosed to any of the group members, which would allow bypassing technical enforcement of the organizational purpose binding.

age of the employees of enterprises were used as clear text data attributes for fraud screening. On the other, hand fraud screening facilitates the discovery of crimes. In analogy to the intention of law text on telephone and video surveillance, a comprehensive screening on clear text personal data puts the data subjects, i.e. the employees, under an undesired general suspicion. Hence, German law has been concretized to allow personal data for fraud analysis only, if evidence for a fraud suspicion already exists. As a result, comprehensive fraud screening on clear text personal data as a means to discover such fraud suspicion evidence is prohibited. [FRW09]

The presented architecture and pseudonymization approach replace a fraud screening on clear text personal data with an analysis on pseudonymized personal data. The pseudonyms may only be disclosed for discovered and a priori defined fraud suspicions in order to establish accountability. Disclosing pseudonyms is lawfully allowed, when a fraud suspicion already exists. Fraud screening on pseudonymized data may be used in compliance with privacy law in order to reduce the number of undiscovered fraud cases, while respecting the privacy of the employees not engaging in fraudulent activity. Such a measure can be implemented as a continuous process and may significantly reduce the time to discovery of fraud, since the internal audit group does not need to rely solely on whistleblowers and infrequent financial audits.

References

[95/95]   Directive 95/46/EC of the European Parliament and of the Council of 24 October 1995 on the protection of individuals with regard to the processing of personal data and on the free movement of such data. Official Journal L 281, October 1995. http://europa.eu.int/eur-lex/en/lif/dat/1995/en_395L0046.html.

[Biz07]   Johann Bizer. Sieben goldene Regeln des Datenschutzes (in German). *Datenschutz und Datensicherheit*, 31(5):350–356, 2007.

[FKM⁺10]   Ulrich Flegel, Florian Kerschbaum, Philip Miseldine, Ganna Monakova, Richard Wacker, and Frank Leymann. *Insider Threats in Cybersecurity – And Beyond*, chapter Legally Sustainable Solutions for Privacy Issues in Collaborative Fraud Detection. Advances in Information Security. Springer, New York, 2010. To appear.

[Fle07]   Ulrich Flegel. *Privacy-Respecting Intrusion Detection*, volume 35 of *Advances in Information Security*. Springer, New York, 2007.

[FRW09]   Ulrich Flegel, Oliver Raabe, and Richard Wacker. Technischer Datenschutz für IDS und FDS durch Pseudonymisierung (in German). *Datenschutz und Datensicherheit (DuD)*, 33(12):735–741, December 2009.

[FVB10]   Ulrich Flegel, Julien Vayssière, and Gunter Bitz. *Insider Threats in Cybersecurity – And Beyond*, chapter A State of the Art Survey of Fraud Detection Technology. Advances in Information Security. Springer, New York, 2010. To appear.

[GDW09]   Alexander Grosskopf, Gero Decker, and Mathias Weske. *The Process: Business Process Modeling Using BPMN*. Meghan Kiffer, 2009.

[Gem97]   Peter Gemmel. An introduction to threshold cryptography. *Cryptobytes*, 2(3):7, 1997.

[KGT06]   Andreas Knöpfel, Bernhard Gröne, and Peter Tabeling. *Fundamental modeling concepts: Effective communication of IT systems*. Wiley, 2006.

[oCFE06]   Association of Certified Fraud Examiners. Report to the nation on occupational fraud and abuse, 2006.

[Reu09]   Reuters. German snooping scandal engulfs Airbus, April 2009.

[Sha79]   Adi Shamir. How to share a secret. *Communications of the ACM*, 22:612–613, 1979.

[Wel09]   Deutsche Welle. Spy scandal widens at German rail Deutsche Bahn, February 2009.

Threats and Countermeasures

Malware Detection and Prevention Platform: Telecom Italia Case Study

Luciana Costa · Roberta D'Amico

G. R. Romoli 274, 10148 Turin, Italy – Telecom Italia SpA
{luciana.costa | roberta.damico}@telecomitalia.it

Abstract

This paper illustrates the botnet problem, its impact and the need of security measures. By reviewing the existing literature regarding the botnet detection solutions the paper evidences the important role an ISP could take to better safeguard the user reducing in the meantime the spreading of the botnet phenomenon. The malware detection and prevention platform that Telecom Italia has defined is described. The aim is to minimize the potential harm that bots can inflict upon Internet infrastructure and to provide a detection and notification way to the users when their machines try to access a malware domain or when there is evidence that their computers have been compromised.

The idea is not necessarily to block or delay the users' traffic but to inform the users about the potential security risk on navigating on compromised sites, leaving anyway to the users the final choice to access the malicious domain. A security portal is accessible from a user detected as potentially infected with the aims to provide a common, well-organized set of information useful to clean the compromised system. Following this approach TI intends to prevent damage to its infrastructure while contrasting the malware infection spread.

1 Introduction

Bot networks proliferation and their evolution represent one of the most current alarming security threats for Internet users and also for Internet Service Providers (ISP). Differently from other types of malware, a bot is designed to infect a host and connect it back to an entity called botmaster, using a specific Command-and-Control (C&C) infrastructure. In such way the compromised hosts periodically receive binary updates and attack instructions. The greatest danger is represented by the minds behind those bot networks and the ability through which they can control their infrastructures by preserving their anonymity.

During the last years, we have assisted to a shift of the objectives that motivate the malicious activities of cybercriminals. They are not in search of notoriety but rather they are increasingly focusing on attaining financial gains. This shift is characterized by a new generation of cybercriminals. They don't act individually, but to ensure a stable business model, they began to create sophisticated organizations with different players whose relationship and co-operation is based on a trading system. On one hand there are the suppliers of services, ranging from the malicious code writers to the developers of exploit packets. On the other hand there are the consumers of these services ranging from spammers to cybercriminals that use extortion or the stolen data to make profits. Within this business system, botnets represent the element of interaction between the service suppliers and the concerning consumers.

The reason is simple. Botnets make possible to the cybercriminals to gain high profits at low costs, if compared to the involved risks. They represent a malicious infrastructure able to provide flexible resources usable to exploit new types of vulnerability and new malware techniques. By relying on the use of malware armies, the botnet owners become the preferred purchasers of malware services, not only to propagate the infections on new hosts and to retrieve new resources but also to perform criminal activities. This increased demand of malicious code has led to an evident and rapid malware evolution regarding the techniques used to avoid antivirus detection and removal and to hinder analysis of malicious code. The use of packing, stealthing, polymorphism and metamorphism are only some examples. For the botnet owners the cooperation with the supplier of malware services gives some economic benefits. Botnet operators can now rely upon the quality of the malicious code that reduces the risks involved in its use. This is very important because the profits of the botnet owners are entirely reliant on the availability, stability and integrity of the botnet infrastructure. Financial gains are achieved by the sell of an entire botnet or by the temporary rent of a group of compromised hosts to third parties, usually used for sending out spam messages or for performing denial of service attacks against a remote target. There is a fast-growing online cybercrime market based on this model of 'botnet-as-a-service' that, just like legitimate commercial Internet service, offers helpdesk support, Service Level Agreement (SLA) and price list. Others services available, in addition to the rent of part of a botnet, include the sale of personal data stolen to the victims (e.g. credit card numbers) and the infection of target systems based on the "pay-per-install" model. The money received by botnet owners, for a successful compromised system, depends on the difficulties in infecting the system.

The evident damage and the potential bad effects of botnets make their detection essential to prevent further infections. Most of the internet users are characterized by low security protection level which allows an attacker to easily penetrate their computers. Internet users are generally not aware of potential risks their malware infected computers are exposed to, such as phishing, online fraud, theft of personal data (like personal credentials for online banking account, credit cards numbers, personal identification data and so on). They can also become an unaware source of spam or a component of online crime network. Most of the time, the actions and measures that the users take to address a machine infection are useful, but have proven to be insufficient to reduce the overall problem. This has shifted the attention to the role that an Internet Service Providers (ISPs) can have as control points for botnet activity.

ISPs, while providing IP connectivity and other services to their Internet customers, are in a privileged position to detect malware infection and propagation in their networks. It is important that the first step toward prevention would be made at the network/ISP level rather than relying only on individual users to keep their machines clean by bot. The benefits are not only related to the Internet users, which would be better protected if their ISPs play a security role, but also for the same ISP.

The presence of a large number of infected hosts is a big problem for an ISP: the bots can be used to send very large volumes of spam, resulting in extra cost for the ISP and in a negative reputation of the IP address space used by the ISP. By causing ISP's mail servers and network links to get blacklisted, bots reduce the quality of service the ISP can provide to its subscribers. For the ISP is then a big benefit to reduce the size of bonets and to mitigate their effects.

The Botnet is known to be an internationally distributed problem which requires a mutual co-operation between all the parties involved: security software vendors, registrars, legal and government entities and also ISPs. Some initiatives in this direction are raised. The Messaging Anti-Abuse Working Group (MAAWG), with the collaboration of the major Internet and email service providers, has issued the first best practices [MoO'09] for managing infected subscribers. Customers with infected computers are redirected to a protected environment, provided by the ISP, where they can download remediation tools to remove the malicious code. The Internet Engineering Task Force (IETF) has published a draft [LiMO09] with recommendations for ISP on the methods usable for alerting the customers whose systems have been compromised. Also the largest ISPs in Australia, under pressure from the government, are preparing a voluntary code, containing guidelines on how ISPs can identify suspicious activity, the contact ways they can use to alert the infected customers and mechanisms for filtering out their connection.

In the next chapter we will provide an overview of the botnet detection approaches currently known. Chapter 3 describes the botnet detection and prevention framework that Telecom Italia has defined with the intent to protect its users and to give them notification of potential security risks. Finally our contribution ends with a conclusion session.

2 Overview of the Botnet detection solutions

The research community is actively looking for effective methods against the botnet phenomenon; in fact the detection represents a complex challenge and some of the proposed solutions cannot sufficiently handle the problem.

Bots can use custom protocols as their communications channel; moreover they can employ encryption and packing mechanism to mask their payload and can use different network topologies to organize themselves. As a result, a number of botnet-specific detection approaches have been proposed. These systems can be applied either on network level or on host level.

Host-based solution can be useful on recognizing malware binaries and anomaly behavior related to system calls or to the creation of specific registry keys. Anyway most of them are signature based and may be ineffective: malware authors are using a vast array of tool and techniques to generate new variants of malware to easily evade their detection. Moreover bots may have the same privilege level of host-based detection systems; they can disable anti-virus tools or use techniques such as rootkits to protect themselves from detection at the local host. Finally, these solutions can involve a system performance overhead which is sometimes significant and not well accepted by the users.

Network-based detection systems that rely on signature have the same problem: they cannot detect new attacks without a proper signature which describes the new threat behavior. On the other hand, anomaly-based detection systems did not have this limitation. Most of these techniques focus on discovering the Command and Control (C&C) channels between botmaster and individual bots. Others approaches look only to specific aspect that characterize the bot infection, for example the detection of scanning activities to detect a local host infection. Because bot agents can infect a system using many different ways other than traditional remote exploitation, there is a risk to have lots of false positives and false negatives.

Others detection techniques are finally based on DNS analysis. Bots need to communicate regularly with the C&C server to receive instructions from the botmaster, so DNS is used by the bots to locate the C&C points. To make a botnet more resilient the botmaster can use different DNS techniques referred to as fluxing. One method known as IP fluxing consists in changing very frequently the IP address associated to a specific domain name. Another technique is domain fluxing which periodically generates a new list of domain names to find the right C&C server. In the contest of DNS analysis, most of the detection approaches focus on identifying unique features of DNS traffic that when observed can denote a botnet presence.

Presently botnets represent a very advanced and flexible form of malware which is able to simply evade detection systems. Thereby detection strategies need likely to evolve to adapt to the new techniques adopted by the cybercriminals to evade their detection. It should also be noticed the difficulties to achieve high accuracy in bot detection, without having high false positive levels.

As said above a service provider can play an important role against malware spread and botnet attacks. Just to give some examples, the Cyber Clean Center (CCC) [JaGo07] is a possible approach that an ISP can adopt. This is based on detecting attack events from bot infected users and on collecting bot samples to analyze with the aim to develop disinfection tools. The infected users are then identified, in cooperation with the ISP participant to the initiative, and alerted by mail. By following the link specified inside the mail, the user can download the disinfection tool from the CCC bot countermeasure page.

Another approach an ISP can use, to reduce the botnet spread inside its networks, is to interfere in the preparation phase of an attack, by trying to stop the malicious code before it makes its way down to the targeted host. By providing a detection service to its users, an ISP can therefore advise its customers when they attempt to access malicious sites. The methods used to carry notification can be different, ranging from a redirection to a security portal to a mail or banner notification. The choice depends also on the service type the ISP intends to offer to its customers: the scope may consist in sending only an advice to the potentially infected user, suggesting possible countermeasures or the service's scope may also include preventing the infection by blocking malicious connections.

The following section will describe the modular platform defined by TI for botnet detection in its network.

3 Telecom Italia strategy

In Telecom Italia, inside Security Innovation department, an internal project was established two years ago focused on the study and analysis of the botnet phenomenon. The aim was to better understand the behavior of the malware code, the level of infection inside TI networks and the different detection solutions available on the market to implement a protection strategy.

After a first period dedicated to this analysis we are now looking to define a modular malware detection and prevention platform mainly based on the monitoring and analysis of DNS and HTTP traffic.

The following picture shows the high level architecture of this platform:

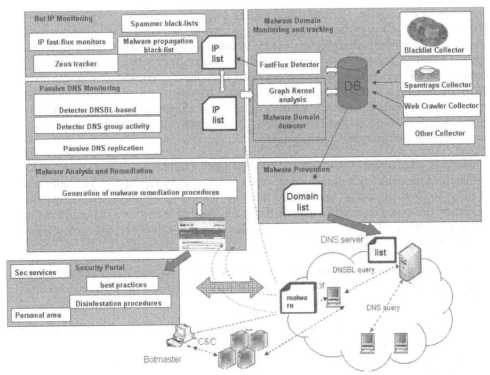

Fig. 1: Malware detection and prevention framework - main modules

In the next sessions each module is briefly described.

3.1 Malware Domain Monitoring

This component is dedicated to the creation and maintenance of a repository of black-list domains. The aim is to have a complete and as accurate as possible list of domain names or URLs which are potentially connected to the propagation of infection vectors, like worms, bots, trojan horses and so on.

One of the currently most used techniques by the cyber-criminal for the propagation of malware code is referred as drive-by download: in such cases some downloads are indirectly authorized by the users, but without understanding the real consequences, or are performed without the knowledge of the user. Drive-by downloads usually happen by visiting a website, which was previously compromised to exploit some vulnerabilities of a web browser, or by viewing an e-mail message or by clicking on a popup window. Typically the downloaded code is any kind of malware.

The black-list of domain names generated and maintained by this module contains not only the sites potentially related to the propagation of the infections, like those related to drive-by download attacks, but also collects the domains used by botmaster as C&C infrastructures, to coordinate and upgrade the infected hosts.

Just to make an example, an increasingly popular technique used to improve the reliability of the C&C infrastructure of the botnet, is known as domain flux. With this mechanism each bot periodically and independently generates a list of domain names that it contacts to seek out rendezvous points in Internet, i.e. location established by the malware authors whenever they like to census their zombies or when they wish to upload a new binary payloads to them. The first host in the list that sends a reply like a valid C&C server is considered genuine, until the next period of domain generation is started. This binary update service essentially replaces the classic command and control function that allow botnets to operate as a collective. This mechanism is used for example by Conficker and Torpig botnets.

From the attacker's point of view, domain flux is yet another technique to potentially improve the resilience of the botnet against take-down attempts. However, to the defender's advantage, once the Domain Generation Algorithm (DGA) is known, it opens up the possibility of „hijacking" a botnet, by registering an available domain that is generated by the botnet's DGAs and returning an answer that is a valid C&C response (to keep bots from switching over to the next domain in the domain list).

Another possibility to take advantage of domain flux is to prevent the access to these domains: in such a case, the Malware Domain Monitoring module must collect the newly generated list of domain names, using the botnet's DGA.

Therefore this specific component is fueled with data coming from different type of sources, like:
- Blacklist Collector,
- Spamtraps Collector,
- Web Crawler,
- Domain flux botnet detector and tracker

Since the quality of black domain name list is a key for the detection based on the monitoring and analysis of DNS traffic, the list should not include false positive nor false negative. For this reason the data fetched from different sources are further processed by specific computation aimed to minimize the false positive while trying to include as much as possible malware related domain.

One of such computation is to verify the presence of each domain name in more than one list, and to assign a kind of score which increases as the matches augment.

Another way is to assign a weight to each source, depending on its reliability and credibility.

Finally other techniques based on DNS analysis can be used to refine the domain-name blacklist. A most interested mechanism is based on using the DNS query graph [KiTM08] that represents a relation between queering hosts and a queried domain name. Specifically the idea is that domain names resolved by hosts that request black domain names are also expected to be black, while domain names resolved by hosts that do not resolve black domain names are expected to be white. So the approach consists in extracting, from the DNS traffic, the query graph and in applying some computations, like the graph kernel, aimed at giving similarities between nodes in graph. In this way, in terms of query graph, nodes (domain names) that are similar to nodes (black domains) are also expected to be black, and vice versa

The Malware Domain List generated by this module is than used as input by the next module.

3.2 Malware Prevention

This component has the purpose to identify the malware related connections originating from hosts inside the networks. The aim of this module is to enable infection prevention or at least to allow a notification alert to the infected users. To perform its task the Malware Prevention module uses the Malware Domain List generated and updated by the module first described.

The detection mechanism identifies the DNS requests concerning to the resolution of malware domains and redirects the users, from which they are generated, to a security portal. Here each user is advised of the potential risk connected to the web site and about the possibility that its machine could be infected with some kind of malware code.

The detection can be performed also analyzing the HTTP traffic: whenever an http request to a black-list domain/URL is found, the connection is prevented and the user is redirected to the security portal.

Obviously in case of HTTP detection, a more granular check is feasible, which means the Malware Prevention module may examine each URL and may enable a block at URL level not just at domain level. Another big advantage is that it works also in case of a domain contacted directly by its IP addresses, hence by-passing DNS protocol. However one of the disadvantages is that it works just for HTTP protocol: in this case, the connections to C&C servers that use protocols different from http, such as the IRC protocol, are not blocked.

For this reason the plan is to extend the Malware Prevention module in order to capture and analyze both DNS and HTTP traffic.

3.3 Bot IP Monitoring

Currently many projects and initiatives are dedicated to the generation of IP addresses black-lists, usable also as DNSBL (DNS BlackList). They are a collection of public addresses identified as source of spam or email harvester, or whose behavior is very similar to a host used for the malware propagation.

Many of these services offer a web interface for querying the database, while others support different interaction protocols, like rsync.

Moreover some of them are focused mainly in tracking Internet's spam senders and spam services, like for example spam bots, used to send spam messages or used to scrape addresses form websites. Exemplary of these specific services are offered by Spamhaus project, UCEPROTECT and Project Honey Pot: they generate lists of public IPs, in different format, depending on the usage (DNS zone, or just a flat list).

Other services are more general purpose than the previous ones: they take a census of infected IPs, dedicated to the propagation of different malicious code, not only spam bot, but also worm, virus or some types of Trojan-horses or stealth spamware, dictionary mail harvesters and so on. To give just an example, Composite Blocking List (CBL) offers this kind of list: it takes input data from large spamtraps and email infrastructures and lists only the IPs exhibiting characteristics specific to open proxies and spam-bot used to send malicious codes. Moreover the CBL also lists portions of spam-bot infrastructure, such as web site or name servers exclusively dedicated to the use of spam-bot or used for the download of infections.

Besides those, others initiatives are devoted to the monitoring and tracking of specific malware. A good example of this category is the "abuse.ch ZeuS Tracker" which provides the possibility to track ZeuS C&C servers and malicious hosts which are hosting ZeuS files. In particular the ZeuS Tracker monitors the ZeuS C&C servers, checking at regular time the status of each ones and the associated files/URIs. A ZeuS host (C&C server) can be a domain name or just an IP address.

Finally others projects track botnes and malwares that take advantage of fast-flux services: for example "dnsbl.abuse.ch" is a free DNSBL-service which offer a FastFLux Tracker of bots in real time: it lists public IP addresses that are part of a Spam, Malware, Phishing or Scam related Fast-Flux botnet.

The first action of the Bot IP Monitoring module is to collect, from different sources, these various IP black lists: than, as a second step, it performs a check to verify which of that IPs belong to Telecom Italia, for example looking at the Autonomous System Number (ASN) membership. Only the TI's IPs are kept, since of interested, while the others are filtered out.

The final goal of this module is to enable the notification to the users, which were using these fetched black-listed IPs. In particular the advice wish to inform a user that his IP is inside a black-list, because of a possible malware infection of its machine. Giving also the information about the specific list in which the IPs was found, the user can also have an idea of the possible infection type in which he is encountered. That means if the source is SpamHaus, probably the machine has a spam-bot; otherwise if its IP is inside the list produced by ZeuS Tracker, the infection is related to Zeus malware.

Assistance is then offered to the user to resolve the security problem in which he encountered: the user is invited to visit the security portal in which he can find all the information he may need.

3.4 Security Portal

The goal of the Security Portal is to offer a sort of centralized site where a user can find all the information he may need to better understand the security risks related to Internet usage, he can receive general security best practiced to follow and he can look for protection solutions and systems to improve the reliability of its machine.

Users that have access to the Security Portal, by an automatically redirection or following a received notification, can find a specific dedicated area where they can know the kind of infection encountered, bot or other type of malware. This information is very useful from the end users perspective. Once they are aware of the problem, they can decide what actions to perform to remove the malicious code from their machine. In this sense, a user may eventually request, from the security portal, a check of its machine to identify and remove the malware binary installed in the host. Being more conscious of the security risks, the users can also adopt some form of protection for the future. In fact, the idea is to give the user also the opportunity to choice between different type of security solutions and services, like for example the installation of anti-malware software or personal firewall suite, etc.

The security portal is also designated to let the users to choice the preferred way to receive alert notifications: he can privilege an e-mail advise (a sort of post notification alert) or a direct redirection to a captive portal (like a prevention advice, before accessing the malicious site). He may also choice to not receive this malware alert notification, because he isn't interested in this kind of advice.

3.5 Passive DNS Monitoring

DNS represents an interesting protocol to monitor and analyze for botnet detection. Unlikely other kind of malware, bots are coordinated and updated by a botmaster therefore they periodically must connect to a C&C server to get new instructions about the malicious tasks they have to perform or to receive new upgrades for their payload.

This module is therefore dedicated to the monitoring of DNS traffic: objective is to passively capture DNS data to further process in order to identify communication pattern typical of botnet infections. These information are useful to identify users infected with bots inside Telecom Italia networks, and also may be used to improve the quality of domain-name blacklist.

Since DNS usage is much localized and specific to the network in which the monitoring takes place, it is preferable to have a local sensor device to perform the task of DNS data capture instead of using data collected on other networks.

In the scientific literature many techniques are dedicated to this kind of analysis.

Just to give an idea, we mention some of them which we hold as a good representative of this approach and as possible methods for the future analysis of our DNS traffic.
- Passive DNS Replication: this is a technology aimed to construct zone replicas based only on captured name server responses, and without cooperation from zone administrators. The rational behind this approach is that DNS data is often volatile, and there are many unwanted records present in the domain name system. With the passive DNS replication domain name system data from production networks are captured and stored in a database for later reference. This data are very useful to support various security-related processes; for example one usage is related to the discovery of the domain-name used as C&C server. Some bot may contain one or more hard-coded domain names instead of IP addresses. Each domain can resolve to multiple IP addresses. Blocking a single IP address often does not prevent hosts from joining the botnet. If the domain name is knows than it is possible to accommodate better filters, based on the domain name. One way to recover domain names from IP addresses consists in capturing DNS packets and looking for the IP address you are interested in. DNS caches may delay the reappearance of resource records for hours. Idea: Capture DNS records in advance and store them in a database for later reference. This leads to "passive DNS replication".
- DNS-based blackhole list (DNSBL) [RaFD06]: another good example of DNS based technique, is based on monitoring the DNSBL lookups to expose botnet membership. This approach consists in performing a sort of counter-intelligence based on the idea that botmasters themselves perform DNSBL lookups to control if their spam bots are blacklisted. Some heuristics are applied to distinguish DNSBL lookups likely perpetrated by a botmaster, carrying out such reconnaissance, from those DNSBL lookups done by legitimate mail server. By monitoring these queries it is possible to obtain a list of potential bots.

- Botnet Detection by monitoring DNS traffic in search of group activities [HHHH09]: the idea is to identify several features of botnet DNS that are distinguishable from legitimate DNS traffic. Only botnet members for example send queries to the domain name of C&C server; therefore, the number of different IP address which queried botnet domain is normally fixed. On the other hand, the legitimate sites are queried from anonymous users (random) at usually. Another properties from which can be derived a group activity due to a botnet is the occurrence of DNS query. In the case of botnet, DNS queries occur temporary and simultaneously. The fixed members of botnet act and migrate together at the same time. However, most of legitimate DNS queries occur continuously and do not occur simultaneously. Based on those features the detection algorithm can identify the domain names connected to botnet and also the IP addresses from which the requests are originated. Probably these IP addresses belong to bot nodes.

3.6 Malware Analysis and Remediation

This is the most challenging module of our botnet detection and notification framework. Its goal is to classify the different malware code types, identifying the behavior of each malware sample in order to derive appropriate signatures usable to facilitate the detection of such a specific malware.

Moreover the idea is also to identify the right procedures which can be suggested to the victim users to clean the machines from the malicious codes. In fact, once a specific malware is correctly classified, it is easier to suggest the best measures and actions to execute to remove the malware from the infected machine.

This block performs also analysis to try to identify and understand the type of malware linked to a specific black-listed domain name (which is listed in the Malware Domain List): the intent is to collect as much relevant information as possible useful to fill out an accurate cleaning procedure to suggest to the infected users.

A good example of what we have in mind is represented by the Cyber Clean Center (CCC), a project which sees the participation of the Japanese Computer Emergency Response Team Coordination center (JP-CERT) and a collection of 76 Japanese ISPs covering about 90 percent of the nation's Internet users [JaGo07].

Specifically this center connects Internet lines of the project participating ISPs and "decoy" machines (Honeypot) to capture bot samples. The various malicious code collected are then analyzed by skilled teams with the aim to create specific disinfestations tools for the captured bot samples. These tools are then offered for free to the infected users, which are, in some way, alerted of the infection of their machines. In the advice the identified victim users are invited to visit a specific URL where they can downloads the free bot disinfestations tool to use to clean its computer from the identified bots.

4 Conclusion

The aim of this contribution is to introduce botnet detection challenge, the motivation behind the success of this threat and the role an ISP can play to keep down its spread. In this context Telecom

Italia has designed a modular architecture to detect and prevent bot infections inside its networks and to enable a notification to the potentially infected users.

We are gradually developing and testing each component of this framework: since last year a first version of Bot IP Monitoring has been in execution. By monitoring different types of black-lists, this module identifies the blacklisted IP addresses belonging to TI and keeps trace of the level of infection inside TI networks.

We are now working on the Malware Domain Monitoring, with the goal to generate an optimized list of domain names and URLs classified as malicious. This list will be used by the Malware Prevention module: currently we are evaluating the different possible ways to implement the detection and notification component of this block.

Since our regulatory framework is very strict, due to Italian privacy concerns, we have to pay attention in implementing all the measures to guarantee the anonymity of the data and their usage in accordance with our laws.

References

[MoO'09] Mody Nirmal, O'Reirdam Michael: Messaging Anti-Abuse Working Group Common Best Practices for Mitigating Large Scale Bot Infections in Residential Networks, July 2009, V1.0.0.

[LiMO09] Livingood Jason, Mody Nirmal, O'Reirdam Michael: Recommendations for the Remediation of Bots in ISP Network, September 2009, V03.

[JaGo07] Japanese government, Cyber Clean Center (CCC) Activity Report, FY 2007, https://www.ccc.go.jp/en_report/h19ccc_en_report.pdf.

[RaFD06] Ramachandran Anirudh, Feamster Nick, Dagon David: Revealing Botnet Membership Using DNSBL Counter-Intelligence, July 2006.

[HHHH09] Choi Hyunsang, Lee Hanwoo, Lee Heejo, Kim Hyogon: Botnet Detection by monitoring group activities in DNS Traffic, 2009

[KiTM08] Keisuke Ishibashi, Tsuyoshi Toyono, Makoto Iwamura: Botnet Detection combining DNS and Honeypot Data, 2008

[Weim05] Weimer Florian: Passive DNS Replication. April 2005

Defining Threat Agents: Towards a More Complete Threat Analysis

Timothy Casey[1] · Patrick Koeberl[2] · Claire Vishik[1]

[1]Intel
[2]Intel Innovation Lab
{timothy.casey | patrickx.koeberl | claire.vishik}@intel.com

Abstract

There has been significant progress in defining and developing viable approaches to threat modeling and risk assessment techniques for a wide range of IT applications and computing environments. However, we observe that the focus of most studies continues to be on asset or vulnerability analysis, leaving the analysis of threat agents out of scope. The motivations of the attackers are predominantly economic, and the mitigation techniques and planning approaches depend heavily on the intent and resources available to the attackers. Although threat agent taxonomies may be simple, they are necessary for the development of both theoretical studies of vulnerabilities and practical analyses of the measures necessary for the remediation and mitigation. In this paper, we are taking a more careful look at the typology of threat agents that can provide considerable insights into the likelihood, seriousness, and specific nature of security attack. We also evaluate the context where these taxonomies operate. Finally, we describe Intel's Threat Agent Library (TAL) and its applicability to various situations in dynamic threat analysis.

1 Introduction

Considerable progress has been achieved in numerous areas of threat analysis and threat modeling in recent years. Most of the approaches continue to be qualitative, due to the difficulties in quantifying all the aspects of the threat analysis, but some quantitative techniques, e.g., based on the analysis of the cost of security, have been developed, including "Total Cost of Security" described in [THOM09]. The adjacent field of requirements engineering has flourished also [CHEN07].

In qualitative studies, the focus continues to be on introducing new taxonomies and ontologies [FENZ09], applying threat modeling techniques to new areas [CARD09], e.g., ad-hoc networks or improving usability and effectiveness of existing approaches, such as the Common Vulnerability Scoring System [FRUH09]. Interest in developing models to address hardware and software threat analysis in a combined fashion is beginning to emerge [DARU09] as well.

However, we observe that the focus of most studies continues to be on asset or vulnerability analysis, and the types of threat agents are frequently treated as supplemental. We believe that the mitigation techniques and planning approaches depend on the intent and abilities of the attackers, and therefore a greater emphasis on the analysis from this angle is important. We also note that the focus on the threat agents permits the researchers to harness cyber-economic studies into a more comprehensive analysis of threats and vulnerabilities. The practitioners are thus permitted to allocate resources to the components that can move the advantage in cybersecurity from the attackers to the defenders and lead to "game change" in cybersecurity.

In this paper, we are taking a more careful look at the typology of threat agents that can provide considerable insights into the likelihood and specific nature of an attack and can inform the planners about the best and most pragmatic mitigation techniques. In our discussion, we focus on TAL (Threat Agent Library), a threat assessment tool developed at Intel that describes taxonomy of attackers. Additionally, we describe simplified example applications of Intel TAL to illustrate its utility as part of an extensive threat analysis in an organization.

1.1 Game Change in Cybersecurity and Threat Modeling

In order to evaluate the role and importance of a security tool, we need to place it in a larger context. The current focus in security is frequently on very narrowly defined projects because such projects are more tractable and offer a greater probability of success. However, to move the advantage from the attackers to the defenders of the cyberspace, we need to address hard problems of cybersecurity in a larger context. The US Federal R&D strategy includes game-changing approaches (specific measures that can result in a strong advantage for the defenders). Comprehensive threat modeling is foundational for evaluating the big picture and identifying areas that need to change in order to transfer the advantages in cybersecurity from the attackers to the defenders.

Game change was defined during the National Cyber Leap Year (NCLY) organized by NITRD, a Federal agency in the US.[1]

The NCLY effort has proceeded on the premise that, while some progress on cybersecurity will be made by researching better solutions to today's problems, some of those problems may well be too hard. The Leap Year has pursued a complementary approach: a search for ways to bypass the intractable problems. This approach we call changing the game, as in "if you are playing a game you can't win, change the game!"[2]

In 2009, the NCLY Summit, a meeting of more than 100 subject matter experts, developed concrete ideas on five topics that could move the advantage in cyberspace to the defenders:

- **Digital Provenance** → basing trust decisions on verified assertions
- **Moving-target Defense** → attacks only work once if at all
- **Hardware-enabled Trust** → knowing when we've been had
- **Health-inspired Network Defense** → move from forensics to real-time diagnosis
- **Cyber Economics** → crime doesn't pay

Anish Chopra and Howard Schmidt describe the results of the NCLY and Summit in the White House Blog as follows:

In a challenge to the research and development community, the President's Cyberspace Policy Review (near-term action item #9) called for a strategy for new, game-changing technologies that give the advantage to beneficial use. This challenge complements and extends the call in the Comprehensive National Cybersecurity Initiative (CNCI goal #9) for "leap-ahead" technologies,

---

1 Network and Information Technology Research and Development (NITRD) program.
2 National Cyber Leap Year Summit: Background is available at: http://www.nitrd.gov/NCLYBackgroundInfo.aspx

strategies, and programs. The National Cyber Leap Year responded to this challenge, gathering input from the community through concept papers and a national summit[3].

Three more refined game-changing concepts emerged from the continuation of this process in 2010:

- **Moving Target** – Systems that move in multiple dimensions to disadvantage the attacker and increase resiliency.
- **Tailored Trustworthy Spaces** – Security tailored to the needs of a particular transaction rather than the other way around.
- **Cyber Economic Incentives** – A landscape of incentives that reward good cybersecurity and ensure crime doesn't pay[4].

These broad themes aim at changing the foundations of cybersecurity R&D and the deployment of the results of such research. Foundational changes are always difficult to achieve, and taking these ideas from a brainstorming stage to concrete projects, technology development, implementation and deployment, processes and incentives will require considerable effort and resources. Clearly, defining and evaluating the threat landscape for each of the topics is necessary for success. Each threat model, identifying and describing threat agents, in addition to threats to assets and technologies, will be key to building a framework to capture and analyze potentially game changing components that should represent a future focus of research and technology development.

1.2 Economic Aspects of Threat Analysis

One other reason we need to focus more on the threat agents is the economic motivation for most of the security attacks. Secure practices must be incentivized to encourage quick development and introduction of new technologies and practices. And these technologies and practices must include the reduction of the economic incentive for the attackers, in addition to technical deterrents. New theories and models are needed looking at social dimensions of both good and bad cyberspace behavior. In this context, knowing the profile and capabilities of perpetrators is necessary to select the right kinds of mitigations.

Research in cybersecurity economics has been growing rapidly, yet we continue to debate the fundamental issues in applying economic methodologies to cybersecurity technology development. Today, we focus on protection of components that are readily available to attackers from other sources, perpetuating some types of security attacks. In the underground economy, in areas where security mitigation efforts are the strongest, such as protecting user accounts or clients, the cost of user records, user credentials, and access to the breached clients is minimal. A stronger emphasis on the attackers can help define economically viable models in organizational security that will impact the attackers economically.

Some challenges need to be addressed to understand the threat agents better; these challenges may have an indirect connection to the agents themselves, but have a clear impact on agent analysis. Among the challenges, we can name:

---

3 Chopra. A., and Schmidt, H. Help Change the Game in Cybersecurity! Available at: http://www.whitehouse.gov/blog/2010/05/19/help-change-game-cybersecurity
4 http://www.whitehouse.gov/blog/2010/05/19/help-change-game-cybersecurity

- *Improved access to cyberspace data*
  There are numerous legal and ethical issues around the collection, protection and distribution of data while at the same time we must ensure that all data types/categories are available to the R&D community, including international cross-border sharing[5],[6],[7]. We need to encourage sharing of appropriate data to support effective economic analysis.
- *Viable economic models for threat analysis and mitigation*
  We need to have a foundation to take the deployment decisions based on reliable forecasting of the consequences of various scenarios. Different organizational missions for all stakeholders providing a comprehensive basis for choosing courses of action that have the highest return on investment can be identified using the new generation of economic models [AbSM2009].

2 Approaches to Threat Agents

When risk managers assess threats to information assets, they have to understand the nature of potential human threat agents: the categories of people and organizations that can harm the information assets of an enterprise. This is a challenging task. A key problem is the lack of industry standards or reference definitions of agents as well as the dynamic nature of many threats. Assessors often have different concepts of even the most common agents, making it difficult to share information or apply it consistently.

Many classifications of threat agents and their activities have been developed, such as the IBM classification [ABRA91]. This taxonomy includes "clever outsiders", "knowledgeable insiders" and "funded organizations". The simplicity of this approach is attractive, but real world threat agents have widely differing intents, capabilities and access to resources. A threat taxonomy proposed by ISSS (Information Security Society of Switzerland) [RUF03] describes agents, their motivations, and localization. The taxonomy addresses three factors only: the identity of the agent, origin or place of the operations, and the nature of the intent. Although this type of characterization is useful, the proposed parameters are not sufficient to offer detailed analyses of many situations. Some other classifications, such as [KIM07] focus on the goals of threat agents: unauthorized access, unauthorized modification or destruction of important information assets, and denial of authorized access.

Work is being done today in profiling cyber-criminals, an adjacent area to threat agent analysis. [KWAN08] stresses the complexity of the area. In order to profile cyber-criminals, we need to first define cyber-crime, a difficult task considering geographic and legal diversity and the dynamic nature of the field. The first step, according to Kwan et al., is to develop the profile of the attack, moving then to the attackers. This is not an unusual approach, but independent development of the attacker profiles seems necessary in order to make progress and avoid dependence on the subjective perceptions of the importance of certain types of attacks.

---

5 Albena Spasova, "Tackling cyber crime together," http://www.guardian.co.uk/commentisfree/2009/jun/25/cyber-crime-europe

6 Kevin Poulsen, U.S. defends cybercrime treaty," http://www.securityfocus.com/news/8529, 2004-04-23

7 Richard Adhikari, "Report Warns of More Cybercrime," http://www.esecurityplanet.com/news/article.php/3790191/Report-Warns-of-More-Cybercrime.htm

With increased availability of attack tools and lower barriers to entry for the attackers, a layered structure of the threat agents has emerged, with those executing attacks not always the „owners" of the attack space (see,. e.g., [BIER08].

We think that in order to effectively allocate security resources in an organization, finer grained threat agent taxonomy is useful. In addition to its comprehensive nature, a threat agent classification needs to be:

- Capable of describing the key characteristics of threat agents
- Extensible, allowing new threat agents to be added if needed
- Qualitative rather than quantitative. A quantitative approach requires values to be defined which are subjective in nature. A descriptive, label based approach is preferable.
- Composed in a fashion that can add new and useful dimensions to risk and threat analysis
- Flexible in a way to permit us to address changes in the environment
- Capable of addressing economic issues in threat analysis
- Able to function as a complete model or a component in other models as needed
- Capable of reflecting trends in the evolution of common threats
- Not ambiguous, ensuring that the main definitions are specific enough and do not need to be renegotiated for different situations
- Composed of re-usable standard components

Fig. 1: TAL Structure

We believe that the last point is very important: even well designed risk management projects often experience threat creep - threat definitions are repeatedly re-negotiated as the assessment progresses, making the outcomes and recommendations difficult to interpret. Publicity about some threat agents tends to inflate their potential weight in the analysis, leading to further skewing of the results. Frequently a factor that appears to be the biggest threat because of disproportionally large attention may not be a significant risk in a particular situation if all the elements of the situation are analyzed. Finally, it is important to remember that threat agents evolve as they are influenced by diverse economic, societal, political, and technological trends. In the end, a viable threat analysis can begin only with a non-ambiguous, but flexible representation of the big picture, and the analysis tools for threat agents can permit us to control the other factors, protecting them from being inflated or under-estimated.

The TAL (Threat Agent Library) introduced in Figure 1 above has many of the useful features of threat agent taxonomies discussed in this section.

2.1 Approach in Intel TAL

The TAL is a standardized set of threat agent archetypes defined to improve the accuracy and efficiency of the threat analysis [CASE07]. A cross-disciplinary team at Intel developed a Threat Agent Library of 23 agent archetypes, each uniquely defined. TAL takes a detailed view of potential attackers describing multiple attributes of threat agents. There are 20+ types of hostile and non-hostile agents e.g., mobster, legal adversary, terrorist, cyber vandal, corrupt government official, government cyberwarrior, disgruntled employee or distracted, untrained or reckless employees. Each agent is described uniquely using the attributes listed below:

- Intent (hostile/accidental)
- Access (internal/external)
- Outcome (threat agent's goal)
- Limits (legal and ethical limits constraining threat agent)
- Resource level (organizational level)
- Skill level
- Objective (attack strategy)
- Visibility (overt/covert/clandestine)

	Insider	Common Tactics/Actions	Description
Civil Activist		Electronic or physical business disruption	Highly motivated but non-violent supporter of cause
Cyber Vandal		Network/computing disruption, web hijacking, malware	Derives thrills from intrusion of property, no strong agenda
Government Spy	■	Theft of IP or Business Data	State-sponsored spy, supporting idealistic goals
Government Cyberwarrior		Organizational, infrastructural, and physical business disruption	State-sponsored attacker with significant resources
Internal Spy	■	Theft of IP, PII, or business data	Professional data gatherer as a trusted insider
Irrational Individual		Personal violence resulting in physical business disruption	Someone with illogical purpose and irrational behaviour

Fig. 2: Sample subset of threat agents

The attribute set can sufficiently differentiate threat agents and is easily understood and applied by even novice security practitioners. In addition to taxonomy attributes, outcome attributes are used for analyses, permitting the assessors to further refine the picture.

The attribute set defined earlier can support the development of a library of threat agents, where each threat agent is defined by its unique set of characteristics as illustrated in Figure 2. Starting with a simple description of each agent, an iterative process was defined to refine the agent definitions. Threat agent creation is a data-driven exercise; in-house experience is supplemented with outside expertise and research data. Based on this information, trending (as illustrated in Fig. 3) is determined. Trending is situation and organization specific.

Agent	Recent Activity	Predicted Trend
Agent A	→	→
Agent B	→	↘
Agent C	↗	↗
Agent D	↗	↗

Fig. 3: Trending in agent behavior (environment specific)

Once defined, agents are assessed on the strength of their threat as it changes over time; a threat agent rating is defined by factors including the agent's recent activity. The rating is on a scale from low to high and is re-evaluated at regular intervals to ensure continued high relevance of the library. This approach facilitates risk assessments and enables trending.

Thus, the library is a catalog of diverse agents describing strengths and weaknesses of major threat sources. Archetypes of these agents, inclusive of their attributes, are designed based on normal behaviors, not outliers. In a similar fashion to the "persona" technique increasingly used in product development, each archetype includes a detailed description of typical characteristics and behaviors, to improve further analysis. The resulting threat "persona" can aid analysis by providing a clear picture of the attacker mindset.

3 Uses of TAL

Developing an appropriate threat model is a key element of operations. When conducting threat and risk assessments, we need to rank the risks in order to understand the needs for resource allocation, strength of mitigation and other parameters relevant for an organization or an environment. Threats are ranked in terms of probability and damage potential; mitigation for less probable threats may not be addressed by the security teams, and the elimination is frequently ad-hoc. The TAL can improve the approach by providing a consistent library, from which to select a subset of most likely threat agents. Analysis and design decisions can then focus on these threat agents only. In this way, a more consistent, faster, and repeatable threat modeling process is supported.

How can we use the TAL to obtain new information about a security threat to an organization? The evaluation of the threat to the organizational IT for an average enterprise from a government cyberwarrior may be a good example. Cyberwarfare threats rightfully receive a lot of media attention, but this, until recently, was mostly applied to operations associated, directly or indirectly, with defense activities or government operations. Consequently, enterprise IT could conclude that the need to form strong defenses from government cyberwarfare is not a priority. However, recently reported events indicated that such views may need to be revised. The users of TAL, under these circumstances, can easily revise the ranking and trending in the library and rethink the applicability of this threat to regular threat assessments because of the uniform and standardized method of defining the agent.

3.1 Components of threat assessments

Several stages can be identified when using TAL for different types of threat analyses. These stages are briefly described below for two example assessments.

Small domains can benefit from narrowing the focus onto a subset of 'most likely' threat agents:

- Subject matter experts examine the problem set and select a subset of 2-4 likely agents from the Threat Agent Library.
- Further analyses focus on the selected agents only.
- The descriptions of agents can be incorporated into other assessment tools, streamlining this component of the analysis. Intel is using this approach as part of a number of internal assessments, such as TARA risk assessment methodology [ROSE09].

In large domains, where all threats need to be considered, the analysis may follow a different process:

- Subject Matter Experts build a model (e.g. attack tree) to determine the most likely avenue of attack
- Agents associated with the likely avenues are included in the models, presenting the generic level of attacker skill, expertise, and economic capabilities.

Below, we apply the TAL to a couple of example cases associated with threats that are not frequently analyzed through other means, to demonstrate the adaptability of the approach.

3.2 Using TAL to analyze known threats: insights that we can gain

We will now apply TAL to the analysis sample of threats: device remarking and cognitive hacking.

3.2.1 Device Remarking

In a device remarking attack, the IC is "upgraded" by removing the existing device markings and replacing them with markings indicating a higher value device, for example changing the temperature rating from a commercial to an extended temperature range. The remarked device is then sold on to unsuspecting customers at a premium. For a simple screen printed marking, the skill level and equipment required for such an attack are not significant.

Subject matter experts begin the analysis by selecting a suitable subset of threat agents from the TAL. It is important to emphasize that threat agents be selected by attributes rather than by name. The threat agent name is simply a label identifying a set of attributes; selecting by agent name can lead to misinterpretation and overlooking of less obvious options.

Two threat agents are selected from the TAL, Mobster and Thief. Their attributes are listed in Table 1. Both agents represent a viable device remarking risk in terms of intent and capabilities; however the higher organizational resources and skills of 'Mobster' allow this agent to produce and distribute a much greater number of remarked devices in the short time span before the remarking operation is located and shut down. As a result of using the TAL, the technologists engaged in threat analysis can determine pragmatic strategies to address more sophisticated threat agents.

Using the current and predicted threat rating associated with each agent the TAL based assessment can determine which agent to focus on.

Table 1: Looking closely at potential perpetrators in device re-marking

	Mobster	Thief
Intent	Hostile	Hostile
Access	External	External
Outcome	Acquisition/Theft	Acquisition/ Theft
Limits	Extra-legal	Extra-legal
Resources	Organization	Individual
Skills	Adept	Minimal
Objective	Take	Take
Visibility	Covert	Clandestine

What insights can we gain by applying the TAL? The analysis of threat agent attributes, ratings and "personas" supports informed decision making when assessing the need to introduce anti-remarking technologies. In particular, the "Skills" and "Resources" attributes of the appropriate threat agent will determine the appropriate response. In addition to the technological aspects, the appropriate level of supporting legal and law enforcement activities can be assessed. The threat "persona" provides the necessary insight into the threat agent's mindset, operations and interactions. In this way, the TAL approach enables the formulation of a coherent and consistent anti-remarking strategy.

3.2.2 Cognitive Hacking: Another Example

Cognitive hacking is a term used by George Cybenko to describe attempts to influence the activities of the users through fraudulent information delivered to them [CYBE02]. Examples could range from selling the stock based on a fraudulent press release describing serious issues in the company in question to attempting to change outcomes in elections by planting videos and other information misrepresenting the candidates. Other scenarios can include misrepresentations of technologies or products.

The fraudulent information can be planted by defeating access control systems or appropriating valid access credentials from other parties or could be made available through legitimate channels. As examples show (EMULEX stock lost 70% of its value in 2 hours after fraudulent information on the company's performance was posted as a legitimate press release), the results of cognitive hacking can be devastating, and it represents a classical example of today's security attacks where social, economic, and technical factors combine to offer novel opportunities to the attackers.

In addition to the intent, we can assess the skills and resources necessary to a cognitive hacker. We will discover that, depending on the situation and object of the attack, resources and skills will vary from significant to negligible. The wide range of attackers' ccharacteristics as illustrated in Table 2 (and consequently mitigation techniques) makes cognitive hacking a threat that is very difficult to address. The TAL will be helpful to devise a viable mitigation strategy in this case.

In situations of this nature, where technical measures and best practices to address the vulnerabilities are incomplete without the evaluation of the attackers, their skills and resources, we need to shift the focus to the evaluation of the potential attackers in order to mitigate the risks.

Table 2: Evaluating Cognitive Hacking

		Threat Agent				
		Civil Activist	Internal Spy	Mobster	Radical Activist	Cyber Vandal
Motivation	Political	■			■	
	Theft		■	■		
	Fraud			■		
	Prestige					■

4 Conclusions and Future Work

The standardized approach to threat agent analysis is already making an impact. It was incorporated into Intel's main business security and acquisitions risk assessment tools where it contributed to streamlining associated processes. A key manufacturing group reported a 60% improvement in total threat assessment time, reducing the negotiation period from months to days. The agent archetypes also enable focused data collection and accurate threat ranking, allowing Intel IT architecture and mitigation groups to better prioritize resources. Externally, the US DHS has incorporated the library as a methodology of the IT Sector Baseline Risk Assessment [INFO09].

It is clear that a sophisticated and dynamic threat agent taxonomy fills a gap in threat analysis. Work on TAL at Intel continues, to better adapt the library for broad baseline analyses and for using it as part of other ontologies to provide a comprehensive analysis of the threat space.

The approach is being fine-tuned to support new applications in today's dynamic technology environment. The new ambitious goals in cybersecurity as exemplified by the US game change efforts offer opportunities to use threat agent analysis in new settings that permit the technologists to address the economic and technical aspects of cybersecurity threats.

References

[THOM09] Thomas, R. C. 2009. Total cost of security: a method for managing risks and incentives across the extended enterprise. In Proceedings of the 5th Annual Workshop on Cyber Security and information intelligence Research: Cyber Security and information intelligence Challenges and Strategies (Oak Ridge, Tennessee, April 13 - 15, 2009). F. Sheldon, G. Peterson, A. Krings, R. Abercrombie, and A. Mili, Eds. CSIIRW '09. ACM, New York, NY, 1-4.

[CHEN07] Cheng, B. H. and Atlee, J. M. 2007. Research Directions in Requirements Engineering. In 2007 Future of Software Engineering (May 23 - 25, 2007). International Conference on Software Engineering. IEEE Computer Society, Washington, DC, 285-303.

[FENZ09]   Fenz, S. and Ekelhart, A. 2009. Formalizing information security knowledge. In Proceedings of the 4th international Symposium on information, Computer, and Communications Security (Sydney, Australia, March 10 - 12, 2009). ASIACCS '09. ACM, New York, NY, 183-194.

[CARD09]   Cardenas, A. A., Roosta, T., and Sastry, S. 2009. Rethinking security properties, threat models, and the design space in sensor networks: A case study in SCADA systems. Ad Hoc Netw. 7, 8 (Nov. 2009), 1434-1447.

[FRUH09]   Fruhwirth, C. and Mannisto, T. 2009. Improving CVSS-based vulnerability prioritization and response with context information. In Proceedings of the 2009 3rd international Symposium on Empirical Software Engineering and Measurement (October 15 - 16, 2009). ESEM. IEEE Computer Society, Washington, DC, 535-544.

[DARU09]   Daruwala, B., Mandujano, S., Mangipudi, N. K., and Wong, H. 2009. Threat analysis for hardware and software products using HazOP. In Proceedings of the international Conference on Computational and information Science 2009 (Houston, USA, April 30 - May 02, 2009). V. Zafiris, M. Benavides, K. Gao, S. Hashemi, K. Jegdic, G. A. Kouzaev, P. Simeonov, L. Vladareanu, and C. Vobach, Eds. Recent Advances In Electrical Engineering. World Scientific and Engineering Academy and Society (WSEAS), Stevens Point, Wisconsin, 446-453.

[AbSM2009]   R. K. Abercrombie, F. T. Sheldon, and A. Mili, "Managing Complex IT Security Processes with Value Based Measures," Proceedings of 2009 IEEE Symposium on Computational Intelligence in Cyber Security, Nashville, TN, April 1, 2009

[RUF03]   Lukas Ruf, Consecom AG, Anthony Thorn, ATSS GmbH, Tobias Christen, Zürich Financial Services AG, Beatrice Gruber, Credit Suisse AG, Roland Portmann, Hochschule Luzer. Threat Modeling in Security Architecture -The Nature of Threats. ISSS Working Group. Available at: http://www.isss.ch/fileadmin/publ/agsa/ISSS-AG-Security-Architecture__Threat-Modeling_ Lukas-Ruf.pdf

[KIM07]   Kim, Y., Park, G., Kim, T., and Lee, S. 2007. Security Evaluation for Information Assurance. In Proceedings of the the 2007 international Conference Computational Science and Its Applications (August 26 - 29, 2007). ICCSA. IEEE Computer Society, Washington, DC, 227-230.

[KWAN08]   Kwan, L., Ray, P., and Stephens, G. 2008. Towards a Methodology for Profiling Cyber Criminals. In Proceedings of the Proceedings of the 41st Annual Hawaii international Conference on System Sciences (January 07 - 10, 2008). HICSS. IEEE Computer Society, Washington, DC, 264. Williams, L. Y. 2007 A Taxonomy of Network-Perpetrated Criminal Activity: Developing an Empirically-Based Model for Recourse Strategies. Doctoral Thesis. UMI Order Number: AAI3259653., Capella University.

[ABRA91]   DG Abraham, GM Dolan, GP Double, JV Stevens. 1991. Transaction Security System. In IBM Systems Journal Journal, v 30 no 2 (1991), 206–229.

[BIER08]   Bierman, E. and Cloete, E. 2002. Classification of malicious host threats in mobile agent computing. In Proceedings of the 2002 Annual Research Conference of the South African institute of Computer Scientists and information Technologists on Enablement Through Technology (Port Elizabeth, South Africa, September 16 - 18, 2002). ACM International Conference Proceeding Series, vol. 30. South African Institute for Computer Scientists and Information Technologists, 141-148.

[CASE07]   Casey, Timothy. Threat Agent Library Helps Identify Information Security Risks. Available at: http://communities.intel.com/docs/DOC-1151

[ROSE09]   Rosenquist, Matt. Prioritizing Information Security Risks with Threat Agent Risk Assessment. Available at http://download.intel.com/it/pdf/Prioritizing_Info_Security_Risks_with_TARA.pdf

[CYBE02]   Cybenko, G., Giani, A., and Thompson, P. 2002. Cognitive Hacking: A Battle for the   Mind. Computer 35, 8 (Aug. 2002), 50-56.

[CHEM07]   Chen, Y. 2007. Stakeholder Value Driven Threat Modeling for Off the Shelf Based Systems. In Companion To the Proceedings of the 29th international Conference on Software Engineering (May 20 - 26, 2007). International Conference on Software Engineering. IEEE Computer Society, Washington, DC, 91-92. DOI= http://dx.doi.org/10.1109/ICSECOMPANION.2007.69

[HASA09] Hasan, R., Sion, R., and Winslett, M. 2009. Preventing history forgery with secure provenance. Trans. Storage 5, 4 (Dec. 2009), 1-43.

[INFO09] Department of Homeland Security. Information Technology Sector Baseline Risk Assessment. August 2009. Available at: http://www.dhs.gov/xlibrary/assets/nipp_it_baseline_risk_assessment.pdf

[MAYB05] Maybury M., Chase P., Cheiker B., Brackney D., Matzner S., Hetherington T., et al. Analysis and detection of malicious insiders; 2005.

[ROSE09] Rosenquist, Matthew: Whitepaper: Prioritizing Information Security Risks with Threat Agent Risk Assessment. Available at: http://communities.intel.com/docs/DOC-4693

[THUR09] Thuraisingham, B. 2009. Data Mining for Malicious Code Detection and Security Applications. In Proceedings of the 2009 IEEE/WIC/ACM international Joint Conference on Web intelligence and intelligent Agent Technology - Volume 02 (September 15 - 18, 2009). Web Intelligence & Intelligent Agent. IEEE Computer Society, Washington, DC, 6-7.

[WALF10] Walfish, M., Vutukuru, M., Balakrishnan, H., Karger, D., and Shenker, S. 2010. DDoS defense by offense. ACM Trans. Comput. Syst. 28, 1 (Mar. 2010), 1-54.

[WALK08] Walker, T. 2008. Practical management of malicious insider threat - An enterprise CSIRT perspective. Inf. Secur. Tech. Rep. 13, 4 (Nov. 2008), 225-234.

A Mechanism for e-Banking Frauds Prevention and User Privacy Protection

Rosalia D'Alessandro · Manuel Leone

G. R. Romoli 274, 10148 Turin, Italy – Telecom Italia SpA
{rosalia.dalessandro | manuel.leone}@telecomitalia.it

Abstract

In this paper we will discuss how recent trends in malware evolution will probably require a change of the internet banking security paradigms currently in use. Specifically, we will demonstrate how next generation malware may defeat the most recent strong authentication mechanisms put in place by several financial institutions. These new attacks clearly require a change on current schemes and, at the same time, a definitive reduction in the final user responsibility. Too often the user's behavior adds a weak layer which can be exploited by several techniques, such as Social Engineering attacks. Therefore, a new generation of automatic and hardware-based mechanisms should be deployed, in order to both increase the security level intrinsically offered by the technology, and reducing the exposure to Social Engineering risks. They have to work transparently, minimizing any kind of misuse that could be source of vulnerabilities.

1 Introduction

Convenience is the key reason of why millions of people are opting out of traditional banking services for the online version. This change is promoted by banks and other financial institutes in order to make saving on operating costs. However, fraudulent activities have recently increased just due to this migration, at least according to most analysts.

Traditional online frauds typically occur in a two-step process. Firstly, the offender steals the customer's account information (e.g. her credentials); secondly, the offender will use that information to move victim's money to another account or withdraw it, usually involving some other third party.

The most popular schemes include:
- Phishing or Passive Attacks Scheme: representing a well-known technique to retrieve confidential information from a user by posing as a trusted authority. Most often, with the help of a deceptive email, the attacker redirects the victim to a mirror site to obtain the consumer's personal information such as online banking username and password. Typically this type of attacks is clientless because it does not make use of any software component installed onto the user's PC.
- Trojan Horse or Active Man In The Middle Attack (MITM) Scheme: unfolds when malicious software (malware) embeds to a consumer's PC without the user's consensus. Trojans often come in links or as an attachment from unknown email senders. After installation, the software detects whether a person is accessing banking sites and, in this case, it records

username, password and any other user's sensitive data. Soon after, the stolen data will be transmitted to a collector component notifying the attacker on the availability of new data.

Since the end of the last year, a new malware trend has been showing an interesting switch from the traditional passive scheme to an active form, the pharming attack. In this case, typically with the help of a Trojan, an attacker can take the control of the link between the IP address and the DNS server name it is responding to. In this way, any data sent and received by the legitimate server can easily be manipulated in real-time.

A case in point is the ZEUS Trojan (also known as Zbot, PRG, Wsnpoem, Gorhax and Kneber), firstly identified in July 2007 but mainly spread in 2009 through drive-by downloads and phishing schemes. It has been estimated this Trojan infected, at the end of 2009, approximately 1% of the PCs in the US (around 3.6 million) [RfRl09] and it is still active in 2010. This malware family can be considered the largest botnet over the internet (although the estimation of a botnet size is still an open problem in literature).

Top 10 Victim Countries

Fig. 1: Top 10 country affected by the Zeus botnet [NetW10].

It infected consumer PCs, waited for them to log onto a list of targeted banks and financial institutions [StDo10], and then stole their credentials, sending them to a remote server in real time [FaCh10]. The estimated targets counted about 960 different financial institutes.

Zeus provides a ready-to-deploy package easily purchased and also freely traded online, so that for hackers is very easy to distribute their own botnet. In addition, the ease-of-use of Zeus means the malware can be used widely and is highly prevalent, allowing the most novice hackers to easily steal credentials and other sensitive data for financial gain.

Furthermore, its malware family was totally undetectable by the traditional anti-virus [Trus09]. Due to the most recent techniques, such as polymorphism, metamorphism, packing and emulation, traditional anti-malware solutions are unable to detect completely new or just variants of well-known malware. In a recent study, NSS Labs [NssL10] shows, starting from well-known malware based on Operation Aurora payload (Hydra variant), how simple is building malicious code unidentifiable by anti-malware products. Although the original version was caught by six out of seven anti-viruses tested, just one product had been able to detect the NSS' variant, too.

In this scenario, several countermeasures have been proposed and deployed to reduce the risk related to online banking frauds. One of the most adopted schemes is the strong authentication mechanism based on the one-time passwords (OTPs). According to this scheme, the authentication/authorization credentials are generated "on the fly" by either hardware or software tokens, or according to an algorithm which typically takes in input the time and a secret key. Because the OTPs can be used just once within a limited time window, this mechanism has been widely accepted as a definitive answer to this issue. Unfortunately, this position is right in a passive attack model, but it cannot be of any help against pharming. An unaware user supplies her credentials to the pretended site; the attacker receives this information and submits it, automatically and in real-time, to the real site, getting the access and taking the complete control over the communication, within the OTP validity period. Besides the traditional OTP token-based, OTP SMS-based must be reminded. Such a solution uses SMS channel, typically out of attackers' control, to send an OTP combined with a transaction summary. This approach is effective against both passive and pharming attack, very simple to provision and manage, but it counts some limitation. In particular, it is totally ineffective to detect fake websites and to preserve the user privacy. In fact the attacker can implement a MITM attack, working as a proxy for the real site. In this case, he cannot authorize operations without the knowledge of new OTPs, but he can get access to the user's banking account, and consequently, is able to read the user's data (e.g. transactions, money transfer destinations and reasons and so on…). Unfortunately, the efficacy of this mechanism is strongly based on user verification and collaboration. Moreover, it lacks a good user-experience, especially when the user is accessing the internet banking service directly through his mobile phone. Finally, it is strongly dependent on the availability and the performance of radio channel, in terms of coverage, congestion, latency, and roaming between different Mobile Operators.

As an alternative to OTP, sometimes banks propose mutual authentication schemes using SSL/TLS certificates. But, unless we hypothesize to automate the server's certificate validation at the client side, the scheme is unable to provide the expected security level. Again, it relies on a manual user validation of the server certificate which rarely takes place. As a consequence, fraudulent web sites can use self-issued certificates to fool them. In addition, some other specialized attacks could be performed. Taking advantage of specific cryptographic weaknesses related to hash functions (such as MD5, still used by some Certificate Authorities), attackers can generate a fake certificate which can be verified by the user through the default client root certificates. In that case just a deep validation, which is typically not performed by standard users, could reveal the fraud.

At last, mutual authentication schemes often use machine authentication as primary mechanism and knowledge authentication just as a backup. In that case, the attack becomes even simpler. The adversary has just to present to the victim the backup questions required by the legitimate site. Since there is a lack of consistency in this method, the mutual authentication becomes suspect.

Said that, it becomes clear that despite both strengthened user and mutual authentication methods, a session hijacking Trojan attack is feasible and it could empty an online account; consequently, in our opinion, transaction authentication and integrity check cannot be eliminated in the online banking services.

In this context, we propose a novel mechanism able to satisfy the main following requirements:
- It can be used with mobile phones as well as PCs and laptops;
- It does not rely on explicit user verification or, at least, it minimizes the risk of attacks tied to the user behavior.
- It must be able to guarantee the user privacy, alerting the user when she's connecting to an untrusted site;
- It must be able to prevent both passive and active MITM attacks.

The approach, proposed and described in the next sections, combines several factors: mutual authentication with digital certificates, a smartcard with microSD form-factor, a custom browser extension (Internet Explorer helper object, Firefox add-on, etc.), a mobile phone and an additional security layer, in order to provide transaction authentication and integrity verification.

Therefore the paper is organized as follows: in the Section 2 we describe the proposed approach and provide details concerning the prototype developed in our labs. A brief discussion on the security of the solution, its usability and deployment issues are provided in Section 3, while conclusions and future work are presented in Section 4.

2 Proposed Solution

The mechanism we propose in this paper combines several factors: mutual authentication based on digital certificates, a smartcard with microSD form-factor, a custom browser extension (Internet Explorer helper object, Firefox add-on, etc.), a Web Server extension, a mobile phone and a second layer of security above and beyond the simple user authentication, consisting in transaction authentication and integrity verification. In Fig. 2: Bootstrap phase: user experience ., synthetically, the user experience relating to the mutual authentication phase is shown.

We choose to implement the client component as a browser extension for two main reasons. Firstly, this choice provides a great user experience, being integrated within a well know application from the user viewpoint. Secondly, the browser extension approach can provide a very simple and intuitive graphical feedback on the trustiness tied to the site the user is visiting.

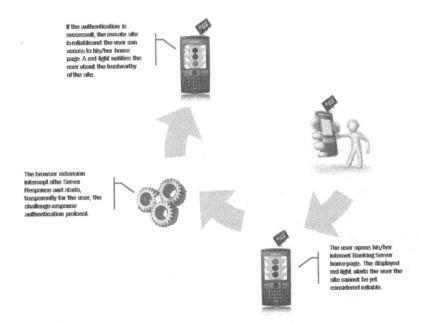

Fig. 2: Bootstrap phase: user experience .

A user can access her internet banking service by her PC or mobile phone via HTTPS, including mutual authentication. When accessing the service through a PC, the mobile phone will play the role of a smartcard reader connected to the PC by a USB cable, although the microSD card can also be inserted directly in the PC, if equipped with a proper slot. The smartcard component stores, respectively, the Bank's Server certificate, the user's RSA keys and X.509 certificates. Fig. 3: Solution modules.3. displays, graphically, the involved components within the solution.

Thanks to the browser extension, the browser shows a toolbar which, by default, displays a red ball to notify the user that she/he is connecting to a website not yet considered trusted. As said before, even if a valid TLS/SSL session is running, typically the user does not check any certificate. To prevent this threat, the browser extension intercepts the URL the user is willing to connect to and, in first instance, verifies whether it has been blacklisted by means of Google Safe Browsing API [Goog10]. If this is not the case, it then verifies if the URL matches the common name field of the server certificate stored into the smartcard (usually this is the standard to way to request a Web Server Certificate). If there is a match, the browser extension will take the control starting an in-line challenge-response authentication protocol with the Bank's Server detailed in the following subsection. If the authentication process will be successful, then the user home page will be displayed and the user will be notified about the trustworthy of the site by a green ball in the toolbar. If there is no match between the requested URL and the server certificate stored locally in the smartcard or the authentication fails, then the user will not be able to access to her home page.

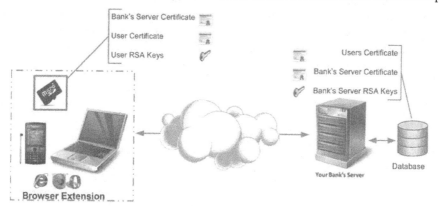

Fig. 3: Solution modules.

After this bootstrap phase, the user is logged into her home page where any transaction can be securely issued. In particular, the solution implements a transaction authentication and validation mechanism involving, again, the components of Fig. 3: Solution modules.3. For instance, in case of a bank transfer, the Bank's Server will send back to the user the received data for approval; the browser extension will receive the data and will ask the user for an explicitly confirmation of the transaction displaying data summary in a popup dialog window on her mobile phone. At this point, the browser extension will also calculate a transaction authorization code used by the Bank's Server to validate the operation.

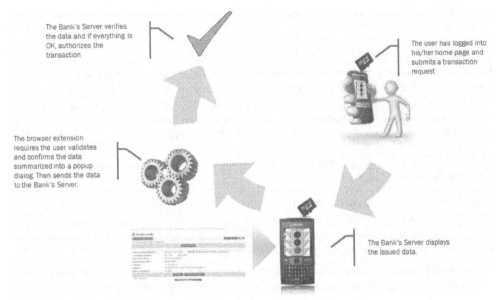

The Bank's Server verifies the data and if everything is OK, authorizes the transaction

The user has logged into his/her home page and submits a transaction request

The browser extension requires the user validates and confirms the data summarized into a popup dialog. Then sends the data to the Bank's Server.

The Bank's Server displays the issued data.

Fig. 4: Transaction phase: user experience.

Now we will go into the protocol details related to both the bootstrap and the transaction phases.

2.1 Protocol Details

The proposed solution is based on the well-known challenge-response paradigm.

In the following subsection, more details concerning protocol design and implementation will be provided. Please, note that the prototype developed in our labs, counts, in first instance, the Microsoft platforms (XP for PC/Laptop and Windows Mobile 6 for mobile phone).

2.1.1 Bootstrap Phase

The most effective way to prevent and detect complex phishing attacks is a deep validation of the Bank Server SSL certificate. Even if this seems potentially easy to realize, in practice is impossible a standard user will do. Most users typically do not have the required skill to securely check the server's certificate. They usually ignore public key concepts and cryptographic notions. Some users just rely on the browser validation. They only verify that no warnings are raised by the browser. Unfortunately, they do not perform any real check to be sure that the current server's certificate is the right one (for instance checking the hash) and not simply a certificate "browser validated", thanks to some root certificate contained in the local certificate store. Therefore it becomes crucial the development of certificate validation mechanisms, totally automatic and transparent for final users.

To achieve this goal it is necessary, in our opinion, to introduce an additional security layer able to verify the trustworthy of the Bank's Server the user is connecting to. In our solution this extra layer is based on the well-known challenge-response authentication mechanism (starting soon after the SSL/TLS session has taken place) and it is totally and transparently handled by the browser extension.

Supposing the user started a connection towards the Bank's Server, firstly the browser extension intercepts the request, retrieves the URL and verifies if in the smartcard exists a server certificate associated to this remote site. In case, it retrieves the relating public key for later use. If this phase fails, the user will be able to navigate the remote site but the browser extension will signal the risk showing a red ball in the toolbar. It will also remains in an "undefined" internal state (Fig. 5: Browser Extension diagram.5). In both cases, the SSL/TLS handshake starts.

In the current implementation, mutual SSL/TLS authentication is configured on the server side based on digital certificates.

If the SSL/TLS authentication is successful, the login home page will be sent back to the user. In this page, the Bank Server will embed the subject name of the user certificate captured during the SSL/TLS phase and a random number (SID) identifying the session in place. The browser extension, once retrieved these data, will perform the following steps

1. Selects, in the smartcard, the RSA keys $< PK_U, pK_U >$, where PK_U is the user's public key and pK_U the corresponding private key, corresponding to the user identity the Bank's Server has just verified. If any key pairs doesn't exist, the connection will be stopped and the user notified;

2. Generates a random value r;

3. Generates a random session key K_s;

4. Sets two variables: one containing K_s encrypted with the server's public key and the other containing the challenge GLG = $Encr_{K_s}(SID \parallel r \parallel Sign_{pK_U}(SID \parallel r))$, where $\parallel$ denotes the cSncatenation operator and $Encr_K(P)$ the encryption of the plaintext P under the key K.

5. Posts back to Bank's server these data and transits in a waiting internal state (Fig. 5: Browser Extension diagram.5).

The Bank's Server firstly retrieves K_s decrypting the incoming data with its private key pK_s and then it decrypts the challenge CLG. At this point it verifies the digital signature by means of the user's public key contained within the certificate associated to the SSL session in place, the SID and, if any check is right, it then calculates the following response to send back the client component:

$$Response = Encr_{K_s}(SID \parallel UID \parallel r \parallel Sign_{pK_s}(SID \parallel UID \parallel r))$$

Where $Sign_{pK}(D)$ denotes the signature of the data D under the private key pK and the UID variable is the subject name of the user certificate, introduced to achieve an additional and strong protection layer against reply and MITM attacks. The browser extension receives this data and verifies the correctness of each value. If the validation is successful, it transits to the authenticated internal state (Fig. 5: Browser Extension diagram.5), and sets a green ball in the toolbar letting the user to enter in her home page.

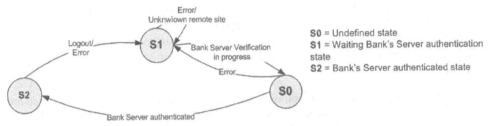

Fig. 5: Browser Extension diagram.

2.1.2   Transaction Phase

The user can issue transactions only if each involved part (the remote Bank's Server and the user) has been properly authenticated (e.g. the internal state must be Authenticated for the browser extension and the Bank Server has authenticated the user, Fig. 5: Browser Extension diagram.5). When the user requires a transaction, for instance a bank transfer, she compiles and submits to the Bank's Server the request. The Bank's Server sends back to the user (e.g. in a new web page) a summary and asks the user for a confirmation. In particular, a dialog window showing the incoming data is displayed. The user must read the transaction summary and press the button OK if everything is ok. At this point the browser extension serializes the data into a stream-buffer TD, including also a timestamp. It also concatenates TD with the SID relating to the session and digitally signs this buffer with pK_U. Finally, the original data and the following cipher text TAN are sent back to the server's Bank:

$$TAN = Encr_{K_S}(TD \mathbin{\|} Sign_{pK_S} (TD)).$$

The Bank's Server receives the data and verified their correctness, it authorizes the transaction completion.

3   A Brief Solution Analysis

The proposed approach can prevent complex phishing, pharming and reply attacks. Advanced malwares, such as the Zeus Banking Trojan, is totally ineffective. In fact, thanks to the provisioning phase (where the Bank's Server certificate is securely stored onto the card) and to the automatic certificate validation, the browser extension can detect and alert the user when she is connecting to a fake site. Furthermore, because the user authentication is based on digital certificates, a hacker cannot impersonate the user to access her home page; in this way, the solution can also guarantee the user privacy.

Furthermore, the use of a cryptographic microSD is needed to further increase the security level of the overall solution. In fact, the hardware approach is, at the moment, the best way to protect keys and other sensitive data. This approach can prevent several attacks, such as the brute force attack which typically affects pure-software solutions, even if based on digital certificates. Moreover, in this scenario the mobile phone plays the role of an advanced security token. It can present the user with a summary of the transaction.

Of course, several countermeasures could be added. For example, in order to prevent malware running on the PC from trying to steal and use the smartcard PIN without the user's consensus, the user can type this one directly on the mobile phone. This choice is motivated by the common opinion which considers the mobile phone as an environment more secure if compared with the standard PC/Laptop. In fact, it should be noted that the number of known malware programs for mobile phones is several orders of magnitude lower than the number related to the PC/Laptop environment.

For the same reasons, when a transaction summary is sent to the microSD to be digital signed for user approval, a component on the mobile phone will display the summary, jointly with the PIN insertion request, to confirm the transaction. Consequently, the user is given a chance to detect any change on the real transaction data simply verifying the summary, which is a quite simple operation do not requiring particular technical skills.

As a consequence, the attacker, in order to be undetectable by the user, should compromise both the PC and the mobile phone. Nonetheless, we feel this event much more complex and unlikely if compared with traditional attack scenarios.

4 Conclusion

Nowadays the attack trend is clearly changing. Large global events, massive worms to make headlines are decreasing giving way to identity thefts, financial frauds, and malware designed to make money. Attackers have now strong financial motivations and more and more advanced technologies. Thereby, on one hand customers depend on online services and, on the other hand, financial institutes are forced to work and invest to maintain and increase confidence in this type of services. This represents a strong incentive to introduce new and more secure mechanisms in order to face untraditional attack techniques. Moreover, this choice could also be used as a marketing lever. Users could decide to subscribe a specific service because they feel it more secure and able to protect their money.

As said, three possible paradigms are considered: user authentication, mutual authentication, and transaction authentication and integrity. All these mechanisms suffer of many limits and drawbacks. In our work, we have tried to face and overcome these ones, developing a mechanism based on mutual authentication with automatic and user-aware server check, transaction integrity and authentication. This solution represents a valid defense not only against phishing and pharming but also against user privacy breaches. An attacker, thanks to the mutual authentication, cannot access the personal page of a legitimate user, so user privacy can be preserved from illegitimate access. Finally, the solution can also be used to secure the access directly from the mobile phone as well as from a personal computer connected to the portable device.

In our labs a first prototype has been developed using a standard Windows XP and Samsung i-780 mobile phone, equipped with a cryptographic smartcard. The user certificate has been enrolled using a standard Microsoft Certification Authority, while, at this moment, the server registration has been performed manually. In the next release, an automatic procedure to register the trusted remote sites' certificate will be released, for example using a simple and user-friendly Over-The-Air (OTA) mechanism.

References

[RfRl09]   Rsa Fraud Action Research Lab: Zeus Trojan Leverages IM Software to Forward Stolen Online Account Data, RSA, 2009.

[Trus09]   Trusteer Report: Measuring the in-the-wild effectiveness of Antivirus against Zeus, Trusteer Inc., 2009

[FaCh10]   Falliere Nicolas, Chien Eric : Zeus: King of the Bots. Symantec, 2010.

[StDo10]   Stevens Kevin, Jackson Don: Zeus Banking Trojan Report. SecureWorks, 2010.

[NssL10]   NssLab Report: Vulnerability-Based Protection and the Google "Operation Aurora" attack. NssLab, 2010.

[TreM10]   TrendMicro Treath Research Team: ZeuS: A Persistent Criminal Enterprise. TrendMicro Inc., 2010.

[NetW10]   NetWitness Press Release: Kneber Botnet. http://www.netwitness.com, 2010

[Goog10]   Google Safe Browing API v2. http://code.google.com/apis/safebrowsing/, 2010

Countering Phishing with TPM-bound Credentials

Ingo Bente · Joerg Vieweg · Josef von Helden

Fachhochschule Hannover – University of Applied Sciences and Arts
Ricklinger Stadtweg 120, 30459 Hannover
{ingo.bente | joerg.vieweg | josef.vonhelden}@fh-hannover.de

Abstract

As electronic banking is one important field in e-commerce, it becomes more and more a target of attackers. The majority of those attacks try to steal credentials, usually pins and tans, from the user. In this paper, we propose to use a machine's Trusted Platform Module to bind an electronic banking account onto a certain machine. Doing so, an attacker is unable to use stolen credentials for malicious transactions as long as he/she doesn't control the machine to which the account is bound to. The platform-authentication is based on a non migratable TPM key in conjunction with a client certificate. This client certificate is used for authentication purposes within the SSL/TLS handshake during session establishment of an online banking session.

1 Introduction

As the Internet is accessible nearly everywhere, online banking is one major application nowadays. It is advertised by banks and widely used as well as accepted by customers. A study from the PEW Internet Research Center [Fox06] shows that in 2006 about 43% of the American people who have access to the Internet use online banking services on a daily basis. This shows that online banking is one of the mainstream Internet activities.

Online banking allows the remote management of bank accounts, e.g. performing transactions or checking the account balance, in a convenient way by using a conventional PC. Usually, this PC is located at the customer's home. The actions that can be performed via online banking are nearly the same as those which are offered at the bank's office. This is one of the reasons why online banking has become an important business for banks and a "must-have" feature for customers.

In order to use online banking, a customer typically needs, besides the valid bank account, appropriate authentication credentials. Those credentials ensure that only the account owner is able to view the balance and perform actions like money transfers. In order to log-in to the bank's online service and to perform basic, passive tasks like viewing the account balance, the user typically needs to provide a personal identification number (PIN) or password, together with his account number. When the customer wants to perform active tasks like money transfers, he needs to provide another type of credential; the so called transaction numbers (TANs). Each TAN is a one-time credential and used only once. In the classical version, TANs are taken sequentially or arbitrarily from a previously generated list of TANs. Those credentials (PIN and TANs) are only known to the customer and must not be given to a third party.

In order to access online banking services, the customer normally uses a web browser and opens the bank's website, which in turn requests the customer's credentials. The online banking application consists of several websites, representing the account and the possible actions. As already stated, the credentials are needed to log-in and to perform actions.

As online banking is widely adopted, it also imposes the threat of losing or leaking the credentials, thus attracting the criminal scene. A common offense which targets the customer as an attack vector is phishing. With phishing, the attacker tries to steal the user's online banking credentials. This is usually done by sending an email to the victim, pointing to a counterfeit website looking like the bank's online banking site. This site invites the customer to enter banking credentials under a pretence. If the customer enters the credentials, the attacker is able to use them later for malicious activities, e.g. a money transfer to his own bank account. Even if the rogue site doesn't own the bank's certificate, typically producing a certificate warning on the browser, there are some customers who still enter their credentials. This renders phishing a real problem for the customer as well as for the bank. Recent activities for improving the customer's awareness against such attacks, like emphasizing the certificate warnings, only fight the symptom, not really the cause.

While phishing attacks need the customer's active cooperation to obtain the banking credentials, there are other attack possibilities which run without notice of the customer. These kinds of attacks are often performed by an appropriate malware component on the customer's machine. Examples for such malware would be a Trojan horse or a Bot running silently on the machine. Those malware steals the credentials when the customer is going to use them for online banking. The stolen credentials are commonly transferred to a so called drop zone, where the attacker gathers them for later usage. The bottom line is that since credentials for online banking services are normally solely based upon knowledge, there are ways for attackers to steal and misuse them.

Due to these lacking or incomplete security mechanisms and the not to be underestimated amount of money getting lost by successful phishing attacks [Krebs07][BSI10], new measures to improve the security of online banking services while maintaining their usability are needed.

2 Related Work

Some research and related work has been done on the topic of using online banking via websites, which is the most commonly used technique. Falk, Praksh and Borders show [Falk08] that there are often design flaws in security critical websites. Those flaws result in the situation, that even an attentive user, who normally would not easily be fooled by a false website, might fail in recognizing an attack due to severe design flaws.

Related work has also been done within the fields of securing e-commerce and online banking by the use of Trusted Computing mechanisms. The most interesting approach to mention here is S. Balfe's idea [Balfe08] of securing so called "card not present" transactions, mainly in the area of credit cards, by using trusted computing mechanisms. With his idea of binding such "card not present" transactions to a certain machine, he tries to minimize the problem when card information is stolen and misused by a third party. The threats he tries to mitigate apply also to our scenario. Crucial information for performing a "card not present" transaction may also be stolen using phishing or by placing malicious software on the victim's computer. From a banks point of view, his approach is rather complex due to the usage of Trusted Computing capabilities. Besides the different target scenarios, our approach tries to be as simple as possible. We only rely on a TPM with a non migratable signing key while Balfe uses Attestation Identity Keys in conjunction with a trusted third party and the TCG's subject key attestation identity extension for X.509 certificates.

There has also been work in the area of authenticating platforms by using TPM mechanisms. Song et al. [Song08] proposes a two step approach, part of the so called TrustCube. First, a registration phase, which runs offline and only happens once, followed by an authentication phase which happens each time the identity of a platform is verified. While our approach only relies on a non-migratable TPM key and the standard SSL/TLS-handshake, the TrustCube approach uses the Trusted Network Connect architecture [TCG08] to communicate and for verification. As Trusted Network Connect is originally not intended for communicating between arbitrary networks, i.e. within an internet based environment, this approach is not easily adoptable to secure online banking. Rehbock and Hunt showed an approach for using Trusted Network Connect within Web based environments [Rehbock09]. But even if extending Trusted Network Connect to work within our scenario, it adds a significant amount of complexity to the architecture.

Besides the approaches of using a secure platform authentication, there is a lot of other work focusing on securing the customer's platform and verifying the identity of the bank server to prevent data leakage. Stumpf et al. proposes to use virtualization and attestation in combination with a trusted third party to prevent compromise of the client and man-in-the-middle attacks in e-commerce environments [Stumpf08]. This idea relies strongly on the features of a trusted platform. Although this would be a reasonable approach, at the moment there are a lot of components missing, e.g. a widely adopted Trusted OS, to implement this idea.

3 Online Banking in a Nutshell

As already stated, online banking is widely used. Main purpose is the remote management and overview of banking accounts. One is for example able to transfer money to another account or to manage bank transfers. Such actions are directly performed upon the account balance. If an unauthorized person would gain access to the account, he could transfer money to his own account, i.e. stealing the money from the owner of the account. To prevent this, there are several common mechanisms. Those mechanisms protect the account against unwanted access (1) and restrict account operations to the owner or an authorized person of the account (2).

To use the account, the owner has to authenticate himself, fulfilling (1). This is usually done by providing a secret to the owner which is only known to him. Normally a so called personal identification number (PIN) is used for this. Using this PIN and the account identifier (typically the account number) the owner can access the account. To perform operations, the owner needs more information. This information, the so called transaction number (TAN), authorizes the operation, fulfilling (2). It acts as the customers sign, which means that it ensures that the customer really intended the operation. Technically, the TAN is realized as a completely random one time password. Often it is, as well as the PIN, just a number.

There are several approaches to improve the security of online-banking, in particular against the already mentioned phishing attacks. Refinements of the classical TAN method are the so called indexed TAN (iTAN), TANs with acknowledgement and mobile TANs (mTANs). Besides PIN/

TAN some enhanced standards like the German Financial Transaction Services (FinTS) use cryptographic authentication methods like digital signatures.

A problem with these approaches is that the majority of the banks still offer the conventional PIN/TAN-method, thus rendering the enhancements mentioned above obsolete. But even when using the enhanced TAN-methods, the problem with the PIN remains. Although an attacker would be unable to perform actions with the account, he still could retrieve sensitive information, for example the account balance. This is a general problem affecting all authentication methods which are based on the knowledge of username and PIN/password credentials. Approaches to fight the malware problem are rather general, like the installation of an Anti-Virus Scanner or a Personal Firewall, thus aiming at the overall security situation of the customer's machine.

3.1 SSL/TLS Usage

Technically, online banking is typically based on a secure channel. This secure channel is established between the bank's server and the browser of the customer. SSL/TLS is used for this purpose. Figure 1 gives a simplified overview of the SSL/TLS-handshake. There are four typical phases:

1. Initial communication between client and server, this is done within a *client_hello* and a *server_hello* message. Besides others, this is used to choose one appropriate cipher suite for the following steps.

2. The server sends its own certificate to the client, thus allowing the client to verify the server's identity.

3. Within our scenario, the customer's browser typically checks the certificate against one or more well known trusted parties. If this check fails, which could happen if someone tries to compromise the secure channel establishment (man-in-the-middle attack), the browser will prompt a warning to the customer stating that the authenticity of the bank servers certificate could not be verified.

4. After the SSL/TLS-Handshake is finished, both parties communicate over an encrypted channel. The handshake may finish if the browser's check of the certificate was a success or the user has chosen to ignore the warning about the authenticity of the certificate.

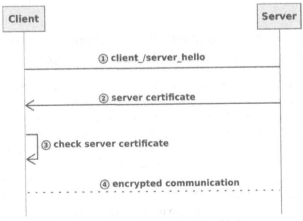

Figure 1: Simplified SSL/TLS-Handshake

3.2 Threats

As already pointed out, threats are arising when using online banking with the background described. This section gives an overview of those threats.

3.2.1 (T1): Misuse of Authentication Data

When a customer uses online banking, he or she needs to provide information to perform an authentication. As already mentioned this authentication data is typically the account number and an appropriate PIN as secret. Combining both, the customer is able to access the account. At least the PIN should only be known to the account holder. If somebody else gains the authentication information he or she is able to access the account. As the attacker is not able to perform operations with the account due to the missing authorization proof (TANs) there is a major privacy problem as account details like recent transactions and the balance are visible. The attacker may use this information to compromise the customer.

3.2.2 (T2): Misuse of Authentication and Authorization Data

The second threat, leakage of both authentication and authorization data extends the threat (T1). While already possessing authentication data and therefore being able to access the account, the attacker now also holds the proof to authorize a account operation- usually a certain amount of TANs. Besides the privacy problem of (T1), the attacker is now able to do arbitrary things, like stealing money, with the account.

Both threats (T1) and (T2) arise due to data leakage of sensitive information which should only be accessible by the legitimate account holder and due to having only knowledge based authentication as well as authorization.

3.2.3 (T3): Unauthorized manipulation of online banking sessions

Regarding the first two threats (T1) and (T2) attackers act in two time-separated steps: (1) stealing sensitive data and (2) (mis)use this data at a later time. This threat (T3) indicates a kind of real-time attack: the attacker is able to manipulate an online session of an authorized user during the session itself. This can be done by a remote man in the middle attack or by a local malware attack.

3.2.3.1 (T3.1): Unauthorized manipulation of online banking sessions by performing man in the middle attacks (remote)

In this threat the attacker is in a man in the middle position between the client and the server of an online banking session (i.e. all packets of the session will be transferred via the attacker's machine). He or she splits up the SSL/TLS session between client and server into two: one between client and attacker and a second one between attacker and server. The attacker spoofs the server's identity against the client e.g. by showing the client a wrong certificate and hoping that the customer ignores the warnings or the customer's machine (the client) silently accepts the spoofed certificate (due to (mis)configuration or vulnerabilities). If the customer accepts the spoofed certificate and enters his/her credentials the attacker passes them to the server for authentication and authorization. The attacker is then able to manipulate the transaction being done during this session e.g. changing the destination banking account of a money transfer.

3.2.3.2 (T3.2): Unauthorized manipulation of online banking sessions by performing malware attacks (local)

In this threat, the attacker successfully installs a malware component on the customer's machine. After the customer successfully opened his/her online banking session using his/her credentials the malware manipulates the transaction being done during this session e.g. changing the destination banking account of a money transfer.

4 Binding banking accounts to specific platforms

To mitigate the threats mentioned above, we propose the idea of binding a certain online banking account to one or more well known platforms. This results in a situation where, even if an attacker is able to gather the sensitive information, he is unable to misuse them as long as he cannot control the platform the account is bound to. The authentication process does not solely rely on knowledge anymore, but also includes access to the respective, authorized platforms. That is, typical phishing attacks, where the customer reveals information to the attacker are no longer successful. In order to access the online banking account, an attacker would now need both, the credentials as well as a malware component running on the customer's machine, thus rendering the attack a lot more sophisticated.

From the technological point of view, we propose the use of the Trusted Platform Module in conjunction with a non-migratable TPM-key in order to extend the client authentication within the SSL/TLS-handshake. Our idea consists of two phases:

- First, a deployment phase which binds the banking account to a platform and
- second, the authentication phase which verifies the binding established within the first phase.

The deployment phase needs to be performed to setup the customer's machine, i.e. to create the signing key on the platform and to bind this platform to the account. The authentication phase will be performed each time the customer uses his/her banking account via online banking.

4.1 Deployment Phase

To use the proposed approach, this phase is mandatory as it establishes the link between the online banking account and the platform which should be allowed to perform banking actions. To achieve this linkage, there are several steps which need to be carried out. Figure 2 gives an overview about this phase. Those steps affect the customer's machine as well as the Bank's online accounting environment.

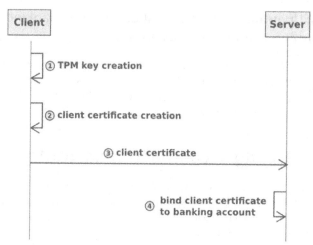

Figure 2: Deployment Phase

The first step is the creation of the key. This is done by using the platform's TPM, ensuring that the private part of this key is bound to this TPM. This means that the public key part may be used outside of the TPM while the private key part cannot be used outside, thus binding it to the platform the TPM is attached to. In the next step, the public part is encapsulated into a X.509 certificate and transferred to the bank. Finally, the bank is now able to integrate this certificate into the accounting system. This step needs to be done only once for each machine which will be used for online banking by the customer. The generated certificate is assigned to the banking account, thus implementing the binding between the machine and the account.

4.1.1 Key creation Problems

While the key storage inside the TPM is rather strongly protected against Software-based attacks, the creation process (including the transfer of the certificate to the bank's server) itself isn't. This leads to the problem that if the creation process as well as the certificate transfer get's manipulated, the created key is not trustworthy anymore as the key is possibly not created by the TPM. Further work needs to be done to avoid this problem but one short-term approach to solve it would be the use of a special environment for key creation. This is possible as the key is stored within the TPM. To perform this, the bank must provide this environment, for example as a Live-CD which is able to create this key without relying on already installed software components on the platform.

4.2 Authentication Phase

The second phase takes place when the customer is using online banking. Normally, there would only be two verifications:

- First, while establishing the SSL/TLS-channel the server certificate would be checked.
- After the secure channel is established, there would be a verification of the customer's credentials.

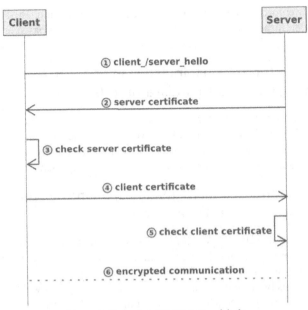

Figure 3: Extended SSL/TLS-Handshake

When using our proposed approach, there is a third verification step: The bank now requires a client authentication within the SSL/TLS-handshake, depicted within Figure 3. That is, the bank first demands the client certificate and uses this to identify the machine by comparing it against the already known certificates (see phase one). In the next step, the client sends this certificate again, but now combined with the Pre Master Secret and signed by the private part of the TPM-key. When the bank receives this signed message, it can use the public part of the key to verify it. If the certificate matches the expected one, the concerning machine is known and has been bound to the customer's bank account. As one is unable to retrieve the private part of the used TPM-key, it is ensured that it must be the platform where the key was deployed on in the first phase. When the customer enters his account number, the bank verifies that the account was bound to this machine. This means that there are two requirements which must be met to access the account:

- The machine which is used to perform the online banking must be known and
- it must be the machine which is bound to the account.

If those requirements are fulfilled and the credentials are the expected ones, the access to the account can be granted.

4.3 Security Consideration

This section describes how our approach mitigates the threats introduced in section 3.2.

4.3.1 (T1) Misuse of Authentication Data and (T2) Misuse of Authentication and Authorization Data

Our approach successfully mitigates both threats (T1) and (T2). While it is still possible for an attacker to steal authentication and authorization data it isn't possible to misuse them. Our approach additionally enforces the verification of the customer's machine. The attacker will not be able to spoof the identification of the customer's machine because it is based on a non migratable TPM key bound to the real customer's machine itself.

4.3.2 (T3.1): Unauthorized manipulation of online banking sessions by performing man in the middle attacks (remote)

Our approach successfully mitigates threat (T3.1). Verification of the customer's machine is embedded into the SSL/TLS client authentication. Even if the attacker is in a man in the middle position he/she will not be able to successfully perform the client authentication step because it is based on a non migratable TPM key bound to the real customer's machine.

4.3.3 (T3.2): Unauthorized manipulation of online banking sessions by performing malware attacks (local)

Our approach does not directly address threat (T3.2). In this threat the attacker may gain full control over the customer's machine through his/her malware directly operating on this machine. Thus the malware will be able to successfully perform the client authentication step as well as to manipulate transactions because it can act on the machine before data will be encrypted for the SSL/TLS tunnel. Nevertheless with a TPM equipped machine there are much better possibilities for protection against malware infection.

There is another very important security consideration to be mentioned here: The security improvements will only be effective if the deployment phase (see 4.1.1) as well as the bank server's are protected against unauthorized manipulation.

4.4 Practicability Consideration

An overall prerequisite to the practicability of our proposed solution is of course the availability of TPM equipped clients. The US market research company IDC believes that the number of TPM penetration in client PCs and x86 servers will approach 100 million systems by the end of 2009 [TCG09].

Regarding practicability one has to take into account two target groups: (1) users as customers and (2) banks as service providers.

4.4.1 (1) Practicability to users

Once the system is set up, changes to the authentication phase are totally transparent to the user, i.e. there is no practicability impact to the user while operating his or her online banking transactions. Nevertheless the following impacts caused by system setup and administration have to be taken into account:

- The flexibility of the user to use online banking spontaneously from arbitrary machines is reduced. We don't believe that this a significant limitation because most of the users will anyway use only a few dedicated machines for online banking. Furthermore banks could provide our approach as an optional service.
- The user has to operate the deployment step each time he or she wants to add or delete machines as valid clients for online banking. The impact to practicability highly depends

on the details of this deployment phase which isn't subject to this paper. We consider the impact as being low because the deployment step is likely to be performed quite seldom.

- One has to define some smart procedures for the user to recover from failures and system crashes on the client machines. This isn't subject to this paper, too. It has to be done during further refinements of this approach.

4.4.2 (2) Practicability to banks

Generally it's the same for banks as for users: Once the system is set up, changes to the authentication phase are totally transparent to the user, i.e. there is no practicability impact to banks while operating online banking transactions. Nevertheless the following impacts caused by system setup and administration have to be taken into account:

- Banks have to setup and administer an infrastructure (resp. integrate it into existing infrastructure) as well as procedures for management of client certificates. The amount of overhead heavily depends on existing infrastructures and the possibilities for integration of the deployment phase in existing infrastructures and procedures. The detailed inspection and definition of the deployment phase is subject to future work.

5 Conclusion and Future Work

The main threat when using online banking arises if an attacker is able to steal the customer's credentials. With those credentials, arbitrary actions ranging from viewing the account balance to making money transfers may be performed. Common techniques to steal those credentials are phishing, man in the middle, malware and social engineering. Our proposed approach counters those attacks by binding the online banking account to specific machines. Even if the attacker is able to retrieve the credentials he would need the valid machine specific (private) key to proof that he/she is using an authorized (registered) machine. As this key is non migratable and protected by the TPM, the attacker is unable to complete this step within the mentioned phishing scenario.

While this provides a good approach, there are some open questions. The first thing to mention here is the problem of securely creating the TPM key. If this phase is manipulated, the account binding cannot be trusted, thus rendering the whole process useless. As already mentioned, one simple approach would be to use a special environment for key creation. Further questions come up when thinking about practicability for users as well as for banks. Future work has to be done to quantify the practicability impact as well as the overhead to be done by banks for setting up and management of the system.

Besides the open question, one thing noticeable about the proposed approach is that it is not only suitable at the online banking scenario. It can also be used for arbitrary scenarios where a user has to authenticate itself by providing a knowledge based secret like a password. Recent phishing attacks like the ones launched against Twitter users [Stone09] or the European Unions Emission Trading [Eitzen10] could have been avoided by using our approach. The attackers would still have been able to acquire the user's secret but would have been unable to use it as the authentication is only possible by using a registered machine. There are a lot more possible scenarios where this approach could lead to an improvement of the overall security situation.

References

[Balfe08]   S. Balfe. Secure payment architectures and other applications of trusted computing, 2008.

[Falk08]   L. Falk, A. Prakash, and K. Borders. Analyzing websites for user-visible security design flaws. In SOUPS '08: Proceedings of the 4th symposium on Usable privacy and security, pages 117–126, New York, NY, USA, 2008. ACM.

[Fox06]   S. Fox and J. Beier. Online banking 2006. http://www.pewinternet.org/Reports/2006/Online-Banking-2006.aspx?r=1, June 2006.

[TCG08]   Trusted Computing Group. TNC Architecture for Interoperability. http://www.trustedcomputinggroup.org/resources/tnc_architecture_for_interoperability_version_13, April 2008. Specification Version 1.3 Revision 6.

[TCG09]   Trusted Computing Group. TCG Media Room, http://www.trustedcomputinggroup.org/media_room/news/95, April 2009.

[Rehbock09] S. Rehbock and R. Hunt. Trustworthy clients: Extending tnc to web-based environments. Computer Communications, 32(5):1006–1013, 2009.

[Song08]   Z. Song, J. Molina, S. Lee, H. Lee, S. Kotani, and R. Masuoka. Trustcube: An infrastructure that builds trust in client. In Future of Trust in Computing, pages 68–79. Vieweg+Teubner, 2008.

[Stumpf08] F. Stumpf, C. Eckert, and S. Balfe. Towards secure e-commerce based on virtualization and attestation techniques. In Proceedings of the Third International Conference on Availability, Reliability and Security (ARES 2008), pages 376–382, Barcelona, Spain, Mar. 2008. IEEE Computer Society.

[Eitzen10] C. von Eitzen, Hackers paralyse emissions trading scheme, H-online, http://www.h-online.com/security/news/item/Hackers-paralyse-emissions-trading-scheme-921075.html, Feb. 2010.

[Stone09]   I. Stone, Gone Phishing, twitter Blog, http://blog.twitter.com/2009/01/gone-phishing.html, Jan, 2009

[BSI10]   Federal Office for Information Security (BSI), Quartalsbericht 1/2010, https://www.bsi.bund.de/cae/servlet/contentblob/1117344/publicationFile/89792/Quartalslagebericht_1_2010_pdf.pdf ,pages 5-7, Bonn, 2010

[Krebs07]   B. Krebs, Study: $3.2 Billion Lost to Phishing in 2007, Washington Post, http://blog.washingtonpost.com/securityfix/2007/12/study_32_billion_lost_to_phish_1.html, Dec. 2007

Smart Grid Security and Future Aspects

Security Challenges of a Changing Energy Landscape

Marek Jawurek · Martin Johns

Vincenz-Priessnitz-Straße 1, 76131 Karlsruhe, Germany SAP Research
{marek.jawurek | martin.johns}@sap.com

Abstract

The German electric energy industry is under change. The Smart Grid, Smart Metering and electric mobility are being researched and implemented. It will have implications for the security and privacy of our every-day-lives if security and privacy are not taken into account during this change. Therefore the identification and mitigation of security and privacy issues of prospective technologies is essential before respective systems are built. In this paper we identify the current legislative measures to induce change, derive the necessary technical changes and analyze them with respect to security and privacy challenges. We identify several security and privacy challenges: New paradigms like mobile energy consumers or bidirectional communication with electrical meters, isolated systems like Industrial Control Systems or Home Automation Networks that will eventually be connected to public networks and huge amounts of privacy-related data that will be created by respective systems. We conclude that the energy sector is an interesting field for security and privacy research and that now is the time to ensure a secure and private future of energy supply.

1 Motivation

In ten years, we drive electric cars with renewable energy. We are now at the point in time where we, as security researchers, need to ensure that this will happen in a secure and privacy-aware manner.

Due to legal and technological changes the electric energy industry is changing rapidly at this very moment to accommodate topics like volatile renewable generation, electric mobility on a wide scale or consumer load shifting while still maintaining stability, affordable electric energy and safety for our society. For the realization of these topics IT-systems will play a crucial role and their security will in turn play a crucial role for the safety of electrical grids. Security in IT-systems for the energy industry is a very interesting topic, as these systems will unlock certain markets for the energy industry that will have impact on our every-day-life and as currently many new technologies are explored in research projects. Different constraints make this endeavour challenging: legal constraints, safety, availability and real-time requirements, the heterogeneity of involved players and the variety of potentially malicious users and their attack vectors.

In this work we list the relevant legal changes for the German energy sector and derive resulting changes for its IT-systems. Based on these prognosed changes we identify emerging security challenges that need to be taken into account now in order to ensure a secure and privacy-aware transformation of the energy sector.

The rest of this paper is structured as follows: Firstly, we list several legislative impulses and their affect on the energy landscape with the help of three snapshots in Section 2. Secondly, in Section 3, we analyze the potential resulting changes in IT-systems. In Section 4 we depict which security challenges can be deducted from the aforementioned changes in IT-systems and give some specific new attack vectors. Finally, after reviewing related work (Section 5), in Section 6 we conclude with a summary.

2 The Energy Landscape under Change

The energy landscape has been under major change in Germany since 1999 although first ground-work was already laid as early as 1991. These changes are mainly driven by politics which in turn realize standards set by the European union and its road map for the energy sector [EUCO06]. The following is an incomplete list of legal changes that have been mayor drivers for the change of the energy sector:

L1: Liberalization of energy markets: The goal of liberalization was to enable energy consumers to introduce competition into the energy sector and thereby foster efficiency and economic viability. What was previously considered a natural monopoly was divided into pieces where the only natural monopoly, the transport of energy, was subjected to regulation. Vertically organized corporations that owned the whole value-chain from production over transport to sales had to unbundle their operations to correspond to roles that the legislation created. See [Krisp07] for a detailed analysis of legal change.

L2: Support for the decentralized generation of renewable energy: Since 1991 several financial and legal measures were introduced by the legislative to support the decentralized production of renewable electrical energy. The implemented measures have led to an increased amount of decentrally produced renewable energy [BMUE10].

L3: Further liberalization of meter operations: In 2008 a law introduced two new roles for the area of meter installation, operation and meter reading: The metering point operator is responsible for installation, operation and maintenance of the meter while the measurement services provider is responsible for reading the data off the meter and transferring it to respective authorized receivers [GeLe08].

L4: Introduction of Smart Meters: Houses that are newly-connected to the electrical grid or that have been renovated since 2010 must be equipped with a special meter (§21b of [GeLe05]). Although, remote-reading is not mentioned as a requirement in the law, metering point operators want to upgrade directly to full Smart Meters with remote-reading capability (advanced metering).

L5: Free choice of metering point operator: According to §21b (2) of [GeLe05] house-owners have the choice of metering point operator. The metering point operator has to use a meter that fulfils the legal requirements and the technical requirements of the local grid operator.

L6: Tariffs to encourage energy saving: From end of 2010 energy suppliers must offer at least one tariff that supports the saving of energy. This might either be a load-dependent or a time-dependent tariff (§ 40 (3) of [GeLe05]). This might support L4 in the wide-scale distribution of Smart Meters as load/time-dependent metering requires this hardware.

L7: Legislative support for the introduction of electric mobility: Following their development plan for electric mobility [GeGo09] the German government created a research framework program for electric mobility [BMWi09]. The idea is to foster research programs that deal with electric cars and the necessary infrastructures.

After having depicted the legal measures introduced to make change happen the following three sections 2.1, 2.2 and 2.3 describe different stages, before, in the mid of and after the introduced change. They will help us to identify (Section 3) the emerging changes in technology that might have security implications (Section 4).

2.1 Yesterday: Few Players, Strong Ties

We consider the year 1990 for our 'Yesterday'-scenario. Energy markets were considered natural monopolies. That means, it was taken for granted that one corporation owned the local distribution grid and had a monopoly on the energy supply to the residents and industries of that area.

Back then energy was produced, transported, distributed and sold by few big integrated corporations. As they held the whole value chain this had mayor consequences for the structure of the market, the customers and the internal processes. Only few actors were active in the market with clearly defined areas of influence.

As energy suppliers were integrated corporations and produced for own use their power plants did not need interaction and were controlled by isolated computer systems with manual interaction: Industrial control systems (ICS). Demand control of major consumers of energy was performed via telephone.

Metering was performed with Ferraris meters and meters were read manually either by a representative of the supplier or by the customer himself. Customers had usually one fixed price for energy that did not change over the course of the day or year and had no way of knowing the current demand.

Decentralized generation of energy from renewable sources was effectively non-existent with only 3.1% of Germany's total demand fulfilled by renewable energy [BMUE10] (Table 5).

Electric mobility, as in electric cars, scooters or buses was nearly non-existent.

2.2 Today: Totally Liberalized ...

We consider the year 2010 for our 'Today'-scenario. Energy markets are liberalized and unbundled where possible. Liberalization led to the emergence of more suppliers who procure energy either directly over-the-counter from producers or at energy stock markets like the EEX. Customers have the choice of supplier independent of the customer's/supplier's location.

The control of demand still works like in the 'Yesterday'-scenario with one important addition. Consumers of large amounts of energy participate directly in the trade of energy and control their demand in response to market prices.

From 2010 on, owners can choose to equip newly built or renovated houses with Smart Meters (see [WoCP09] for a short definition). Different research and commercial projects are deploying Smart Meters [SMPM10] and allow residents to view real-time energy consumption data [Yello10]. Some research projects also try to figure out how volatile prices induce changed customer behaviour [PrIn10] or how controllable devices on the consumer side can be leveraged by suppliers to shift loads [PMRe10].

Decentralized generation of energy from renewable sources is currently emerging. Energy generated from renewable sources in Germany amounts to 16.1% of Germany's total demand in 2010 [BMUE10].

Electric mobility is being supported by the government with a research program framework [BMWi09] Car manufacturers and energy corporations are researching the integration of electric mobility into the Smart Grid (see [WoCP09] for a short definition) of the future in [PMRM10].

2.3 Tomorrow: Smart Grid Utopia

We consider the year 2020 for our 'Tomorrow'-scenario. For this scenario we base our predictions conclusions on the legal changes being introduced as laid out in Section 2 and experience from research programs where we actively participate. Expected developments are marked with H1.. HN standing for hypothesis 1 to N to be referenced later:

H1: The proportion of renewably generated energy will increase further. The volatile nature of renewable generation will put a significant strain on the grid. Therefore controllable generators will be tied to the smart meter and can be part of a controllable virtual power plant (see H2).

H2: The market will feature more market roles, those that have been realized so far in the 'Today'-scenario, those that are being introduced in L4 and those that probably will be introduced by electric mobility. Electric mobility might necessitate roles for the provisioning of mobility services across electric grid boundaries with support of roaming similar to roaming in the mobile telephony market, e.g. electric mobility provider. Roaming across different electric grids and national borders might also necessitate independent third parties that facilitate this roaming by transparently providing services for international billing and other bookkeeping tasks, e.g. clearing houses. The installation and operation of charging points could be handled by charging point operators. With an increasing amount of devices participating in demand response an aggregation role could simplify communication: the demand side manager. The demand side manager has a number of controllable appliances under his command and sells this potential in load change to customers like suppliers or grid operators. On the other hand, a virtual power plant (run by an aggregator company) [FENI10] role will do this for decentral producers of generators.

H3: Demand response for big consumers will probably be entirely controlled by the market price and direct procurement of energy by the big consumer. However, demand response (the response of the demand side to loads on the grid) could be a beneficial endeavour for small/medium enterprises and even for consumers. Alternatively it could be made a requirement as the strain on the grids will increase due to H7 and H1. That means, that appliances can be scheduled to run at a specific time or be delayed during times of high demand. At consumer level dishwashers, refrigerators or washing machines could be scheduled / delayed by a demand side manager inside the parameters given by the owner (e.g. wash dishes until 8 pm).

H4: It can be expected that every household will be equipped with a Smart Meter and that this Smart Meter will be remotely-readable, manageable and upgradeable (L4). This will enable energy prices for end-users that are either load-dependent or time-dependent (L6). The Smart Meter will be act as a gateway for receiving and forwarding price/control signals from demand side managers/aggregators/grid operators to appliances in Home Automation Networks (HANs).

H5: An integration of the Smart Meter with the HAN will enable residents to get direct feedback regarding the current energy usage of their appliances and the current energy price. In addition to that, residents of houses equipped in this manner will be able to 'program' their appliances and plan their usage patterns either in compliance with their supply contract or in expectation of future market prices.

H6: Electric mobility will be deployed one a wide scale [GeGo09]. Advances in technology will make up for low range/long charging times. For instance, travel schedules derived from commuting habits and personal/professional calendars could help to plan charging along the day's route and respective charging points could be reserved. Charge points will be distributed on a wide scale and most of them will also offer cars to introduce energy back into the grid to provide service to the grid as a storage system, bundled together by aggregators.

H7: Due to a large amount of new, potentially autonomous, devices connected to the grid that will allow controlled generation, storage and demand the current management of the grid will not be feasible anymore. Old power plant management systems, 'old' grid control devices and new devices must become inter-connected to allow shifts in demand and supply in order to ensure stability, economic viability and environmental sustainability.

3 Emerging Technological Changes

In this Section we attempt to analyze the intermediate impact the legal changes and the changes we observe between today and the predicted 'Tomorrow'-scenario will likely have on IT systems.

3.1 More Communication Relationships with Heterogeneous Partners

Due to L1 already in the 'Today'-scenario we see more roles in the energy market than we had in the 'Yesterday'-scenario. From L3 and some predictions in H2 we can see that the market of the future will feature even more different roles with potentially many companies fulfilling these roles. That means, that some roles will communicate with a number of different (w.r.t. role) partners which implicates different communication protocols/interfaces and therefore more involved IT-systems.

3.2 Interfaces where No Interfaces Existed Before

Newly introduced interfaces between different systems always involve a significant amount of work and coordination (w.r.t. standardization). However, these interfaces could be of utmost importance to a successful realization of the Smart Grid and surrounding technologies:

- Old legacy ICS systems (Section 2.1), were never meant to be connected to the outside of the power plant [RIPT01]. Despite that, [RIPT01] states that ICS in fact are already connected to corporate networks as management habits change and engineers monitor their systems remotely.

- Suppliers used to enter customer's consumption data into their billing systems manually. But indirection of meter data reading by measurement service providers (L3) and the change in type of data (from kWh to energy usage profiles L6 in high resolution) implicate that supplier's billing systems must offer automatic interfaces for measurement services provider to transmit these profiles.
- HANs will form an important basis for the Smart Grid as the network of controllable appliances with a Smart Meter as gateway to the Smart Grid. The necessary connections between HANs and Smart Meters for this purpose have to be analyzed and standardized.

3.3 New Communication Paradigms

New communication paradigms will dramatically change the way IT-systems operate in the energy sector:

- Communication will not be unidirectional anymore (H3), but control/price signals will be send back to the consumer.
- With emerging electric mobility (see H6) a great number of energy consumers will not be bound to a specific location anymore. As a plug-in hybrid electric vehicle (PHEV) moves around and charges at different charging points the communication endpoint for its mobility provider or other necessary communication partners moves around as well. A clearinghouse might mitigate the number of involved communication parties (see H2) but the location will still implicate the local communication partners (charging point operators, grid operators). These systems must accommodate for international roaming and differently structured energy markets in different countries.

3.4 High Amounts of Privacy Related Data

Due to the ability of Smart Meters to record fine grained profiles of energy consumption (see L4) and the necessity to do so (see L6) huge amounts of data will arrive at suppliers' IT-systems eventually. Legally imposed data retention times will only worsen the situation.

Electric mobility also creates additional data tuples: Data about when and where someone charged a certain car and where he plans to go (reservations of charging points).

3.5 Overarching Architecture

The idea of the Smart Grid implicates some form of intelligence in the grid. Because central intelligence is just not feasible for a grid of this size a way must be found to decentrally control the whole either directly with control messages or indirectly with incentives and market prices.

4 Security Challenges

In this Section we derive the security challenges that are implicated by the emerging changes for IT-systems from Section 3. For every area of changes as laid out in Section 3 a corresponding subsection provides the respective security implications.

4.1 More Communication Relationships with Heterogeneous Partners

Automated communication relationships with heterogeneous partners implicate several severe IT-security challenges. Due to the high numbers of (potentially changing) partners ensuring authenticity of a communication partner is not trivial. This relates to the actual technology used (e.g. PKI, shared secrets) to protect against attacks aimed at the technology and it also relates to keeping respective connection details up-to-date (e.g. contact persons, telephone numbers) to protect from social engineering attacks. Authorization for data/system access has to be crafted to every specific role/company and has to be managed over the lifetime of the communication relationship. Special care has to be given privacy related data which is, at least in German, subject to data privacy law w.r.t. creation, transport and alteration.

4.2 Interfaces where No Interfaces Existed Before

As already mentioned in Section 3.2 ICS were not designed to be connected to public networks but in fact are connected to corporate networks which in turn have connection to public networks. They have not been designed and implemented with a remote attacker model in mind and therefore contain blatant vulnerabilities [WeFS06]. Changing the systems appropriately might face a severe problem: There are few control system security experts available [Weis09]. The point which makes this security challenge so significant is that these systems control important real-life systems like coal plants but also critical systems like nuclear power plants or hydro power stations. Failure of these facilities might result in loss of money, infrastructure or even lives. The software interfaces constitute another attack vector which could be used for mischief, extortion or terrorism.

The fact that billing systems (and other systems) need to be interfaced opens up attack vectors similar to those in Web Security: Data that is transmitted must not be trusted and handled as potentially malicious data to protect from injection attacks. These attacks must not necessarily originate from the transmitting system but could come from transitively connected IT-systems.

The connection of Home Automation Networks (HANs) and Smart Meter (H5) also implicates several challenges: Apart from the obvious challenges like standards for their communication and the correct implementations of these standards the linking of HAN and Smart Meter connects the HAN to other networks. This is a similar situation as with ICS systems (HAN and ICS systems are similar in the way that both control physical devices). The HAN was probably not designed to be connected in such a way and furthermore it now also has several masters - the home owner via his legacy interaction methods and the party that would like to control appliances inside the HAN. Authentication, authorization, trust and privacy issues emerge.

4.3 New Communication Paradigms

The new communication direction of the emerging bidirectional communication, from demand side managers/suppliers to customers brings interesting challenges: The Smart Meter (or the HAN controller) must be able to authenticate and authorize the commands that enter the HAN from outside (w.r.t. the view of the customer). The Smart Meter might play the role of a firewall for the HAN.

With respect to control/price signals the sender of these signals must employ measures to ensure safe transport and to prevent repudiation of receipt. Otherwise, the customer could try to commit fraud by intercepting the signals and pretending that they never arrived. Fallback handling has to be developed for times of accidental loss of communication connection. Confidentiality of (existence of) these signals should also be preserved. By intercepting control signals attacker might either deduct appliances in use at the receiver's house or, even worse, deduct times of absence: When the residents are on vacation their washing machines will not require scheduling and therefore will not receive signals.

The mobility of energy consumers opens up a whole new field for IT although solutions could be heavily borrowed from the mobile phone industry: The mobility requires an authorization and billing infrastructure that features high-availability and confidentiality and potentially spans several countries or whole continents. Here it is crucial to keep costs of such infrastructures low (without sacrificing security) as the profits from mobile charging will also be significantly lower than with conventional refueling. The actual charging procedures and systems must ensure that neither involved parties can commit fraud (charging point operator by simulating a charging procedure, the customer by repudiation, supplier by claiming false charging records) nor that outsiders threaten the acceptance of electric vehicles by attacking the availability/credibility of the system.

4.4 High Amounts of Privacy Related Data

The problem about this data is that it can be used to create personal profiles of residents and can be subject to national data privacy laws which can differ from country to country. The energy usage profiles indicate when people wake up/go to bed, when and if they cook and whether they stay at home or go out at nights [Sulta91]. The data might also indicate how appliances are used [BaSL09].

Electric mobility creates even more privacy related data. Information about the position of past and future charges could be used for extortion (husband at unambiguous location) or industrial espionage (employee of company Y at headquarters of company X).

It is crucial that architectures (or organizational measures) that are developed for the handling of this data account for its importance and prevent leakage of data to unauthorized parties or retention times longer than necessary.

4.5 Overarching Architecture

Security challenges related to the overarching architecture are very hard to predict. It is safe to say that it will face the same challenges that all distributed systems face w.r.t. security. One point that should be stressed here is the following: When the Smart Grid is fully realized it will probably be the largest logical network of embedded devices (charging cars H6 and Smart Meters H4), control systems (ICS) (H7) and traditional IT-systems with a real impact on our everyday-life [CISC09]. That means, that a failure of such a system, however it was produced, would lead to a complete standstill of our society, unlike with similar networks (mobile phones, the Internet). Containment strategies of the implemented controls have to be devised in order to limit the impact range of attacks/failures. The idea to support decentralized generation (L2) will already facilitate this.

5 Related Work

We could identify several areas of related work: Firstly, there are several articles that identify risks for the Advanced Metering Infrastructure (AMI)/Smart Grid superficially [GaRo08] and [CISC09], in more depth [Anton09], [KHLF10], [ASAP10] and [OoLT09] and for specific systems (Dutch Smart Metering) [RoKe08]. [ASAP09] identifies very detailed relevant components of AMI systems and provides guidance on how to secure them. However, we did not find any work on the integration of an infrastructure for electric mobility into the Smart Grid.

Secondly, the area of ICS security is covered by [WeFS06] which describes the vulnerabilities that were found in different ICS systems under analysis, by a NIST recommendation/guide [ScSF08] on how to secure ICS systems and by a short blog post in [DaBo10] at 2009/12/16 indicating the differences between traditional IT-systems and ICS systems.

Thirdly, privacy of Smart Grids in particular is discussed shortly in [McMc09], [ASAP10] and very detailed in [WoCP09]. The 'Smart Grid Security Blog' [DaBo10] is also a wealthy source of information regarding the security of the Smart Grid.

However, we could not find related work that deals with the integration of electric mobility into Smart Grids and with privacy and security issues of electric mobility.

6 Conclusion

From legislative measures implemented by the German government to fulfill a European/German agenda for technical/organizational evolution in the energy sector and from data regarding the future of electric mobility [WWFD09] and data about the proportion of renewable energies [BMUE10] we derive emerging changes in relevant technical systems. Based on these changes we identify implications for the security of these and of new technical systems.

In particular we identify the need for communication protocols and a corresponding infrastructure that allows secure and privacy-aware roaming of electricity consumers (electric vehicles) and their integration into the Smart Grid. Ideas for this infrastructure could be borrowed from mobile telecommunication solutions but must account for the differences between the domains and for differences in energy industries of different countries. Furthermore, we identify two fields where legacy technological systems will be connected to public networks although they have not been designed for this. Industrial Control Systems and Home Automation Networks were designed to work isolated from other networks but will be connected to the Smart Grid to fully unlock its potential. The problem of data privacy spans all identified new problem areas. As IT-systems will operate the energy industry of the future, the collection, transport and processing of huge amounts of data will become feasible and interested parties might either experiment carelessly with this data or even try to capitalize on it.

Finally, we point out that the Smart Grid will form one of the largest networks with every-day-life physical implications in case of failure or successful attack. Interestingly enough, we are at a point in time where things are still in development and where research and development of security and privacy solutions for the respective areas will have an impact.

7 Acknowledgment

Martin Johns' work in this paper was partly funded by the German Federal Ministry of Economics and Technology (BMWi) as part of the e-mobility project with reference number 01ME09012.

Marek Jawurek's work in this paper was partly funded by the German Federal Ministry of Economics and Technology (BMWi) as part of the MEREGIOmobil project with reference number 01ME09007.

References

[Anton09] Antoniadis, Denise: Identify Inherent Security Risks: Advanced Metering Infrastructure and Smart Meters. 2009.

[ASAP09] The Advanced Security Acceleration Project (ASAP-SG): Security Profile for Advanced Metering Infrastructure. Technical report, December 2009.

[ASAP10] Advanced Security Acceleration Project (ASAP) – Smart Grid The Cyber Security Coordination Task Group: Smart Grid Cyber Security Strategy and Requirements. February 2010.

[BaSL09] Bauer, Gerald, Stockinger, Karl, Lukowicz, Paul: Recognizing the Use-Mode of Kitchen Appliances from Their Current Consumption. In EuroSSC, 2009, pages 163–176.

[BMUE10] Naturschutz und Reaktorsicherheit (BMU) Bundesministerium für Umwelt: Entwicklung der erneuerbaren Energien in Deutschland 1990-2009. 2010.

[BMWi09] BMWi. IKT für Elektromobilität. http://www.ikt-em.de/de, 2009.

[CISC09] CISCO: Securing the Smart Grid. Technical report, 2009.

[DaBo10] Danahy, Jack, Bochman, Andy: The Smart Grid Security Blog. http://smartgridsecurity.blogspot.com/, 2010.

[EUCO06] EU Commission: European SmartGrids Technology Platform: Vision and Strategy for Europe's Electricity Networks of the Future. Technical report, 2006.

[FENI10] The FENIX Project. Flexible Electricity Network to Integrate the eXpected 'energy revolution'. http://www.fenix-project.org/, 2010.

[GaRo08] Garrison Stuber, Michael, Robinson, R. Eric: Advanced Metering Infrastructure Risk Analysis for Advanced Metering. Technical report, 2008.

[GeGo09] German Government: Nationaler Entwicklungsplan Elektromobilität der Bundesregierung. August 2009.

[GeLe05] German Legislation: Energiewirtschaftsgesetz. 2005.

[GeLe08] German Legislation: Gesetz zur Offnung des Messwesens bei Strom und Gas für Wettbewerb. September 2008.

[KHLF10] Khurana, Himanshu, Hadley, Mark, Lu, Ning, Frincke, Deborah A.: Smart-Grid Security Issues. In: IEEE Security and Privacy, pages 8:81–85, 2010.

[Krisp07] Krisp, Annika: Der deutsche Strommarkt in Europa : Zwischen Wettbewerb und Klimaschutz. PhD thesis, 2007.

[McMc09] McDaniel, Patrick, McLaughlin, Stephen: Security and Privacy Challenges in the Smart Grid. In: IEEE Security and Privacy, pages 7:75–77, 2009.

[OoLT09] M. Oostdijk G. Lenzini, W. Teeuw: Trust, Security, and Privacy for the Adanced Metering Infrastructure. Technical report, July 2009.

[PrIn10] Project Intelliekon: http://intelliekon.de/intelliekon, 2010.

[PMRe10] Project MeRegio. http://meregio.forschung.kit.edu/, 2010.

[PMRM10] Project MeRegioMobil. http://meregiomobil.forschung.kit.edu/, 2010.

[RIPT01] Riptech Inc.: Understanding SCADA System Security Vulnerabilities. http://www.iwar.org.uk/cip/resources/utilities/SCADAWhitepaperfinal1.pdf, January 2001.

[RoKe08] Roos, Bart, Keeming, Sander: Security analysis of Dutch smart metering systems. Technical report, July 2008.

[ScSF08] Scarfone, Karen, Stouffer, Keith, Falco, Joe: Guide to Industrial Control Systems (ICS) Security. Technical report, September 2008.

[SMPM10] Smart Metering Projects Map http://maps.google.com/maps/ms?ie=UTF8\&oe=UTF8\&msa=0\&msid=115519311058367534348.0000011362ac6d7d21187, 2010.

[Sulta91] F. Sultanem: Using appliance signatures for monitoring residential loads at meter panel level. In: Power Delivery, IEEE Transactions on, 6(4):1380 –1385, October 1991.

[WeFS06] Wells, Rita A., Fink, Raymend K., Spencer, David F.: Lessons learned from Cyber Security Assessments of SCADA and Energy Management Systems. Technical report, September 2006.

[Weis09] Weiss, Joe: Cyber Security of Industrial Control Systems for Air Force and other Military Bases. June 2009.

[WoCP09] Wolf, Christopher, Cavoukian, Ann, Polenetsky, Jules: SmartPrivacy for the Smart Grid: Embedding Privacy into the Design of Electricity Conservation. November 2009.

[WWFD09] WWF Deutschland. Auswirkungen von Elektroautos auf den Kraftwerkspark und die CO2-Emissionen in Deutschland. March 2009.

[Yello10] Yellow Strom GmbH: Seeing and controlling electricity. http://google.yellostrom.de/index_en.php, 2010.

Privacy by Design: Best Practices for Privacy and the Smart Grid

Ann Cavoukian

Information and Privacy Commissioner of Ontario
2 Bloor Street East, Suite 1400, Toronto, Ontario, Canada, M4W 1A8
info@ipc.on.ca

Abstract

The Smart Grid has the potential to deliver substantial value, but is a significant endeavour that will require privacy risk mitigation measures to be taken. The infrastructure that will support the Smart Grid will be capable of collecting detailed information on energy consumption use and patterns within the most private of places – our homes. We must ensure that the cornucopia of personally identifiable data is managed in a trustworthy and transparent manner. Embracing a positive-sum model whereby privacy and energy conservation objectives are achieved in unison is key to ensuring consumer trust and confidence. Privacy standards are needed against which utility stakeholders can map their Smart Grid developments and implementation.

With the expertise and leadership of the two major electricity providers in Canada, the Information and Privacy Commissioner of Ontario has applied the principles of *Privacy by Design* (the Gold Standard for data protection) to develop a practical roadmap – a set of seven best practices for embedding privacy into the design of the Smart Grid. Now is the time to bake privacy into the Smart Grid, while it is in its nascent stages of development and implementation.

1 Introduction

Planning and development of the Smart Grid is occurring widely throughout North America and the European Union, with Smart Grid technology being supported by significant public and private investment [Onta09a] [USDe09] [Econ09a] [AnFu10]. Companies are also pursuing new products in the area of electric vehicles, smart appliances, and energy production technology, such as solar panels for household roofs, as well as new service offerings in the management of energy capacity, location, time, rate of change and quality.

With the modernization of the electrical infrastructure, utilities will also be faced with new challenges as more granular data than ever before on customers' energy consumption will soon become available. Taking a "business as usual" approach to data protection will no longer be sufficient. Utilities must embrace a new positive-sum business model — one that respects both the interests of electrical reform and privacy — or risk losing consumer confidence and the public's trust.

With virtually every home and business in Canada's most populous province now having a smart meter, Ontario is a strong leader in laying the Smart Grid infrastructure that is essential to the future of electricity provision and conservation (see Appendix) [UtPr10]. We are also a leader in the area of privacy and Smart Grid policy, having published a white paper in 2009 with the U.S. Future of Privacy Forum that brought to light the privacy issues that arise from the increase in the quantity and the granularity of personally identifiable information being collected, used and disclosed by electrical utilities and other providers [InTh09]. The logical next step was to provide utilities with a practical road map on how to apply *Privacy by Design* to the Smart Grid.

This paper begins with an overview of the Smart Grid, outlines the privacy issues related to the capturing of more detailed data on consumer electrical consumption and finally, identifies a set of best practices, developed in conjunction with the two major electricity providers in Canada, for privacy in the Smart Grid [InHT10]. These best practices, or what is intended to be the Gold standard for privacy and the Smart Grid, will assist utilities around the world to understand how to incorporate Fair Information Practices (FIPs) and *Privacy by Design* into the design and architecture of Smart Grid systems so that privacy becomes the default rather than an afterthought.

2 The Smart Grid

The "Smart Grid" refers to the modernization of the current electrical grid so that there is bi-directional flow of information and electricity in order to achieve several goals, including: providing consumers with more choices on managing their electricity usage; bringing more transparent pricing strategies that can lead to up to five to fifteen per cent in energy consumption reduction; self-healing in case of physical attacks, cyber attacks or natural disasters; linking with a wide array of energy sources such as renewable energy producers, in addition to energy produced by power plants; providing better power quality and reliability; more efficient delivery; and lowering expenses for grid operators who are better able to use their assets, and more efficiently run the grid [USDe08] [Illi09].

Information communications technology (ICTs) and a networked infrastructure is at the heart of improvements to the electrical grid that will enable collation of data provided by smart meters, sensors, computer systems, and other devices into understandable and actionable information for consumers and utilities [Econ04] [Econ09b]. Choices regarding communications improvements "will rely on a variety of technologies including cellular spectrum, fiber optics, power line carrier (including broadband over power line), microwave, radio (licensed and unlicensed), WiMax, WiFi and others" [Onta09b]. In the U.S., broadband over power line is a consideration that could help utilities monitor and manage various elements of their electric power distribution operations, and may provide broadband internet access over electrical lines, helping to provide broadband internet access to rural areas [Fede06].

Given the existing number and range of communications, operational and information systems being used by utilities, there will be challenges related to interoperability and the level of integration between systems to achieve suitable utilization of the available information. The amount of data available from smart metering and Smart Grid devices will grow substantially and may require a significantly more robust means of validating, storing and filtering this data for optimal use. Additionally, two-way, high-data volume and frequency, and low-latency communications may be required to support many of the Smart Grid operations, protections and control functions.

New technologies may be introduced arising from changes experienced by utilities in implementing the Smart Grid. In some instances this may involve using specific smart devices to monitor and/or adjust voltage levels and similar power conditions across lines and connection points. Smart energy regulators, capacitors, switches and power line monitors are technologies that can be used to support energy conservation by reducing energy losses, distributed generation penetration, plug-in vehicles, and improved reliability and management of utility assets. For Smart field devices, challenges may lie in integrating diverse existing systems as well as applying information into new systems and services.

Many of these technologies and associated Smart Grid standards are still in their early stages of development, and not all will move into commercialization or reach a suitable practice point for mass deployment. The costs and time required, as well as the benefits attained, will depend on the scope and pace of implementation, technology trends, and consumer acceptance and adoption of this new approach to electricity consumption and related services.

3 Personally Identifiable Information and Privacy on the Smart Grid

Consumers are an important focus of electrical grid improvements because they represent almost a quarter of all energy consumed [Ener09]. End-user components and activities will tend to increase the collection, use and disclosure of personal information by utility providers, and perhaps, third parties. For example, instead of measuring energy use at the end of each billing period, smart meters will provide this information at much shorter intervals. Accordingly, it is predicted that "[a] Smart Grid is expected to generate up to eight orders of magnitude more data than today's traditional power network" [Acce10].

In some current Smart Grid environments, consumers have already begun to receive information about their own electricity use, as compared to other consumers in their geographic area. When these data points become more specific (i.e., perhaps broken down by income, age, household size, etc.), what are the benefits and risks to the dissemination of more granular data? Privacy concerns arise when there is a possibility to discover personal information such as the personal habits, behaviours and lifestyles of individuals inside dwellings, and to use this information for secondary purposes, other than for the provision of electricity.

The definition of "personal information" varies across jurisdictions. In Ontario, personal information refers to any recorded information about an identifiable individual. In addition to one's name, contact and biographical information, this could include information about individual preferences, transactional history, record of activities or travels, or any information derived from the above, such as a profile or score, and information about others that may be appended to an individual's file, such as about family, friends, colleagues, etc. In the context of the Smart Grid, the linkage of any personally identifiable information with energy use would render the linked data as personal information.

Research suggests that consumer lifestyles could be gleaned from this information, such as: Whether individuals tend to cook microwavable meals or meals on the stove; whether they have breakfast; the time at which individuals are at home; whether a house has an alarm system and how often it is activated; when occupants usually shower; when the TV and/or computer is on; whether appliances are in good condition; the number of gadgets in the home; if the home has a washer and dryer and how often they are used; whether lights and appliances are used at odd hours, such as in the middle of the night; whether and how often exercise equipment such as a treadmill is used [Hart92] [Leo01] [LiWi08] [LLC+03] [Quin09].

In combination with other information, it may be derived that: the homeowner tends to arrive home shortly after the bars close; the individual is a restless sleeper and is sleep deprived; the occupant leaves late for work; the homeowner often leaves appliances on while at work; the occupant rarely washes his/her clothes; the person leaves their children home alone; the occupant exercises infrequently [Quin09].

Even if electricity use is not recorded minute by minute, or at the appliance level, ongoing monitoring of electricity consumption may reveal the approximate number of occupants in a household, when they are present, as well as when they are awake or asleep [Jami09] [Mart09] [Mayk09]. This will resonate as a 'sanctity of the home' issue, where such intimate details of daily life should not be accessible without the knowledge of the occupant(s).

It is not yet clear who along the grid will have access to a user's personal information and where on the grid such access will be possible. Some utilities have indicated that they have no need or desire for device level electricity usage for their grid management needs. A recent study out of the Cambridge University Computer Laboratory notes that in the U.K., the government wants gas and electricity meter reading from every household in the country every half hour [AnFu10]. This same study notes that in 2009, as a result of the Dutch Consumers' Association opposition, the Dutch government declined to approve a Smart Metering Bill that would make smart meters mandatory for all households in the Netherlands.

There is a risk that personally identifiable information will be used for purposes other than that for which it was originally collected [Cali10]. Examples of such secondary purposes may be: bundling personally identifiable information into several different data products such as energy usage or appliance data, either in identifiable customer-level, anonymized or aggregate form; third parties making important decisions regarding individuals without their consent, such as in the case of determining insurance risk; utilities and third parties using the data to seek consent for other services; and third parties seeking to engage the user directly for commercial gain (e.g., targeted advertising).

Even data that has been anonymized may still raise privacy issues. Researchers have documented the ease of identification of users, even when a minimum of non-personal information about them is available [Ohm09]. As has been the case in the on-line behavioural advertising arena [Fede09a], there may be a need for enhanced privacy protections.

Utility providers' efforts at identifying threats will become increasingly important as the electrical grid becomes more complex and interconnected. With additional entry points and data paths, the vulnerabilities increase as well, involving "the potential for compromise of data confidentiality, including the breach of customer privacy" [Elec09]. As the risk management framework for the Smart Grid continues to develop, designers of the Smart Grid and utility providers must ensure that unauthorized access to personal information traveling through the electrical grid is minimized, as much as possible. For example, a hacker with access to smart meters could tamper with billing information, device control, privacy, identity information and communications [KeRo08]. Wireless networks used by the utility to communicate with smart meters can expose control signals and consumption data to such threats as eavesdropping, interception, or message forgery.

While significant attention is being given to securing Smart Grid components, we note that technical security does not equal privacy. Rather, security is one of several important considerations in protecting privacy. Privacy subsumes much more than protecting the perimeters of a system, network or enterprise. Attention should be paid to insider threats within utilities and those organizations that provide services using consumers' energy consumption information. Rogue insiders, with legitimate rights and privileges to access personal information may be found at any level of an organization, including employees, contractors, business partners, auditors, and even alumni [Inst09].

The information collected on a Smart Grid will form a library of personal information, the mishandling of which could be highly invasive of consumer privacy. There will be major concerns if consumer-focused principles of transparency and control are not treated as essential design principles from beginning to end. Once energy consumption information flows outside of the home, the following questions may come to the minds of consumers: Who will have access to this intimate data, and for what purposes? Will I be notified? What are the obligations of companies making smart appliances and Smart Grid systems to build in privacy? How will I be able to control the details of my daily life in the future? Organizations involved with the Smart Grid and responsible for the processing of customers' personal information must be able to respond to these questions.

"Utilities, regulators and governments will need to give consumers confidence that their usage data is being handled by authorized parties in an ethical manner. Such assurances will be the key when developing the public perception of these new technologies" [WoAc09]. The best response is to ensure that privacy is embedded into the design of the Smart Grid, from start to finish.

4 Privacy by Design and the Smart Grid

Privacy by Design: The 7 Foundational Principles [Cavo10] is the next wave of privacy. They incorporate universal principles of fair information practices, but go well beyond them, to seek the highest global standard possible, representing a significant raising of the bar [OpUl09]. We believe that *Privacy by Design* should be adopted as the Gold Standard for the Smart Grid.

I developed the concept of *Privacy by Design* back in the 90's, to address the ever-growing and systemic effects of ICTs, and of large-scale networked data systems. *Privacy by Design* advances the view that the future of privacy cannot be assured solely by compliance with regulatory frameworks; rather, privacy assurance must ideally become an organization's default mode of operation. Initially, deploying privacy-enhancing technologies was seen as the solution. Today, we realize that a more substantial approach is required. *Privacy by Design* extends beyond information technology to include accountable business practices and physical design (includes networked infrastructure). The objectives of *Privacy by Design* – ensuring freedom of choice and personal control over one's information and, for organizations, gaining a sustainable competitive advantage — may be accomplished by practicing the 7 Foundational Principles.

5 Best Practices for Privacy and the Smart Grid

1. *Smart Grid systems should feature privacy principles in their overall project governance framework and proactively embed privacy requirements into their designs, in order to prevent privacy-invasive events from occurring*

Smart Grid projects involving consumer information require privacy considerations to be integrated into their development, right from the project inception phase. Identifying and incorporating privacy considerations into such requirements provides a solid foundation for *Privacy by Design* principles. Project development methodologies are commonly used for the successful development of any large scale networked data system solution (e.g. ISO12207 [Inte08], Unified Process, etc).

Include the 7 Foundational Principles of *Privacy by Design* [Cavo10] in the requirements development and design processes, and subsequently to the building and testing systems for alignment with those requirements. The utility should conduct Smart Grid project privacy impact assessments (PIA) or similar type of assessments as part of the requirements and design stages, to allow incorporation into requirements and plans — right from the outset. For in-flight projects, the PIA or similar type of assessments can be conducted at a later time in the program if necessary, with any corrective actions incorporated at that time.

2. *Smart Grid systems must ensure that privacy is the default — the "no action required" mode of protecting one's privacy — its presence is ensured*

Consumer information, specifically personally identifiable information on the Smart Grid, must be strongly protected, whether at rest or in transit. Personally identifiable information that is communicated wirelessly or over wired networks should be encrypted by default — any exceptions should be assessed (risk-based) on the impact to customers of third party access.

It is much harder to protect personal information when it is stored in multiple locations — keep personal information in a minimal number of systems from which it may be securely shared.

Similarly, allowing need-only access to this information will provide an extra layer of protection. It is important to consider the manner in which third parties will be allowed to gain access, for various legitimate support purposes — there must be appropriate language built into the contractual agreements to safeguard consumers. For example, third parties should agree not to correlate data with data obtained from other sources or the individual, without the consent of the individual.

There should be as little persistency of personal information as possible. At the end of the cycle, personal information must be securely destroyed, in accordance with any legal requirements.

3. *Smart Grid systems must make privacy a core functionality in the design and architecture of Smart Grid systems and practices — an essential design feature*

Privacy must be a core functionality in the design and architecture of new Smart Grid systems and practices. However, these often involve refreshing the existing asset base, which previously had no real need to carry or transmit consumer information. It is understood that many utilities will be building onto existing legacy systems and that few will be able to work with a clean slate, but instead will need to introduce *Privacy by Design* principles into legacy systems as opportunities arise, to ensure the overall architecture is secure. It is important to understand how personal information is being handled within the enterprise and determine whether any adjustments need to be made due to challenges raised by new Smart Grid initiatives.

Research suggests that it is worthwhile to consider designing in technological solutions to preserve privacy when disclosing consumer energy consumption data to third parties -- for example, using signal processing to: decrease the resolution of the data; filter out high-frequency events, or; introduce noise into the data [LiWi08].

4. *Smart Grid systems must avoid any unnecessary trade-offs between privacy and legitimate objectives of Smart Grid projects*

Beyond making privacy the default by embedding it directly into systems, achieving *Privacy by Design* entails the ability to embed privacy without any loss of functionality of Smart Grid related goals.

5. *Smart Grid systems must build in privacy end-to-end, throughout the entire life cycle of any personal information collected*

Ensure that the people, processes and technology involved in Smart Grid projects consider privacy at every stage, including at the final point of the secure destruction of personal information.

6. *Smart Grid systems must be visible and transparent to consumers — engaging in accountable business practices — to ensure that new Smart Grid systems operate according to stated objectives*

Records must be able to show that the methods used to both incorporate privacy as well as the Smart Grid objectives will meet the privacy requirements of the project. Ensuring such "requirements traceability" between the foundational privacy principles and each stage of Smart Grid project delivery will ensure that one is ready for a third party audit at any time.

Any non-compliant privacy deliverables will require an immediate remediation plan to correct the deficiency and provide an acceptable means of redress.

Informing consumers of the use to which personal information collected from them will be put is a key objective in achieving visibility and transparency.

7. *Smart Grid systems must be designed with respect for consumer privacy, as a core foundational requirement*

From a consumer perspective, it is essential to provide the necessary information, options, and controls so that consumers may manage their energy, costs, carbon footprints, and privacy.

For example, third parties should not request information from the utility about an individual – rather the individual must be able to maintain control over the type of information that is disclosed to third parties by the utility.

We agree that there should be "documented requirements for regular privacy training and ongoing awareness activities for all utilities vendors, and other entities with management responsibilities throughout the Smart Grid" [Nati09]. However, even if notice is provided regarding data use and disclosures, communicating the policies to consumers is not easily achieved. The emerging Smart Grid ecosystem is an opportunity for commercial entities to improve the methods by which they convey their data use practices to consumers so that consumers can make fully informed decisions regarding the use of their information.

The public must also be educated about the need to protect their privacy when engaging the Smart Grid services of third parties, who will have access to their energy consumption information. Utility providers and vendors cannot assume that individuals will inherently know how to protect their personal information. We know this is not the case. Studies show that privacy policies are often inadequate methods of disclosing the uses of personal information by commercial entities [Fede09b]. Utilities and third party service providers should provide clear instructions to the consumer as to how to use the privacy safeguards offered, such as a secure login and password, as well as how to un-enroll and delete their personal information.

6 Conclusion

The inside of a dwelling is the most private of places, and is recognized at the highest judicial levels [LaFo95] [Scal01]. The overarching privacy concerns associated with Smart Grid technology are its ability to greatly increase the amount of information that is currently available relating to the activities of individuals within their homes.

Utilities will face many challenges during this transformation. While a significant portion of the Smart Grid implementation will not involve consumer information, the amount of personally identifiable information being collected and the digital nature of that information will precipitate internal changes within utilities that go well beyond individual IT departments. A point which bears repeating is that we must take great care not to sacrifice consumer privacy amidst a sea of enthusiasm for electricity reform and conservation.

These 7 Best Practices for Smart Grid *Privacy by Design* were developed by the Information and Privacy Commissioner of Ontario (IPC) in collaboration with Canada's two major electricity providers, Hydro One and Toronto Hydro, to be used by utilities in Ontario and elsewhere, that will be facing these challenges. The time to do this is now – to enhance consumer trust and confidence by building *Privacy by Design* directly into the development and implementation of Smart Grid systems.

7 Appendix

7.1 The Smart Grid in Ontario

In Ontario, organizations have been working on the question of privacy and the Smart Grid for several years. Hydro One Networks and Toronto Hydro — both subject to the privacy laws that the IPC oversees compliance with — began their Smart Grid projects knowing at the outset that privacy became an essential component any time that personal information was involved. The IPC embarked on work when first approached by the government several years ago on Bill 21, the *Energy Conservation Responsibility Act, 2006* [Bill06], which added amendments to the *Electricity Act, 1998* [Elec98] relating to smart meters and a Smart Metering Entity.

Major components of the future grid in Ontario will include advanced metering infrastructure, time-of-use pricing, demand management, and the Smart Metering Entity. Ontario's time-of-use pricing goal is to have 3.6 million customers on time-of-use pricing by June 2011. In order to implement time-of-use prices, electricity distribution companies must achieve four things: install smart meters, enrol those smart meters with the Meter Data Management Repository ("Repository") maintained by the Independent Electricity System Operator (IESO), incorporate time-of-use prices within their services, and file their program with the Ontario Energy Board (OEB). The Ontario government has established a plan that draws on customer demand management and renewable generation to help meet projected electricity demand over the next 20 years. This is projected to enable the shut down of coal plants in Ontario by 2014 [Puxl07].

Electricity distributors in Ontario are required to adhere to functional specification criteria when installing smart meters, metering equipment, systems and technology [Mini06]. The specifications require a minimum functionality of hourly meter reads, and the ability to transmit this information without field visits. Smart meters contain an advanced metering communication device, and each has a visible display that includes its identification number and meter serial number. Transmission of meter reads may be as frequent as necessary to meet requirements, and must be done using an approved protocol and file structure. Distributors with advanced metering control computers may store up to 60 days worth of meter reads, and must not aggregate meter reads into rate periods or calculate consumption data prior to sending the information to the IESO's Repository. The smart meter system must also report on confirming data linkages between the advanced meter communication device, the meter serial number and the customer's account. The smart meter system, including some parts the Repository must also log successful transfer of meter reads as well as log unsuccessful attempts, including the cause and status of such attempts. In addition, the system must confirm the accuracy of meter readings and report suspected cases of meter theft, tampering or interference.

An Advanced Metering Infrastructure (AMI) is required to have "security features to prevent unauthorized access to the AMI and meter data and to ensure authentication to all AMI elements" [Mini06]. The IESO uses a unique ID for each electricity point of delivery (physical or virtual), including individual residences or multiple meters. The Repository maintains internal links that relate each point to metered quantities. The master directory links all points, meters, and utilities. Meter reads are stored in the Repository including interval consumption data and billing quantity data. It can support meter reads from 5 to 60 minute intervals. Meter data is aggregated for reporting and analysis. The Repository can flag data as outdated and schedule it for re-aggregation when it is required. The Repository supports overrides to allow for the utility to update inaccurate information.

The province's specifications also require that an AMI meet all applicable federal, provincial and municipal laws, codes, rules, directions, guidelines, regulations and statutes, including requirements of regulatory authorities and agencies such as the Canadian Standards Association and Measurement Canada.

The IESO is designated as the Smart Metering Entity under Ontario Regulation [Onta06]. The Smart Metering Entity was created by legislation to accomplish the government's smart metering initiative [Elec98]. The entity has responsibility for the collection, management and storage of information related to the metering of consumers' consumption or use of electricity in Ontario, including data collected from distributors. In order to do this, the entity can operate one or more databases to facilitate collecting, managing, storing and retrieving smart metering data. The entity is required to provide and promote non-discriminatory access, on appropriate terms and subject to any conditions in its licence relating to the protection of privacy, by distributors, retailers, the Ontario Power Authority (OPA) and other persons. The Smart Metering Entity may also manage and aggregate the data related to consumers' electricity consumption or use. Distributors, retailers and other persons must provide the entity with the information it requires in fulfilling its objects or conducting its business activities.

References

[Acce10]   Accenture: Accenture Launches Smart Grid Data Management Solution to Reduce Risks and Costs of Smart Grid Deployments. Accenture, 2010.

[AnFu10]   Anderson, Ross and Fuloria, Shailendra: On the security economics of electricity metering. In: Proceedings of the Ninth Workshop on the Economics of Information Security (WEIS 2010), 2010.

[Bill06]   Bill 21, Energy Conservation Responsibility Act, 2006. Legislative Assembly of Ontario, 2006.

[Cavo10]   Cavoukian, Ann: Privacy by Design: The 7 Foundational principles, Implementation and Mapping of Fair Information Practises. Information and Privacy Commissioner of Ontario, Canada, 2010.

[Cali10]   California Public Utilities Commission: Decision Adopting Requirements For Smart Grid Deployment Plans Pursuant To Senate Bill 17 (Padilla), Chapter 327, Statutes Of 2009. California Public Utilities Commission, 2010.

[Econ04]   The Economist: Building the energy internet. The Economist. May 11, 2004.

[Econ09a]   The Economist: Wiser wires. The Economist, October 8, 2009.

[Econ09b]   The Economist: Building the smart grid. The Economist, June 4, 2009.

[Elec98]   Electricity Act, 1998, S.O. 1998, c. 15, Sched. A.

[Elec09]   Electric Power Research Institute: Report to the National Institute of Standards and Technology on the Smart Grid Interoperability Standards Roadmap. Electric Power Research Institute, 2009.

[Ener09]   Energy Information Administration: Annual Energy Review 2008. Energy Information Administration, 2009.

[Fede06]   Federal Communications Commission: Memorandum and Opinion, FCC 06-113. Federal Communications Commission, 2006.

[Fede09a]   Federal Trade Commission: FTC Staff Revises Online Behaviour Advertising Principles. Federal Trade Commission, 2009.

[Fede09b]   Federal Trade Commission: FTC Staff Report: Self-Regulatory Principles For Online Behavioral Advertising. Federal Trade Commission, 2009.

[Hart92]   Hart, George: Nonintrusive Appliance Load Monitoring. Proceedings of the IEEE, Vol. 80, No. 12, December 1992.

[Illi09]   Illinois Smart Grid Initiative: Empowering Consumers Through a Modern Electrical Grid. Report of the Illinois Smart Grid Initiative, 2009.

[Inst09]   Institute for Information Infrastructure Protection: Human Behavior, Insider Threat and Awareness. Institute for Information Infrastructure Protection, 2009.

[Inte08]   International Organisation for Standardization: ISO/IEC 12207:2008. International Organisation for Standardization, 2008.

[InTh09]   Information and Privacy Commissioner of Ontario, Canada and The Future of Privacy Forum: SmartPrivacy for the Smart Grid: Embedding Privacy into the Design of Electricity Conservation. Information and Privacy Commissioner of Ontario, Canada, 2009.

[InHT10]   Information and Privacy Commissioner of Ontario, Canada, Hydro One Inc. and Toronto Hydro Corporation: Privacy by Design: Achieving the Gold Standard in Data Protection for the Smart Grid, 2010.

[Jami09]   Jamieson, Alastair: Smart meters could be 'spy in the home'. Tony Gallagher: The Telegraph, October 11, 2009.

[KeRo08]   Keemink, Sander and Roos, Bart: Security analysis of Dutch smart metering systems. Universiteit van Amsterdam, 2008.

[LaFo95]   La Forest, Gérard (J): R. v. Silveira, [1995] 2 S.C.R. 297, 23 O.R. (3d) 256. 1995.

[LLC+03]   Laughman, Christopher; Lee, Kwangduk; Cox, Robert; Shaw, Steven; Leeb, Steven; Norford, Les and Armstrong, Peter: Power Signature Analysis. IEEE Power & Energy Magazine, March/April 2003.

[Leo01]   Leo, Alan: The Measure of Power: Non-Intrusive Load Monitoring Gives Detailed Views of Where Power is Going, With Payoffs for Utilities, Consumers, and maybe Big Brother. Technology Review Magazine, June 28, 2001.

[LiWi08]   Lisovich, Mikhail and Wicker, Stephen: Privacy Concerns in Upcoming Residential and Commercial Demand-Response Systems. IEEE Proceedings On Power Systems, Vol. 1, No. 1, March 2008.

[Mart09]   Martin, Peter (J.A): R. v. Gomboc. 2009 ABCA 276, 247 C.C.C. (3d) 119. 2009.

[Mayk09]   Maykuth, Andrew: Utilities' smart meters save money, but erode privacy. The Philadelphia Inquirer, September 6, 2009.

[Mini06]   Ministry of Energy and Infrastructure: Functional Specifications for an Advanced Metering Infrastrucutre. Ministry of Energy and Infrastructure, 2007.

[Nati09]   National Institute of Standards and Technology: Draft NIST Interagency Report (NISTIR) 7628, Smart Grid Cyber Security Strategy and Requirements. National Institute of Standards and Technology, 2009.

[Onta06]   Ontario Regulation 393/07 of the Electricity Act, 1998.

[Onta09a]   Ontario Energy Board: 2010/2011 Distribution Rate Application (EB-2009-0096), Exhibit F1, Tab 1, Schedule 3. Ontario Energy Board, 2009.

[Onta09b]   Ontario Smart Grid Forum: Enabling Tomorrow's Electricity System. Ontario Smart Grid Forum, 2009.

[Ohm09]   Ohm, Paul: Broken Promises of Privacy: Responding to the Surprising Failure of Anonymization (Legal Studies Research Paper No. 09-12). University of Colorado Law School, 2009.

[OpUl09]   OpenSG Subcommittee and Utility Smart Grid Executive Working Group: Smart Grid Standards Adoption: Utility Industry Perspective. UCA International Users Group, 2009.

[Puxl07]   Puxley, Chinta: Ontario Promises to Close Coal Plants by 2014, Reduce Greenhouse Emissions. RedOrbit.com, 2007.

[Quin09]   Quinn, Elias Leake: Privacy and the New Energy Infrastructure. Centre for Energy and Environmental Security, Working Paper Series, 2009.

[Scal01]   Scalia, Antonin Gregory (J.A.): Kyllo v. United States, 533 U.S. 27 (2001), 190 F.3d 1041. 2001.

[USDe08]   U.S. Department of Energy: The Smart Grid: An Introduction. U.S. Department of Energy, 2008.

[USDe09]   U.S. Department of Energy: Smart Grid System Report. U.S. Department of Energy, 2009.

[UtPr10]   Utility Consumers' Action Network and Privacy Rights Clearinghouse: Comments by Utility Consumers' Action Network and Privacy Rights Clearinghouse on the Assigned Commissioner's February 8th Scoping Memo. Utility Consumers' Action Network, 2010.

[WoAc09]   World Economic Forum and Accenture: Accelerating Smart Grid Investments. World Economic Forum, 2009.

A Policy-based Authorization Scheme for Resource Sharing in Pervasive Environments

Roberto Morales · Jetzabel Serna · Manel Medina

Technical University of Catalonia
Computer Architecture Department
Jordi Girona 1-3, 08034
Barcelona, Spain
{rmorales | jetzabel | medina}@ac.upc.edu

Abstract

Ubiquitous environments require special properties that traditional computing does not support. The high diversity of mobile devices and the marked rise in ubiquitous resources have originated a great variety of challenges such as a proper resource management which plays a fundamental role in pervasive computing, where adaptation and dynamic re-configuration of resources take place. In previous works [MoGi08], [MoOG10] we have presented CARM (Composable-Adaptive Resource Management), a new adaptive resource management approach that supports adaptation for the required resources. CARM constitutes a component-based model to abstract system's ubiquitous resources in a transparent and uniform way to the applications. Due to its network heterogeneity and the dynamic population of nomadic users, important security challenges arise; therefore, in this article we address CARM's primary security concerns towards the development of a "Security module" capable of certifying the eligibility of devices to join a personal network without compromising privacy. Our approach is analyzed in terms of Authentication and Authorization, essentially consisting of an authorization scheme using Attribute Certificates (ACs) and supported by control policies that define all authorization decisions needed among unknown devices. This paper mainly describes ongoing work towards a proof-of-concept implementation in the given scenarios; initially considering two CARM enabled mobile-phones with Bluetooth connectivity and enforcing security without altering the bandwidth efficiency.

1 Introduction

As the computing and communication infrastructures continue to expand and diversify, environments get populated of a great diversity of heterogeneous devices. People are already carrying mobile phones, mp3 players or even wearing smart-jackets with a lot of small sensors, thus providing a huge pool of available resources. In these environments also called *ubiquitous* or *pervasive environments,* devices with limited or scarce resources can benefit from devices with high resource capabilities, in such a way that they can use a larger display or higher definition ones, high capabilities devices can also benefit from limited devices by for example delegating tasks for remote execution. Unfortunately, current applications only make use of resources that are by default attached to the device, thus limiting the extraordinary potential out there. In previous works we have defined the CARM middleware, able of providing a flexible infrastructure where personal devices use resources by opportunistically annexing friendly devices they encounter. The CARM middleware is comprised of two main modules, namely: *i) the Core*, which interacts directly with ubiquitous devices to provision shared resources among applications, providing high-level management of such resources, and *ii) the Resource Abstraction Layer*, which allows the access to the specific functionalities of each device. Even though CARM offers a plethora of applications and benefits; for the successful exploitation of this middleware security concerns must be properly addressed.

This research work focuses on the security issues of the CARM middleware. Our approach is analyzed in terms of authentication and authorization; under the assumption that users are willing to share their resources, but being aware that permissions to use them are more likely to be granted if it is under the owner's control and causes no ill effects.

The proposed authorization scheme is able of managing devices which do not have any authentication information in advanced in order to create secure personals networks even when no infrastructure is available; we point out the main requirements related to the implementation of a prototype considering CARM and its different scenarios. To support the lack of infrastructure we combine different components: a *Credential Validator (CV)* that keeps in cache the public key of the Certification Authority for credentials validation; an *Attribute Certificate Manager (ACM)* where the user acts as an Attribute Authority (AA) and issues ACs based on pre-defined policies, a *Privilege Manager (PV)* which defines all authorization decisions, and finally an *Alerting System (AS)* that allows users to work in a collaborative mode by warning others of misbehaving nodes, updating and distributing the corresponding blacklists.

The rest of this paper is organized as follows: The CARM use case scenarios are describe in Section 2. Section 3 outlines the main security challenges. The security model design and testbed implementation are described in Section 4. Related work is briefly overviewed in Section 5 and finally the main conclusions and future directions are drawn in Section 6.

2 Use Case Scenario

Several potential applications could benefit from CARM's middleware, imagine users sharing their local resources and using those available from others in the vicinity, allowing you to walk around and use the neighbor's high definition video display, use other's hardware positioning system (GPS), high quality audio, or the possibility of sharing wireless Internet connection; a set of optional sharing resources is depicted in Figure 1. With the high diversity of resources many use case scenarios are suitable to these environments; a shopping center's infrastructure *"shops"* could benefit from CARM by displaying in transparent mode sales information (i.e. shops information, sales opportunities, advertising, etc.) in users shared display. By using only the device's display user information will not be compromised, and the user will not receive any additional packages or installation files. In turn, by allowing the shop center to use the shared display, shops may grant bonus points or additional discounts to collaborative users. Despite the wide range of possible scenarios for the sake of simplicity, in the initial CARM testbed implementation we will focus on just one resource, thus evaluating the high quality audio shared resource considering that granted audio resources on mobile phones are at the moment extremely tight due to size and power constraints.

Figure 1: Resource sharing in a CARM enabled mobile

Our scenario consists of a Personal Area Network (PAN) with a group of users and a set of known components (e.g. mobile phones). With CARM it is possible to extend the audio capabilities and have real time control of multiple sound channels positioned and moving dynamically around the user, providing an immersive 3-dimensional sound environment, allowing amazing effects, and optimizing user's audio listening experience.

The following scenario involves communication and collaboration between distinct devices:
- A group of friends has just sat down at its favorite restaurant and Claire decides she wants to play her last favorite song to the group. As Bob owns a high quality sound device and after they push a few buttons on their phones and engage their built-in micro-speakers they are ready to play the music on Bob's phone.
- At the same time an unknown user sitting in the near is able to use Claire's GPS shared resource.

More critical scenarios involving audio sharing could be applied; for example in a catastrophe where no signal coverage is available, personnel from rescue teams could detect audio sharing resources (speakers and microphone) and locate people stuck in spaces surrounded by collapsed walls, in order to rescue them.

3 Security Challenges

Despite the benefits of CARM's implementation, owners are reluctant to allow the use of their shared resources for fear of potential adverse effects; the use of peripherals is more likely to be granted if it's under owner's control and causes not ill effects. Therefore for the successful exploitation of CARM's applications, providing security is fundamental. In this study we have identified a set of security issues as described next:
- How to prevent unauthorized access?
- How to restrict access to certain resources?

- How many resources should be granted to a specific device?
- How to revoke permissions once granted?
- How to manage credentials where no central authority is available?
- How to support the lack of infrastructure.

Creating an efficient mechanism which addresses security concerns and isolation while making remote use of i/o devices is still an open problem.

4 CARM's Security Architecture

The proposed architecture will provide all necessary components towards an automatic authentication and the appropriate management of resource's privileges. For any shared resource, each resource's owner will be able to specify the corresponding attributes and credential validation policies for gaining the appropriated access. Next we will introduce the core components of the proposed security architecture.

4.1 Security Module

Given the importance of security and trust in these environments where resource protection is crucial, the CARM's security module will allow devices to decide for each resource, to which devices the credentials will be issued, under what conditions and with which access rights. To achieve this, we propose the use of Attribute Certificates (ACs) [Farr02], and to be able to perform the different validation and authorization processes we proposed a set of components just as sketched in Figure 2, followed by their brief description.

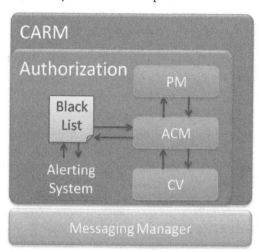

Figure 2: CARM 's Security Module

- **Credential Validator (CV):** Authenticates, validates credentials, signatures and required formats.
- **Policy Manager (PM):** the PM makes all authorization decisions. Creates, manages and verifies/matches all corresponding permissions, and sends an answer in the form of "granted" or "denied".

- **Attribute Certificate Manager (ACM):** the ACM manages (issue, revoke, validates, etc.) all ACs, updates the revocation list and the blacklist when applicable.
- **Alerting System (AS):** when the ACM warns the AS about a malicious node, the AS then broadcasts an alert message to neighbors to alert them about a potential risk.
- **Blacklist:** keeps record of all nodes which certificates have been recently revoked due to their malicious behaviors (resources' misuse).

4.2 Communication Protocol

Going back to the use case defined in Section 2 we now proceed to describe the basics of our proposed protocol, Figure 3 shows basic user interactions.

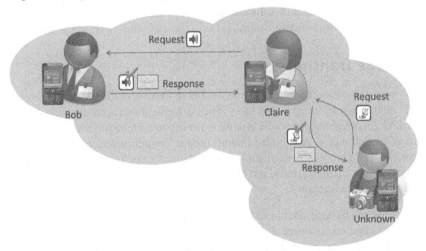

Figure 3: Audio resource sharing communications

Initially Claire requests Bob's shared audio resource, Bob's messaging system service receives Claire's request message M' and forwards it to the security module. M' is signed by Claire SK_{Claire} and includes her public key PK_{Claire} along with the corresponding data and a timestamp. If no AC is provided, after credential validation done by the CV with public key of the issuing CA PK_{CA}, Bob issues an AC to Claire's device (IMEI-based ID) specifying the granted access rights. If a CA is provided, using PK_{Bob} the ACM will validate and forward the AC to the PM for policy matching and the PM will send a *"granted"* or *"denied"* message to the messaging system. Bob's response message M'' will be signed by him SK_{Bob} and encrypted with Claire's public key PK_{Claire}.

On the meantime an unknown user requests Claire's shared GPS resource, Claire verifies if the requester device (IMEI-based ID) is contained in her blacklist or friend's blacklist, if available, checking procedure will also apply for a *"global blacklist"*. Claire then decides whether or not to issue the AC granting permissions. When a resource has been released AC's will be revoked and the revocation list will be updated. In case of misuse the ACM revokes the AC and adds the IMEI-based ID to the revocation list and to the local blacklist, again if the infrastructure is available, the ID will be added also to the global list, the AS is then activated and broadcasts a message to neighbors warning them about a malicious node. By misuse we understand when a malicious node has an inappropriate behavior and generates noise, sends trash, or for example blocks the connection, and last but not least, a special case will be in the situation where Claire should leave, and even though the unknown user is making a proper use of the GPS shared resource Claire can no longer be able to grant the resource. In such a case Claire is able to send her public key to neighbors allowing them to validate ACs issued by her, thus enabling users to continue performing their current tasks. To prevent erroneous validation of revoked certificates issued by another node when no infrastructure is available, a copy of the local blacklist for further queries is also sent.

It is also worth to mention that we believe in privacy as an interesting paradox in authorization environments; therefore the proposed scheme takes into account issuing the AC considering the identifier provided by the user digital certificate based on the device's IMEI thus preserving user's real identity. Note that current mobile PKI solutions do not consider the use of pseudonyms, nevertheless we find the use of pseudonyms very useful and for future work we plan to explore an IMEI-based pseudonym generation solution for automatic authentication. In the next subsection we will briefly describe the available communication channels and message transmission details.

4.3 Message Transmission

In the above mentioned communication protocol and in the overall CARM system, communications are done through an independent layer which is configurable accordingly to user needs or availability. A light-weighted protocol was designed to support high mobility of devices using two communication channels: *i*) A *signaling channel* used to communicate control information to a device, such as ACs and other information that may include configuration or control information, availability, and changing states; and *ii*) a *data channel* to transmit substantive data information relevant to a shared resource.

Messages format will basically include a header and a payload. Header implementation contains packet type information, resource destination and other applicable information necessary for the exchange process. The optional payload will include the message's signature, timestamp and information according to the current process.

4.4 Testbed and Implementation

To evaluate our proof-of-concept proposal, we have used two Nokia mobile phones: an E65 and 6600 models (both devices are based on Symbian OS), Figure 4 shows device's specifications. The prototype was developed on J2ME and additional components were based on Symbian C++ due to platform dependency restrictions. To implement the policy-based authorization mechanism we use ACs [Yeep02], [RaPi06] a well-known format to maintain the information related to a specific user's attributes (access rights). ACs strongly bind a set of attributes to its holder [ZhMe04], and in particular we have chosen ACs because we believe that ACs are relatively *simple* to manage, similar to a session cookie ACs are issued considering a "*short*" validity period, and thus avoiding the whole lifecycle management. Additionally, we use the eXtensible Access Control Markup Language [Oasi05], [MCCP06] for specifying the access control policies.

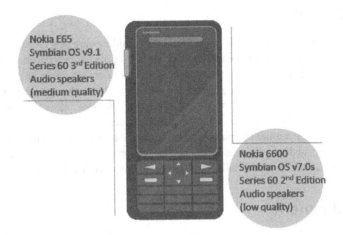

Figure 4: Device Specifications

The experiment setup consisted of a Bluetooth *piconet* with a L2CAP connection between the mobile phones and a typical data transmission rate of 721 kbits/s. Measurements were taken for the following operations (up to 100 tests were performed): *i*) connecting the two devices, *ii*) attribute certificate transmission, *iii*) requesting a resource, *iv*) relinquishing a resource, and *v*) disconnecting. Initial results show that most of the time is consumed by performing the initial Bluetooth connection (2644.8ms), which is independent of the time added by the security model. The resource request was 169.5ms; relinquish and disconnection operations an average of 21.5ms and 30.3ms respectively. The time consumed by the AC's transmission was 111.9ms and which not represents a great time variation and promises to be a good solution for peripherals authorization in a high dynamic environment, however other measurements such as validation and computation time are still needed in order to evaluate more accurately the overall performance.

5 Related Work

The interest in ubiquitous computing environments has given rise to a proliferation of middleware models and programming environments that allows resources to be dynamically discovered and utilized. In current State-of-the-Art projects such as the Dynamic Composable Computing [RTSR08] or MobiGo[XiUm07] share similar directions as CARM, the main difference is that our proposal does not rely on an infrastructure or use any specialized devices. However, none of these projects have considered a security mechanism to authorize devices to use their shared resources. Projects like [ClSh07], [BoRe08], [PaOm04] and [KaFJ01], offer different security solutions generic for data sharing in pervasive environments and are not strategically designed for peripherals sharing which take into consideration other critical constraints strongly dependable on each resource (i.e. power consumption, bandwidth consumption, resource priority, time limitations, etc.) and must be addressed. A security mechanism like PERMIS [CGO+08] intended to distributed environments could be partially adopted into these scenarios; therefore we have taken PERMIS into consideration for the design of the proposed scheme.

6 Conclusions

In this article we have overviewed the basis of CARM's middleware and highlighted important security concerns in pervasive environments. A security module has been proposed mainly consisting of authorization and authentication mechanisms to guarantee resource protection and to prevent unauthorized access. We have suggested a testbed configuration for the evaluation of the proof-of-concept implementation primarily considering the devices authentication and resource privileges management. Future research will include a deeper study in policies formats and representation in order to minimize the power consumption. We also plan to extend the middleware in order to add more devices, other resources and allocation policies. New communication technologies (WiFi or ZigBee) and scalability issues are also considered as future work.

Acknowledgement

This work has been supported by the Spanish Computer Emergency Response Team (esCERT-UPC) and the Mexican National Council for Science and Technology (CONACyt). All products or company names mentioned herein are trademarks or registered trademarks of their respective owners.

References

[MoGi08]   Morales, R. and Gil, M., *CARM: Composable, Adaptive Resource Management System in Ubiquitous Computing Environments*. Advances in Soft Computing. J. M. Corchado, D. I. Tapia and J. Bravo, Springer Berlin / Heidelberg. Volume 51/2009: 335-342, 2008.

[MoOG10] Morales, R., Otero, B. and Gil, M., *Mobile Resource Management for a Better User Experience: An Audio Case Study*, 4th Symposium of Ubiquitous Computing and Ambient Intelligence (UCAmI), 2010.

[RTSR08]   Roy, W., Trevor, P., Sud, S., Rosario, B., et al. *Dynamic Composable Computing*, Proceedings of the 9th workshop on Mobile computing systems and applications. Napa Valley, California, ACM, 2008.

[XiUm07]   Xiang, S. and R. Umakishore, *MobiGo: A Middleware for Seamless Mobility*, Proceedings of the 13th IEEE International Conference on Embedded and Real-Time Computing Systems and Applications, IEEE Computer Society, 2007.

[ClSh07]   Claycomb, W. and Shin, D. 2007. *Towards secure resource sharing for impromptu collaboration in pervasive computing*. In Proceedings of the 2007 ACM Symposium on Applied Computing (Seoul, Korea, March 11 - 15, 2007). SAC '07. ACM, New York, NY, 940-946. DOI=http://doi.acm.org/10.1145/1244002.1244208

[Oasi05]   OASIS. *eXtensible Access Control Markup Language (XACML) Version 2.0*, 2005. OASIS Committee Specification: Tim Moses (editor).

[Farr02]   S. Farrell. *An Internet Attribute Certificate Profile for Authorization*. Network Working Group, Request for Comments: 3281, April 2002. RFC-3281. Online. Network Working Group. Available http://tools.ietf.org/html/rfc3281-section-4.1

[Yeep02]   P. Yee. *Attribute Certificate Request Message Format*. PKIX Working Group, Internet Draft, March 2002. Online. Available http://tools.ietf.org/html/draft-ietf-pkix-acrmf-01

[RaPi06]   C. Francis Raytheon and D. Pinkas Bull. *Attribute Certificate (AC) Policies Extension*. Network Working Group, Request for Comments: 4476, May 2006, RFC-4476. Online. Network Working Group. Available http://www.faqs.org/rfcs/rfc4476.html

[PaOm04] Patroklos G. Argyroudis and D. O'Mahony. *ÆTHER: an Authorization Management Architecture for Ubiquitous Computing*. In Proceedings of 1st European PKI Workshop: Research and Applications (EuroPKI04), 246-259, Springer-Verlag 2004.

[BoRe08] A. Boukerche and Y. Ren *A trust-based security system for ubiquitous and pervasive computing environments*. Computers and Communications 31: 4343-4351, 2008.

[KaFJ01] L. Kagal, T. Finin and A. Joshi *Trust-Based Security in Pervasive Computing Environments*. Computer, vol. 34, no. 12, pp. 154-157, Dec. 2001.

[CGO+08] D. Chadwick, Z.Gansen, S. Otenko, R. Laborde, L. Su and T. A. Nguyen. *PERMIS: A Modular Authorization Infrastructure*. Concurrency and Computation: Practice & Experience - Volume 20 , Issue 11 1341-1357, August 2008.

[ZhMe04] W. Zhou and C. Meinel *Implement role based access control with attribute certificates*. In Proceedings of the 6th International Conference on Advanced Communication Technology - Volume 1, 536-541, Feb. 2004.

[MCCP06] U.M. Mbanaso, G.S. Cooper, D.W. Chadwick and S. Proctor *Privacy Preserving Trust Authorization Framework Using XACML*. In Proceedings of the International Symposium on on World of Wireless, Mobile and Multimedia Networks. 673 - 678, 2006.

Visual Representation of Advanced Electronic Signatures

Nick Pope

Thales Information Systems Security
ETSI ESI STF364 Leader, United Kingdom
nick.pope@thales-esecurity.com

Abstract

This paper considers the issues concerning the visual representation of cryptographic based digital signatures (referred to as advanced electronic signatures in the European legal context). Two particular aspects are considered: firstly the visual appearance of the signature as part of the document as applied by the signatory at time of signing, secondly the representation of the digital signature when verified by the recipient. The paper proposes principles for these two aspects of visual representation to ensure that the normal user of electronic documents, who has little or no knowledge of digital signature technology, can best understand the signature whilst enabling forensic experts to investigate the details of the signature in case of dispute over a signed document. The paper also touches on a further aspect of signature representation, which is still the subject to ongoing debate. This paper is based on work carried out in ETSI on standards for visual representation of advanced electronic signatures in PDF with input from European projects using signed documents (see acknowledgements at end of paper).

1 Introduction: From Paper to Electronic

Traditionally a signature is a visible mark placed on paper as a stylized form of a person's name or even a simple "X". This can be used, for example, to give evidence of the provenance of the document (i.e. identify the source) or provide an indication of the intent of the person applying the mark. This is placed at a particular point in a document to associate particular meaning with the signature based on its context.

For example an auditor's report may end with the following:

> This report is constitutes a true and proper report of the IT audit carried on ABC's eInvoicing service today 25th October 2010.

> J Smith

> *John Smith*
> *Smith Independent Auditors*

The mark is taken by the recipient as an indication of the identified person has consented to whatever statement is associated with the signature. The meaning associated with the presence of the signature can often have legal implications indicating that the identified person signed the document with some intent. The prime reason for placing the signature within a document is to provide a clear indication of intent by the identified person by placing the signature within a certain context. This indication is often assumed to be authentic although protection against forgery can be an issue.

Signed paper documents do provide some protection against forgery. Integrity of the content can be provided by the properties of the paper and ink making changes evident, although this has been somewhat weakened by the use of modern digital copying techniques. The signature can be visually checked against known copies and there is a reasonable chance that the style of the signature will reveal whether the signature was created by the identified person.

In the paper domain, an inexpert user can by visual examination get some confidence that the signature and document are authentic, and can clearly understand the intent implied by the signature. With appropriate expertise this is still possible to a level that gives confidence to be accepted in court.

Digital signatures technology can provide the integrity and authenticity in the electronic domain, as paper and verified handwritten signatures do in the physical domain, if not better. Any change in the document is detectable using the digital signature value, and the public key certificate can authenticate the source of the document. The digital signature assures the integrity of the document, any change is immediately detectable. Similarly, the public key certificate assures the identity of the signatory, in the same way a handwriting expert can verify the authenticity of the handwritten signature. The legal acceptance of such signatures has been adopted into European legislation through the Directive on Electronic Signatures [EUSig99], and standards developed for their use in ETSI and a number of other internationally recognised bodies.

However, this technology should be represented to the user in a way that it is:

a. Clearly visible within the document in a way that indicates the intent of the signature,

b. Easily understood whether the signature is valid.

Security experts have spent many years, if not decades, honing the use of public key techniques to provide security which is probably many times better than handwritten signatures. However, little or no consideration has been given to how these signatures are represented to the human user in a way that is easily understood by the untrained user.

It is suggested that for digital signature technology to be used to provide the electronic equivalent of handwritten signatures (i.e. legally recognized electronic signatures) the visual representation of the digital signature also needs to be considered. Digital signatures have properties that make them difficult to represent visually in a way that is easily comprehended.

Digital signatures are invisible. On their own they leave no visible mark on the document. Any visual appearance of the signature is added as an addition to the encoded digital signature. Whilst systems exist to add a signature appearance to a document (see description of PDF and Microsoft Office below) these elements are added to the document before the digital signature. Whilst they may share information the appearance and the digital signature are not the same.

Digital signatures are complex. When verifying a digital signature to high degree of certainty several factors need to be taken account:

- Is the algorithm and key length strong enough?
- Is this strength sufficient for the lifetime of the document?
- Is the certificate revoked?
- Did this occur before the signature was created?
- What should go in the various naming fields called "CN", "OU", Serial Number?
- etc, etc.......

So when verifying signatures detailed information is provided on the signature which often is meaningless to all but the few of us experts in public key technology. If the signature validates successfully then this is generally straightforward, but if there is any aspect that fails the user is left uncertain as to whether this is significant.

This paper suggests a few simple principles for the visual representation of electronic signatures to provide an electronic equivalent of existing conventional visibly written signatures, called under the EU Signatures Directive [EUSig99] an Advanced Electronic Signature. The principles aim to assist the normal untrained user to better comprehend the intent of a signature and to easily check its authenticity, whilst where necessary providing further information where detailed forensic analysis is required.

This paper is based on work carried out in ETSI (European Telecommunication Standards Institute) Specialist Task Force 364 on PDF Advanced Electronic Signatures, to develop standards for visual representation of advanced electronic signatures in PDF, as well as ongoing work in the European collaborative project SPOCS and earlier work in the Austrian government which defines visual Official Signature. This paper also takes into account recent work in the IETF with the definition of means of linking a visual representation of an X.509 certificate with the certificate itself.

2 Visual Aspects of Electronic Signatures

2.1 Visual Appearance vs Verification

This paper will consider two primary aspects of visual representation of advanced electronic signatures:

a. The visual appearance of the signature within the document.
b. The visual representation of the signature verification.

The first aspect is important for representing the intent of the signatory. It is suggested that the full meaning of the signature can only be understood by its context within a document. Whether the signature placed below a statement such as "I agree to terms and condition listed above", or "I witness that the above document was agreed to by the identified parties who were present before me" makes a significant difference. The signature appearance is applied by the signatory at the time of signing.

The second aspect is important in enabling the recipient of the document to authenticate if the identity claimed by the signatory is correct. It is also indicates that the document has not been tampered with since it has been signed. Traditionally, this has been provided by the medium carrying the document with the signature; that is by the paper on which the document is written. In the case of digital signatures this function is closely linked since authentication and integrity are applied together by a single mechanism. Verification is applicable to the recipient at the time of reading the document when needing assurance that the signature is authentic.

2.2 Visual Appearance

There are two widely available examples of the visual appearance of documents firstly signatures in PDF (Portable Document Format) documents using, for example, Adobe Acrobat, secondly in documents created using Microsoft (MS) Office 2010.

An example of a signed PDF document is shown below:

I hope that you find this paper interesting and informative.

The PDF signature can include (depending on configuration):

a. selected information from the digital certificate;

b. a graphic of, for example, a handwritten image or logo,

c. the time of signing (using a local clock),

d. Other information entered by the signatory such as reason

An example of a signed MS Office document is shown below:

I hope that you find this paper interesting and informative.

The MS Office signature consists of a "signature line" including:

a. Information about the expected signer added during document editing (e.g. "To be signed by Nick");

b. Text or an image added by the signer whilst creating the signature;

c. Basic naming information (e.g. common name) within the digital signature certificate.

d. The date when the signature was created.

e. Other information entered by the signatory such as reason

In both examples, the visual appearance of the signature is under control of the signatory. The visual appearance is created before the digital signature. Thus, even though the information displayed may be derived from the certificate, there is no guarantee that the name certified by the certificate is what appears in the signature appearance. In addition, because the appearance is created before adding the digital signature this appearance only shows the claimed time which comes from a local clock rather than a trusted time source. So if the signature is time-stamped this time may be different from the time displayed in the signature appearance.

In both examples, the visual appearance is linked to a digital signature which is "hidden" in the encoding of the document. The digital signature protects the document including the signature appearance. Within the document itself, any certified identity information encoded in the digital signature is not directly visible; it depends on the creator of the document to extract information from the certificate later used to sign the document and copy it into the visual appearance of the signature.

2.3 Signature Verification

Whilst the digital signature is hidden it provides information that can be used to authenticate the signatory.

In both Adobe Acrobat Reader and MS Office, when the document is viewed the digital signatures associated with the signature appearance can be verified by clicking on the "signature".

In the case of Acrobat a separate verification window is shown as below when the user clicks to verify the signature:

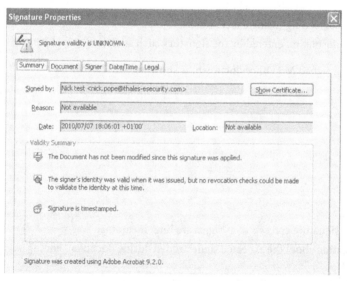

This starts with a summary giving the identity of the signer with other details about the signature and its validity. Note that the time shown in the verification is different from that shown by the signature appearance within the document, and whilst there is a correspondence between the signature appearance and the digital signature verification information they are not shown in an identical way.

Further details of the digital signature and the certificate is shown in Acrobat through additional tabs and click through buttons.

With MS Office a verification window is also shown when clicking on the signature appearance (signature line in MS Office terms) as follows:

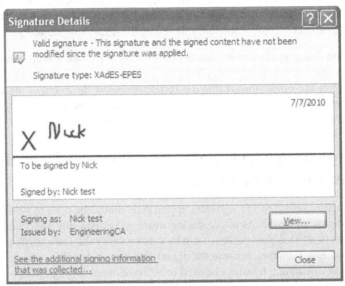

This again shows basic information about the validity of the signature and identity, as derived from the certificate. Further information on the certificate and the scope of the protection can be provided by click through buttons / links.

In the case of the Acrobat reader the user is left to relate the verified information to the appearance in the document. In the case of MS Office both the appearance and information derived from the digital signature are displayed but it is not immediately clear what information is derived from the digital signature (and hence trusted), and what information is derived from the signature appearance.

3 Principles

From a consideration of the implementation of signatures as described above, and more particularly working in ETSI on the standardisation with regards to visual representation of Electronic Signatures in PDF, ETSI TS 102 778-6 [ETSI10], the following principles have been identified. These principles recognise the two distinct aspects of the electronic signature representation: signature appearance and signature verification. They aim to make signatures understandable to users untrained in signature technologies and assist them in making appropriate decisions regarding the authenticity of the signature.

3.1 The Signature Appearance is Only a Claim

Any name or other information, such as signing time, that appears in a document is not by itself necessarily any proof of identity etc. Information placed in the signature appearance is under control of the party creating the signed document. In the case of Acrobat the signer can configure the appearance to be what he wants, and similarly in MS Office the signer can provide text / graphics as required. Even if such configuration controls were not available in the application, because of the features that electronic document commonly have of being able to represent information in any form that the author requires, it would not be possible to assure that any automatically created appearance cannot be manually forged by the document signatory.

This fact does not denigrate the importance of the signature appearance in providing a means for the signatory to indicate intent when applying the signature. The very fact that the appearance is under control of the author means that it directly represents the intent of the signatory. The signature appearance must be considered as distinct from the digital signature which is linked to the appearance and provides a means of verifying its authenticity.

3.2 The Signature Appearance should be visually verified against the Digital Signature

The digital signature linked to the signature appearance should be used to verify that the signature appearance is authentic. As the digital signature is created using a certified key, which is known to belong to an identified person, it can be used to verify the authenticity and integrity of the signed document. However, because the digital signature is invisible, and does not directly appear within the document, it cannot be used to indicate intent through its appearance within the document.

Verification of the signature appearance against the digital signature can be done visually when reading a document by displaying the signature verification information. The reader may visually check the verification information against the signature as it appears in the document.

Consideration had been given to the possibilities of automatically checking the signature appearance against the digital signature by the ETSI team working on PDF Advanced Electronic Signatures (PAdES) standards. However, it was considered that a fraudulent signer could provide information in a way that may mislead the verification as to what is displayed and how this is linked to the digital signature. Hence it was decided that the surest way is to check the appearance and the verification information visually. Rather the human reader should be assisted in carrying out a visual comparison of the verification information derived from the digital signature against the signature appearance by providing information in a way that the two can be easily related.

3.3 Human Understanding of Advanced E-Signature Verification

As verification of the digital signature against the signature appearance is to be carried out by a human, who may not be aware of digital signature technology, the verification needs to be presented in a way that can be clearly understood. Generally, the person reading a document and wishing to verify the signature will have little or no understanding of digital signatures and certificates.

The reader clearly needs to be shown whether the signature is valid. However, there will be situations where the validity of the signature is unknown or even the signature is considered invalid. In which case, some basic information needs to be provided to help the reader understand the reason for the signature not being known as valid. If possible this should be provided in simple non-technical terms so that a basic assessment may be made by the reader, but this has to be backed up by detailed information that can be used by an expert in the situation where validity of the signature is of paramount importance (e.g. in case of legal dispute).

The reader also needs to be provided with information regarding certified identity that can be checked against the claimed identity in the signature appearance. This may be provided at a basic level that can be easily related to the identity in the signature appearance but should be backed up by detailed information on the full identity in case of dispute.

If the information displayed in the signature verification is consistent with the appearance of the signature in the document then the user can be assured of the authenticity of the signature as it appears in the document.

3.4 Consistency of Visual Representation of Electronic Signatures and Familiarity

With the current Acrobat and MS Office software the signature appearing within the document can be different from that provided in verification through the certificate. Whilst this is reasonable from the point of the signatory having control to apply the signature to indicate intent, this makes it difficult for the reader to compare the signature appearance against the signature verification.

The signatory should be helped to sign a document in a way that reflects the information used in the digital certificate. In Acrobat this is achieved by the default appearance including information from the certificate. With MS Office the common name field in the user's certificate is included at the bottom of the "signature line". The ETSI specification [ETSI10] by providing a common standard assists in achieving consistency and familiarity.

This can be further assisted by the use of a simple visual representation of the certificate being included with the certificate when it is issued. This enables the same image to be used in creating the visible signature when signing a document as can be verified by the electronic signature. The IETF have proposed a standard means of achieving this in the Certificate Image specification [LePR09].

3.5 Layered Approach to Advanced E-Signature Verification

As digital signature technology is based on a number of complicated concepts (public/private keys, certificates, revocation, timestamps etc) that cannot be easily comprehended by non-experts it can be difficult to provide information in a way which is easily understood and yet has the detailed information necessary for forensic investigation.

The approach recommended by the ETSI standards team is to provide a first layer of information that is understandable by the untrained user, with additional layers of information enabling detailed investigation by experts.

At the first layer the reader may be shown basic information about the signature validity, signer identity and possibly signing time when provided by a trusted source. Additional information such as algorithms and certificate details could be provided by subsidiary layers accessible via buttons, additional tabs etc. Through this approach the naïve user can be shown the basic information needed to confirm that the signature is valid and the expert can drill down into the detailed information if there is dispute over the signature.

3.6 Verification Clearly separate from Document Visible Content

The verification of digital signature should be viewed as separate from the document content. The document content is information created by the author to be displayed as intended by the author. The digital signature verification is information created by the system reading the document to confirm the authenticity of the document as displayed, including any signature appearances.

If the signature verification information is mixed with information provided by the author it can be very difficult to clearly differentiate "trusted" information provided by the reader from "un-trusted" information provided by the author. For example, if a "tick" mark is provided automatically over a document signature by the reader software to indicate that the signature is valid, the author can place an identical tick graphic over what seems to be a normal appearance of the signature but could be a forgery.

When viewing a document if the user requires to check the validity of the document this should be done outside the document, not by overlaying the document with verification information.

3.7 See what was signed

With PDF documents it is possible to sign a document at different stages of a workflow with only some form of data protected by the signature. For example, the first signature in a workflow may apply to a basic document with empty comment fields, and a second signature may apply to the document with comment fields completed.

Wherever there may be uncertainty over the scope of the information protected by a digital signature it should be possible to check this as part of verification. Without this the user could be fooled into believing that information is correct where it has been added after signing. For example, with the document with comments described above the comment fields may be completed and it is assumed that these comments form part of the original document.

With Acrobat it is possible to go back and view the document as was signed. In MS Office by clicking on the link *"See additional signing information that was collected ...."* the user is shown a statement about the scope of the signature.

4 Further Aspects of Electronic Signature Representation

During the development of the ETSI document on PDF signature representation a number of further requirements were brought to the attention of the team which could not be simply address by existing PDF standards. This is due to the current PDF document encoding not supporting the inclusion of information directly derived from the digital signature in the document appearance, and in particular in a printed copy of the document which no longer includes the digital signature. For example, to demonstrate that a printout of a document is uniquely derived from a given signed original, a digest of the binary signature value might be included in the signature. A further example is in Austrian system described in [LePR09]. Similar requirements exist to display in the document the time of signing as in the signature time-stamp.

Neither the current PDF nor MS Office signature schemes support such additions to the appearance of the document. Also, the use of such schemes confuse the current clear separation between the signature appearance, which is directly applied by the signatory, and the digital signature, which is hidden and can be used to verify the appearance. However, there is still some interest in this area by some countries and it may be addressed as part of the SPOCS European collaborative research programme.

5 Conclusions

This paper aims to clearly delineate the two representations of an electronic signature: the appearance of the electronic signature within a document and the representation of the digital signature verification. It is hoped that by concentrating on these visual aspects this paper works towards improving what is possibly one of the areas of greatest vulnerability in how electronic signatures are currently used. Many years of in-depth research has gone into the technology of digital signatures, scant regard has been given to how this relates to how signatures are represented.

It is suggested that the appearance of a signature within a document is very important for indicating the intent of the signature, but without support of an invisible digital signature there may be little protection against fraud. Digital signatures are widely accepted as a means of verifying the integrity of document, and confirming the authenticity of a signature applied to a document.

It is important that the relative roles of signature appearance and signature verification is understood and that the signature appearance can be easily verified against the verification information by an untrained user. A number of principles are identified in the paper for ensuring proper use of both aspects. These are all addressed to an extent by both Adobe Acrobat Reader and Microsoft Office. Improvements could be made by ensuring that users are aware of the implications of both aspects and assistance is given in relating the two together.

Two recent advances in standardisation will help the two aspects to be used together in a coherent manner. Firstly, the ETSI specification on "PDF Advanced Electronic Signatures - Visual Representations of Electronic Signatures" [ETSI10] provides assistance in how to provide the two aspects in PDFs. Secondly, the IETF has recently developed an Internet draft, soon to be proposed as a standard, for use of "Certificate Image" [SHBR] whereby an X.509 standard certificate can include an image which can be used both in the signature appearance and for signature verification.

By addressing both aspects of visual representation, signature appearance and signature verification, signatures can be practically applied to systems in a way that gives signatures proper meaning and can easily be verified as being authentic.

6 References:

[EUSig99] EU DIRECTIVE 1999/93/EC of the European Parliament and of the Council of 13 December 1999 on a Community framework for electronic signatures

[LePR09] Herbert Leitold, Reinhard Posch and Thomas Rössler: "Media-break resistant eSignatures in eGovernment – an Austrian experience" In: IFIP Advances in Information and Communication Technology 2009

[ETSI10] ETSI TS 102 778-6 PDF Advanced Electronic Signatures - Visual Representations of Electronic Signatures (draft to be published)

[SHBR] Stefan Santesson, Russ Housley, Siddharth Bajaj, Leonard Rosenthol "Internet X.509 Public Key Infrastructure - Certificate Image" IETF Internet Draft (to be published as IETF Proposed Standard RFC xxxx)

7 Acknowledgements

This paper is based on the work on a technical specification on "PDF Advanced Electronic Signatures - Visual Representations of Electronic Signatures" carried out by ETSI STF 364. Members of the team are:

Alexander Funk	TeleTrusT Deutschland e. V.
Giuliana Marzola	InfoCert s.p.a.
Juan Carlos Cruellas	DAC-UPC
Julien Stern	Cryptolog International
Leonard Rosenthol	Adobe Systems
Marc Straat (co-lead)	Adobe Systems
Nick Pope (co-lead)	Thales

About ETSI:

ETSI produces globally-applicable standards for Information and Communications Technologies (ICT), including fixed, mobile, radio, converged, broadcast and internet technologies and is officially recognized by the European Commission as a European Standards Organization. ETSI is a not-for-profit organization whose 700 ETSI member organizations benefit from direct participation and are drawn from 60 countries worldwide. For more information, please visit: www. etsi.org

About ETSI Specialist Task Forces (STF):

STFs are teams of highly-skilled experts working together over a pre-defined period to draft an ETSI standard under the technical guidance of an ETSI Technical Body and with the support of the ETSI Secretariat. The task of the STFs is to accelerate the standardization process in areas of strategic importance and in response to urgent market needs. For more information, please visit: http://portal.etsi.org/stfs/process/home.asp

Also, the author acknowledges the important work of the SPOCS EU collaborative project and the Austrian government on official signatures which has influenced this work.

DSKPP and PSKC, IETF Standard Protocol and Payload for Symmetric Key Provisioning

Philip Hoyer

Senior Architect – Office of CTO
ActivIdentity (UK), 117 Waterloo Road, London SE1 8UL
phoyer@actividentity.com

Abstract

This paper will describe the work currently being completed by the IETF 'keyprov' working group to create a standard online protocol and payload to provision symmetric keys. Dynamic Symmetric Key Provisioning Protocol - DSKPP provides an open and interoperable mechanism for initializing and configuring symmetric keys to cryptographic modules that are accessible over the Internet. The portable Symmetric Key Container - PSKC specifies a symmetric key XML format for transport and provisioning of symmetric keys (for example One Time Password (OTP) shared secrets or symmetric cryptographic keys) to different types of devices. The paper will outline the mechanisms of DSKPP and its main application use cases. It will also describe the PSKC payload format and its applicability for use within the DSKPP protocol or as a standalone format for off-line key provisioning and transport.

1 Introduction

Securing modern application and technology infrastructure components is mainly based on cryptography using keys. Even though advances have been made in implementation by adding asymmetric (PKI) and symmetric key based security and cryptographic mechanisms, one main area that keeps an overall system secure is the availability of fresh uncompromised keys. To achieve this effective key management and provisioning is essential.

When a symmetric key is used in application it is usually used with a specific algorithm. Some algorithms require additional parameters or values (key meta-data) that are used as input in the computation of the algorithm (for example a counter for a one time password algorithm). Additionally it might be desirable to restrict and govern the usage of the key in terms of time period when the key can be used or number of times a key should be used (key policy). It is hence highly desirable during key provisioning to be able to provision the additional key meta data and policy to the application using the key.

The state of affair when the 'keyprov' working group was founded was that mostly provisioning of symmetric keys was performed using proprietary and hence non-interoperable protocols and transport formats. This meant that in the majority of cases, applications requiring keys would not be able to interoperate with key provisioning infrastructure from other providers. This meant that more often than not key provisioning was either completely lacking or suboptimal from a security perspective.

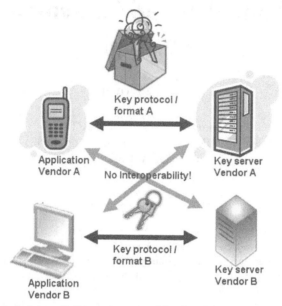

Fig 1: Historical state of affair, no interoperability between proprietary symmetric key provisioning

The need for provisioning protocols in PKI architectures has been recognized for some time. Although the existence and architecture of these protocols provide a feasibility proof for the work in the IETF 'keyprov' working group, assumptions built into these protocols mean that it was not possible to apply them to symmetric key architectures without substantial modification.

In particular the ability to provision symmetric keys and associated key meta-data (attributes) dynamically to already issued devices such as cell phones and USB drives was highly desirable. The IETF working group was hence set-up to develop the necessary protocols and data formats required to support provisioning and management of symmetric keys and related meta-data, both proprietary and standards based.

The following highlight two major use cases of the ones that have been considered:

1. **Online symmetric key provisioning** – this is when an application has network connectivity and requires symmetric keys for application functionality. In this case the application would connect over the network using the symmetric key provisioning protocol to retrieve one or more symmetric keys and related meta-data. One example could be an application on a mobile phone capable of generating One-Time-Passwords using an algorithm that utilizes symmetric keys and a counter.

2. **Offline bulk key provisioning** - this use case is when applications or devices that harbor symmetric keys, injected at manufacturing, need to be imported into an infrastructure for usage. The knowledge of the keys and their related meta-data need to be securely imported from the manufacturing to the infrastructure components. One example would be

One-Time-Password tokens that come with related keys and counters (seed data) and are imported into a validation server possibly for securing remote access VPNs.

1.1 History of the 'keyprov' working group

The state of affair when the IETF 'keyprov' working group was founded in early 2007 was of an ecosystem of vendor-specific solutions for provisioning of symmetric keys (and meta-data) but no standardized solution was available.

The main key provisioning scenarios required included
- over the wire (an application with network TCP/IP connectivity)
- over the air (an application on a mobile phone)
- or offline (bulk, multiple keys securely transported for example on a CD-ROM)

Not only was there no standardised online protocol but there was no standardized container for keys and meta-data available either. Resulting in a state of no interoperability between client and servers for provisioning symmetric keys.

Hence in February 2007 the IETF 'keyprov' working group was founded with input from Veri-Sign (DSKPP), RSA (CT-KIP), and OATH (PSKC) with the following main deliverables:

1. An online XML based protocol to allow online provisioning of symmetric keys – The Dynamic Symmetric Key Provisioning Protocol [DSKPP]
2. An XML based symmetric key payload (transport) format – Portable Symmetric Key Container [PSKC]
3. An ASN.1 based symmetric key payload (transport) format – Symmetric Key Package Content Type [SKPC]

2 The Dynamic Symmetric Key Provisioning Protocol (DSKPP)

DSKPP [DSKPP] is a XML based client-server protocol for initialization (and configuration) of symmetric keys to cryptographic modules or applications requiring symmetric keys.

It is intended for use within computer and communications systems employing symmetric cryptographic modules that are locally (over-the-wire) or remotely (over-the-air) accessible.

The protocol can be run with or without private-key capabilities in the cryptographic modules, and with or without an established public key infrastructure.

2.1 DSKPP Protocol variants

DSKPP protocol variants support multiple usage scenarios:
- Four-pass variant enables mutual key generation by the provisioning server and cryptographic module in near real-time; **provisioned keys are not transferred over-the-wire or over-the-air**.

- Two-pass variant enables generation and transport of symmetric keys to a cryptographic module in environments where near real-time communication is not possible.
- Two-pass variant also enables transport of pre-generated (e.g., legacy) keys to a cryptographic module.

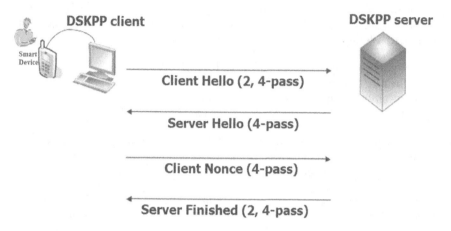

DSKPP client   **DSKPP server**

Smart
Device

Client Hello (2, 4-pass)

Server Hello (4-pass)

Client Nonce (4-pass)

Server Finished (2, 4-pass)

Fig 2: DSKPP: 2 pass and 4 pass protocol variant comparison

2.2 Cryptographic properties

DSKPP allows for:

Key confirmation of the provisioned keys (proof that the key reached the destination)
- In both 2 pass and 4 pass protocol variants via a MAC on the exchanged data

Replay protection (protection against another rogue client asking for the same key)
- In both 2 pass and 4 pass variants through inclusion of client-provided data in MAC

Server authentication (making sure that the client is communicating with the correct key provisioning server instead of a rogue key server impersonation)
- In both 2 pass and 4 pass variants through MAC in ServerFinished message when replacing existing key

Protection against Man-In-The-Middle (MITM)
- In both 2 pass and 4 pass variants through use of shared keys, client certificates, or server public   key usage

User authentication (make sure that the right user is operating the receiving application / cryptographic module)
- In both 2 pass and 4 pass variants using a user entered authentication code

Device authentication (make sure that the keys reach the correct device)
- In both 2 pass and 4 pass variants if based on shared secret key or if device sends a client certificate

2.3 DSKPP bindings

Security Binding
- Transport level encryption (e.g., TLS) is not required for key transport, the protocol protects the keys in transit with in-built key protection mechanisms
- TLS/SSL is required if other parameters/attributes must be protected in transit

HTTP Binding
- It is recommended to use the Special Content-Type header defined in [DSKPP]
- Examples are provided in the specification [DSKPP]

3 Portable Symmetric Key Container (PSKC)

Portable Symmetric Key Container (PSKC) [PSKC] is a standardized XML-based document for transporting symmetric keys and key related meta data.

PSKC specifies the information elements (meta-data) that may be required when the symmetric key is utilized for specific purposes, such as the algorithm type or the initial counter in the HOTP [HOTP] algorithm. It also allows transmission of a PIN that will protect the usage of the key and related PIN policies such as maximum and minimum length of PIN.

PSKC also allows transmission of key policies and key utilization purpose aligned with NIST SP800-57 "Recommendation for Key Management" [NISTSP800-57]. This allows the transfer of the purpose of utilization of the key, for example 'authentication'.

It became clear that for keys that are intended for a specific purpose and use a specific algorithm the transported key and meta-data would conform to a set of mandatory meta data elements that have been defined as a PSKC profile.

This means that a receiver of a PSKC transport document for a specific purpose will know exactly which of the meta-data elements are present.

To define a centralised open reference of such profiles the PSKC specification requested to IANA the creation of a IANA maintained registry for PSKC algorithm profiles:
- Such a profile contains a common name, pointer to a stable reference, URN for reference to the profile, information about PSKC XML elements and attributes being used, and examples.
- PSKC spec defines two PSKC algorithm profiles: HOTP and KEYPROV-PIN
- Further algorithm profiles are described in [PSKC-PROFILES]

A symmetric key container using an ASN.1 based encoding instead of XML, bust completely aligned with the definition and specification of PSKC is available with [SKPC].

3.1 PSKC Data Model

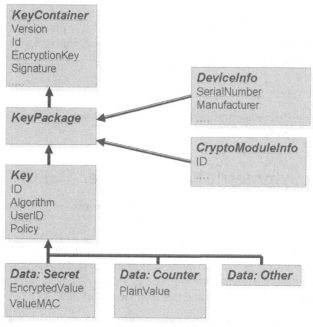

Fig 3: PSKC Data Model

The portable key container is based on an XML schema definition and contains the following main conceptual entities:

1. **KeyContainer** entity - representing the container that carries a number of KeyPackages. A valid container MUST carry at least 1 KeyPackage.

2. **KeyPackage** entity - representing the package of at most one key and its related provisioning endpoint or current usage endpoint, such as a physical or virtual device and a specific CryptoModule

3. **DeviceInfo** entity - representing the information about the device and criteria to uniquely identify the device

4. **CryptoModuleInfo** entity - representing the information about the CryptoModule where the keys reside or are provisioned to

5. **Key** entity - representing the key transported or provisioned

6. **Data** entity - representing a list of meta-data related to the key, where the element name is the name of the meta-data and its associated value is either in encrypted form (for example for Data element <Secret>) or plaintext (for example the Data element <Counter>)

3.2 PSKC Example

```
<KeyContainer Version="1.0" xmlns="urn:ietf:params:xml:ns:keyprov:pskc" … >
 <EncryptionKey><ds:KeyName>Pre-shared-key</ds:KeyName></EncryptionKey>
  <KeyPackage>
   <DeviceInfo><Manufacturer>Manufacturer</Manufacturer><SerialNo>987654321
    </SerialNo>
   </DeviceInfo>
   <CryptoModuleInfo><Id>CM_ID_001</Id></CryptoModuleInfo>
   <Key Id="12345678" Algorithm="urn:ietf:params:xml:ns:keyprov:pskc:hotp">
    <Issuer>Issuer</Issuer>
    <AlgorithmParameters><ResponseFormat Length="8" Encoding="DECIMAL"/>
    </AlgorithmParameters>
    <Data>
     <Secret>
      <EncryptedValue>
       <xenc:EncryptionMethod Algorithm="http://www.w3.org/2001/04/
       xmlenc#aes128-cbc"/>
       <xenc:CipherData><xenc:CipherValue>pgznhXdDh…. </xenc:CipherValue>
       </xenc:CipherData>
      <EncryptedValue>
      <ValueMAC>ooo0Swn6s/myD4o05FCfBHN0560=</ValueMAC>
     </Secret>
     <Counter><PlainValue>0</PlainValue></Counter>
    </Data>
  <Policy><KeyUsage>OTP</KeyUsage></Policy>
   </Key>
   </KeyPackage>
</KeyContainer>
```

3.3 PSKC Key protection methods

PSKC allows for various options to protect symmetric keys in transit:
- Protection by underlying transport protocol (for example TLS)
- Protection based on pre-shared symmetric keys
  - For those cases where the encryption algorithm does not provide integrity protection an additional MAC key and MAC algorithm
- Protection based on Password Based Encryption (PBE)
  - Key derived from password based on PKCS#5.
  - XML Encryption 1.1 element structure is used.
- Protection based on Asymmetric Keys (PKI)
  - Information about the used certificate must be included in the Key Container

Encryption of secret within the PSKC document is performed by leveraging XML Encryption.

Digital signature can be applied to the entire <KeyContainer>.

3.4 PSKC additional features

- PSKC can be used for offline Bulk provisioning of keys
  - Multiple Key Packages referencing different provisioning endpoints (devices) within a single Key Container document.

- PSKC has the ability to carry a key policy determining usage of the key in the application or the device.
  - Start & Expire Date of a key
  - Restriction on the number of key usages
  - PIN protection policy
- Registry for key usage, such as "OTP", "CR", "Encrypt" (based on NIST SP800-57 "Recommendation for Key Management" [NISTSP800-57]).

4 Conclusion

The work of the IETF 'keyprov' working group has delivered three main building blocks to allow standardised interoperable key provisioning for symmetric keys, their meta-data and related key policies. These specifications are open and royalty free to implement:

1. An online XML based protocol to allow online provisioning of symmetric keys – The Dynamic Symmetric Key Provisioning Protocol [DSKPP]
2. An XML based symmetric key payload (transport) format – Portable Symmetric Key Container [PSKC]
3. An ASN.1 based symmetric key payload (transport) format – Symmetric Key Package Content Type [SKPC]

Implementations from different vendors will be interoperable allowing for the first time to decouple securely symmetric key clients (applications/crypto modules) and provisioning servers.

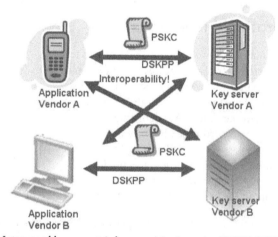

Fig 4: Interoperable symmetric key provisioning using IETF DSKPP & PSKC

Interoperable Symmetric Key Provisioning is possible using IETF 'keyprov' standards, spread the word and implement!

References

[OATH]   The Initiative for Open Authentication, In: www.openauthentication.org.

[DSKPP]   IETF: Dynamic Symmetric Key Provisioning Protocol, In: https://datatracker.ietf.org/doc/draft-ietf-keyprov-dskpp/ ,2010.

[PSKC]   IETF: Portable Symmetric Key Container, In: https://datatracker.ietf.org/doc/draft-ietf-keyprov-pskc/ ,2010.

[SKPC]   IETF: Symmetric Key Package Content Type, In: https://datatracker.ietf.org/doc/draft-ietf-keyprov-symmetrickeyformat/ 2010.

[HOTP]   IETF: HOTP: An HMAC-Based One-Time Password Algorithm, In: http://www.ietf.org/rfc/rfc4226.txt , 2005.

[NISTSP800-57] NIST: Recommendations for Key Management, In: http://csrc.nist.gov/publications/nist-pubs/800-57/sp800-57-Part1-revised2_Mar08-2007.pdf , 2007

[PSKC-PROFILES] IETF: Additional Portable Symmetric Key Container (PSKC) Algorithm Profiles, In: http://tools.ietf.org/html/draft-hoyer-keyprov-pskc-algorithm-profiles-01 , 2010.

Silicon PUFs in Practice

Patrick Koeberl · Jiangtao Li · Anand Rajan · Claire Vishik

Intel Corporation
{patrickx.koeberl | jiangtao.li | anand.rajan | claire.vishik}@intel.com

Abstract

Low cost computing devices have become a key enabler of the digital economy, supporting everyday activities such as banking, access control, and travel. These devices often present highly resource constrained environments which impede the introduction of technologies that can improve the safety of the transactions performed on them. Several approaches have been proposed which strive to enhance the security of the user application without significantly increasing the associated cost, for example foregoing the use of higher grade smart cards supporting efficient public-key cryptography. In high volume scenarios the cost saving associated with such a decision can be compelling and security is invariably compromised as a result. This paper proposes realistic scenarios for the use of silicon PUFs (Physically Unclonable Functions) to enable lower cost and more secure implementations of smartcards and similar technologies. Silicon PUFs leverage the unique manufacturing variation present on all ICs to support authentication that is conceptually similar to biometric functionality as well as the generation of cryptographic key material. We recognize that significant improvements in PUF implementation will need to be achieved in order to make the technology commercially deployable. With these improvements, we can anticipate the potential applicability of PUFs to meeting the authentication, confidentiality and integrity requirements of many everyday transactions. In addition, the volatility of PUF-based secrets offers an attractive alternative to storing cryptographic keys in non-volatile memory.

1 Introduction

Modern cryptographic methods have become a key enabler of the digital economy, supporting everyday activities such as banking, mobile communication, access control, and travel. In order to perform encryption, decryption, and authentication functions each party must store key material or other secrets securely; any compromise would result in attacks such as communication eavesdropping and impersonation. As mobile computing devices become ubiquitous it is not possible to ensure their physical security and they may become subject to attacks which attempt to extract the key material or other secrets. Such attacks can be broadly classified as passive, where the attacker uses non-invasive methods to extract keys by methods such as memory dumping, side channel attacks [KoJJ99, Koch96, BeSa97], API attacks [BmAr01] and others. Active attacks, on the other hand, are invasive and require that the attacker open a device to gain access to its internals. For large form factors, defenses against active attacks can take the form of immediate key erasure on detection of a tamper event, the canonical example being the IBM4758 [SmWe99]. However, such measures are more difficult to implement on small form factors where the cost, size, and power requirements of an active tamper response are not economical. As an example, most smartcards lack the continuous power supply required to implement key erasure on tamper (key erasure on the next power up is possible but may be too late). In general, the continued proliferation of lower power devices creates novel security challenges that have not yet been adequately addressed.

Recently, silicon PUFs (Physically Unclonable Functions) have been introduced which promise lower cost and more secure implementations of key storage and authentication functions. Silicon PUFs leverage the unique manufacturing variation present on all ICs to support biometric-like authentication functions as well as the generation of cryptographic key material. In this paper we explore some of the properties which make PUFs attractive as a replacement or augmenting technology for secure key storage and authentication functions, focusing on the issues which might arise in a real-world implementation. We also outline some of the difficulties presented by current silicon PUF implementations.

1.1 Background

Physically Unclonable Functions were introduced by Pappu [Papp01] and can be informally described as physical systems which when measured or challenged provide unique and unpredictable responses. Creating a physical copy of the PUF with an identical challenge-response behaviour is also hard, thus resulting in a structure which is unclonable even by the manufacturer. Pappu proposes a PUF implementation based on optical techniques where a transparent medium with embedded light scattering particles is 'challenged' by a laser and the resultant speckle pattern is captured to form the response. The laser interacts in a complex way with the scattering particles and produces a speckle pattern which is unique to the particular PUF instance. The implementation of optical PUFs poses some challenges particularly around the requirements for high tolerances in laser positioning with respect to the light scattering particles.

Gassend et al. introduced silicon PUFs in [GCDD02a]. Silicon PUF implementations are desirable as they leverage the CMOS manufacturing technology used to fabricate the majority of ICs today. Silicon PUFs exploit the uncontrollable manufacturing variations which are a result of IC fabrication. Manufacturing variation of parameters such as dopant concentrations and line widths manifest themselves as differences in timing behaviour between instances of the same IC. These timing differences can be measured using a suitable circuit. Ideally, a silicon PUF should not require a deviation from the normal CMOS processing steps, as well as be implementable using standard EDA design flows.

In [GCDD02a] two types of silicon PUFs are introduced which can be classified as delay-based silicon PUFs. The first example, the arbiter PUF (see Fig. 1), consists of a number of four-terminal switching elements connected in series. These pass a signal straight through or switch it to the other output terminal based on a configuration bit. The challenge for this PUF consists of a vector of configuration bits which are applied to the switch elements. A race condition is set up in the circuit by injecting a rising edge, and the faster propagation path determined by a terminating arbiter. This results in a single bit response for a particular challenge which can be scaled up to a multi-bit vector by duplicating the circuit.

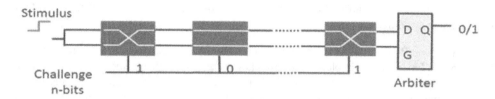

Fig. 1: Arbiter PUF

The second delay-based PUF, based on ring oscillators, uses a circuit construct already in common use as an IC test and characterisation mechanism. The ring oscillator (see Fig. 2) is a self oscillating delay loop commonly constructed from inverters. In the ring oscillator PUF the frequencies of logically identical ring oscillators are compared to produce a single response bit. The operating frequency of the ring oscillators will be influenced by manufacturing variation and the frequency difference between two oscillators can be measured using a counter. A single response bit can thus be generated for a pair of oscillators.

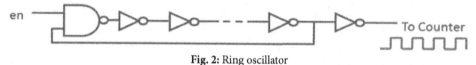

Fig. 2: Ring oscillator

In [GKST07], Guajardo et al. introduce a new PUF type. Here the power-up state of uninitialised 6T SRAM cells is used as the PUF response. The challenge in this case can be considered to be a set of SRAM addresses. The storage mechanism in an SRAM cell consists of a pair of cross-coupled inverters which have one of two stable states after power-up. Which state the cell enters is largely determined by the relative characteristics of the inverters, which in turn is influenced by manufacturing variation. This type of PUF can be classed a cross-coupled PUF and has inspired a number of alternatives based on the cross-coupled primitive. The first of these, the butterfly PUF [KGM+08] uses cross-coupled latches within an FPGA in a similar fashion. The motivation behind the butterfly PUF is to work around a limitation which prevents an SRAM PUF implementation in FPGA architectures where SRAM is initialised automatically on configuration.

In fact, any digital storage element constructed from static logic will use a cross-coupled structure as its basis and one can envisage cross-coupled PUFs based on the many flip-flop and latch variants. An example of a cross-coupled PUF based on D-type flip-flops can be found in [MaTV08]. In the years since the introduction of the PUF concept by Pappu, the PUF landscape has widened considerably with proposals for PUFs based on a wide variety of physical phenomena and materials including IC coatings [TSS+06], acoustics [Vrij04], radio frequency signatures [DeKi07] and phosphors [JiCh08]. The PUF landscape continues to widen.

1.2 The Focus of This Paper

PUFs exhibit a range of potentially attractive properties that make them a potential replacement for current authentication, confidentiality and integrity mechanisms. However, a cost benefit analysis of PUF deployments in the context of real world use cases has not been consistently carried out, with the PUF literature thus far focusing on theory, architecture and implementation at the PUF level. While many researchers make conjectures concerning the use of PUFs, the assumptions made are mostly theoretical, and even the first PUF products on the market focus on the possibility of an implementation more than they focus on certain realistic uses of PUFs that are compelling. The main contribution of this paper is to examine silicon PUFs in the context of potential applications and explore the requirements for silicon PUF deployments that will make the technology attractive for larger scale commercialization. We will restrict our definition of silicon PUF to apply to those silicon PUFs that are implementable in standard CMOS processes using digital design flows.

2 PUF Properties

A consistent view of what constitutes a PUF from the formal standpoint does not exist at this point in the literature although there have been some previous attempts [Papp01, GCDD02a, GKST07]. In [RuSS09] the existing definitions are reviewed and an appraisal of some of the shortcomings given. Noting the difficulties with developing a formal PUF definition, we will restrict ourselves to the following informal description:

A Physically Unclonable Function is the physical embodiment of a function which reacts with a response when a stimulus is applied. The stimulus C and response R are termed a challenge-response pair (CRP). A PUF may possess one or more CRPs.

It is assumed that:

1. Given a challenge C the probability of predicting the response R to that challenge is negligible.
2. The response R to a challenge C reveals negligible information on the response R' to challenge C'.
3. It is practically infeasible to construct a copy of the PUF which exhibits the same challenge-response behaviour i.e. it should be physically unclonable even by the original manufacturer.

As we will see, silicon PUF implementations deviate from the above definition and requirements in a number of ways which impact the security properties of the PUF and the system embedding it. For many applications, PUFs must be combined with additional functionality, increasing the total cost of a PUF-based solution. On the other hand, such a solution may have significantly enhanced security properties justifying the increased cost.

2.1 Noise

All known PUF implementations exhibit non-ideal reproducibility; the PUF response to a challenge is noisy. In silicon PUFs, this noise is a result of environmental factors such as power supply and temperature fluctuations. Errors may also be introduced by the PUF measurement strategy. For example, since it is not possible to construct a metastability free arbiter in the asynchronous domain [KiWo76], the arbiter PUF's response will be random or highly biased for those challenges which fall within the 'window of uncertainty' of the arbiter.

For most applications the noisy nature of the PUF response requires a post-processing step with the goal of producing a noise-free output with a uniform distribution. The generation of cryptographic keys is an example. What is required is an error correcting code similar in nature to the forward error correction schemes commonly used in telecommunications engineering, whereby redundant data is added allowing for errors to be detected and corrected within some bound. For cryptographic applications, it is important that the redundant information or helper data have the additional property that it reveals no information about the PUF response, since if it were to do so it would imply a secure storage requirement for the helper data. Dodis et al. introduced *fuzzy extractors* in [DORS08] to meet this secure error correction requirement.

The fuzzy extractor consists of two algorithms, *enrolment* where the noisy PUF response is measured and the helper data generated. The helper data does not reveal any information about the PUF and can be stored in the clear. The second algorithm, *reconstruction* takes a noisy PUF measurement together with the helper data and reconstructs a noise free response. The fuzzy extractor must be sized such that it can correct for the expected noise level of the PUF. In practice the long term stability of the PUF must be taken into consideration with aging effects as electromigration, hot carrier injection and negative bias temperature instability (NBTI) being of particular importance for silicon PUFs.

2.2 Challenge-Response Space

An important aspect of a PUF is the size of the challenge-response space it possesses. For the silicon PUFs under consideration, Table 1 shows the number of challenges exhibited. The size of the challenge response space has a number of implications for the PUF itself and the system enclosing the PUF. From the perspective of emulating a PUF it is clear that possessing an exponential number of challenges is preferable; this prevents the emulation of the PUF by way of a lookup table. This property is also important for some PUF applications, as we will see later PUF-based lightweight authentication requires a large challenge-response space. PUF types which exhibit a polynomial number of challenges (or just one challenge) may be used for the generation of secrets, such as cryptographic keys, and impose a hard requirement for supporting error correction and cryptographic functions which must reside locally to the PUF. This strongly influences the security assumptions that must be made on the system enclosing the PUF.

Table 1: Number of available challenges for silicon PUFs

	PUF Type	Number of Challenges	Notes
Delay	Arbiter	2^c	c = number of challenge bits. The number of independent responses is polynomially bounded.
	Ring Oscillator	1	
Cross-coupled	Flip-flop	1	
	SRAM	1	

2.3 Unpredictability

For an ideal PUF, the probability of an attacker correctly predicting the PUF response to a given challenge is negligible even if the attacker has access to a set of previously used CRPs (assuming the PUF possesses more than one CRP). It was shown early on that this does not hold for the arbiter PUF [GLC+04], where a numerical modelling attack against the arbiter PUF was shown to be feasible using machine learning techniques. In a modelling attack a relatively small number of CRPs is used to build a model capable of emulating the PUF challenge-response behaviour for any challenge. Clearly, this is an unsatisfactory situation for any application built on top of such a PUF. Various modifications to the basic arbiter circuit have been proposed, based on introducing nonlinearities into the circuit [GLC+04, SuDe07]. However, many of these have also been shown to be susceptible to modelling attacks [RuSS10]. Another approach to hardening the arbiter PUF against such attacks is to place a non-linear function such as a hash before the PUF, correcting the noisy PUF output with an error correction unit and placing a hash function on the output. This approach is termed a controlled PUF [GCDD02b]. Such an approach increases the security assumptions that must be made about the new construct, for example the communication pathways between PUF and hash units must be assumed to be secure. It is assumed that the PUF and hash units can be somehow physically intertwined to increase the resistance to an invasive attacker; in practice this is unlikely since the arbiter PUF has very strict routing requirements.

For cross-coupled PUFs, such as the SRAM and Flip-flop PUFs purely model building attacks are not relevant since they have only one challenge. Although both PUF types exhibit a bias at the bit level to 0 or 1, when large numbers of bits are combined into the single response using post processing [MaTV08] the output is effectively random and unpredictable.

2.4 Physical Unclonabilty

The PUF property of physical unclonabilty is sometimes termed *manufacturer resistance*. It is assumed that even the manufacturer of the system containing the PUF cannot create another instance of the system with the same PUF challenge-response behaviour. For some contexts, this is a reasonable assumption, as in the case of a deliberate silicon manufacturing overrun intended to produce unlicensed copies of a device. Here the embedded PUF guarantees that each instance is unique in terms of its PUF challenge-response characteristics. When contrasted with classical methods of silicon product serialisation, for instance one-time programmable (OTP) or many-time programmable (MTP) fuses, the advantage offered by a PUF-based solution is clear since it is not possible to clone a device by programming or reprogramming the fuses.

The feasibility of other attack types should be considered. Although the PUF itself may be physically unclonable, it may be possible to emulate the PUF with a simple table approach if the attacker can exhaustively read out all PUF responses. Clearly the exponential number of challenges possessed by the arbiter PUF makes such an attack intractable. However, the ring oscillator PUF is vulnerable, as are the cross-coupled PUF types. Emulation attacks using a PUF model derived from a subset of CRPs as described above are another route to cloning a PUF.

2.5 Tamper Evidence

The tendency of a PUF to substantially change its challenge response behaviour in response to an invasive attempt to analyse its structure i.e. to be *tamper evident* is assumed in much of the PUF literature [GKST07, KGM+08, RuSS09, AMS+09]. Experimental results of a focussed ion beam (FIB) attack on a coating PUF are reported in [TSS+06], however this remains an isolated case and is not relevant to the purely silicon PUFs under consideration here. While it is conceivable that any direct probing or damage to a silicon PUF's structure would change its challenge-response behaviour, it is unlikely that an attacker would choose this route in a real-world attack. It is more likely that an invasive attacker would focus on the functionality downstream of the PUF such as the error correction unit or attempt to intercept a PUF derived cryptographic key at the point of use, for example at a decryption unit. Moreover for the silicon PUFs under consideration here, the tamper evidence claim assumes that an attacker will choose the *frontside* of the die as the entry point. *Backside* techniques where the entry point is through the die substrate are widely used in silicon debug and failure analysis applications and allow access to circuit nodes without disturbing the metallisation layers which define the device interconnect. When combined with probing technologies such as Time Resolved Emission (TRE) [SSH+05] and E-beam Probing (EBP) [SLK+07], the backside approach enables circuit analysis with minimal or zero impact on the node under observation.

Finally, the sensitivity of a PUF to direct i.e. mechanical probing may be less than expected due to implementation side-effects. In the case of the ring oscillator PUF proposed reliability enhancement techniques such as only choosing oscillator pairs whose frequencies are far apart [SuDe07], decrease the PUFs sensitivity to the electrical load imposed by a mechanical probe. Similarly, if an attempt were made to characterise the timing of the delay elements comprising the arbiter a subset of the CR space might be unaffected, specifically those timing paths which have differences larger than the load imposed by the probe. It is worth noting that the arbiter PUF inherently places a lower limit on the timing differences it is capable of resolving due to the 'window of uncertainty' imposed by the arbiter implementation, typically a synchronous element such as a level sensitive latch or D-type flip-flop. To summarise it cannot be assumed that PUFs are inherently tamper evident; they may only be tamper evident within the scope of a specific threat model, for example one which excludes backside attacks using non-mechanical probing techniques.

2.6 Area Efficiency

Area efficiency is an important aspect of any hardware implementation and has received little attention in the PUF literature. As noted above, other factors will strongly influence the selection of a particular silicon PUF type for an application, particularly the size of the challenge response space. However, it is instructive to compare the area efficiency of silicon PUFs in terms of the number of transistors required to generate one raw bit of response as shown in Table 2. This is a lower bound on the number of transistors required as it neglects the area overhead of PUF measurement circuitry, SRAM row/column decoders, error correction, etc. Transistor counts are based on typical standard cell and SRAM transistor counts (12 for a two input multiplexer, 24 for a D-type flip-flop).

Taking each PUF's challenge response space into account (Table 1), it is clear that the exponential number of challenges exhibited by the arbiter PUF has a considerable hardware cost. The additional cost of any supporting logic such as error correction and cryptographic functions is not considered here. The question of whether the hardware resources used to construct the silicon PUF can be reused for other purposes should be considered. In the case of the cross-coupled PUFs (SRAM and flip-flop) if the PUF response is required only once during the runtime of the system, then it is conceivable that the resources concerned could be reused for other purposes thus increasing the area efficiency of these silicon PUF types.

Table 2: Area efficiency of silicon PUFs

	PUF Type	Area Efficiency (transistors/ raw response bit)
Delay	Arbiter	$24N_{challenge\text{-}bits}$
	Ring Oscillator	$4N_{inverter\text{-}stages}$
Cross-coupled	Flip-flop	24
	SRAM	6

3 PUF Applications

PUF-based solutions have been proposed for many problems including anti-counterfeiting [DSP+08], device authentication and secure key storage [SuDe07] as well as IP protection [GKST07]. All silicon PUF applications hinge on the ability to convert the inherent manufacturing variation present on silicon devices into one or more unique digital secrets. We will divide the silicon PUFs into two classes; those possessing a very large number of CRPs and those possessing a single CRP. This distinction is important since it defines whether the PUF is simply functioning as a secure storage mechanism for a single secret or in the other case enabling applications based on the ability to store a very large number of secrets in an area efficient manner.

3.1 Large Challenge-Response Space PUFs

Of the silicon PUFs considered in this paper, only the arbiter PUF exhibits an exponential number of challenges. It should be noted that the number of independent CRPs that the arbiter possesses will not be exponential, since the information content of a physical system is polynomially related to the volume. For a discussion of this point see [RuSS09]. Nevertheless, possessing large numbers of CRPs is an interesting property which potentially enable a class of lightweight (at the PUF side) applications.

3.1.1 Lightweight PUF Authentication

The ability to authenticate a device in a low-cost and secure manner is a requirement for many applications. In particular, resource constrained environments such as passive RFID tags, have stringent power and area budgets where the cost of cryptographic authentication methods may exceed power and area budgets. In [SuDe07], a low cost authentication scheme is proposed which leverages PUFs to implement a challenge-response authentication protocol. In this scheme, the manufacturer or a trusted third party applies a set of randomly chosen challenges to the device containing the PUF and records the responses in a secure database. The device then enters the untrusted supply chain. At a later date, in order to verify the authenticity of the device, the verifier selects a challenge from the database, applies it to the device to be authenticated and compares the stored response with that of the device. If they match the device is authentic. Challenges and responses can be sent in the clear, however, once used, a challenge must be removed from the database in order to prevent man-in-the-middle attacks.

There are a number of constraints that this scheme places on the PUF and the overall system. The deployed PUF must exhibit a large number of CRPs, since CRPs are discarded after use. The ring oscillator PUF is probably ruled out on these grounds, and cross-coupled PUFs with single challenges are excluded. In practice only the arbiter PUF meets this requirement with its exponential number of challenges. Also, since silicon PUF responses are noisy, they require error correction. In the lightweight authentication scheme considered here, this functionality could be implemented at the verifier, it is not a requirement to have error correction local to the PUF.

The requirement for a secure database of potentially large numbers of CRPs is likely to be the most serious impediment to the adoption of this authentication scheme. For a high volume application the number of CRPs required is likely to be prohibitive. While it is conceivable that a smaller number of CRPs be stored and then the database refreshed, such an approach may not be suitable for some applications. In addition, the online nature of the authentication scheme places constraints on database availability.

Finally, the vulnerability of the arbiter PUF to modelling attacks as discussed in the previous section is a serious weakness for any protocol that transmits challenges and responses in the clear. While the secure database requirement may be acceptable for a particular application, the risk of a modelling attack places serious doubts on any implementation of such an authentication scheme.

3.1.2 Controlled PUFs

Some of the shortcomings discussed above are addressed by the controlled PUF concept introduced in [GCDD02b]. Here, a PUF (with a large challenge-response space) is improved by placing a hash function in front of the PUF in order to prevent a chosen-challenge attack. To decouple the controlled PUF's outputs from the actual PUF responses, a hash function is placed on the outputs after noise removal by an error correction unit. These additions serve to increase the controlled PUF's resistance to model building attacks.

A number of protocols are defined in [GCDD02b] which allow a shared secret to be established between the device embedding the controlled PUF and a remote user, enabling applications such as certified execution and smartcard authentication. A complete implementation of these protocols requires the presence of a trusted third party and supplemental asymmetric encryption and MAC functions.

Clearly, a controlled PUF implementation cannot be considered 'lightweight' as area and power budgets must be increased to accommodate the additional functionality. Since the overall security no longer only relies on the security properties of the underlying PUF, the number of security assumptions that must be made is increased. Computational assumptions on the security of the cryptographic primitives used to implement the controlled PUF and the protocols built on them must be made. In addition the resistance of these primitives to side channel and invasive attacks must be considered.

3.2 Single CRP PUFs

The ring oscillator PUF and cross-coupled PUFs (SRAM and flip-flop) effectively possess a single CRP. This precludes their use in any protocol requiring large numbers of CRPs such as the lightweight authentication scheme presented above. However, the requirement to store a secret (or key) securely is a feature of all modern cryptosystems and these PUF types find application as secure key storage mechanisms where the single response is used as the secret. Note that it is possible to use an arbiter PUF in a single challenge mode; however this would not be an efficient use of silicon area (see Table 2).

3.2.1 PUF Based Secure Key Storage

Secure key storage using PUFs is implemented using a small challenge-response space PUF and an error correction unit to correct the noisy PUF response. The resulting secret can then be used to enable an overlying traditional cryptosystem. The value of a PUF derived secret is that it is not present in a digital form on the device embedding the PUF when power is absent. It is volatile in this sense. Furthermore, it is possible to ensure that the secret is only derived from the PUF when required (for example by clearing it from any temporary storage after use). This is in contrast to storing secrets in non-volatile memory such as fuses or floating-gate memories (EEPROM, flash) where the secrets remain in digital form even when the device is powered off. Secrets stored in this fashion may be more vulnerable to an invasive attack; the PUF-based solution thus raises the effort level for an attacker.

As an example, a device authentication application is conceivable where the PUF derived secret is known to the verifier who stores the secret in a secure database. The verifier then executes a symmetric authentication protocol on the basis of the shared secret. Such an application has some of the drawbacks of the lightweight authentication scheme outline above i.e. it requires a secure, available database. Moving to a model where the PUF secret is used to implement a secure key store rather than using the secret directly enables a much wider range of applications. The secret might be used to decrypt the private portion of an asymmetric key pair or a set of issued conditional access keys (the key pair or keys would have been previously encrypted during the enrolment phase of the PUF). Such a secure key store could be implemented with a PUF and error correction unit in combination with a symmetric encryption unit and non-volatile memory serving as the key store.

The security of a PUF based secure key store is subject to the same assumptions as the controlled PUF above i.e. computational assumptions on the security of the cryptographic primitives as well as assumptions on the resistance of these primitives (and the communication pathways between them) to side channel and invasive attacks.

4 Conclusions

In this paper, two PUF applications have been analyzed, a lightweight authentication scheme using PUFs possessing many CRPs and a secure key storage application using PUFs with a single CRP. Of these, the secure key storage application appears promising for currently known silicon PUFs. PUF based secure key storage enables a wide range of solutions, but also increases the security assumptions that must be made on the system embedding the PUF. In this context the value of a PUF deployment is related to volatility of the PUF derived secret which is only present in digital form when the device is powered up. This raises the effort level of the invasive attacker in that he must mount the attack on a functional, running part. Assuming the key is generated only when required adds a temporal requirement; the attacker must also intercept the key at the correct time adding to the complexity of the attack.

The promise of PUFs to provide security based on the high physical complexity of the structure implementing the PUF with minimal additional assumptions remains attractive. The arbiter PUF exhibits some of the required features, but its vulnerability to modelling attacks precludes its use in practical applications. Further research to identify large challenge-response space PUFs that are more resistant to modelling attacks is required.

We conclude that, while theoretical examination of PUFs needs to be considered, more work focusing on practical usages is required to ensure greater probability for the commercialization of PUF applications.

References

[KoJJ99]   Kocher, P., Jaffe, J., Jun, B.: Differential power analysis. In CRYPTO '99. LNCS, vol. 1666, Springer, 1999, p. 388–397.

[Koch96]   Kocher, P.: Timing attacks on implementations of Diffie-Hellman, RSA, DSS and other systems. In CRYPTO '96. LNCS, vol. 1109, Springer, 1996, p. 104–113.

[BeSa97]   Biham, E. and Shamir A.: Differential Fault Analysis of Secret Key Cryptosystems. In CRYTPO '97. Springer, 1997.

[BmAr01]   Bond M. and Anderson R.: API-Level Attacks on Embedded Systems. Computer, vol. 29, 2001, p. 67–75.

[SmWe99]   Smith, S.W. and Weingart, S.H. 1999. Building a high-performance, programmable secure co-processor. Computer Networks (Special Issue on Computer Network Security) 31, 8 (Apr.), 831–860.

[Papp01]   Pappu, R.S.: Physical one-way functions. PhD. Thesis, Massachusetts Institute of Technology, March 2001.

[GCDD02a] Gassend, B., Clarke, D., van Dijk, M., Devadas, S.: Silicon physical random functions. In Proceedings of the 9th ACM Conference on Computer and Communications Security. 2002.

[GKST07]   Guajardo, J., Kumar S., Schrijen, G., Tuyls, P.: FPGA intrinsic PUFs and their use for IP protection, CHES, 2007.

[KGM+08]   Kumar, S.S., Guajardo, J., Maes, R., Schrijen, G.-J., Tuyls, P.: The Butterfly PUF: Protecting IP on every FPGA. In IEEE International Workshop on Hardware- Oriented Security and Trust, HOST 2008, p. 67-70.

[MaTV08]   Maes, R., Tuyls, P., Verbauwhede I.: Intrinsic PUFs from Flip-flops on Reconfigurable Devices, In 3rd Benelux Workshop on Information and System Security (WISSec 2008). 2008.

[TSS+06]   Tuyls, P., Schrijen G.-J., Škorić, B., van Geloven, J., Verhaegh, N., Wolters, R.: Read-proof hardware from protective coatings, Cryptographic Hardware and Embedded Systems Workshop, 2006.

[Vrij04]   Vrijaldenhoven, S.: Acoustical Physical Uncloneable Functions. Master's Thesis, T.U.Eindhoven, 2004.

[DeKi07]   DeJean, G., and Kirovski, D.: RF-DNA: Radio-Frequency Certificates of Authenticity. CHES, 2007.

[JiCh08]   Jiang, D., and Chong, C.N.: Anti-counterfeiting using phosphor PUF, ASID, 2008.

[RuSS09]   Ruhrmair, U., Solter, J., Sehnke, F.: On the foundations of physical unclonable functions. In: Cryptology ePrint Archive Report 277, 2009.

[KiWo76]   Kinniment, D.J., Woods, J.V.: Synchronisation and arbitration circuits in digital systems. In Proc IEE, Vol 123, No 10, 1976, p. 961 - 966.

[DORS08] Dodis, Y., Ostrovsky, R., Reyzin, L., Smith, A. 2008. Fuzzy Extractors: How to Generate Strong Keys from Biometrics and Other Noisy Data. SIAM J. Comput. 38, 1, 2008, p. 97-139.

[GLC+04] Gassend, B., Lim, D., Clarke, D., van Dijk, M., Devadas, S. 2004. Identification and authentication of integrated circuits: Research Articles. Concurr. Comput. : Pract. Exper. 16, 11, 2004, p. 1077-1098.

[SuDe07] Suh, G.E. and Srinivas Devadas, S.: Physical Unclonable Functions for Device Authentication and Secret Key Generation. DAC 2007, p. 9-14.

[RuSS10] Ruhrmair, U., Solter, J., Sehnke, F.: Modeling Attacks on Physical Unclonable Functions, In Cryptology ePrint Archive: Report 2010/251, Tech. Rep.

[GCDD02b] Gassend, B., Clarke, D., van Dijk, M., Devadas, S.: Controlled Physical Random Functions. In: 18th Annual Computer Security Applications Conference, 2002, p. 149.

[AMS+09] Armknecht, F., Maes, R., Sadeghi, A., Sunar, B., Tuyls, P.: PUF-PRFs: A New Tamper-resilient Cryptographic Primitive. In Advances in Cryptology - EUROCRYPT 2009, Poster Session, V. Immler, and C. Wolf (eds.), 2009, p. 96-102

[SSH+05] Stellari, F., Song, P., Hryckowian, J., Torreiter, O.A., Wilson, S., Wu, P., Tosi, A.: Characterization of a 0.13 um CMOS Link Chip using Time Resolved Emission (TRE), In Proc. of European Symposium on Reliability of Electron Devices, Failure Physics and Analysis (ESREF), Arcachon, France, 2005, p. 1550-1553.

[SLK+07] Schlangen, R., Leihkauf, R., Kerst, U., Boit, C., Kruger, B.: Functional IC analysis through chip backside with nano scale resolution - E-beam probing in FIB trenches to STI level, In 14th International Symposium on Physical and Failure Analysis of Integrated Circuits, 2007, p. 35-38.

[DSP+08] Devadas, S., Suh, E., Paral, S., Sowell, R., Ziola, T. Khandelwal, V.: Design and Implementation of PUF-Based "Unclonable" RFID ICs for Anti-Counterfeiting and Security Applications. In: IEEE International Conference on RFID, 2008, p. 58-64.

Biometrics and
Technical Solutions

Visa Applications in TG Biometrics for Public Sector Applications

Dr. Sibylle Hick[1] · Fares Rahmun[2] · Ernest Hammerschmidt[3]

[1,3]secunet Security Networks AG, Kronprinzenstrasse 30, 45128 Essen
{sibylle.hick | ernest.hammerschmidt}@secunet.com

[2]Bundesverwaltungsamt, 50735 Köln
fares.rahmun@bva.bund.de

Abstract

The application, issuance and usage of modern electronic identity documents that are connected to biometric data is only possible after a complex process of requirements and regulations has been carried out together with the establishment of a respective infrastructure. Although different governmental eID documents are connected to various requirements, the structure and approach of the modus operandi is quite similar. Therefore, synergistic effects can be used to represent the processes connected to these documents.

In Germany, the Federal Office for Information Security has published a Technical Guideline "Biometrics for Public Sector Applications" that encloses requirements, recommendations, and best practices to design processes for the handling of the afore described documents within the context of biometrics. Not only electronic documents but also different applications have to be considered. As a result, a number of Application Profiles have been provided covering these circumstances. The description is based on experiences that were gained in several projects: e.g. the introduction of electronic passports in 2005, the preparation of new electronic national identity cards in Germany, and the experiences gained in the European BioDEV II pilot project for Visa which has been carried out to prepare the central European Visa Information System.

1 Introduction

Introducing new identity documents connected to biometric data, such as e.g. electronic passports (ePassports) in Europe, the new German national identity card, and furthermore visa and electronic residence permits, is a comprehensive and challenging task. Several perspectives as well as a great number of requirements have to be considered on an organisational, technical, and legal level. Agreements have to be made with the target groups; involved processes and the underlying infrastructure have to be adjusted.

In order to develop a common theme and satisfy all different requirements the German Federal Office for Information Security (BSI) has published a number of technical guidelines. For issues concerning biometrics the technical guideline "Technical Guideline TR-03121 Biometrics for Public Sector Applications" [TR_03121] (TG Biometrics) has been developed and published together with a Conformance Test Specification [TR_03122] each consisting of three parts. These documents combine the requirements and recommendations that are relevant for a specific target group in a modular and structured way. After a short overview of the overall process and further general details the respective party can easily obtain the relevant information.

In this contribution the objectives within the scope of application for a biometric visa are described in section 2 against the background of the technical guideline TG Biometrics [TR_03121]. Afterwards the structure and approach of this guideline are part of section 3. In order to promote reusability, investment security, flexibility, and interoperability a software architecture had to be designed that is able to support all of the afore listed requirements. Therefore, a detailed overview regarding a flexible software architecture is given in section 4. A deeper insight in the approach can be achieved by looking at an example that shows how requirements of the relevant public sector applications are included for biometric visa. This is done in section 5 where experiences from the European pilot project BioDEV II have been taken into account. Finally, a conclusion is given in the last section.

2 Objectives

The association of biometric data with electronic identity documents faces several challenges. A very important part is the acquisition of biometric features within enrolment in order to achieve a uniform and adequate quality of data. It is a precondition in order to apply biometrics in different public sector applications e.g. identification and/or verification in border control scenarios. While ePassports in Europe and the German national identity card store the biometric features in the electronic identity document itself, the visa data including the bio-metric data is stored within a central Visa Information System (VIS) which is operated together with a Biometric Matching System (BMS). Besides quality issues, time needed for the acquisition of fingerprints of an applicant is also an important factor, in particular when it comes to optimised and user friendly processes. Quality and time constraints are in general opposed factors that have to be considered when requirements and recommendations shall be expressed.

Furthermore, addressing the different kinds of involved target groups, such as vendors of hardware and software components, public authorities as well as agencies and integrators is crucial, because the functions and perspective have to be distinguished in such a way that it is obvious to the entities what is relevant to them.

In order to apply an uniform approach the underlying software architecture shall build a solid framework that allows to integrate different kinds of identity documents and public sector applications dealing with biometrics at the same time. Interfaces shall be specified that allow a high flexibility, interoperability, and protection of investment. Thereby, well established international and national standards shall be taken into account. As a consequence, certification procedures and conformity testing can be established for hardware and software components.

3 Overview of the TG Biometrics

As described before, requirements regarding the documents in combination with public sector applications need to be described in a structured but at the same time modular and independent way because different kinds of hardware and software components are used for each specific context. Additionally, organisations and vendors may only be interested in a defined set of requirements regarding their application environment.

Therefore, a three-part document was developed. The motivation, objectives and a manual are introduced in a framework document of the technical guideline which can be found in part 1 of the TG Biometrics.

Furthermore the concept of Application Profiles (AP) and Function Modules (FM) was chosen. An Application Profile encloses a specific use case. In part 2 all Application Profiles can be found that have been specified so far for the respective electronic identity document. Before all technical details are presented, a short introduction and a process overview considering the biometric features are given. An AP is structured as follows:

- Introduction (legal requirements)
- Process overview
- Target audience
- Software Architecture Overview
- Relevant standards and conditions
- Information regarding the Function Modules

Based on the Application Profile, all relevant requirements and recommendations can be assigned to logical units which are called Function Modules (FMs). The advantage of this approach is in particular that e.g. a hardware vendor does not need to analyse all requirements as being relevant to the product, but can directly select the requirements specified for the hardware. Furthermore, the partitioning into small units allows applying the set of requirements in different kinds of APs whenever possible. Biometric features, such as facial images and fingerprints, are considered separately. While the Function Modules are listed in part 3 like in a reference book, it is the objective of part 2 to identify at first all relevant Function Modules and list those for the reader. As a consequence, an organisation that wants to identify the relevant Function Modules can do so by obtaining this information from a mapping table at the end of each AP. At the end of part 2 of TG Biometrics, an overall mapping table is presented containing all assignments made so far for all APs and all documents.

In the mapping tables the assignment between AP and FMs is made based on unique identifiers which are composed of three parts. The first part characterises the abbreviation of the Function Module e.g. COD represents FM Coding. For visa this means that the FM Coding describes how the biometric feature has to be coded together with the respective quality information in order to be processed later on. The second part of the identifier addresses the biometric feature, where FP was chosen for fingerprint and PH was selected as representation for a biometric photo. The last part of the Function Module characterises the use case, e.g. the enrolment of ten fingerprints within a visa application (VAPP). As a result the identifier COD-FP-VAPP describes the coding requirements that have to be followed if fingerprints shall be coded for the application of visa while COD-PH-VAPP describes the same for the coding of a facial image.

After a user has analysed which Function Modules are relevant to his product or application the detailed technical or organisational information can be found in part 3 of TG Biometrics by referencing the unique identifiers. Thereby, a Function Module combines all requirements, recommendations, and best practices for a special defined unit within the complete process. The classification of Function Modules was carried out based on different products that are already available on the market. In general, a FM Process describes the work flow and sequence in which the according FMs need to be applied. In the case of fingerprint acquisition this can also mean that FMs are called several times because due to quality assurance reasons a fingerprint of each hand is captured three times. At the moment Function Modules have been identified for the following areas:

- Process
- Acquisition Hardware
- Acquisition Software
- Biometric Image Processing
- Quality Assurance
- Compression
- Coding
- Reference Storage
- Logging
- Evaluation
- Operation
- User Interface

4 Software Architecture

The requirements that are defined by different Function Modules have to be implemented by the respective hardware and software components. As shown in section 2, electronic identity documents are used in different applications. Thus, a uniform approach for the underlying software architecture has to be chosen. The concept of the Software Architecture is described in section 2 of part 2 within TG Biometrics and is based in particular on proven international standards. It allows the possibility to offer standardised interfaces for the different applications and at the same time manage the different hardware technologies that are used. Furthermore, the scope of applications of the different involved parties can be clearly defined within the respective APs.

The Software Architecture that is described in this article is based in particular on the ISO standard BioAPI 2.0 [ISO_19784-1] (and [ISO_19784-4] is considered as a future possibility) allowing biometrics to be integrated in different kinds of applications such as enrolment, verification and/ or identification. The idea behind the software architecture is to encapsulate the biometric functions in a way that the developer of the application simply requests the biometric data through defined interfaces. The software and/or hardware vendor on the other side has to provide the biometric functions and has to comply with the respective comprehensive requirements. This is achieved through a three layer software architecture. On the upper layer the governmental public sector application, e.g. application of biometric visa, is provided. The middle layer is represented by a BioAPI 2.0 framework and can be understood as a high-level C-API that connects the upper and the lower layer. On the lower layer the biometric functions are encapsulated in Biometric Service Providers (BSPs). For every biometric feature a separate BSP shall be considered. The enrolment for a biometric visa would thus be realised using two BSPs. One to obtain a facial image and another BSP to capture up to ten fingerprints. The application can access the relevant biometric data by implementing a defined set of BioAPI interfaces (BioAPI_*) that allow to obtain the data from the according BSP over the BioAPI 2.0 framework. The framework manages the different BSPs which have to provide specific interfaces (BioSPI_*) for this. An overview of the software architecture for the example "Application for Biometric Visa" is given in figure 1.

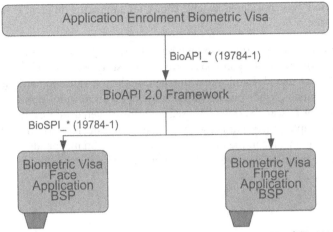

Fig. 1: Software Architecture of the Application for Biometric Visa [TR_03121]

5 Introducing Visa applications in the TR Biometrics

In Europe a new generation of short-stay visas will be introduced which feature the use of biometric data. European Regulation No 767/2008 [EC-767-2008] has been published establishing a central Visa Information System (VIS) which works together with a Biometric Matching System (BMS). The acquisition and central storage of all available fingerprints of almost every visa applicant is connected to a number of requirements and will change the already existing processes for visa significantly.

In order to learn more about these requirements and to gain experiences on how the new processes can be designed in an adequate way, the European Commission has initiated the pilot project BioDEV II (Biometric Data Experimented in Visas). The German federal government has taken the opportunity to gain comprehensive experiences from the secure acquisition (i.e. enrolment) to verification at border control by taking part in the project and implementing the complete process. The enrolment was tested at the German consulates in Damascus (Syria) and Ulan Bator (Mongolia). Verification of the issued biometric visa was then conducted in Germany at the airports Berlin-Schoenefeld and Berlin-Tegel. For the purpose of verification and identification the German Federal Office of Administration (BVA) operated a national VIS. In order to successfully pass through the complete process, it has been important to identify consistent requirements and recommendations for the acquisition and decision about the quality of biometric data. In particular, the contradicting constraints time, quality assurance, and usability had to be taken into account.

BioDEV II consisted of two phases. During the first phase a basic version of an enrolment client software was used at the consular posts. This solution provided only basic quality assurance mechanisms using the NIST NFIQ fingerprint quality algorithm and involved the operators in the decision whether the quality of captured fingerprints was sufficient. The performance of the system was measured both with respect to the fingerprint quality achieved and the time needed to process a visa application. Quality was determined using the Sagem Kit 4 QA solution which will be used in the central European VIS. As this system will determine which standards to meet, using this algorithm was considered a viable choice for comparing different enrolment applications and processes.

The basic enrolment scenario resulted in high rejection rates of up to 82% (cf. Fig 2). In order to improve system performance a second phase was set up testing two different advanced enrolment clients. These clients differed technically with regard to the software and hardware features used for quality improvement. While one client made use of hardware auto-capture capabilities provided by the fingerprint scanner, the other used software-triggered auto-capture. Both processes involved multiple slap captures and the generation of composite records. In order to determine which fingerprints to include in the final set, one client relied on independent quality assurance mechanisms, while the other used a technique known as cross-matching.

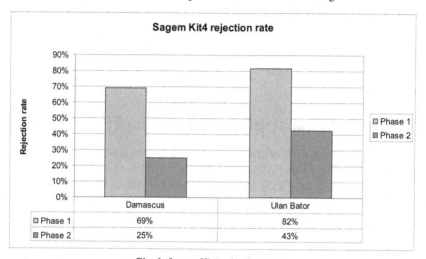

Fig. 2: Sagem Kit4 rejection rates

Among other parameters, the study also evaluated the impact of different segmentation and quality-assurance algorithms, both open-source and vendor specific, as well as possible correlations between their decisions.

Apart from technical considerations, organisational efforts also played an important role during the pilot project. Posters were designed and produced that supported the applicant and the official during the enrolment process and helped identifying and preventing typical mistakes. Tools were provided that allowed to influence the image quality if the applicant had wet or dry fingers. The results of the different mechanisms were logged and analysed afterwards.

Both improved enrolment scenarios showed a massively better performance with regard to fingerprint quality. Kit 4 rejection rates dropped to 43% and 25% in Ulan Bator and Damascus, respectively. After Sagem had introduced a new version of the Kit 4 algorithm, rejection rates even went down to about 3%. Still, the more sophisticated processes also took their time. Enrolment duration increased significantly compared to the first project phase (cf. Fig 3).

The experiences that were gathered during the enrolment processes in the BioDEV II pilot form a solid base to describe well-engineered requirements, recommendations, and best practices within the scope of TG Biometrics. Considering the structure of the technical guideline (as described in section 3) TG-03121-2 has been extended by an additional section describing the Application Profiles for Biometric Visa. At first the enrolment process has been considered in the subsection "Application for Biometric Visa". During the BioDEV II pilot project it has been discovered that logging and evaluation are very powerful mechanisms enabling member states and the European Commission to assess the performance of their respective systems. In particular, if errors occur or results seem not to be feasible, adequate data is available that allows suitable counteraction. Thus, requirements and recommendations regarding logging and evaluation have been described while also considering data privacy at the same time.

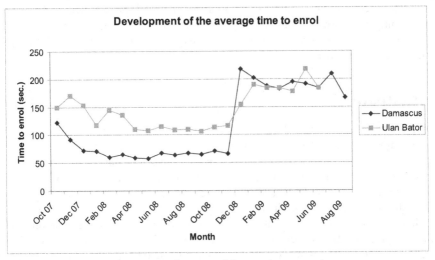

Fig. 3: Development of the avg. time to enrol

This observation led the authors to include an optional instance in the AP describing the Biometric Visa Application process. Apart from the necessary (visa) application office and the VIS/BMS, a Biometric Evaluation Authority (BEA) can be advantageous to collect the additional logging information (mainly regarding quality assurance) and generate respective reports. The Application Office and the VIS/BMS are connected through the National Central Authority (NCA).

On the other side, Function Modules regarding Logging (FM LOG-FP-VAPP and FM LOG-PH-VAPP) describe the values that shall be collected and coded. Function Modules for Evaluation (FM EVA-FP-VAPP and EVA-PH-VAPP) describe the further processing of quality information.

The organisational mechanisms have mainly influenced the specification of the Function Modules Operation and User Interface. For quality reasons, the FM Operation suggests including visual examples of how to position the fingers or the complete hand on the scanning surface. This simple measure greatly increases the success rate of fingerprint acquisition.

The results of conducting the complete process chain for enrolment have been taken into account in the Process description (in particular FM P-FP-VAPP). For example, the concept of composite records based on cross-matching is introduced and described, as this measure has shown to be most promising during the pilot study. Reference is made to Function Modules such as Acquisition Hardware (AH), Acquisition Software (AS), Biometric Image Processing (BIP), Quality Assurance (QA), Compression (COM), and Coding (COD). Function Module Coding combines all additional (quality) information that has been described in FM Logging and which has been collected in these FMs.

The approach for the acquisition of a facial image has mainly been influenced by the experiences that were gathered describing the process of applying for German Identity Documents. Nevertheless, experiences from the BioDEV II pilot project have also been considered (e.g. FM COM-PH-JPG).

The approach which has been described in this section has shown how the results of BioDEV II have been integrated into the TG Biometrics and have enhanced the technical guideline to version 2.0, defining both technical and organisational standards and giving helpful suggestions as to define and implement efficient processes for the use of biometric features in public-sector applications and electronic identity documents.

6 Conclusion

This contribution has shown that different kind of technical and organisational safeguards can have a great impact on the enrolment for a biometric visa. While requirements such as time and quality assurance interact, further factors such as usability (e.g. how information for the acquisition is given to the applicant and the official) need to be considered. This has been conducted for example in the pilot project BioDEV II which has been introduced and de-scribed in section 5. In order to be able to transform the result of this pilot project for the further application of biometric visa requirements, recommendations, and best practices have been specified and accommodated within the scope of TG Biometrics which offers a modular and flexible way to describe public sector applications for different kinds of electronic identity documents. As a next step, the results of the border control processes will be added to the technical guideline.

References

[TR_03121] Federal Office for Information Security: Technical Guideline TR-03121 Biometrics for Public Sector Applications. Part 1: Framework, Part 2: Software Architecture and Application Profiles, Part 3: Function Modules. Version 2.0, 2010.

[TR_03122] Federal Office for Information Security: Technical Guideline TR-03122 Conformance Test Specification for Technical Guideline TR-03121 Biometrics for Public Sector Applications. Part 1: Framework, Part 2: Software Architecture – BioAPI Conformance Testing, Part 3: Test Cases for Function Modules. Version 1.0, 2010.

[ISO_19784-1] ISO/IEC 19784-1:2006 "Information technology – Biometric application programming interface – Part 1: BioAPI specification".

[ISO_19784-4] ISO/IEC CD 19784-4: "Information technology – Biometric application programming interface – Part 4: Biometric sensor function provider interface".

[EC-767-2008] Regulation (EC) No 767/2008 of the European Parliament and of the council of 9 July 2008 concerning the Visa Information System (VIS) and the exchange of data between Member States on short-stay visas (VIS Regulation).

Taking Signatures Seriously – Combining Biometric and Digital Signatures

Santiago Uriel Arias

Confederación Española de Cajas de Ahorros
(Spanish Confederation of Savings Banks)
Caballero de Gracia 28-30 28013 Madrid - Spain
suriel@ceca.es

Abstract

The implementation of Biometrics is no longer seen as an isolated "security project" rather as a part of workflow optimization with a strong focus on the human factor. The project proofs a paradigm shift when dealing with handwritten signatures. While for many years the general idea was to replace the handwritten signature, "Firma Digitalizada" proofs that the handwritten signature can be embedded in a digital workflow in a trustworthy manner. After nine months of real production with millions of clients, CECA experience is one of the leading projects in the usage of these new technologies to provide real business value.

1 Introduction

In October 2009 TeleTrusT has awarded its innovation award to CECA for its project "Firma Digitalizada" at ISSE in The Hague for successfully combining the benefits of biometric signatures and cryptographic techniques in one application. The award reflects the increasing importance of electronic signatures based on handwritten signatures and their integration in the digital workflow. This document will provide the current state of the project and the achievements in the Savings Banks sector.

The Spanish Confederation of Savings Banks is the National Association of 45 Spanish savings banks with its headquarters in Madrid, Spain. The confederation represents about 50% of all the Financial Sector in Spain, with more than 130.000 employees, 1.3 Trillion € in Assets and 1.1 Trillion € in deposits.

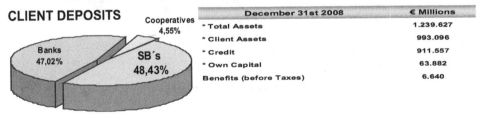

CLIENT DEPOSITS	December 31st 2008	€ Millions
Cooperatives 4,55%	* Total Assets	1.239.627
Banks 47,02%	* Client Assets	993.096
SB´s 48,43%	* Credit	911.557
	* Own Capital	63.882
	Benefits (before Taxes)	6.640

Fig.1: Spanish Savings Banks Sector Figures.

All 45 savings banks are involved in the project presented here. These savings banks have 25.000 branches in the Spanish territory and process more than one Billion transactions/contracts per year.

CECA is also a credit institution with no specific limitation which provides the Savings Banks and other subjects who act in the market with very competitive products and services within the technological and financial area.

The project is a result of a unique cooperation of 45 Savings Banks working together to reach a common objective. This level of cooperation can leverage the individual IT capabilities to reach the highest numbers in terms of financial returns, cost savings, ROI and many other savings. Gartner Group [Newt09] produced a report on this business case that can be found in the Gartner Website.

2 The Digitalised Signature Project

2.1 Original Objectives

The aim to go paper-less with signing procedures is in higher demand than ever and there is one common goal: To achieve trustworthy processes that are safe, secure and conducive to proving an individual's true intent. In applications where handwritten signatures are established as the de facto means of confirming the intent of an individual, Dynamic Signature Recognition offers a pretty smooth migration from paper to electronic processes. At the end of the day it's not all "fully blown Biometrics" in the first stage rather than a step-by-step movement away from paper. The presentation suggested for ISSE in Berlin covers various aspects worth considering when working with handwritten signatures. Please find below an outline of aspects which are intended to be covered.

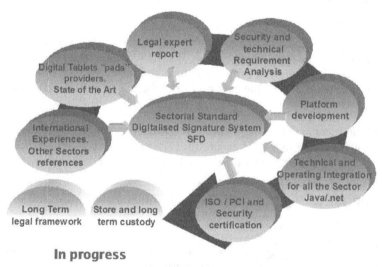

Fig.2: Key aspects of the Project.

The development of the Solution has been leaded by CECA itself with the collaboration of an expert team from MatchMind (a Telvent Company) and a Steering Committee of 25 Savings Banks. The Project Director has been the Deputy CEO of Caja de Avila one of the Spanish Savings Banks.

2.2 Paradigm Shift: Embedding handwritten signatures in digital processes instead of replacing them

Initial requirements from Savings Banks specified that a client coming into a branch must be able to sign by any of the following three means:

1. New Spanish electronic ID, an e-ID card with a smartcard including two PKI certificates (one for identification and the second one for signing).
2. A EMV Card, identifying the client by its PIN.
3. The classic handwritten signature.

Spain has already roll-out more than 15 Mio electronic ID-cards, similar to the new ID card planned for roll-out in Germany in November 2010. Although a lot Spanish citizens already posses a "DNI electrónico" (e ID-card) they do prefer to sign with the handwritten signature. As digital signatures based on certificates on smart-cards are still struggling for acceptance the Spanish Savings banks decided to seek a trustworthy solution to digitize the handwritten signature throughout the writing process, store this information together with the electronic document and secure its authenticity and integrity.

2.3 The Challenge: Documents requiring a Signature

Spanish Savings Banks have been increasing the automation level in branches for many years. They have in place various types of scanning systems, workflow systems, BPM tools and content management systems. But there are documents that cannot be eliminated: Those which need to be signed by clients. These documents must be stored, moved, manually reviewed and kept during the complete life of the legal period (from six years to some decades). The main objective of the project is to get rid of the paper in Savings Banks branches, eliminating physical documents which are still produced for the sole purpose of capturing handwritten signatures. The aim is to work end-to-end with electronic documents. Employees in Spanish Savings Banks should be unburdened from paper handling and gain time to focus on excellence in customer service. Thus it is necessary to capture the handwritten signature in a trustworthy manner and embed it into the document workflow in a reliable way to achieve proof of non-repudiation.

2.4 Inspiration from German Experience

When investigating for potential solutions CECA detected that a huge initiative for a similar approach was under way in German Savings Banks, supported by their German supplier SOFTPRO. The initiative "Elektronische Unterschrift" (Electronic Signature) is part of the project "Model P" for cost-cutting in the workflow of German Savings Banks. As ISSE is held in Berlin in 2010 we assume that it may be interesting to reflect the inspiration we got from Germany and in particular from Berliner Sparkasse and their processing centre Finanz Informatik.

Doris Görke of the German Savings Banks Association (DSGV) summed up their experience with E-Signing in production at Berliner Sparkasse in an article on March 20, 2009 in their weekly newspaper Sparkassenzeitung: It was titled "E-Signing makes slim". Although in many processes a signature is not mandatory in the context of the corresponding legal framework, Doris Görke of DSGV states that electronic signing with the handwritten signature is also beneficial from a marketing and sales perspective. The signing ceremony is an act of appraisal of the relationship between customer and bank. We can also testimony that the ritual of the signing ceremony is re-discovered as an important act. As a consequence CECA's presentation will also reflect the acceptance of security measures and their usability.

2.5 Award-Winning Solution receiving worldwide attention

Apart from the TeleTrusT award mentioned before, "Firma Digitalizada" has been mentioned in late 2009 as Highly Commended by the UK magazine Banking Technology in the Best Use of IT category.

Fig.3: TeleTrusT Award

Additionally, the monthly magazine spin-off of the US daily finance newspaper "American Banker" – "Bank Technology News" (btn) listed CECA as one of the "Top 10 Companies and Technologies of 2009".

Fig.4: Bank Technology News – Top 10 Technologies 2009 Award

On March 25 "Firma Digitalizada" received the status of a commended project in the 2010 awards of the UK-based Finance-IT magazine "Financial Sector Technology" for in the category "Security/Anti-fraud Strategy of the Year".

Fig.5: Last three Awards.

The last recognition of the project has been the "Innovation in Information Security" Award, published by "The Banker" – Financial Times in its June 2010 Issue regarding Innovation in Banking Technology.

2.6 The Track Record so far

CECA is about to achieve its goal of setting the de-facto the standard for E-Signing throughout Spain in financial and other sectors. Clients will feel comfortable having the same signature process regardless if they go to their bank or to a shop next door. To reach this goal, the project was approached across several phases where caution and incremental success histories phases, has been the driver of the implementation.

2.6.1 Project Phases:

2.6.1.1 Phase 1 (November 2007 to February 2008) – Design, Analysis and Build:

Establishment of references and associated experiences, investigation of legal and regulatory requirements, mapping of the technology state of play, detailing security requirements, and articulating the long-term custody considerations for storing the documents.

Once the design and the legal feasibility of the project was proven then a first pilot of the whole system has been created to test the client behaviour.

2.6.1.2 Phase 2 (March 2008 to October 2008) – Pilot Testing:

The first version of the system was tested in seven savings banks, with 15 branches fully operational with clients. More than 50,000 transactions were signed during this phase. Here we obtained the main feedback from clients and employees, resulting in a high satisfaction and acceptance of the new procedures.

2.6.1.3 Phase 3 (October 2008 to June 2009) – Full Development and Second Pilot:

In this phase all the components of the system were completed and it was extended to new banks & branches, involving 14 banks and more than 60 branches. More than 150,000 transactions were signed with clients during this phase.

With a full feedback from all banks, from all client segments (age, position, wealth, risk…) and a huge range of employees, the main Savings Banks felt comfortable to start the full deployment to their networks.

2.6.1.4 Final phase: Full Production (September 2009 onward):

It involved 14 banks and 1,400 branches, and 4 million transactions/contracts were signed and stored.

As of June 2010 the solution is fully deployed in 17 of the 45 Savings Banks. In 2010 another 15 Savings Banks will deploy the solution. The objective is to reach near 10,000 branches before year end.

In 3Q2010 more than 70 Spanish Banks (besides Savings Banks also Cooperative Banks and Retail Banks) will implement the solution. More than ten Thousands of SignPad eSignio tablets have already been rolled out. Since the start of the project more than 55 Millions of electronic documents were signed digitally. At the end of 2010 the number of signed documents is expected to exceed the 100 Million documents mark.

The project already attracted a lot of attention outside the financial industry. Contract management is a topic in a lot of industries. Some examples where "Firma Digitalizada" is under investigation these days too: Telecommunication Providers, retailers, companies for temporary employment and the public administration sector including tax authorities, to mention a few.

2.6.2 Project Management:

The project management was established through the auspices of the CECA management team and consisted of:

Project user committee:
- Steering committee, comprising representatives of participating banks, responsible for the high-level management and strategy for the project. 25 Top managers from CIOs to COOs of these Savings Banks participated.
- Project Director Jose Luis Martín Velayos – Deputy CEO of Caja de Avila
- 32 additional members – CIOs, CTOs and COOs from participating savings banks

Project office team:
- Led by Santiago Uriel and with Project Manager Juan Pablo Yague, both from CECA,

Additional project resources:
- Phase 1 used two full-time equivalents (FTEs)
- Phase 2 used four FTEs
- Phase 3 used 8.6 FTEs (including outsourced development of the applications)

2.6.3 Significant Cost Reductions

The Spanish Confederation of Savings Banks estimates that introducing electronic signing for banking transactions in their branches saves its 45 members of up to 26 Million Euros every year. These savings are calculated based on direct paper savings alone. Additional savings are expected as paper forms disappear in internal workflow reducing the efforts for printing, storing, preparing, signing, routing, shipping, scanning, indexing and physical archiving.

The first business case prepared for the initial phase of the project showed an average of 3 cents per document (from small forms to large contracts) on direct paper savings. This figure increased as additional savings are introduced as order control improvements, less operational risk, audit transformation, ex-ante controls, order processing improvement (in terms of time & human error reduction), and many other improvement areas are identified.

As the project gains in experience and real implementation data is becoming available, it is possible to refine the initial business case, adding to the model the additional cost savings. A very conservative approach update of the business case has raised the savings per document in more than ten times the initial savings, leveraging the initial numbers to more than 30 cents per document. This means savings near 300 Million Euros per year.

The Spanish project is still far beyond the 1.5€ per document that the German Savings Banks Association (DSGV) identified in their Model-P project, described before, but a range between 30c and 1.5€ of savings per document enable ROI (Return on Investments) less than 1 year. Taking a real example of a medium sized Savings Bank in Spain, the business case obtained a ROI of 8,3 months considering only paper direct costs, and a medium of 3 cents per document. Such case including savings in other resources, plus process transformation can reduce the ROI to a few months.

2.7 The Components of the Solution

Prior to CECA's "Firma Digitalizada" there were no packaged solutions providing such capabilities in the European market. Today CECA offers a solution highly customized to the financial sector and its transactions and contracts - running as a "black box" in the user terminal, where a signature pad is attached, with capabilities to scan biometric signatures or to read the client's smartcard "eDNI" (the Spanish eID), and also the client EMV Credit Card as means to sign the document. CECA has integrated SOFTPRO's SignPad eSignio and the Software Development Kit SignWare into its document workflow solution, among other technology suppliers like Ingenico, ePadLink/Interlink, VeriFone, Topaz, etc.

The solution has been packaged and is not only being implemented in the Savings Banks Association sector, but distributed to other Spanish & International Financial institutions and outside the financial sector (telecom, retailers, public administration ...).

2.7.1 Client component

Today signatures of customers and employees of Spanish Savings banks are digitized using the signature pads (SignPad) immediately throughout the writing process. The SignPad captures signals of time, location and pressure and an individual signature profile is created. Hence a signed document includes more than what meets the eye in the first stage. Besides the signature image, it also contains biometric characteristics captured throughout the signing process. Software components cater for the authenticity and integrity of the electronic documents. The captured data are linked with the signed document content. Based on the individual biometric signing characteristics an "electronic signature" is created. Modifications of documents after the signing ceremony are recorded and the documents' integrity is protected.

2.7.2 Server component

The security Model is the key part of the system that guarantees the compliance with the contract and digital documents regulations. Here is where the usage of Biometrics combined with the usage of Digital Certificates provide a robust solution that can achieve the integrity, non-repudiation and identity of the client.

The server module provides both the Certificates infrastructure and the public/private key secure management, as well as the communications management with the provider of content management to store the tenths of millions documents that are generated by the system.

2.7.3 Administration & Signature Analyzer

As biometric signatures are uniquely linked to a document, and they are protected by strong encryption technologies, the system provides the means of extracting the signatures under a controlled environment. The administration module is intended to be used by the audit, legal or security departments to extract the Biometrics from a document providing the private encryption keys. The result of the extraction is sent securely to the Signature Analyzer which provides biometric signature verification using all the signature properties of position, speed, pressure and time.

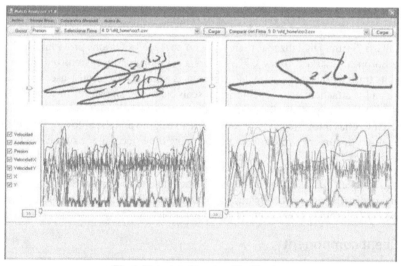

Fig.6: Biometric Signature Verification

2.8 Creating an optimized Workflow Through Process Transformation

Having all documents digital from the origin with the capabilities of automatic signature checking, enable the capabilities of:
- Validating the authenticity of the signature,
- The feature of being able to check if there is a signature or not

Both new features can transform dramatically many processes, introducing new levels of automation, incident reduction resulting in a reduced operational risk:
- New contract opening automation, since original signatures can be checked automatically against the clients' signatures.
- Joint signatures can be applied in different time & location on the same digital document without moving papers.
- Agent mobility enhanced, since no printers are needed.
- No errors resulting from the content transfer from paper files to electronic files
- On-Line signature verification (not only visual checking, but automatic biometric validation).
- Enhanced security for better quality of reference signatures allowing automatic signature verification in paper based payment processing (check processing)

2.8.1 Making the Auditing Department happy

Audit processes extremely simplified since signature review can be done with a simple query against all database contracts. Automatic archiving in a centralized digital custody allows instant recovery of original documents (not a scanned copy). Ex-ante compliance checks can be executed at the click of a button: Who (required number of signatures) signed transactions, contracts, agreements, etc. what where (track of the signature location) and when (time stamp control).

The requirements of MiFID and AML regulations are met thanks to these improved audit processes. There is no longer a need to rely on confidence on tellers/agents as signatures can be automatically checked prior to formalizing contracts or executing transactions with the method of pre-embedded automatic signature verification.

3 Creating a "Green Workflow"

Electronic signing became one of the most vital assets in CECA's overall Corporate Social Responsibility strategy: CECA and the environment benefit from a significant reduction in paper usage and have created a truly "green workflow". Less paper means less pollution, saving trees, and water waste reduction – it is one major aspect of "Green IT".

Let's touch base with some facts: Our associates produce 1 Billion documents every year, from small forms to large hundred-page contracts. This means about 6800 Tons of paper every year, equivalent to the net weight of 28 Airbus 380-800F aircrafts.

Getting rid of this documents means saving more than 121 thousand trees, equivalent to 10 km2 (4 mile2) of dense forest. It also will prevent the emission of 43 thousand tons of CO_2 to the atmosphere equivalent to 20,000 cars or 39,000 houses (a medium sized city).

Fig. 7: Savings of 10 Km² of Forresf or 20.000 Cars

Our track record in April 2010 (when this application was compiled): CECA has achieved more than 1/6 of the paper reduction goals with the current deployment of the solution.

4 The Future Directions

In June 2010 CECA has deployed the solution in around 25% of its association. The goal is to reach by year end 2010 at least 10.000 branches that means 40% of the sector. Technology evolves very quickly so in the meantime the project is implementing new devices (like Tablet PCs, new Pads, Mobile phones...) to capture client biometrics and digital IDs. 2010 will also be the year of going from just getting rid of paper to start transforming processes in a new project with the 45 savings banks.

4.1 Impacts beyond banking

CECA is about to achieve its goal of setting the de-facto the standard for E-Signing throughout Spain in financial and other sectors. Clients will feel comfortable having the same signature process regardless if they go to their bank or to a shop next door. The project already attracted a lot of attention outside the financial industry. Contract management is a topic in a lot of industries. Some examples where "Firma Digitalizada" is under investigation these days too: Telecommunication Providers, retailers, companies for temporary employment and the public administration sector including tax authorities, to mention a few. Without any doubt the project has a lighthouse effect for going paper-less.

5 Conclusion

After 3 years from the first meeting of the CECA steering committee where the idea of the signature digitalisation was raised, we can conclude that the project has been a complete success and the initial objectives have been met completely. The four pillars of the project mission have leveraged the high level of implementation today in Spain:

- Security architecture as a basis for the Legal validity of the solution.
- True cost savings with an aggressive ROI proven by several Savings Banks.
- Client (more than 10 million) and Employee (in more of 5000 branches) acceptance.
- Environmental - Green IT - real results, far beyond just marketing.

The project has proven that in any kind of company, in any activity and in any sector, it can obtain great benefit from the implementation of "Firma Digitalizada".

References

[Newt09]   Newton, Alistair: Case Study for Industry Collaboration: CECA Signature Solution Cuts Costs and Drives Revenue. Gartner Group, 5 October 2009, ID:G00171092

Automatic Configuration of Complex IPsec-VPNs and Implications to Higher Layer Network Management

Michael Rossberg[1] · Günter Schäfer[1] · Kai Martius[2]

[1] Telematics/Computer Networks Research Group
Ilmenau University of Technology
{michael.rossberg | guenter.schaefer}@tu-ilmenau.de

[2] secunet Security Networks AG
kai.martius@secunet.com

Abstract

As the Internet emerges to be, not only the most important, but in many areas the only way of efficient communication, it becomes also vital for business and government institutions to securely exchange data via this medium. This led to the development of virtual private networks (VPNs). However, security in this aspect does not only refer to confidentiality, integrity, authentication, and access control, but also availability; a subgoal of increasing importance due to cheap and simple execution of denial-of-service (DoS) attacks.

In order to increase the DoS-resilience of VPNs, the topology of this overlay network must react flexible to circumvent affected network parts and to reintegrate systems, which become available after the DoS attack ended or have been moved to different address ranges. Therefore, we developed a fully distributed IPsec configuration mechanism, which is able to react to failures dynamically and is yet scalable, efficient, and secure.

Nonetheless, the usually required higher layer services do not work in a distributed way. Thus, a failure may still cause availability issues as services like Domain Name System (DNS) may become inaccessible, even though a network connection is still present.

This article introduces distributed VPN auto-configuration and goes into detail on distributed network services.

1 Introduction

Over the last decade, the Internet has advanced to a low-priced and globally available communication medium. So it is only a consequence that companies and governmental institutions are changing their strategy and switch from dedicated leased lines to the more open, more flexible, and cheaper paradigm of communicating even internal, possibly confidential information via the Internet. Additionally, the Internet also raises the desire of geographically distributed communities without large funding for secure and affordable communication and exchange of files.

Both scenarios can be supported by the creation of virtual private networks (VPNs) on top of the IP layer, e.g. by making use of the IPsec protocol suite. Every participant in such a VPN is given a certificate or password that enables him to securely communicate with others by presenting a compatible certificate or the same password. Security in the sense of VPN primarily concerns confidential data transmission, but often also integrity protection and authentication.

Even though security is naturally handled very well by IPsec VPN, many operational problems remain: Where shall a VPN device connect to? Which VPN device represents which IP address range within the VPN? Over which path data shall be relayed through the VPN, if no direct connection through the network exists? – All of these questions must be covered by a VPN configuration mechanism. However, VPN standards like IPsec do not address the configuration from a macroscopic point of view, but rather rely on the static, manual configuration of each VPN association.

This manual configuration approach has several drawbacks. First, the administrative overhead grows by the power of two with the number of VPN devices, if each VPN device shall be able to communicate with every other VPN device. This will not only lead to higher expenses, but also to more errors caused by human failure. Second, the robustness of the VPN is not as high as it could be, e.g., in case of partial failures of the transport network some VPN devices could redirect traffic for other devices that cannot reach each other directly anymore. Even though IPsec could support such a resilient behavior by utilizing nested security associations, a manual reconfiguration prohibits a timely reaction. Third, manually configured security associations cannot be adopted with sufficient flexibility to support mobile VPNs appropriately. It is not possible to just configure security associations between two mobile devices as both regularly change their external IP addresses.

The large administrative overhead and the limited flexibility of manual configuration approaches lead to a demand for the automation of VPN configuration. Thus, Secure OverLay for IPsec Discovery (SOLID) [RoSS10], was developed, which – in difference to other IPsec configuration mechanisms – does not rely on dedicated servers or hubs and simply uses the public Internet infrastructure.

SOLID is able to automatically configure complex IPsec VPNs, even in scenarios that require the configuration of nested networks and mobile IPsec gateways. For this purpose, it only requires valid certificates to autonomously establish VPNs, thus causing a bare minimum of manual intervention. It is inspired by established peer-to-peer principles and it structures the overall configuration problem into five subtasks: The bootstrapping of joining or restarting IPsec gateways, assignment of address ranges to these gateways, control and optimization of the VPN topology, discovery of private address ranges, and routing in the overlay. SOLID creates topologies that are very resilient towards single or correlated failures of IPsec gateways, and even towards denial-of-service (DoS) attacks.

The full distribution of all configuration tasks is the key to automatically achieving many of the fulfilled objectives, such as scalability, robustness and DoS-resistance, as the planning of central instances requires careful manual planning. Thus, in order to fully exploit SOLIDs capabilities, not only the configuration of the VPN protection mechanisms themselves must be distributed. It is also required to distribute supplementary higher layer services, such as the Domain Name Service (DNS), time synchronization and logging, so that they also work when parts of the VPN are unavailable due to mobility reasons or DoS attacks. By embedding structured and unstructured communication paradigms into the IPsec overlay itself, SOLID can also transparently provide some of these higher layer services.

The next section covers a brief overview on the objectives of VPN auto-configuration, followed by section 3 with a discussion of related work in reference to science and commercial development. Afterwards, a round-up view for an own approach for a self-configuring VPN – SOLID – and its availability properties are discussed. The fifth section goes into detail on three network services that are implemented within SOLID-VPN in a distributed way. Additionally, open issues regarding other network services are also covered. Finally, the article closes with a conclusion.

2 Objectives

From an end-user perspective a VPN should have the following properties:

- **Simplicity:** Users of a system do not wish to configure the VPN itself or a complex configuration mechanism manually, but want it to automatically work and adapt to its current environment.
- **Versatile network environment:** The VPN services are for example expected to work in global, unicast-only networks, shall configure VPN gateways and single nodes, handle internal private address ranges and cope with network address translation (NAT).
- **Transparency:** As existing protocols and applications are unlikely or at least expensive to be adapted for VPN awareness, configurations systems as well as network services must emulate accepted interfaces.
- **Scalability:** Large VPNs may consist of many hundred or even thousands of participants. A fact that does not only have to be considered for automatic configuration, but also by distributed services.
- **Security:** Like indicated in the introduction, the major functional goal of VPNs is the ensuring of data confidentiality, data integrity and authentication, as well as access control. All of these properties can be achieved by mandatory data protection, e.g. by IPsec or TLS. In comparison to manually deployed VPNs, it must be ensured that the configuration mechanism does not weaken the security. Even more difficult is the realization of availability, which can be dissected into the subgoals of:
  - **DoS resistance:** The ability to withstand sabotage by external as well as internal attackers requires VPNs to organize themselves and its services a fully distributed manner.
  - **DoS recovery:** Fractions of a VPN suffering from DoS attacks shall be able to be relocated to different addresses in the transport network, and seamlessly reintegrate into the VPN.
  - **Graceful Degradation:** Even if some components are compromised, the overall security of the rest of the VPN shall stay unaffected.

All in all, this article focuses on availability aspects of automatically deployed VPNs and the defense against internal attackers.

3 Related Work

Current topologies of VPNs can mostly be broken down into fully meshed site-to-site VPN on the one hand and "Hub-to-Spoke" architectures on the other hand (see Fig. 1). The major drawback of site-to-site VPNs is the limited scalability as $O(n^2)$ security associations must be configured and maintained. Due to this property the dynamic reintegration of mobile nodes or a fast DoS recovery is considered to be infeasible.

Hence, the more common topology implies the use of one or more static hubs and dynamic spoke nodes [RRKC04, Flur07, Bhaj08], which is also easier to configure automatically. However, the central coordinator is also a potential weakness in terms of scalability and availability. Furthermore, it is not possible to integrate VPN nodes without a direct connection to the hub, which is essential for attack resilient topologies. Graceful degradation is an additional problem, because hubs are able to decrypt all traffic that is passed through them.

Fig. 1: Example topologies of a site-to-site VPN (left) and a hub-to-spoke VPN (right)

Other VPN topologies that can be configured automatically [Tran05, Aura05, Flur07, Bhaj08] depend on special services of the underlying transport network, e.g. public routable IP addresses within the VPN or globally available multicast. Thus, they only work in certain scenarios and are not suitable as a general replacement for manual VPN configuration. Furthermore, a widespread system showed severe security deficits [RoSc09].

None of the known systems and concepts is optimized on providing availability [RoSc10].

4 Secure OverLay for IPsec Discovery (SOLID)

In contrast to these sketched approaches our presented approach SOLID, creates a self-organizing overlay network, which includes functionality for the discovery of VPN gateways, routing and topology control. In order to construct a VPN overlay, SOLID creates initially only two security associations per gateway proactively, so that an ordered ring structure emerges. As all gateways are ordered by the internal IP address ranges of their private networks, the responsible destination gateway for each data packet can be determined by simply searching along the ring structure.

This search algorithm requires $O(n)$ overlay hops on average, but can be reduced to $O(\log n)$ by introducing cross-connections through the ring. This structure is similar to Chord [SMK+01] or I3 [SAS+02]. However, IPsec gateways cannot be ordered in the ring by random or hashed identifiers, as this would not allow for a variable subnet match. Thus, SOLID cannot rely on the uniform distribution of the looked up keys. Instead random samples are taken estimate the real distribution of inner IP addresses and later used to ensure a good placement of cross-connections over the address space.

Another problem of systems like Chord is their non-applicability to nested security gateways or transport networks in which not all participants can communicate directly with each others, e.g., due to security constraints, mobility, or potentially ongoing routing attacks. Hence, SOLID's topology control creates security associations between affected systems through the VPN itself. The required data exchange is routed through the paths, looked up during the discovery step and thus the ring structure is actually folded into the topology of the transport network like illustrated in Fig. 2.

In order to perform an actual forwarding of user data, a routing mechanism must be deployed to find paths that are as short as possible. However, security associations may change quickly, and the usual routing algorithms depend on a distribution of link knowledge within the whole network, which is slow and must be performed proactively. Thus, in SOLID the forwarding of the actual data packets is initially performed over the security associations used during the discovery, which may be relatively long at first. If needed these paths are later on reactively optimized and within the typical topologies of substrate networks this mechanism leads to ways of ideal length with regards to the hop count. An important property is SOLID's guarantee for end-to-end security as routed data packets are delivered inside a nested IPsec association.

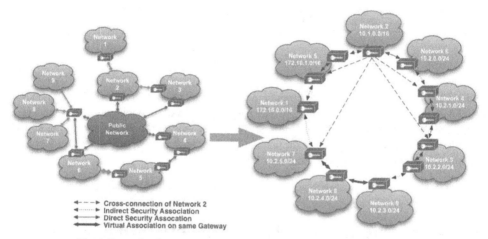

Fig. 2: Example of a transport network and the resulting overlay structure

5 Network Services

Its distributed structure and the possibility to create indirect security associations enable SOLID to react rather robust against DoS attacks as for example node failures affect only the directly hit parts of the VPN and selective link failures can be bypassed. However, problems arise when considering the support of services like DNS, NTP, or the distribution of certificate revocation lists as the devices in a VPN still depend on the availability of these decentralized or even central services. Thus, in order to take full advantage of a distributed and flexible VPN, these services also need to be implemented in a distributed way, while still considering the objective from section 3.

We started tackling the challenge of developing distributed services by implementing a set of entirely different services into SOLID's overlay network. In particular these were a time synchronization service, a name resolution system and a rudimentary network monitoring system. All three distributed systems have very different communication schemes: to perform time synchronization all systems must agree on a single time and frequency, name resolution requires the realization of a distributed database, and the monitoring facilities require a reverse multicast mechanism.

5.1 Time Synchronization

In order to provide distributed time synchronization services between VPN devices, SOLID uses a diffusion model in which each node constantly measures delays to its neighbors and exchanges timestamps [Gole10]. The required information is piggybacked in the dead peer detection mechanism, so that no additional message overhead occurs. If a VPN device measures an offset to its neighbors, it will automatically adjust the value of its own clock and the corresponding frequency correction by a fraction of that offset.

This rather simple mechanism ensures a convergence of time and frequency of all devices within a VPN to a common arbitrary value, depending on initialization values and user communication patterns. Thus, the mechanism performs only an internal synchronization and depends on a different scheme to also allow for an external synchronization. As illustrated in Fig. 3, this is achieved by synchronizing a few VPN devices with external sources, such as GPS, or better by an authenticated source via modem or terrestrial signals.

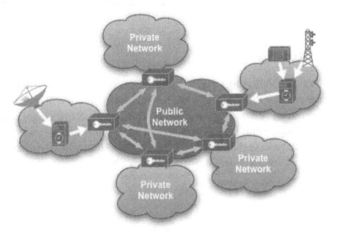

Fig. 3: Illustration of time synchronization infrastructure

In order to protect against external and internal attackers, all exchanged packets are protected by an end-to-end IPsec encapsulation. Furthermore, statistical tests ensure that associations with a high delay or jitter are not used for time synchronization, so that the convergence of the process cannot be threatened by external attackers.

The protection mechanisms against internal attackers are more complex. First of all, statistics are performed on the reasonability of the exchanged time data, i.e., other nodes must show a consistent behavior over time and if more than half of the neighbors are in a stable state, strongly deviating values are not taken into account. Hence, the influence of a potential internal attacker can be strongly limited. Second, a node only synchronizes with nodes that are marked for proactive creation by the topology control algorithm, ensuring that attackers cannot widen their influence by connecting to more nodes. The influence of any potential attacker is thus bound to a logarithmic number of peers.

5.2 DNS Name Resolution

A second, perhaps even more important mechanism copes with the problem of name resolution. If SOLID is configured to perform this task, every VPN client or VPN gateway will get one or more name ranges it is responsible for, e.g., `*.accounting.vpn` [Schu10]. These ranges must be attested by a certificate authority to prevent internal attacks. Clients within the private networks may then either be statically appointed with a name from a set or register one dynamically utilizing the Dynamic Host Configuration Protocol (DHCP).

All VPN devices will aggregate the names they are responsible for, sign sets of DNS records, and publish them in a distributed hash table (DHT), which is embedded within the VPN overlay. Replication mechanisms and on demand re-registrations ensure that the required information is available, when considering node and link failures.

Using the name service is transparent to end-systems: every VPN gateway is registered via DHCP to be a local DNS server, and queries are automatically handed to the SOLID daemon, which will either reply with a cached value, or by querying the DHT and verifying the answers.

5.3 VPN Monitoring

A further problem of distributed topologies is the more complicated monitoring and problem solution. In the context of VPN this includes, for example, the surveillance of the processing and network load of the VPN devices as well as the stability of security associations. Instead of creating a centralized monitoring facility, SOLID can report its status to one or more probes by utilizing an independent reverse multicast tree to each one. Administrators may then connect to these probes and obtain a live overview over the whole VPN.

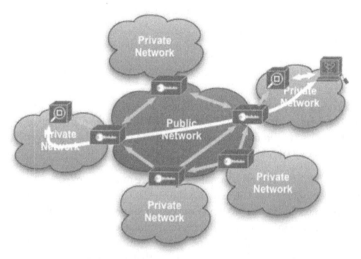

Fig. 4: Creation of two reverse multicast trees for live monitoring

Again, all messages are protected by IPsec and contain a timestamp so that external attackers are assumed to be able to delay messages for a short time or suppress them at most. As there can be multiple independent distribution trees, chances of a successful suppression can be further lowered. The possible influence of internal attackers is also bound to the messages that are passed through them, and as control information and data is protected by asymmetric signatures within the trees, data authentication and integrity is ensured. Thus, compared to external attackers, the only advantage of internal ones is possibility to drop packets more selectively. Furthermore, is the connection between probes and administrators is protected by Transport Layer Security (TLS).

5.4 Other Services

Just like the presented examples for the distributed realization of network services within VPNs, other mechanisms are needed to distribute software and certificate data, perform logging, and to provide means for distributing access control lists (ACLs), which configure client-side firewalls within VPN gateways, or revoking potentially compromised certificates (e.g. by CRLs).

And while a feasibility of service applications with very different distribution patterns has been illustrated in this article, especially the ACL and CRL functionality does not only require an integrity protected and authenticated delivery, but also a certain guarantee that all affected VPN devices are informed. Hence, the focus of our future research activities will concentrate on the scalable and secure creation of node-disjoint delivery paths through the VPN in order to tolerate a certain fraction of compromised nodes.

6 Conclusion

While the automatic deployment of VPNs has been discussed in science as well as network industry for already a decade, many of the availability issues cannot be resolved without fully distributed approaches like SOLID. However, the discussion in this article shows that a distributed configuration can only be a first step, because many higher layer network services are currently not fully accustomed to flexible network changes. Hence, the mechanisms of distributed alternatives to three common, diversely structured services were presented.

As also outlined, the decentralization of CRL and ACL transmission requires a scalable system to distribute them over node-disjoint paths in order to achieve a tolerance against internal attackers. Further research will also concentrate on more resilience against external DoS attacks, by automatically creating stable topologies. The creation of distributed network services allows also for the ad-hoc creation of mobile VPN, i.e., in disaster scenarios, which will be also in focus of our further research.

References

[SMK+01] Stoica, Ion ; Morris, Robert; Karger, David ; Kaashoek, M. F.; Balakrishnan, Hari: Chord: A scalable peer-to-peer lookup service for internet applications. In: ACM SIGCOMM Computer Communication Review 31 (2001), Nr. 4, S. 149–160

[SAS+02] Stoica, Ion ; Adkins, Daniel; Shenker, Scott ; Surana, Sonesh; Zhuang, Shelley: Internet Indirection Infrastructure. In: Proceedings of the 2002 conference on Applications, technologies, architectures, and protocols for computer communications (SIGCOMM), 2002, S. 73–86

[RRKC04]   Raghunath, Satish; Ramakrishnan, K. K.; Kalyanaraman, Shivkumar; Chase, Chris; Measurement based characterization and provisioning of IP VPNs, ACM SIGCOMM, 2004.

[Tran05]   Tran, Trung: Proactive Multicast-Based IPSEC Discovery Protocol and Multicast Extension, IEEE MILCOM, 2005.

[Aura05]   Aura, Tuomas: Cryptographically Generated Addresses (CGA), IETF RFC 3972, 2005.

[Flur07]   Fluhrer, Scott: SYSTEM AND METHOD FOR PROTECTED SPOKE TO SPOKE COMMUNICATION USING AN UNPROTECTED COMPUTER NETWORK, United States Patent US 2007/0271451 A1, 2007.

[Bhaj08]   Bhaiji, Yusuf: Network Security Technologies and Solutions, Cisco Press, 2008.

[RoSc09]   Rossberg, Michael; Schaefer, Guenter: Ciscos Group Encrypted Transport VPN – Eine kritische Analyse, D-A-CH security, 2009.

[Gole09]   Golembewski, René: Live Visualisierung virtueller privater IPsec Netzwerke, Student Research Project, Ilmenau University of Technology, April 2009.

[Schu10]   Schüttler, Florian: Sichere dezentrale Namensauflösung in IPsec-Infrastrukturen, Bachelor Thesis, Ilmenau University of Technology, January 2010.

[Gole10]   Golembewski, René: Sichere, verteilte Zeitsynchronisation in virtuellen privaten Netzwerken, Diploma Thesis, Ilmenau University of Technology, March 2010.

[RoSS10]   Rossberg, Michael; Schaefer, Guenter; Strufe, Thorsten: Distributed Automatic Configuration of Complex IPsec-Infrastructures, To appear: Journal of Network and Systems Management, Septermber 2010.

[RoSc10]   Rossberg, Michael; Schaefer, Guenter: A Survey on Automatic Configuration of Virtual Private Networks, Submitted to: Computer Networks, 2010.

SCADA and Control System Security: New Standards Protecting Old Technology

Scott Howard

Byres Security Inc.
scott@byressecurity.com

on behalf of

the Trusted Computing Group
3855 SW 153rd Drive
Beaverton, Oregon 97006 USA
admin@trustedcomputinggroup.org

Abstract

Industrial control systems were designed and built with a primary focus on performance, availability and reliability - not security. As these systems integrate with corporate networks (and become indirectly connected to the Internet) and their vulnerabilities become more widely known, they are exposed to a variety of threats, from general network probes and denial of service attacks to custom malware that specifically target their components and protocols.

A new generation of standards-based security offerings lets operators defend their control system networks using the same technology that protects telecommunications, banking, and other critical IT infrastructure. The general principles are the same: keep outsiders out, keep insiders honest, keep an eye out for trouble, and keep communications open, clear, and fast - especially during emergencies. Open standards originally designed to enable intelligent, responsive NAC solutions are leveraged by security solutions specifically designed to protect control system environments.

1 Cyber Security in Industrial Control Systems

A wide variety of public and private infrastructure is managed by Industrial Control Systems (ICS), including electrical power generation and distribution; water and waste water; mining operations; chemical and petrochemical plants; pulp and paper plants; and a huge variety of manufacturing operations. These plants typically use highly specialized embedded computers called Programmable Logic Controllers (PLCs) that have been programmed by control system engineers to control and monitor the plant processes. Many of these plants incorporate multi-layered networks of PLCs and Distributed Control Systems (DCS) to implement plant-wide Manufacturing Execution Systems (MES).

Although these digital Industrial Control Systems have been used successfully since the 1970s, it was not until the late 1990's that significant evidence began to emerge of cyber security issues in these systems. In recent years, anecdotal evidence such as press reports, and highly publicized system failures such as the wide-scale electrical blackout in the North-eastern USA and Canada in 2003, have brought this issue to the attention of the general public, system operators, and government regulatory agencies.

1.1 ICS Security Incidents On the Rise

During the period 2001 through 2005, researchers at the British Columbia Institute of Technology managed a project called the Industrial Security Incident Database (ISID) to collect hard data on these cyber security incidents. The database is now called the Repository of Industrial Security Incidents (RISI) and is managed by the non-profit Security Incidents Organization[1].

RISI collects data from approximately 30 member organizations. All data is carefully scrubbed so that the contributing organization cannot be identified. It is the world's largest database of industrial security incidents.

Cyber security incidents impacting control systems is not a new problem – the earliest incident recorded in RISI occurred in 1982, over a quarter century ago. However, these early incidents were sporadic and the period of continuous annual incidents (i.e. where there is no year without a reported incident) didn't begin until 1994. The first year to see a significant increase in the frequency of cyber-security incidents being recorded in the RISI as compared to earlier years was 1998.

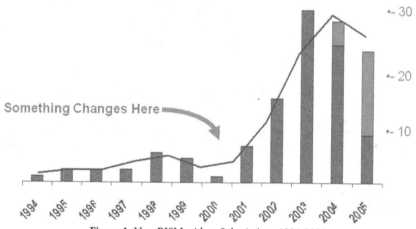

Figure 1: New RISI Incident Submissions 1994-2005

There is a striking increase in the annual incident rate starting in late 2001 or early 2002. Even though the 4 1/2 year period from 2002 to June 2006 represents less than 20% of the total time scale, it contains almost ¾ of incidents reported up to that time. Clearly it appears that the time period between late 2001 and early 2002 marks a significant watershed for SCADA and controls security.

---

1   www.securityincidents.org

Later analysis indicates that the rate of new incident reports has not dropped as was earlier predicted: as of late 2009, the member organizations were reporting 10 to 15 new cyber security incidents per quarter.

1.2 New Technologies Expose Old Vulnerabilities

This sudden rise in security incidents coincides with the introduction of new technologies into ICS networks. In the 1990's, control equipment vendors began adopting Commercial Off-the-Shelf (COTS) technologies, such as Windows PCs and TCP/IP networking, to offer new capabilities such as remote management and interfaces to enterprise data systems. This technological shift has brought tremendous improvements in plant productivity and performance; however, the complexity and "interconnectedness" of SCADA and control systems have increased by orders of magnitude. As a result, these control systems now exhibit many of the same vulnerabilities seen in enterprise networks. In addition, the controllers in these networks are now subjected to new threat sources that they were never designed to handle.

1.3 What's Happening Out There?

An analysis of the RISI database in late 2009 provides some compelling insights into the nature of these incidents. Although some might be tempted to blame hackers and terrorists, the vast majority (76%) of the incidents were accidental in nature. Of these accidents, 65% were caused by device or software failure in the plant; 11% due to human error; and 24% caused by PC malware (viruses, trojans, and others).

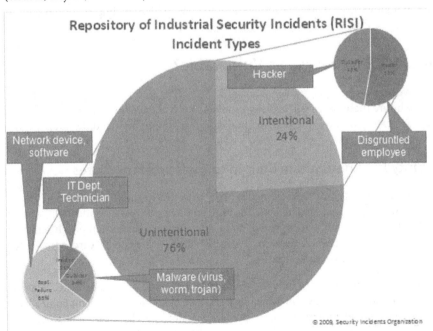

Figure 2: 2009 breakdown of incidents by type and source

Some examples of the types of incidents recorded in RISI:

- An I.T. consultant, hired to update the PCs at a food manufacturer, accidently scanned a range of IP addresses assigned to the control network. The scanning caused every PLC in the plant to crash, resulting in the loss of over $1M of product on the factory floor.
- An engineer at an oil company uploaded a new program to a PLC that he believed was on a test network; however, due to a software configuration error, the new program was actually uploaded to a PLC controlling an oil pipeline. The pipeline was shut down for 4 hours while the problem was resolved and approximately 10,000 barrels of oil production was lost due to the shutdown.
- In 2006, operators at the Browns Ferry nuclear power plant (Alabama, USA) had to perform a manual shut-down of the reactor when it was discovered that there was insufficient cooling water flowing through the reactor core. The subsequent investigation indicated that the likely cause was a malfunction of a PLC in another part of the plant, creating a network traffic storm that caused both the primary and backup cooling drive controllers to crash.
- In 2005, 13 US auto plants operated by Daimler Chrysler were shut down by an infection of the Zotob worm. Despite the presence of professionally installed firewalls, the worm somehow made its way into the control network (probably via a laptop) and was able to travel from plant to plant in seconds. Approximately 50,000 assembly line workers ceased work for about one hour while the malware was removed and affected systems were restarted.

Clearly there can be some very serious financial impact from these security incidents. However, managers at many facilities such as chemical, petrochemical, power utilities and other plants must consider not only the financial impact, but also the potential safety impact, of these types of incidents.

1.4 Why are ICS Networks So Vulnerable?

IT managers have been largely successful in managing this type of security threat, so the question may be asked 'why are these issues still causing problems for ICS operators?' The answer lies in the type of equipment used, and some fundamental design assumptions, that differ dramatically between ICS and IT networks.

1.4.1 Security Assumptions are Built-in to Tools and Procedures

Most IT engineers are familiar with the assumed security priorities in enterprise systems: "C.I.A." or "Confidentiality, Integrity, and Availability". The number one priority is Confidentiality – protect the data at all costs. Network operators will go to any length, including completely shutting down a server or an entire network, to prevent sensitive data such as credit card numbers or personnel records from being compromised.

In contrast, the priorities are almost exactly the opposite for many ICS operators: "A.I.C." ("Availability, Integrity, Confidentiality") where availability and safe operation of the plant control system trumps all other considerations. For example, an operator at a chemical plant would not be overly concerned if an attacker was able to discover how much chemical was contained in a particular storage tank; but if the attacker opened the wrong valve, or started a pump at the wrong time, the plant could grind to a halt very quickly or even degrade into a serious safety or environmental incident.

Table 1: Security Priorities are Inverted between IT and ICS Networks

Priority	Enterprise IT	ICS
1	Confidentiality	Availability
2	Integrity	Integrity
3	Availability	Confidentiality

The "CIA" assumption is built into most security devices available today. IT-focussed firewalls and routers typically have no facility to permit configuration, testing or updating of the device without at least a temporary network traffic blockage or, more commonly, a complete system shutdown. These shutdowns are typically scheduled overnight or on weekends when few users are likely to be affected. This type of shutdown is just not acceptable for many industrial plants which often must run for months or years between shutdowns. Many industrial plant processes are continuous in nature, and once started they will incur significant financial penalty each time they are shut down.

Another example of the difference in design focus is shown when considering the communication protocols used in IT vs. ICS networks. There is a wide choice of IT security devices that are very adept at scanning e-mail and web traffic for viruses; however, these protocols are not used (and in many cases are completely banned) on the plant floor meaning that this capability provides no value for the plant network operator. Instead, he would benefit greatly from a device that could provide similar capability for common industrial protocols such as Modbus/TCP, DNP3, ProfiNet or Ethernet/IP; unfortunately, this type of capability is almost non-existent.

Compounding this difficulty is the fact that a typical ICS requires equipment that is engineered to operate in extremely harsh environmental and electrical conditions, including wide ambient temperature ranges and severe levels of electro-magnetic interference. Traditional IT security devices are built for an office or server room environment which is much more forgiving. This leads to a situation where a control system engineer cannot adequately secure his plant network - not because he doesn't want to, but because it is just not feasible with the tools and equipment that are available to him. As a result, most ICS systems today run with little or no security measures implemented.

1.4.2 ICS Components are Extremely Vulnerable

The PLCs and Remote Terminal Units (RTUs) in control networks were designed with a primary focus on high-performance real-time I/O, not robust networking. Many of these devices will crash if they receive mal-formed network traffic, or even high loads of correctly-formed data. Typically these devices are based on real-time operating system firmware stored in non-volatile memory rather than a general-purpose operating system such as Linux or Windows, so users are completely dependant upon their equipment vendors to correct security vulnerabilities and issue firmware patches. Although a number of vendors have now begun to include security in the design requirements for new devices, there is a huge installed base of legacy devices that still exhibit serious vulnerabilities. Due to the extremely long life cycle (20-30 years) of typical ICS components, this situation is expected to continue for a very long time.

A useful illustration of these vulnerabilities comes from the CERN laboratories. Several hundred PLCs are used to control and monitor the operation of the CERN particle accelerator. CERN engineers subjected a representative sample of these PLCs to tests [Lüde07] with two widely-used network vulnerability testers, Nessus and Netwox. The results in Figure 3 are sobering to say the least. A good number of these controllers crashed outright, and significant numbers remained on-line but failed to handle the test traffic correctly.

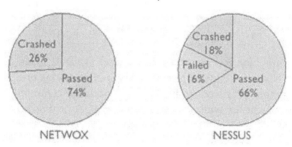

Figure 3: Vulnerability Test Results from CERN

Many of the communication protocols used by these devices were also designed before security was a major concern. For example, the Modbus protocol is one of the most widely supported ICS protocols, starting out as a serial command/response protocol and eventually migrating to TCP/IP. There is no facility for authentication in Modbus, so any device that can establish a network connection to a Modbus controller can not only read data from it but also issue commands to make changes. Needless to say, this has the potential for catastrophic consequences to the equipment or process being controlled by that Modbus PLC.

Another source of vulnerability in ICS networks are the Windows PCs that are widely used to control and monitor the operation of PLC and DCS systems. Like the controllers, these PCs must run for weeks or months at a time without security updates or even antivirus software; these PCs are vulnerable even to outdated malware that would not represent a serious challenge to most enterprise networks.

2 Divide and Conquer: Defense in Depth

The security challenges in ICS networks have not gone unanswered. Industry groups have developed standards and best practices to aid ICS operators in improving the security and reliability of the plants they manage. In addition, equipment vendors are now offering products that adapt cutting-edge security technology to the unique requirements of Industrial Control Systems.

2.1 ANSI/ISA-99 and IEC62443

Many aspects of securing an ICS network are similar to any other computer network. It typically involves a security life-cycle that starts with threat modelling and risk assessment, progresses through deployment of security policy and technology where appropriate, and follows up with management and monitoring of the outcome with the goal of implementing continuous improvement over time.

The International Society of Automation (ISA) have developed one such security lifecycle, ANSI/ISA-99, which is particularly well-suited to the needs of ICS networks and their owners. This standard is now significantly influencing other work in this area such as the upcoming IEC standard 62443.

ICS operators typically have little influence over the vulnerability of the equipment and software that is used in their networks; they are largely dependant upon their equipment vendors to secure these devices. However, the ICS owner can exert significant control over the segmentation and separation of different sub-systems within the network, and this is an area that ANSI/ISA-99 addresses in some detail.

ANSI/ISA-99 introduces the concepts of network 'zones' and 'conduits' as a way of segmenting a network into isolated subsystems based upon the function, location and security capability of the network equipment. In brief, 'zones' are logical or physical groups of network devices that have a common function and security capability. 'Conduits' are the pathways throughout the network that connect these zones together and pass data between them. Once the conduits have been identified, these become ideal 'choke points' in the network where a security device may be used to control what network traffic is allowed to pass between zones. The security device (typically a firewall, but may also introduce other services) will increase the capability of the less-secure zone and reduce the opportunity for a cyber security issue in one zone to spread and cause disruption in other zones. Ideally, the security device would also incorporate real-time alarm generation to alert network operations or security personnel when disallowed or malformed traffic is detected. This is a variation of the 'defense in depth' strategy that has been employed successfully in many enterprise IT environments. The trick is to do it with a device that is rated for the harsh environment found on the plant floor, and to do it with little or no disruption to the traffic passing through the plant network.

2.2 The Tofino Security Appliance

The solution outlined above is implemented today by the Tofino Security Appliance (SA), developed by Byres Security. Tofino is an industrially-rated network security appliance that operates as a layer 2 Ethernet bridge, like an Ethernet switch, so it can be installed in a control network with no pre-configuration and little or no impact to the traffic passing through the network. It provides firewall, asset management and VPN services, and offers modules to perform content inspection on industrial protocols such as OPC and Modbus. The Tofino Central Management Platform (CMP) software enables simple configuration and management of multiple security appliances from a single PC, using concepts and terminology that are already familiar to control system engineers. Finally, the Tofino SA offers a unique 'Test' mode enabling the engineer to test his firewall rules without actually blocking any network traffic, so he can be confident that the rules are correct and complete before they are made operational.

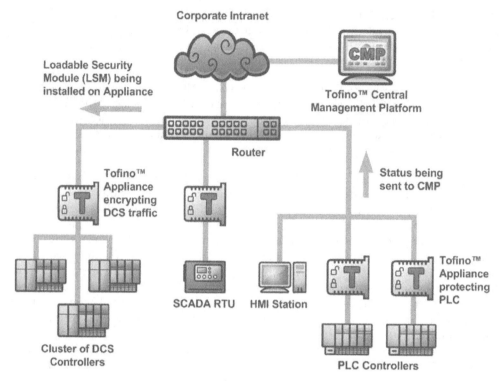

Figure 4: Tofino Security Architecture

3 Trusted Network Connect: the Next Generation

The Tofino Security Appliance has proven to be a simple and effective solution to improve the security of many ICS networks around the world. However, competitive pressures are driving ICS operators to achieve even higher levels of productivity and further cost reductions; these trends cannot continue without corresponding improvements in the security and flexibility of the networks that monitor and manage the plant floor. Trusted Network Connect, from the Trusted Computing Group, offers an innovative solution.

Trusted Network Connect (TNC) is a work group of the Trusted Computing Group (TCG), an industry standards organization focused on strong security through trusted computing. TNC is completely vendor-neutral; the full set of TNC specifications is freely available for anyone to implement, and TNC-based products have been shipping for almost six years. Major vendors such as Juniper Networks and Microsoft are implementing support for TNC standards in their products, and the Trusted Computing Group and the IETF are working to harmonize TNC specifications with IETF Request For Comments (RFCs).

TNC standards provide an architecture and a set of open interfaces that allow interrogation of an endpoint to determine its integrity and compliance with security policies. When an endpoint requests access to the network, a policy server queries the endpoint, determines user identity and endpoint health, and makes an access control decision based on the resulting information. The policy server sends a policy decision to an enforcement point telling it whether to permit access, deny access, or quarantine the endpoint. TNC interfaces standardize communication between these components at the network, transport, and application layers. Legacy devices that cannot participate in the TNC interfaces may be pre-configured in the policy servers or may be supported by TNC-capable proxy devices.

TNC's IF-MAP standard extends the TNC architecture to allow data sharing across a huge variety of security and networking systems. The Metadata Access Point, or MAP, is a central clearinghouse for endpoint metadata; MAP clients can publish, search for, and subscribe to notifications about that metadata. Any networking and security technology can be a MAP client; examples include intrusion prevention system (IPS) platforms, vulnerability scanners, dynamic host configuration protocol (DHCP) servers, physical security systems such as badge access solutions, and even application servers. These components can act as sensors adding data to the MAP, and/or act upon information received from other components.

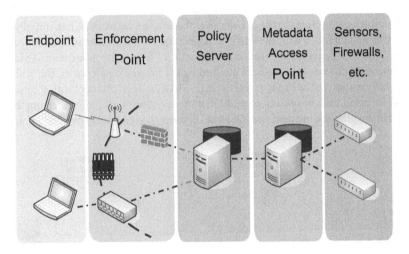

Figure 5: TNC standards enable integration of best-of-breed networking and security products to ensure dynamic, intelligent access control decisions.

Although TNC was originally conceived for protection of IT networks, it addresses many security issues that are also found in control and SCADA networks. Byres Security is working with other members of the Trusted Computing Group, including IT equipment vendors and large user organizations, to adapt the TNC architecture to the special requirements of SCADA and control networks. This offers the potential for significant cost savings in network infrastructure, as well as the ability to manage security policy for both the enterprise and control/SCADA networks from one set of tools. With MAP acting as an event-driven ,clearing house' for products from multiple vendors, TNC enables the deployment of security systems that are much more comprehensive and flexible than those based on proprietary technologies.

3.1 TNC on the Plant Floor

TNC member companies are deploying the TNC interfaces in real plant environments.

An aerospace company needs to implement secure connections between their enterprise network and the manufacturing plant. Due to the size of the product being manufactured, the manufacturing tooling - mounted on mobile crawlers - roams throughout the entire manufacturing facility. Essentially, the product being manufactured remains stationary while the production line moves around the product, the reverse of most production sites. Due to the mobility requirement, the crawler must use wireless, with its potential security challenges, to connect to the network.

Open standards from TNC enable a solution that combines products from multiple vendors, all interoperating via standard interfaces. The cornerstone of this system is the MAP, or Metadata Access Point, which acts as a 'clearing house' for a wide variety of transitory data. A key element in the operation of the TNC-based security solution, the MAP provides flexibility and interoperability that simply cannot be achieved with proprietary solutions.

A Tofino Security Appliance from Byres Security protects each crawler. The Tofino SA provides firewall services to insulate the crawler's legacy PLCs from disruption and permit only the specific network connections required for correct plant operation. In addition, Tofino VPN services secure all network connections to the crawler over the wireless network. When initially deployed, the appliances first check in with the MAP to collect their corporate security certificates. Next, they retrieve their security policy (firewall rules and VPN security associations) via the same server. If unauthorized network traffic is blocked by the firewall on a crawler, the Tofino SA can report this information to the MAP in real time. IF-MAP, an open protocol with support from diverse vendors, could then be used to respond in a variety of ways, including alerting the network security team, logging the incident in a database, or even changing security policy if appropriate.

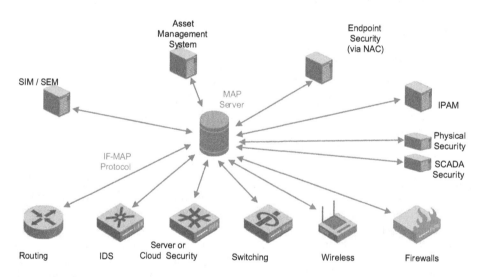

Figure 6: MAP is the information 'clearing house', using a publish-and-subscribe model to share event information among multiple security systems

MAP-based functionality can go far beyond the crawler's security appliance and other network-based security products. A wide variety of MAP-capable devices enable the company to implement highly optimized security solutions, customized to their specific needs. As each crawler moves around the plant, MAP-aware wireless access points report each crawler's location to the MAP; because of the open and flexible nature of IF-MAP, the crawler's security policy can be configured based on the physical location of the crawler. For example, if the crawler is located in a service bay, firewall policy allows a PLC engineering workstation to upload new firmware or logic programming into the controller; such activity is prohibited when the crawler is in use on the plant floor. Other systems that interface to MAP, such as physical plant security systems can be configured to interoperate in ways that would be impractical, if not impossible, using proprietary solutions.

4 Conclusion

Now, more than ever, organizations interconnecting control system networks with corporate IT networks need to be aware of potential risks. To obtain the full benefit of this integration, a complete security life-cycle incorporating planning, processes, and technology is required to adequately reduce exposure, mitigate the risks associated with a hyper-connected environment, and prepare the infrastructure to securely handle change.

The current trend towards higher levels of integration between enterprise and control/SCADA networks will continue to accelerate as operators seek improved productivity and return on investment (ROI). However, this ROI will not be realized without significant improvements in control system security. TNC and MAP provide an open ecosystem of interfaces, tools, and products that enable robust and flexible security architectures to be deployed quickly and cost-effectively. Moreover, integration of specialized security products like the Tofino Security Appliance demonstrates that open TNC standards from Trusted Computing Group enable management of security policy for both the enterprise and control networks from a single set of tools, offering high levels of security in a very flexible and cost-effective solution.

References

[Lüde07]   Lüders, Stefan, "Twelve Steps to Improving Control Systems Cyber Security at CERN", 2007, http://cerncourier.com/cws/article/cnl/31989

A Small Leak will Sink a Great Ship: An Empirical Study of DLP Solutions

Matthias Luft · Thorsten Holz

Laboratory for Dependable Distributed Systems
University of Mannheim
{matthias.luft | thorsten.holz}@informatik.uni-mannheim.de

Abstract

Data Leakage Prevention (DLP) is the general term for a new approach to avoid data breaches. To achieve this goal, all currently available implementations of this concept perform an analysis of intercepted data to detect breaches in a generic way. The analysis is typically based on user-defined policies which specify what data is valuable. There are several different approaches to both define these content policies and to intercept data to enable analysis.

In this paper, we introduce a methodology to evaluate DLP solutions and we exemplify the method by testing two DLP implementations in detail. Our review process is an essential step in the life cycle of every new software or concept: there should be a continuous cycle of test phases and examinations before a solution can be regarded to be dependable. To perform such an analysis in a structured way, we develop a set of generic tests which evaluate critical parts of important functionality in a DLP solution. We focus on the development of a set of tests that evaluate the DLP specific functionality, instead of performing a traditional vulnerability assessment.

Our empirical tests reveal security vulnerabilities in the tested products. The vulnerabilities have different impact, like the fact that data breaches can still happen or even new leakage vectors can arise.

1 Introduction

Data Leakage Prevention (DLP) is the general term for a new technology which has its focus on the important problem of information leakage: many of the problems which emerge from security holes concern the unauthorized access on data. The impact of such incidents ranges from identity theft, stealing of sensitive corporate data to law suits due to data breach rights. DLP provides an approach which should avoid the possibility of data leakage. There are already several products on the market which fulfil the requirements to be called a DLP suite [QuPr08]. Since this technology is novel and still in its early stages, it should be reviewed and tested several times before it could be regarded as a dependable solution for the addressed problem.

In this paper, we introduce an evaluation methodology to review DLP solutions. We focus on the different requirements that need to be fulfilled by such a tool to provide comprehensive protection against this threat. Specifically, we develop a set of generic tests which evaluate critical parts of the functionality of a DLP solution such as for example how data is monitored or how the solutions reacts to leakage attempts. Furthermore, we perform an empirical study to exemplify the methodology: we perform a review of several DLP solutions in face of mainly three questions:

- Is accidental leakage still possible?
- Is it possible to subvert the leakage prevention?
- Are there any vulnerabilities in the software?

The two exemplary DLP solutions that we examined are *McAfee Host Data Loss Prevention* and *Websense Data Security Suite*, which is one of the leading products in this area. Our empirical evaluation reveals several security vulnerabilities in the tested products: we were able to exfiltrate data without the DLP solution noticing these security breaches. The vulnerabilities we have identified have different impact, like the fact that data breaches can still happen or even new leakage vectors can arise due to an increased attack surface. As the examination shows, both solutions contain several flaws which make them fail in important areas. These results allow the abstraction to general problems of the concept DLP and an interpretation of its capabilities.

2 Background: DLP Solutions

In this section, we provide a brief overview of the basic concepts in this area. Data leakage is a very general term which can be used in a variety of meanings. In the context of DLP, it means a certain loss of data or, more precisely, the loss of confidentiality for data. To examine DLP solutions, it is necessary to define the term data leakage to decide, based on this understanding, which threats exist and must be controlled.

2.1 Practical Examples of Data Leakage

There are lots of well-known examples that represent different kinds of Data Leakage. One of the most popular incidents in 2008 was the selling of a camera on Ebay [Guar08]. This camera contained pictures of terror suspects and documents classified as *internal* of the MI6, the British intelligence service.

Another british organization, the General Teaching Council of England, lost a CD containing data of more than 11.000 teachers [BBC08]. The CD was sent to another office via an courier service, but did never arrive. Fortunately, all information was encrypted so that nobody can use the lost data. At this point, it is necessary to distinguish between data and information. The remainder of this paper will refer to the term *data* when the pure content of any kind of media or communication channel is meant. In contrast, data becomes information when it can be interpreted to transport any kind of message.

Other examples of data leakage are even worse because personal data is disclosed. These kind of incidents can result in identity theft for thousands of people. One of the biggest leakages of this kind happened in 2008 to the German company T-Mobile: about 17 million customer data sets were stolen due to the exploitation of security vulnerabilities in different systems and databases [Spie08]. Byers studied information leakage due to hidden (meta-)data in documents and found several interesting cases where sensitive data was leaked this way [Byer04].

Based on this exemplary selection, some of the characteristics of data leakage can be pointed out. These characteristics are independent from the kind of leakage and how it occurred. Leakage happens in an unintentional way, has a certain impact and is inadvertent [JoDy07]. Additionally, leakage is not restricted to any kind of leakage vector like malicious activity or lost devices.

Based on these presumptions and examples, the following, very general, definition of Data Leakage can be derived:

Data Leakage is – from the owner's point of view – unintentional loss of confidentiality for any kind of data.

The remainder of this paper will use the defined characteristics as well as the different ways data leakage can occur. They will also influence the development of appropriate test cases for DLP solutions in Section 3.2.

2.2 Data Leakage Prevention Techniques

After having clarified the definition of data leakage, we can now turn to approaches to prevent leakage. The following definition of DLP solutions by Mogull [Mogu07] is a good source to understand all important aspects of these tools:

Products that, based on central policies, identify, monitor, and protect data at rest, in motion, and in use, through deep content analysis

Based on this definition, it is possible to derive the three main capabilities of DLP solutions: *Identify, Monitor, React*. Each of these steps in leakage prevention has to deal with the mentioned requirements to handle data at rest, in motion, and in use. Thus the remainder of this section explains how the different challenges are handled in each situation. Since the single phases of DLP have very different requirements for both analysis processes and examination, the understanding of these phases is necessary for a structured evaluation in a later step.

If sensitive data should be protected, every kind of control mechanisms needs to know how the valuable data looks like. Thus, in a first step, methods of defining data and scanning for it are needed. It is necessary to provide generic methods to define data both as general and as specific as needed. A very common technique for the identification of data are regular expressions. These expressions can be very generic and therefore potentially produce a high rate of false positives. To apply more fine grained filtering, most DLP solutions provide methods like database fingerprinting or exact file matching. These approaches query either a database or a fileserver and use the stored data for the generation of hash maps of sensitive data. To allow this analysis, the solution must thus be able to understand lots of different file types like Word documents, ZIP archives, or different image formats.

If this identification of data is successful, in a second step, data must be accessible to allow the application of any kind of control: after content analysis the DLP solution now needs to inspect the context of data. The context of data is again related to the different states of data: In motion, at rest, and in use. Data in motion means data that is currently transferred over a network. Consequently, data in rest is data that is stored on a file server. Data in use is data that is currently accessed by users – for example, copied to the clipboard or viewed using an application. Data in every state can be in a different context: Data in motion can have the context of an email or a FTP file transmission. This means a complete solution needs as many approaches for monitoring data as ways of transmitting, storing, or using data exist in the given system.

If a breach of policy is detected using mechanisms to monitor and identify data, an appropriate reaction policy must be applied. For example, it is not appropriate to delete sensible documents which are found on a public file server – this would lead to a radical decrease of the availability of data even if it would avoid any leakage. Depending on the user policy, the reaction policy thus typically needs to be manually specified by the operator.

3 Evaluation Methodology

Since DLP is a new technology, the first step in evaluating a concrete suite is the composition of different requirements that must be fulfilled by a DLP solution to provide comprehensive protection against data leakage. Our developed set of requirements is generic in order to allow the derivation of concrete tests for concrete DLP products.

When evaluating any piece of software, the test cases derive from its application and specification. The security requirements and therefore test cases of a DLP product must cover all use cases which represent typical user behavior, as well as, typical business processes that process data. In doing so, both intentional and unintentional leakage of data must be handled properly. Intentional data leakage includes mainly malicious activities, but also an employee who is restricted by the DLP solution and wants to get his work done, e.g., by sending an email containing important information to a colleague.

Table 1 lists our set of questions that can be used to develop a set of concrete technical tests for a specific DLP application. This set of questions was manually compiled and addresses all relevant security requirements of a DLP solution based on our experience.

Table 1: Generic questionnaire to develop a concrete DLP test cases

Identify	Are all methods to match data properly working? Are all file types handled properly? Are all file extensions handled properly? Are unknown data structures handled properly? Is encrypted data handled properly?
Monitor	Are all removable devices (USB, floppy disc, CD) monitored properly? Are all file systems monitored properly, including all special functionalities? Are all network protocols (Layer 2/3/4) handled properly? Are all application protocols (Layer 2/3/4) handled properly? Are all intercepting network devices monitored properly? Is there a possibility to decrypt files using an enterprise encryption system?
React	Is sensitive data blocked? Are all incidents reported properly? Are there reaction or blocking rules? Allow reaction rules race conditions? Is there a firewall/proxy integration to block network connections?
System Security	Is all sensitive traffic encrypted? Exist any publicly available vulnerabilities? Can vulnerabilities easily found using vulnerability assessment methods? Are all access rights set properly per default? Are the application protocols designed in a secure way? Is there a security certification like a Common Criteria Level?

3.1 Evaluation and Results

In the following evaluation, we examine whether the two DLP solutions *McAfee Host Data Loss Prevention* and *Websense Data Security Suite* are able to protect the confidentiality of data in typical use cases. Since the implementation of DLP components on endpoint systems was one of the main changes in 2008 [QuPr08], the according endpoint agents of the two suites are interesting points of research. To separate the functionality of an endpoint agent and due to the high security relevance, we investigated the protection of sensible data in the context of USB media. To examine these components, adequate test cases for endpoint agents are developed on the base of the generic set of test cases presented in the previous section.

3.2 Test Cases for DLP Endpoint Agents

As mentioned in Section 4, the concrete evaluation of an application derives from its capabilities. The examination of an endpoint agent needs a subset of all test cases. Since only the endpoint agent for removable media monitoring is examined, no network monitoring is performed and thus Table 2 lists the necessary evaluation items.

Table 2: Test Cases for DLP endpoint agents

Discover	Are regular expressions matched and is data blocked? Are all file types handled properly? Are unknown file types handled properly? Are all file extensions handled properly?
Monitor	Are all/multiple devices monitored? Are all file systems monitored properly?
React	Is sensitive data blocked? Are all incidents reported properly?
System Security	Is all sensitive traffic encrypted? Exist any trivial to find vulnerabilities?

We performed concrete technical tests that answered the listed questions. These tests were organized in a hierarchy so that more complex tests must not be run when the basic tests failed. For example, if basic MIME type recognition does not work, it is not necessary to run tests with obfuscated data. All actual tests we performed are listed in Table 3 on page 10, including the results. More complex tests that were obsolete are not listed. In the following, we discuss only the test case in which the DLP solutions failed since these are the most interesting cases.

3.3 Basic Setup and Reporting

To evaluate the capabilities of the DLP solutions, a simple policy was created: Every file that contains the string *SECRET* should be blocked from being written to any removable media. Additionally, a notification message should show up, and the blocked data should be stored for further analysis. We were able to trigger this policy using both DLP solutions (see Figure 1 for the exemplary screenshot of the McAfee solution), and since this basic test was passed, we could perform additional tests.

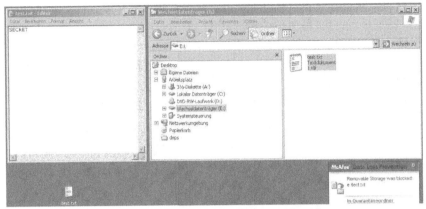

Figure 1: Copying the secret file to an USB stick

The results, which we discuss in the following sections, are again divided according to the three single stages *identify*, *monitor* and *react*.

3.4 McAfee Host Data Loss Prevention

One of the new DLP solutions which arose in 2008 was the McAfee Host Data Loss Prevention suite. We performed our analysis with version 2.2 of the tool. The software exists both as a full DLP suite, including network monitoring and data discovery, and as an endpoint monitoring solution. The central management is realized via a plugin which can be integrated into the general McAfee management console. The solution basically provides the monitoring of removable storage media like USB sticks or floppy discs. All content which should be written to these media is monitored and analyzed based on the central policies.

3.4.1 Identify

Every DLP solution supports lots of file types that can be *understood* and parsed. To check whether a real deep content analysis is performed, a PDF document containing the string *SECRET* was prepared. Then we removed the MIME information of the PDF document – which is, in this case, the first line of the file. This slightly modified file was not detected by the scan engine. In general, this means that unknown MIME types are not monitored. Since meta data can be an important leakage vector [Byer04], a PNG image which contained the EXIF comment (where EXIF is a standard for embedded meta data for images) *SECRET* was copied to an USB stick. This test should examine whether recognized document formats are parsed completely and correctly. As the file can be copied to an USB stick, this is another failing of the solution.

3.4.2 Monitor

One of the most severe vulnerabilities of the solution is the improper handling of USB devices that contain more than one partition. Using an USB hard drive containing three partitions, only the last mounted partition was monitored during each of several attempts, the first two ones were not monitored at all. Therefore it was possible to write arbitrary data containing the secret string to the first two partitions.

A kind of a side channel is the possibility of copying a file which is named SECRET.txt to an USB stick. Even though the file name contains the valuable information *SECRET*, the file is not blocked (see Figure 2).

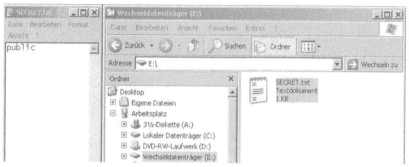

Figure 2: Information contained in file names is not monitored

To ensure the stability of the endpoint agent, it is important to analyze the behavior of the system when a big file must be examined. Since the McAfee Host Data Leakage Prevention does not analyze files which are bigger than 500 MB, it was not possible to run a test using a 5GB file containing random data.

3.4.3 React

As Figure 1 showed, files are deleted if valuable information is discovered. To check whether valuable data is really deleted, a completely empty floppy disk was prepared. Every sector of the memory was overwritten with bytes containing only zeros. When this disk was inserted into the client system, it must be formatted and then could be mounted. A file containing *SECRET* several times was written to the disk and expectedly got blocked and deleted. After this process, the disk was examined in a low level forensic way without using any file system structures. This examination showed that the disk still contained the secret string *SECRET*. Thus it is possible to bypass the DLP solution via recovering the deleted files and a forensic examination of the media since no secure deletion is performed.

In a last step of reaction, the blocked data is stored on a central repository. This central repository is available via SMB and a provided network share. Monitoring this transmission, we noticed that the file is just delivered via the SMB protocol. SMB is mainly used as a plaintext protocol (although this depends on the concrete environment). Therefore, it was no problem to intercept the traffic and extract the sensible information directly from the network traffic.

3.5 Websense Data Security Suite

According to the DLP market overview by Gartner [PrQM07], the Websense Data Security Suite was one of the leading DLP solutions already in 2007. Nevertheless, it just provided network monitoring and discovery functionalities. Since an endpoint agent was added in 2008, it is a suitable completion to the DLP solution by McAfee. Central management both of policies and client administration is realized by standalone or web applications.

Like the McAfee Host Data Loss Prevention, the Data Security Suite monitors all removable storage media so that the same set of test cases can be applied for our evaluation.

3.5.1 Identify

The first test of the data processing was again a PDF document without its magic MIME bytes. Again, this small change was enough to circumvent the DLP solution and the file was copied successfully to the USB stick. This test controls the inspection of files for their MIME type. Since also the McAfee DLP solution did not recognize this file without the correct type information, the same PNG file containing the EXIF comment SECRET was copied to the USB stick. Similar to the previous test, the Websense Data Security Suite did not block the copying and thus this test case also failed.

3.5.2 Monitor

The system monitors all tested channels correctly. For example both NTFS alternate data streams and the Linux ext3 file system were monitored and every information breach was detected. But a test of the stability of the application failed: During the copying of a 5 GB file filled with random data – which contained also the string *SECRET* – to an USB hard disk, the complete operating system froze in all three test runs. Without the endpoint agent running, this process completed without any problems. Thus running the endpoint agent affects the availability of the system and also means a restriction of operation. We did not further examine whether or not this flaw has any other security implications.

3.5.3 React

Per default, the communication between the endpoint agents and the central Websense server is handled using HTTPS. This implicitly means that all communication is encrypted. This encryption can be turned off so that it was possible to analyze the communication protocol. The following listing shows the plain text communication – without its HTTP header information to improve readability – that happens when the endpoint agent registers at the server after each start:

Request (client to server):

```
CPS_CLIENT4626415283943780173|xp-template|N/A|N/A|  .K|....
```

Response (server to client):

```
CPS_CLIENT4626415283943780173|78|.XaO....  ...M.e.s.s.a.g.e.w.a.s..
h.a.n.d.l.e.d.s.u.c.c.e.s.s.f.u.l.l.y..
```

This protocol is vulnerable to at least one attack: if an attacker is able to intercept the traffic from the client to the server and vice versa, the attacker can drop the requests from the client to the server and reply arbitrary answers to the client. The complete response of the Server is predictable since it has the following meaning:

- *CPS_CLIENT4626415283943780173*: Can be extracted from the Client request
- *78*: Answer code which stands *Message was handled successfully*. There are also other message codes like *Incident was handled successfully*
- *Message body*: Derives from the answer code.

Thus an attacker can intercept the reporting of an incident, drop the request and send the answer *Incident was handled successfully* to the client. The reporting of incidents would never reach the server and thus would never been reported and no error would have been reported. Since a default installation uses HTTPS, this vulnerability is not exploitable without a vulnerability in the encryption, however.

It could also be possible that an attacker is able to inject faked messages into the incident reporting system. It was not possible to replay an initial registration request of the client. But since there is no additional client verification using, for example, certificates, the session ID (in the example above: *CPS_CLIENT-4626-41528-39437-80173*) is generated only on the client side. This means that the server has no possibility to prove the identity of the client. If an attacker gets access to the data on the client system, he has access to all data the endpoint agent can use to generate the session ID following a certain algorithm. It could be possible that an attacker explores this algorithm and is then able to generate valid session IDs.

3.5.4 System Security

As mentioned in Section 3.5.3, the communication between the endpoint agent and the reporting server is encrypted due to the use of HTTPS. This protocol is based on SSL, which in turn uses certificates for the authentication of the two stations. Since the Websense Data Security Suite uses a certificate only on server side, the client is not authenticated. Furthermore, the client does not verify whether the server's certificate is valid. Thus an attacker is able to perform an SSL man in the middle attack. This results in the decryption of the protocol and this in turn in the disclosure of sensible data. Since only data that is judged to match the policy is sent, this actually adds an additional vector for data leakage that delivers valuable data directly to an attacker. Additionally, this attack vector makes the replay attacks mentioned in Section 3.5.3 possible.

3.6 Evaluation Summary

The findings from Sections 3.4 and 3.5 show that the DLP solutions are not yet matured. There were far too many possibilities for even accidental leakage (e.g., copying of data to one of the unmonitored partitions of an USB hard drive) in the McAfee Host Data Leakage Prevention that it would be questionable to rely on the system as a part of the security concept. And even if the scan engine of the Websense solution may be able to avoid accidental leakage, it introduces an additional leakage vector to the network due to the lack of mutual authentication.

These findings are summarized in Table 3 to provide a fast overview on the capabilities of the solutions. If the solution passed a test, a PASSED field is used, otherwise a FAILED field takes place. As noted before, we discussed in the previous sections only some of the test cases in which at least one of the solutions failed.

Table 3: Tests and associated results for McAfee Host Data Leakage Prevention and Websense Data Security Suite

Test	McAfee	WebSense
Text file containing *SECRET*	PASSED	PASSED
Text file named *SECRET*	FAILED	PASSED
PDF document containing *SECRET*	PASSED	PASSED
Word file including a embedded Excel table	PASSED	PASSED
Zipped word file including a embedded Excel table	PASSED	PASSED
PDF document without MIME type information	FAILED	FAILED
EXIF comment	FAILED	FAILED
NTFS alternate data streams	PASSED	PASSED
Third party filesystems	PASSED	PASSED
Multiple partitions on USB hard drive	FAILED	PASSED
Blocking of valuable data / secure deletion	FAILED	PASSED
Proper encryption of management communication	FAILED	FAILED
Proper encryption of reported incidents	FAILED	FAILED
Fuzzing	PASSED	PASSED
Handling of large files	FAILED	FAILED

4 Conclusion

Our approach to assess the security of DLP suites allowed the disclosure of several vulnerabilities in the evaluated products. The presented generic evaluation methodology could be used to generate concrete test cases for a structured security assessment of concrete DLP funcionality. The revealed vulnerabilities lead to two conclusions: The McAfee solution is not able to prevent accidental data leakage. In contrast, the Websense Data Security Suite provides good mechanisms for identifying and blocking data, but also fails for general security requirements like the confidentiality of processed data.

Based on our evaluation, it is not possible to judge all DLP solutions, although the exemplary products contained serious flaws. Even if the approach of DLP works for one of the solutions, it must be carefully evaluated whether a DLP solution increases the security of a network. In doing so, also traditional vulnerability assessments should be performed to get a more complete picture of the maturity of DLP solutions. At the moment, it seems like the benefits of a (partially) working detection engine do not compensate the vulnerabilities and the high complexity that is added to a network by implementing one of the evaluated solutions.

References

[BBC08]   BBC. Teacher's details on missing disk. http://news.bbc.co.uk/1/hi/england/west_midlands/ 7636822.stm, 2008.

[Byer04]   Simon Byers. Information Leakage Caused by Hidden Data in Published Documents. IEEE Security and Privacy, 2(2):23–27, 2004.

[PrQM07]   P. Proctor E. Quellet and R. Mogull. Magic Quadrant for Content Monitoring and Filtering and Data Loss Prevention. Technical report, Gartner RAS Core Research, 2007.

[Guar08]   The Guardian. Ebay camera contains secret MI6 terrorist images. http://www.guardian.co.uk/ politics/2008/sep/30/terrorism.ebay, 2008.

[JoDy07]   M. E. Johnson and Scott Dynes. Inadvertent disclosure - Information Leaks in the Extended Enterprise. In Proceedings of the Sixth Workshop on the Economics of Information Security. Carnegie Mellon University, 2007.

[Mogu07]   Rich Mogull. Understanding and Selecting a Data Loss Prevention Solution. Technicalreport, SANS Institute, 2007.

[QuPr08]   E. Quellet and P. Proctor. Magic Quadrant for Content Monitoring and Filtering and Data Loss Prevention. Technical report, Gartner RAS Core Research, 2008.

[Spie08]   Der Spiegel. Diebe klauten 17 Millionen T-Mobile-Datensaetze. http://www.spiegel.de/ wirtschaft/0,1518,581938,00.html, 200html, 200

eID and the new German Identity Card

The New German ID Card

Marian Margraf

Federal Ministry of the Interior
marian.margraf@bmi.bund.de

Abstract

Besides their use in identity verification at police and border controls, national ID cards are frequently used for commercial applications, too. One objective of the introduction of the new national ID card on 1 November 2010 is to extend the conventional use of ID documents to the digital world. In order to meet this objective, the new ID card offers two electronic functionalities for e-business and e-government service providers: an electronic authentication and a digital signature.

In the following paper we describe the electronic authentication mechanism used by the ID card, explain the differences between authentication and signature and discuss the security and privacy properties of the two applications used for e-government and e-business.

1 Introduction

On 1 November 2010 Germany will start issuing new identity cards. One of the main differences compared to the previous version is the integration of an ISO-14443-compliant chip which contains a government application, e.g. for border control purposes, and two applications for e-government and e-business (authentication and signature).

IT security and privacy considerations played a crucial role during the design phase of the electronical functionalities. Reliable protection for personal information required a coordinated approach to legal provisions, organisational measures and technical implementation.

The legislative framework for the (current) national ID card (*Personalausweisgesetz*) already contains various provisions about the use of the national ID card, including restrictions. Thus, only in exceptional cases it is permitted to make a paper copy of the ID document; the serial number of the ID card must not be used for data mining purposes; and the machine-readable zone (MRZ) and the data in it must only be used for government purposes.

These provisions were transferred into the legal framework for the new, electronic national ID card. However, because of the new electronic functionalities, additional security mechanisms have to be specified and implemented. Therefore, the following requirements were taken into account during the design phase of the chip functionalities:

1. all data transmissions must be encrypted;
2. all transmissions of data have to be approved by the cardholder;
3. an illicit use of the ID card by a third party must be impossible;
4. the cardholder must know to whom their personal data will be transmitted;

5. only personal data that are necessary and approved by the cardholder may be transmitted;

6. the usage of the card cannot be monitored by government institutions or other parties;

7. the ID card must enable pseudonymous authentication;

8. lost ID cards must be revocable;

9. unique identifiers must not be used, neither for the citizen nor for the ID card.

The last three requirements, in particular, require a careful design of the revocation management for lost ID cards which is described in [1].

For an overview of the security mechanisms of the German ID card, please refer to [2]. In [6] you will find an overview of the privacy features and data protection mechanisms of European eID cards.

2 Commercial applications

Besides their use in identity verification at police and border controls, national ID cards are frequently used for commercial applications. In all these scenarios, the cardholder identifies him-or-herself, using the ID card (and the biometric information on it), to the business partner or government officer, thereby proving a claimed identity.

In normal situations, the cardholder knows the person to whom he or she proves identity because this takes place either on the premises of the commercial partner or the government, or both persons involved show each other their ID cards. This is usually the basis of the trust between the two persons and/or whether they are acting on behalf of the institution(s) they represent.

In a technical sense, a *mutual* authentication takes place. However, both parties receive just a 'snap shot' of the authentication, and they cannot prove the other person's identity to a third party. A signature, which can, if necessary, be presented to a court or in administrative proceedings, constitutes such a proof.

The objective of the introduction of the new national ID card on 1 November 2010 is to extend the conventional use of ID documents to the digital world. In order to meet this objective, the new ID card offers two electronic functionalities for e-business and e-government service providers:

1. electronic authentication: which enables mutual authentication of two parties via the Internet in such a way that each party knows the person with whom it is communicating;

2. qualified digital signature (Qualifizierte Elektronische Signatur (QES)): which is a digital equivalent to a legally binding, hand-written signature according to the German Digital Signature Act (Signaturgesetz).

The cardholder has full control over the use of both functionalities: the ability of the card to perform an electronic authentication will be enabled or disabled when the citizen receives the card (and can be changed later), and a digital signature requires the prior loading of a (qualified) certificate onto the card.

2.1 Electronic authentication

According to the definitions in the Guidelines for Information Security Audits (*Grundschutz-katalog*) of the Federal Office for Information Security (*Bundesamt fuer Sicherheit in der Informationstechnik (BSI)*) the term *electronic authentication* refers to a procedure or an operation for the verification of an identity.

The current procedure for service providers is normally to check the security features of an ID card that is produced and compare the photo to the customer; an equivalent online procedure requires other mechanisms. Smart-card based cryptographic protocols can replace the verification of security features, i.e., the verification of the trustworthiness of the ID card.

A secret PIN, only known to the cardholder, acts as a substitute for the verification of biometric features (comparing the photo). By proving his knowledge of the PIN, the claimant proves to be the legitimate owner of the ID card.

Another objective, in addition to the authentication of the cardholder to the service, is the authentication of the service to the cardholder. The means for doing this are card-verifiable certificates (CV certificates) which can be verified by the chip on the ID card. Besides the expiry date and the name of the institution that owns the certificate, they contain fine-grained information about which data categories the service provider is allowed to access.

A new government institution, the Issuing Office for Certicates (*Vergabestelle für Berechtigungs-zertifikate (VfB)*) which is part of the Federal Office of Administration (*Bundesverwaltungsamt (BVA)*), issues these certificates to service providers. A service provider applying for a certificate has to submit evidence as to why access to personal data on their customers' electronic ID cards is necessary for the service; the Issuing Office verifies, in a formal procedure, that this evidence meets the requirements.

One of the main aspects of this procedure is the selection of the data fields (of the eID card) to which the access will be granted. The principle of minimal disclosure applies; for example, service providers who only need to verify whether a customer is above a certain age, will only obtain access rights to a binary inquiry function for exactly this purpose (age verification). Other services, for example online shops, might get granted access to additional personal information such as name or address.

Service providers will receive their certificates from one of the trust centers that act as Certification Authorities (eID CA). A trust center that wants to provide certificates for the German electronic ID card must fulfill the requirements for issuing qualified digital signature certificates according to the German Digital Signature Act and be registered at the Federal Network Agency (*Bundesnetzagentur (BNetzA)*)

A special option offered by the German eID card is a card-specific and service-specific identifier which enables pseudonymous authentication. If requested, the chip generates a cryptographic token from the sector ID, which is part of the certificate, and a secret key stored in the chip. Thus, this token is unique for each combination of card and service provider but different for different service providers (even using the same card) or different cards.

This token or pseudonym, therefore, enables a service provider to recognize an eID card without the possibility of cross-referencing with another service provider's authentication data.

2.2 Qualified Digital Signature

As already mention above, for the electronic authentication both parties receive just a 'snap shot' of the authentication, and they cannot prove the other person's identity to a third party. A signature, which can, if necessary, be presented to a court or in administrative proceedings, constitutes such a proof.

Moreover, in an authentication procedure we are going to show who we are, a signature shows our will, for example if we sign a contract. Therefore, authentication and signature are different mechanisms and there are use cases for both mechanisms.

In Germany, qualified digital signatures are regulated by the German Digital Signature Act. By this act, qualified digital signatures are equivalent to hand-written signatures, up to the regularities of some special laws.

The chip of the new ID card is designed to be a signature card in the sense of the German Digital Signature Act, i.e. citizen can use this card to load a qualified digital certificate and to sign electronic documents in the usual way.

3 Realization of the electronic authentication

Main idea of the electronic authentication of the ID card is to establish a trusted and secure channel between the chip and the service provider. This will be done by using an authenticated Diffie-Hellman key agreement protocol. With this, we achieve to goals:

1. Both communication parties know with whom they interact (authentication).
2. The communication parties can establish a secure channel (key agreement).

In order to guarantee authenticity of the communication parties, the public keys must be assigned to the respective party. This will be done, as described in the following subsections, by digital signatures and, to achieve the bond of card and cardholder, by using the secret PIN.

For a description of the cryptographic protocols in detail please refer to [4].

3.1 Enter the PIN (Pass word Authentication Communication Protocol (PACE))

As already mentioned above a communication with the chip of the ID card can only be performed if the cardholder enter his PIN to the chip. This guarantees a so-called two-factor-authentication based on ownership (the ID card) and knowledge (the PIN).

Remember that the chip is contactless, hence the PIN cannot be send "over the air" without additional protection.

The PACE protocol that is used for PIN sharing in this context is a password authenticated Diffie-Hellman key agreement protocol that provides secure communication and explicit password-based authentication of the chip and the card reader.

A proof of the security features as well as a detailed description of PACE can be found in [77].

3.2 Mutual Authentication (Extented Access Control (EAC))

3.2.1 Public Key Infrastructure

In order to guarantee the authenticity of ID cards and service providers, two public key infra-structures (PKI) are used.

Terminal Authentication (see Subsection 3.2.2) requires the service provider to prove to the chip that it is entitled to access data on the chip. A service provider holds at least one certificate encoding its public key and access rights, and the corresponding private key.

The PKI required for issuing and validating certificates for service providers consists of the following entities:

1. Country Verifying Certification Authority (CVCA) hosted by the BSI
2. eID Certification Authorities hosted by the Trust Centers
3. Service Providers

Chip Authentication (see subsection 3.2.3) requires the chip of the ID card to prove to the service provider that it is an official chip belonging to a German ID card. The chip holds a static Diffie-Helmann key pair where the public key is signed by the card-manufactor.

The PKI required for issuing and validating certificates and public keys for chips of German ID cards consists of the following entities:

1. Country Signing Certification Authorithy (CSCA) hosted by the BSI
2. Document Signer (DS) hosted by the card-manufactor
3. ID cards

These PKIs form the basis of Extended Access Control.

3.2.2 Authentication of the Service Provider (Terminal Authentication)

When a citizen wants to use the electronic authentication mechanism of his ID card he usually goes to the web-site of a service provider. The service provider sends its certificate to the citizen. This certificate then will be displayed on the screen to show the content of the certificate (data such name of the institution that owns the certificate, expiry data of the certificate and which data categories the institutions is allowed to read from the chip), the citizen confirms by entering his PIN.

After this, following steps are performed by the service provider and the ID card chip:

1. The service provider sends a certificate chain to the chip. The chain starts with a certificate verifiable with the root public key stored on the chip and ends with the service provider's certificate.
2. The chip verifies the certificates.

3. The chip verifies that the service provider also holds the associated secret key to the public key (by a challenge response protocol).

4. The service provider generates an ephemeral Diffie-Hellman key pair, signs the Diffie-Hellman public key with its secret key and sends both data to the chip.

5. The chip verifies the signature using the public key which is stored in the certificate of the service provider.

If all certificates and keys could be successfully verified, the chip has an authenticated Diffie-Hellman public key from the service provider.

3.2.3 Authentication of the Document (Chip Authentication)

The chip of the ID card has a static Diffie-Hellman key pair. The secret key is stored on a secure storage of the chip, so can neither be read nor cloned. The public key is signed by the card manufacturer (in Germany the Bundesdruckerei) during the production process.

Now the following steps are performed by the ID card chip and the service provider:

1. The chip sends its public key, the signature of the public key and the certificate of the manufacturer to the service provider.

2. The service provider checks the manufacturer's certificate using the root certificate and the signature of the chip's public key using the manufacturer's certificate.

If the public key of the chip could be successfully verified, the service provider has an authenticated Diffie-Hellman public key from a chip of an official ID card.

As we have seen in Section 1 one design principle was the non-use of unique identifiers for the ID card. On account of this, the Diffie-Hellman key pairs are not unique for a chip. Chips that will be produced within a period of three month will get the same key pair to use for chip authentication. As chip authentication does not authenticate the card holder but only shows, that the chip belongs to an official ID card, in fact, this is non-usual, but has no security effect.

3.2.4 Authentication of the Cardholder

At this step chip and service provider have exchanged authenticated Diffie-Hellman public keys to each other. Now they can generate a common secret and derive symmetric keys to establish an encrypted and authenticated channel (using AES as the symmetric cipher and AES-MAC as the message authentication code).

Now the data which can be read by the service provider will be transmitted from the chip to the service provider. As the channel is authenticated, the cardholder is authenticated too. Moreover, since the channel is encrypted, only the service provider that has sent its certificate to the chip can read these data.

3.3 Revocation Management
3.3.1 Revocation of Documents

In order to impede the illegitimate use of lost or stolen ID cards, the cardholder has to be able to revoke them.

A very common mechanism for chip cards, e.g., qualified digital signature cards, is the creation of a global revocation list that includes the (unique) public keys or the serial numbers of all revoked cards and/or certificates. The disadvantage of this mechanism is that a unique public key or serial number constitutes a card-specific identifier which acts as a direct link to the cardholder's identity. Such a mechanism therefore contradicts the design principle of minimal disclosure. For example, if one service provider has only access rights for age verification (see above) whereas another one also has access to other personal information, such as the name, even full access to both service provider's databases must not allow a link to their client's authentication data. This notably applies in the case when pseudonyms are used.

A solution to this problem is the use of service-provider-specific revocation lists, i.e., each card provides a service-provider-specific and card-specific revocation token to the service provider who verifies it against their individual service-provider-specific revocation list. The technical and organizational implementations of this concept are described in [1].

3.3.2 Revocation of Service Providers

Of course, the concession to read data from the ID card must be revocable, too. As it is not possible to store revocation lists on the chip, here another mechanism with a similar security level must be found. CV certificates have a very short validity (depending on the data that can be read from the chip 2 up to 30 days). Therefore, a recall of such a certificate can be realized by the non-issuing of a new one for this service provider.

References

[BKMN10] Bender, Jens; Kügler, Dennis; Margraf, Marian; Naumann, Ingo: Das Sperrmanagement im neuen deutschen Personalausweis - Sperrmanagement ohne globale chipindividuelle Merkmale, Datensicherheit und Datenschutz (DuD), 2010, p. 295-298.

[BKMN08] Bender, Jens, Kügler, Dennis, Margraf, Marian, Naumann, Ingo: Sicherheitsmechanismen für kontaktlose Chips im deutschen elektronischen Personalausweis. Datenschutz und Datensicherheit (DuD), 2008, p. 173-177.

[BeFK09] Bender, Jens, Fischlin, Marc, Kügler Kügler: Security Analysis of the PACE Key-Agreement Protocol. Information Security Conference (ISC) 2009, Lecture Notes in Computer Science, Volume 5735, Springer-Verlag, 2009, p. 33-48.

[Marg09] Margraf, Marian: Der elektronische Identitätsnachweis des zukünftigen Personalausweises. in: 19. SIT-SmartCard Workshop (Fraunhofer-Institut für Sichere Informationstechnologie), Darmstadt 3./4. 2009, p. 3-14.

[BMI 09] Federal Ministry of Interior: Gesetz über Personalausweise und den elektronischen Identitätsnachweis, 2009.

[BSI 10] Federal Office for Information Security (BSI): Technical Guideline TR-03110, Advanced Security Mechanisms for Machine Readable Travel Documents – Extended Access Control (EAC) and Password Authentication Connection Establishment (PACE), and Restricted Authentication, Version 2.03, 2010.

[BSI 10] Federal Office for Information Security (BSI): Technical Guideline TR-03127, Technical Architecture of the New German ID Card, 2010.

[ENIS09] ENISA Position Paper, Privacy Features of European eID Card Specifications, Januar 2009, http://www.enisa.europa.eu/act/it/eid/eid-cards-en.

AusweisApp and the eID Service/Server – Online Identification Finally more Secure

Werner Braun[1] · Dirk Arendt[2]

[1]Siemens AG
Siemens IT Solutions and Services
Otto-Hahn-Ring 6
81739 Munich, Germany
wernerbraun@siemens.com

[2]OpenLimit SignCubes AG
Zugerstr. 76b
6341 Baar, Switzerland
dirk.arendt@openlimit.com

Abstract

Anyone applying for a new ID document in Germany from November 2010 onwards will receive something completely innovative. The new electronic proof of identity comes in credit card format and, in addition to its official functions, can be used as an ID card when visiting the virtual city hall or shopping online, for instance.

The key components involved in using the ID card for identification purposes on the Internet are the AusweisApp and the eID service. These components form the innovative security infrastructure that makes online identification possible. One outstanding characteristic of the German eID model is its excellent interoperability with regard to the integration of smart cards, card readers, platforms and applications. This approach is also suitable for use in other countries.

Siemens IT Solutions and Services and OpenLimit are playing a key role in planning and executing the "new ID" project. Siemens IT Solutions and Services is the general contractor and responsible for the overall architecture of the IT solution, the Web portal, and the creation and integration of the application. Long-standing specialists in the field of signature and encryption technologies, OpenLimit is developing and maintaining the AusweisApp and the eID server middleware.

Application integration of the new ID card is a complex, multi-layered process requiring in-depth industry knowledge and IT expertise. Siemens IT Solutions and Services was able to demonstrate its exceptional know-how right from the very start of the project.

As an experienced supplier of certified software, OpenLimit takes care of all aspects related to the creation and operation of an eID server and development of the AusweisApp and individually adapted eID clients.

1 The new ID card

The new proof of identity comes in credit card format and will replace the existing ID document on November 1, 2010. Germany will set new standards in identity management with this innovative ID card.

Figure 1: New ID card

Like the existing document, the new ID card contains numerous security features that have been developed even further. The new ID card also offers the possibility of applying conventional uses of paper documents to the digital world. Thanks to the contactless chip inside the card, the eID (electronic identity) and QES (qualified electronic signature) functions have also been integrated, offering new potential uses, above all in the Internet.

The new ID card can also still be used for visual identification. Use of the two electronic functions is voluntary and the eID function is even free of charge to citizens.

1.1 Certificated identity makes online services more secure

Key components for online identification are AusweisApp and the associated eID service. This software for the PC or Mac and the authentication solution will enable citizens to use online services such as e-government, e-shopping and e-banking even more securely in future, as well as providing them with a reliable means of verifying the identity of these service providers. As a result, secure mutual identification in the Internet is possible for the first time.

To enable this, the service provider must apply to the Federal Office of Administration for a certificate to read the data. This agency examines who exactly wishes to read what data and why. Without this certificate, no data from the new ID card can be read online. That increases security for citizens, since they have the assurance when shopping online, for example, that their opposite number in the Internet is actually who he or she claims to be. Its identity is proven by means of the authorization certificate. This certificate contains the name of the organization, plus other details such as its registered office, the name of the data protection officer, the duration of the certificate's validity and the purpose of the data transmission. Phishing, i.e. the interception of user data with the aid of false Internet sites, will then no longer be possible.

And the service provider can also rely on the data it receives from the official document being accurate.

2 AusweisApp and the eID service – Online identification

The application software AusweisApp in conjunction with the eID service ensures encrypted communication between citizens and service providers. Using a public key system, the eID service ensures that only authorized enterprises and authorities are able to read details stored on the ID card, while allowing citizens to use the relevant online services securely and confidentially.

2.1 AusweisApp

The application software AusweisApp is provided free of charge to all citizens. AusweisApp is a small all-round talent. The software enables ID card holders to authenticate themselves online using the identification function and to sign transactions using the qualified signature function. AusweisApp also provides a plug-in for signing and encrypting e-mails. Microsoft Outlook, Outlook Express and Mozilla Thunderbird are supported as standard. AusweisApp also runs under just about all operating systems. It is platform-independent and supports Windows®, Linux and Mac OS® X as well as SuSe.

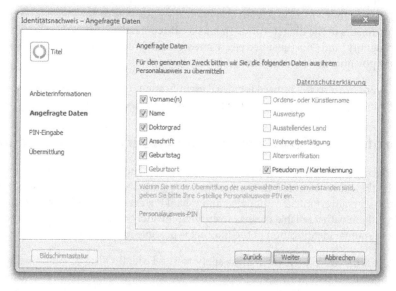

Figure 2: Citizens can decide themselves in AusweisApp what
data fields they wish to transfer to the service provider.

Citizens therefore need just one software to use all the functions with their new ID card. And if they already hold a signature card from a German trust center, they can also use it with

AusweisApp. The open middleware approach based on the eCard API supports all smart cards in German-speaking countries, such as the health professional card and health card.

Security is the main requirement demanded of AusweisApp; however, ease of use and accessibility are key aspects in implementation of the solution. Since administrative tasks are to be separated functionally from the actual application, the solution consists of the two components AusweisApp and an administration client. The latter enables not only user-specific configurations, but among other things also ensures automatic updating as soon a newer version of AusweisApp is available. Their uniform look and consistent menu guidance make it easier for citizens to use both components.

2.2 The eID service

The eID service acts as the link between AusweisApp and the Website, i.e. between the citizen and service provider. It is the instance that establishes trust in the identification process as it verifies whether the service provider has valid authorization to access the ID card and whether the ID card has been forged or reported as stolen.

The eID server is implemented as a logically independent server, which means it can be used by multiple Web applications and also operated remotely, e.g. at the premises of a third party. So that the confidentiality and integrity of the processed data is safeguarded, the data must be encrypted and signed when it is transferred between the eID server and application server if it is transmitted over an open network.

A service provider has the choice of obtaining the eID service from a provider or setting up its own eID service with an eID server. There are many different factors that impinge on this decision: flexibility, traffic (how often the eID service is used), volume of investment, business model, data security, liability, etc.).

Anyone wishing to run an eID server must comply with the technical guidelines of the Federal Office for Information Security (BSI). They stipulate not only that the server must be run at a secured location, but also prescribe the use of a hardware-based security module that prevents any type of external access – both logical and physical. The eID server has multi-client capability. A municipal data center, for example, can lease the service to several other municipalities.

2.3 Interaction between AusweisApp and the eID service

How does communication between citizens and the provider of an online service, such as a municipality, work? Let us take the example of a citizen who visits the municipality's Website, where he/she wishes to use a specific service that requires or enables authentication by ID card. The Website sends its authorization certification (i.e. the municipality's means of identification) to the citizen's PC via a third instance, the eID service. The citizen places his/her ID card on a reader connected to the computer via USB. AusweisApp establishes an encrypted connection to the eID server and the municipality's Website. The eID service checks both identities, as well as the authorization to read and validity of the ID card, and then enables access to the ID card. The citizen confirms that the data on his/her ID card can be read by entering a PIN using AusweisApp.

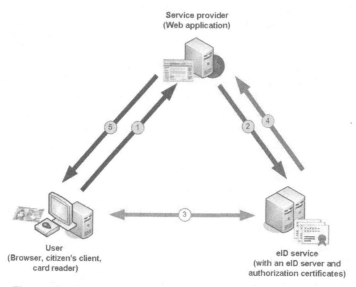

Figure 4: Basic communication process between the parties (end-to-end)
User – Service Provider – eID-Service

Detailed description of the communication process:

1. The user first calls up the service provider's offering over the Internet.

2. After this has been called up by the user, a software component of the Web portal instructs the citizen's PC to establish a connection to the eID service. At the same time the Web portal informs the eID service of the data and function results it wants from the citizen's ID card (authentication request to the eID service).

3. After the connection to the eID service has been established, the enabled AusweisApp shows the citizen whether the service provider is authorized to retrieve his/her data (by displaying the certificate description) and what data is to be read from the ID card. The citizen can object to individual items of data being transferred. The authentication and access process is continued when the user enters his/her PIN. The data is read on the basis of the effective access rights and sent to the eID service.

4. The eID server then passes on this data to the Web portal by means of an authentication response.

5. In response to the received data, the Web portal releases the requested resources and performs the service that has been requested (e.g. release of an order).

Both parties have now securely authenticated their identities to one another. The online transaction or e-government process can then begin. Once someone has authenticated their identity on the online portal of their local government office or insurance provider, they can then quickly access a variety of online services. This saves everyone involved time and money, can be done any time, including evenings and weekends – and is just as secure as going along in person, but is much more convenient.

3 eID and QES

The identification function (eID function) is already on the card when the new ID card is issued by the ID card authority. Citizens can then decide whether the ID function is to remain enabled. They can also subsequently enable and disable the function at any time.

Many administrative processes and commercial services cannot be handled electronically in full at the moment because unambiguous identification of the parties communicating over the Internet is not possible or is possible only to a limited extent. Service providers resort to time-consuming and costly ways of establishing identities by post or simply have to rely on the opposite party actually being who he or she claims to be. The new eID function enables direct, clear, mutual and international authentication.

Like in the real world, identification in the Internet remains a snapshot taken at a particular moment in time. Secure and encrypted transmission of the data via an independent, government-certified third party – the eID service – means the identity of the parties communicating with each other are reliably verified. If prior permission is given, individual data fields read from the ID card can also be stored in a form or database. The act remains a snapshot because both parties do not retain any permanent proof of each other's identity.

An online connection is always required for the purpose of electronic identification. Both parties must be connected to the eID server at the time they are mutually authenticated. ID card holders must give their prior consent every time their data is read and transferred and do so by entering a PIN.

3.1 The qualified electronic signature (QES)

Electronic signatures are used to sign digital documents, for example contracts and legal documents. They also reveal whether documents have been changed after being signed. The same applies to declarations and applications that have to be issued to authorities in written form so as to be legally binding.

The new ID card is ready for use of the electronic signature. The qualified electronic signature (QES) used is a very secure variant. This has the same legal status as a personal handwritten signature. Citizens can use the signature function by acquiring a component for this – a signature certificate – and subsequently loading it on their ID card. The signature certificates are not issued by ID card authorities, but by special service providers – signature providers – approved in accordance with the German Digital Signature Act (SigG).

Citizens can also sign documents electronically with AusweisApp, which is provided free of charge.

3.2 Differences between the identification and signature function

Whereas the eID function is intended to enable mutual identification at a certain point in time, the signatory affirms a unilateral expression of will – one that is permanent and also has probative force in a court of law. A qualified electronic signature is necessary if a statutory requirements for written form in business transactions or administrative processes in accordance with Section 126 a (1) of the German Civil Code (BGB) or a provision in the German Administrative Procedures Act demands permanently attributable proof of an expression of will or an act in the electronic world. Back in 1999, the QES was given the same status as a handwritten signature under law.

Unlike the eID function, the QES can also be used offline. Citizens can sign documents at their computer without being connected to the Internet. In order to sign a contract or form electronically, the ID card holder requires a class 3 card reader that has a built-in display and keypad. A basic class 1 reader where the PIN is entered on the computer's keyboard is sufficient for using the eID function.

Table 1: Comparison between eID and QES

eID		QES
Authentication	*Purpose*	Expression of will
Snapshot	*Timeframe*	Permanence
ID card authority	*Responsibility*	Trust center
Available when the card is issued	*Integration on ID card*	Must be subsequently installed
Free of charge	*Fee*	Subject to a charge
Basic class 1 reader	*Card reader*	Class 3 convenience reader
AusweisApp	*Software*	AusweisApp

4 Application scenarios and testing

The online ID function can also be used by providers who offer online identification in their services. They might be online services from private enterprises, such as online shops, banks, e-mail providers or social networks. Authorities can also offer this function as part of their e-government services, such as for re-registering motor vehicles or applying for birth certificates.

Figure 3: Different application scenarios

However, electronic identification not only works in the internet. The online identification function of the new ID card can also be used at ticket vending machines, for car and bicycle leasing services or for checking into a hotel.

Test and implementation measures were launched in October 2009 to flank and provide ideal support for rollout of the new ID card. The German Federal Ministry of the Interior (BMI) is currently coordinating application testing for AusweisApp and the eID service. Volunteer application testers – companies, organizations and authorities – are testing the infrastructure, initial trial ID cards as well as AusweisApp and the eID service. They are conducting trials of the solution in everyday use, testing its logic and integration. The results are being fed back into further development of the solution. This testing also gives participants the opportunity to be the first to collaborate in rollout of this innovation, to obtain competent support in preparing their applications and adapting systems and to implement a technically mature solution for quick and secure identification of customers or employees. As a result, concrete application scenarios can now be developed and implemented.

The advantages for service providers:
- A customer's identify can be verified, above all for online services
- New service offerings are now possible, e.g. transactions that previously required a signature
- The same authentication mechanism can be used for different applications, which reduces the time and effort involved in integration
- The standardized software interface for using the electronic proof of identity means there is no major integration work involved
- No longer necessary to roll out an "identity card" (customer card)
- High customer potential, since every citizen will have an electronic ID card in future

From November 2010, the AusweisApp software will then be available for citizens to download free of charge from a Web portal. Siemens IT Solutions and Services is the general contractor for the project. It is responsible for the overall IT solution architecture, the Web portal and implementation and integration of the application. OpenLimit will develop and maintain AusweisApp. The German Federal Printing Office (Bundesdruckerei) will provide the eID service for the one-year test phase.

The test phase will be completed at the end of October, so that experience from it can be incorporated before the solution goes live. Various service providers will then offer applications for online identification. However, identification is only one of the possible interesting applications. New ones are: Secure online registration, access using a pseudonym, the electronic signature, age verification, automatic completion of forms, citizen's forms, barrier-free use of Internet services and access control.

4.1 Public authorities

The new ID card can enable process chains and procedural processes without any media discontinuities thanks to the combination of the eID function and QES. That harbors great potential for e-government projects and for optimizing processes. Citizen centricity, service orientation and cost cutting will then also be able to be reconciled with each other.

So that Public Administration 2.0 can unfold its full potential, a comprehensive review of existing laws and regulations which specifically enable the use of online identification and the electronic signature is necessary. Implementation of the new possibilities offered by the new ID card would be particularly important in mass processes at the municipal level, such as in relation to registration of residents, road transport and driver licenses or land survey, fiscal and construction matters. A visit to the virtual city hall is then possible for all citizens at any time and could offer municipalities potential for optimization.

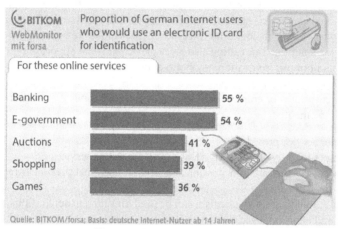

Figure 5: German Internet users

4.2 Enterprises

The ID card and eID infrastructure can help reinforce trust in electronic commerce. After all, enterprises will be able to verify their customers' identify beyond doubt. When a transaction is conducted in their online shop, they can read the name, address and place of residence of the customer from his or her ID card, for instance. As a result, they have the assurance that products and services have actually been ordered by the person who wants to have and pay for them. If payments are overdue, enterprises know who to direct their inquiries to. Customers and shoppers also benefit from online identification with the new ID card: They now know exactly who they are dealing with, from whom they bought something, whom they can turn to for recourse if what they ordered is not delivered, and what data the other party actually obtains from them.

However, the identification function of the new ID card must be integrated in existing processes. One of the key components in the new eID infrastructure is the middleware specified in Technical Guideline TR-03112 of the Federal Office for Information Security (BSI) and based on the stipulations of the internationally coordinated "eCard Application Program Interface Framework" (eCard API). A major advantage of this middleware solution is that it and so its services can be connected simply to other systems. The identification mechanism can thus be used for different applications from different areas. Internal approval processes, login processes, access controls and identification scenarios at organizations can use the infrastructure. The providers no longer have to carry out rollouts of their own because the smart card – in this case the new ID card – will be used comprehensively in a few years' time. The cost and effort of integrating it are also minimal. Services and applications to which the electronic identification function is to be added can fall back on well-documented and standardized interfaces.

These processes have no media discontinuities and not only cut transaction costs, but also create new and innovative sales channels that can be tapped at no great investment.

5 Important issues for service providers

Application integration of the new ID card is a complex, multi-layered process requiring in-depth industry knowledge and IT expertise. Service providers face various questions in this connection:

- What expectations do citizens/my customers and business partners have?
- What applications should I enable for use with the new ID card?
- Should I obtain the eID service from an external source or provide it myself?
- What do I have to do to gain authorization as a service provider?
- What requirements must I meet?
- How do I integrate the new ID card with other identification and authentication mechanisms?
- What role does the qualified electronic signature (QES) play for me?
- What security issues are of what importance and when?

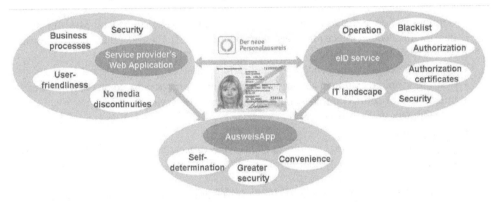

Figure 6: Integration of the new ID card is complex

As companies involved in the AusweisApp and eID service/server project for the German Federal Ministry of the Interior, Siemens IT Solutions and Services and OpenLimit have already been able to demonstrate their outstanding expertise, successfully implementing and flanking complex security processes from the outset. In addition, the two companies supported numerous pilot customers testing the applications and were able to display the competences specifically needed for the issues of importance to you: E-business and e-government services, vending machines, offline systems and other applications.

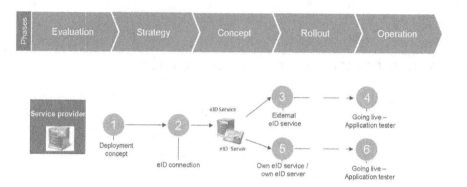

Figure 7: Service Provider have different options and need a holistic approach

The technical expertise and first-hand experience you need to succeed.

Siemens IT Solutions and Services:
- Communication and clarification of questions with the German Federal Ministry of the Interior, the Federal Office for Information Security (BSI), the Federal Office of Administration (BVA), etc.
- Support in designing the concept for applications based on the new ID card
- Consulting on integration of applications and business processes based on the new ID card
- Integration for connecting Web applications to the eID service
- Development of security concepts
- Integration of partners
- Support in integration for creating an eID service, processing of authorization certificates and blacklists
- Creation of an eID service
- Integration of the eID service in existing infrastructures (legacy system integration)
- Experience gained with many pilot customers as a result of testing of the electronic proof of identity for e-business and e-government services, vending machines and offline systems
- Demonstrators for secure registration and authentication by means of the new ID card and much more

OpenLimit:
- Middleware and its implementation and configuration for the eID server
- Training on eID server administration
- Technical consulting on the ID card, identity management, eID, signature, long-term storage
- Adapted components for reading the new ID card (AusweisApp modifications)
- Technical integration of the new ID card and other cards in existing processes
- Middleware and implementation of components for reliable long-term storage
- SDKs for integrating certified signature and authentication components in applications

Rollout of the new ID card will plug various gaps in the identification and signature process in the digital world. Leveraging these new opportunities for you efficiently and securely is our trade: Our expertise and experience help you succeed!

Postident Online with the new Personal Identity Card

Jens Terboven

Deutsche Post AG, Zentrale, Marketing Brief,
Abteilung Zusatz- und Spezialleistungen, 53250 Bonn
j.terboven@deutschepost.de

Abstract

Deutsche Post enjoys a high reputation with its customers for reliability and seriousness, and thus is ideally suited to provide products and services connected with the topic of security. Within their business processes, many companies require certainty about the identity of their contractual partners; especially on the Internet, where the subject of data security has the highest priority, this requirement entails reliable innovations. The established physical product "Postident" is already providing secure, personal identifications of end customers today, in a manner which complies with the law, but the future demands modern electronic solutions.

The challenges for companies as well as for end customers and an increasingly tightening legal framework have led Deutsche Post to think about an online strategy for its Postident product in a digital future. In addition to speed, convenience, savings in cost and effort and the need to comply with the law, the security aspect is to be the focus of the new developments. Because this is the area where Deutsche Post is especially competent!

Using the online identity card function of the new personal identity card, the existing Postident procedure is to be expanded to incorporate the possibility of secure, quicker and more convenient identification on the Internet. The objective is for the private customer to be able to use a computer with Internet access, the new personal identity card and the corresponding card PIN to prove his identity conclusively and as laid down by law. The innovative, forward-looking service offering of Deutsche Post is completed by the provision of an eID server by Deutsche Post's Signtrust business unit, the issuing of authorisation certificates and by data supply to companies "from a single source", in a single format and via one interface.

1 Deutsche Post as an identification service provider

1.1 The situation in today's identification market

For many companies in a whole range of sectors, Deutsche Post is the most important service provider for customer identification. The high reputation for reliability and seriousness built up by Deutsche Post among customers throughout its history makes it the ideal provider of products in the security area. Sectors which lack their own branch network, or whose network is declining, cannot identify their customers themselves, since they do not have any direct contact with them. Banks and insurance companies, but also signature service providers are among those already taking advantage of the products and services offered by Deutsche Post's delivery staff and retail outlets right across Germany, all of which are provided in compliance with the law.

The Postident product in particular has become especially well established in the identification services market; it enables the secure personal identification of end customers and complies with the requirements of the German Money Laundering and Signature Acts. Depending on the legal requirements or the customer's needs, a choice may be made between three different product options - Postident Basic, Comfort and Special. Identification using the identity card data or the customer signature is performed here for the customer by the employee of a Deutsche Post retail outlet or by the delivery staff of Deutsche Post. With this product, Deutsche Post has developed into the leading service provider in the security segment: Currently, Postident provides the indispensible link for all online banks and trust centres between the company and the end customer and is essential for secure identification.

Since Postident has established itself as standard, it is being introduced across entire sectors: Even small companies which would find the setup of their own identification processes a tall order, perhaps an impossible task, are thus able to comply with the standard. So Deutsche Post has a multiplier function in the clear identification of citizens for business purposes.

– Binding, confidential, reliable – these adjectives also apply to Signtrust, which has been convincing its customers for 10 years as a trust centre which handles highly sensitive data. Signtrust operates and manages not only its own trust centre, it provides the same services for the German Federal Chamber of Notaries and for Datev. The main focus involves issuing qualified certificates with supplier accreditation, whose existence can be traced back for 35 years. Other products for the IT security market, such as SSL server certificates, software certificates and an ASP signature service complete the portfolio.

1.2 Future challenges

Consumer protection is an area which is constantly changing: The protection of children, young people, and of data is being regulated more strictly. The tighter laws and restrictions represent especially serious demands for security management; it is necessary to establish the identity of the contractual partner securely, also if this is done electronically. The subject of data security, especially on the Internet, is gaining great significance. It is therefore necessary to develop innovative and reliable solutions.

In addition, companies, such as banks, are transferring their business processes in whole or in part to the Internet, which is resulting in a reduction in branch numbers and points of contact with customers. This deficit for the companies can be compensated by customer-friendly electronic solutions, and that is exactly what Deutsche Post is setting out to achieve. But the end users too would like to follow the trend of the times in favour of quicker, more convenient and "leaner" processes, whilst at the same time also maintaining a more reliable and transparent data transfer in their online communications.

2 The product development of Postident Online

2.1 The online strategy of Postident

Deutsche Post is ready to take on these challenges of the digital future and is increasingly switching from physical products to online creations, to offer its customers a choice of both types of provision.

Companies require their modern, electronic processes to be set up and implemented in a way so that they can communicate with their end customers. These processes will have to take account of the interests of both parties, help to save time and money and meet the requirements of e-commerce.

With the traditional Postident service, the Postident order forms which are used today by the deliverer or the retail outlet employee are scanned by Deutsche Post and the corrected, quality-checked data are provided to the companies electronically. Thus the companies save time by not having to perform their own processes.

But the processes are to be simplified not only for companies, but also for citizens. Deutsche Post would like to reduce the changes in medium in communication on the Internet between the parties, by allowing a single (identification) process to be able to be performed right to the end, without changing the medium or the venue. The introduction of the new personal identity cards and their online identity card function (eID function) will help to implement this intention. Thus the existing Postident process will be expanded by using the new identity card to include the possibility of secure, quicker and more convenient identification on the Internet. Thus customers will be free to use the classic process involving the Deutsche Post retail outlet or the deliverer, or to take advantage of the benefits of the new Postident Online on their computers.

In addition, infrastructure changes are planned in the medium term for the Deutsche Post retail outlets, so that processes such as an ID card check can be performed simply, quickly and securely in an electronic manner, for example when registered post products require a signature.

Following the needs, requirements and developments in the market (e.g. the introduction of the new personal ID card), the strategy was implemented in a concrete product: Postident Online.

2.2 Postident Online in detail

The development of the Postident Online product is Deutsche Post's reaction to the introduction of the new ID cards in Germany from 1 October 2010 and its online ID function. The four components which will be necessary to prove an end customer's identity electronically in the future are as follows:
- The ID card app, previously known as "citizen client" (Bürgerclient): Software components on the system of the ID card holder to access the new ID card;
- The eID server: Server component of the eID service provider, which is made available to the eID service provider in order to enable complex processes when accessing the new ID card and to communicate with it via the citizen client;
- The authorisation CA: A certifying service which issues electronic authorisation certificates for access to the new ID card.

- The actual online service, "Postident Online" which allows the end customer to trigger the identification and which accepts the data from the new ID card.

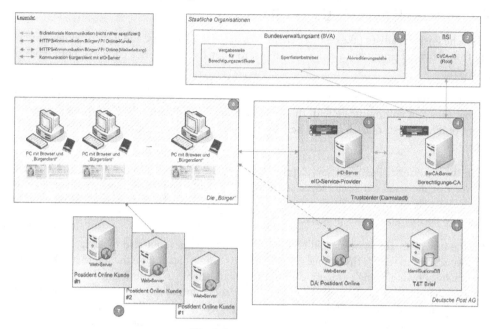

Fig. 1: System overview

The process of identification when opening a bank account will take place in detail as follows:

The companies which use Postident Online operate their own Web application. The end customer is initially situated here, for example to open an account. To open the account he must first provide the necessary data. At the end of the application process, the customer must identify his contractual partner. Now the end customer can decide whether he wishes to perform an online identification using the eID function of his new ID card, or to use the conventional (hard copy) Postident.

If the end customer opts for online authentication, and if he does not have a suitable card-reader, he can order one and continue the identification process after he has received and installed it by using a previously received online ID.

The Postident Online server leads the end customer on to the eID server and specifies the data to be requested from the new ID card. The eID server then launches the end customer's Card app, performs the identification with the new ID card, then transmits the identity data received from the new ID card and leads the end customer back to the Postident Online server.

Depending on the configuration entered for the customer, the end customer now either can or must upload documents which are connected to his identification. Some possible examples are copies of his signature, application forms to open an account or authorisations.

In order for its identification to be recognised as complying with money-laundering legislation, the company using Postident Online requires a transaction which has been performed by an already existing account of the citizen. The transaction is configurative, since not all companies require the transaction or organise it themselves. If the company asks Deutsche Post to perform the transaction and would only like to be informed of the result, Postident Online can take on this process step.

The identity data and the attachments and account details if required will be forwarded by Postident Online to an identification database of Deutsche Post, where the customer can then call it up.

In addition to identification there is an opportunity to perform an age-check. Here a check is made on whether the citizen has reached a specified minimum age or not. The age-check is done by the eID service, which checks whether the date of birth entered in the new identity card lies before or after the cut-off date for minimum age, without actually having to give away the date of birth itself. The result of the age-check is transferred to the identification database of Deutsche Post, and the customer then can check it there.

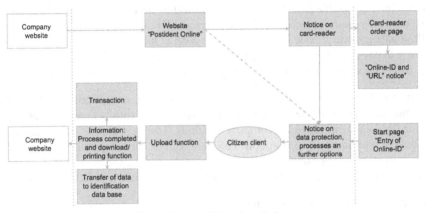

Fig. 2: Process of Postident Online

Within the Postident procedure, a person's ID card data is collected and processed. Because of the sensitivity of the personal ID card data, special conditions are imposed on processing.

For the use of the eID function an authorisation certificate which has been issued for Postident Online is required. The transmission of the data read from the new personal ID card is performed in encrypted form to the Postident Online Web application and will be forwarded from there, also in encrypted form, to the identification database. For the identification database special security requirements apply. These requirements will be satisfied inter alia by a holistic security concept. Monitoring will be carried out by a security architect.

The fulfilment of the data protection requirements is strictly monitored by the internal data protection officer. Confidential treatment of the data will be guaranteed by strict access restrictions, so that only authorised persons receive access and the data can only be used for the stated purpose.

2.3 Benefits of Postident Online for companies

The Postident Online product is also of interest to companies which up to now have not been interested in using the e-ID function of the new personal ID card due to the high investment costs or particularly complex and expensive organisation. By taking on the transaction process – the German Money Laundering Act (§6 II No. 2 GWG) demands an account transaction from the person to be identified – Deutsche Post not only saves the companies expense, but above all saves them a complex task. Deutsche Post performs the entire process, i.e., the legally stipulated collection from the end customer's account and the transfer back to him. Thus Postident Online represents not only a convenient way of implementing the opportunities provided by the new personal ID cards. Also, other conditions are being implemented in the new product, which companies demand from identification for legal or internal operating reasons, such as the already illustrated uploading of documents which are connected to identification. Thus the company receives a completed process and does not have to introduce any additional process steps.

Deutsche Post will provide the eID server – the server component which performs the complex processes when accessing the personal ID card and enables communication with the ID card app – as an ASP service, so that here too no investment will be necessary. The authorisation certificates which are necessary for access to the new Personal ID card are also produced by Deutsche Post. These elements are already integrated into Postident Online, and so companies themselves do not have to pay any attention to these aspects. Also, the eID server and the authorisation certificates are of course offered separately by Postident Online.

Thus Deutsche Post can present itself as a genuine "outsourcer", since it can cover the complete identification process – from the request for data from the end customer's new personal ID card to sending the data identified to the company – with its "Postident Online" offering. The online option and the traditional physical option "Postident" can be used in parallel so that companies can benefit from bundling the collected data: Customers receive the data from electronic and physical identification digitally in the same format and via the same interface.

It is anticipated that companies will be able to increase the number of business transactions with Postident online. The reason for this is that there is no change in medium. The end customers do not have to visit a retail outlet to identify themselves, as is the case now. They can continue the process conveniently and quickly at their PC, motivation will be increased to finish the process immediately, here and now.

By bundling the established Postident and Trust Centre offers, Deutsche Post increases the trust in which it is held both by companies and by end customers, and thus it is particularly suitable to offer an identification service as a responsible provider which can be trusted to handle sensitive data with care.

2.4 Benefits of Postident Online for end users

The end customers also profit from the innovative electronic products of Deutsche Post, and through Postident Online and the online ID card function of the new ID card they have many benefits. By performing everyday tasks on the PC, customers save themselves journeys, processes are done more quickly and conveniently and can be carried out round the clock, irrespective of opening hours. In the future they will have freedom of choice as to how they wish to perform their communication with companies, in the traditional way or innovatively by using the new personal identity card. In addition, the end customer can decide himself which data he is willing to release.

The authorisation certificates, which are applied for from Deutsche Post and are continually renewed, guarantee the identity of the other party, since because of the new functions personal data can no longer be transferred to unknown, anonymous companies; instead the identity of the contractual partner is always authenticated and updated and displayed to the end customer. In addition, the eID function checks whether the online supplier really is the person he claims to be.

In line with the principle of data economy, only such data is requested as is absolutely necessary, i.e., the new personal ID card can, for example, confirm age but not reveal a concrete date of birth. The citizen receives full transparency and control when he completes an identification process, as Deutsche Post explicitly points out why the personal data was collected and what it is to be used for. The data released by the citizen is returned to him as a "confirmation document", which he can print out if desired. There is also the possibility of uploading additional documents connected to the business transaction.

3 Summary and outlook

With Postident Online, Deutsche Post is taking a logical and consistent step forward and facing the challenges of the digital future as an innovative service provider held in unparalleled trust by the general public. Unlike many other suppliers, Deutsche Post is able to build on a stable base of existing customer relationships and strong customer loyalty, and only has to modernise these relationships – a decisive competitive advantage. Through these customer relationships, Deutsche Post can also offer Postident Online to customers who would not otherwise set up their own infrastructure as the cost and effort would be too great. Postident Online thus serves as a multiplier for the new personal ID card, particularly among small and medium-sized enterprises.

The objective of the Postident Online strategy is to take all the opportunities arising from the online ID card function of the new personal ID card and to develop products which are technologically state-of-the-art and satisfy the needs of companies and end customers. With the implementation of Postident Online, that objective is being fulfilled.

But in the future too, Deutsche Post wishes to seize the opportunity to establish itself as one of the leading providers of binding, confidential and reliable services.

The eID Function of the nPA within the European STORK Infrastructure

Volker Reible[1] · Dr. Andre Braunmandl[2]

[1]T-Systems International GmbH, Otto-Röhm-Straße 71 c,
64293 Darmstadt, Germany
volker.reible@t-systems.com

[2]Bundesamt für Sicherheit in der Informationstechnik (BSI),
Godesberger Allee 185-189, 53175 Bonn, Germany
andre.braunmandl@bsi.bund.de

Abstract

Germany will introduce the new electronic ID card (neuer Personalausweis) in credit-card format to replace the existing national identity card starting in November 2010. ID card data will be stored on an ID chip, enabling cardholders to identify themselves online when dealing with government authorities as well as commercial service providers. At the same time, cardholders can be confident that whoever requests their data is also authorized to do so. For official identity checks all electronic ID cards will include a digital photo; optional two fingerprints and/or a qualified electronic signature may also be stored on the chip. To use the new eID card the citizen needs a card reader as well as a client software called "Ausweis-App". Since autumn 2009 an application trial is running to test and prepare the roll-out.

In parallel, the European Commission started in June 2008 the STORK project under the CIP, ICT PSP framework. STORK's main objectives are to identify existing eID infrastructures in Europe, specify and implement a common architecture which allows secure and easy to use eID solutions in Europe, and demonstrate the European interoperability in six application pilots. The outcome of STORK will be a prototypical infrastructure to be a working basis for the pan-European eID architecture.

1 Introduction

1.1 The way from paper-based to electronic ID

In Germany every citizen aged 16 or older is obliged to have an Identity Card (*Personalausweis*). About 60 million paper-based cards have been issued. Since 1987, the German ID Card is issued in the ID-2-format (74 mm × 105 mm). The frontside contains a photo and a signature of the holder as well as last name, first names, date and place of birth and a serial document number and the date of expiry.

Last name, first names, date of birth, document number and the date of expiry are repeated in machine-readable form in the two bottom lines of the document, which are used for border and police controls only.

The backside contains the residential address, the height and eye colour of the holder as well as the authority and date of issue. Therefore, when the residential address has changed, a sticker with the new data is applied to the document.

The new electronic ID card (nPA) to be issued starting on 01 November 2010 will have the ordinary banking card format and will contain a contactless chip hosting some biometric data (digital image and optionally two fingerprints), other data regarding the person and the ID card (first name, given name, academic title, date and place of birth, current address, validity information, maturity information in terms of yes or no regarding a specific age, plus some card and document specific data).

German Identity Cards are issued by the municipality of the residence of the holder, but they are centrally produced by the Federal Printing Office (*Bundesdruckerei*). Stickers containing changed address data are produced locally and vary in size, typeface and quality.

The document number is a unique serial number, which unambiguously identifies the document, that is, it changes with respect to the card holder when the card holder gets a new ID card. During the lifetime of the document (10 years) it constitutes a kind of unique personal identity number. According to § 3 Identity Card Act, it is explicitly forbidden to use this document number for accessing personal data in files or for linking data in different files. The special machine-readable code is technically not suited for online authentication. But this will change, when the present paperbased ID card will be substituted by the nPA from 2010 onwards.

1.2 German field trial

To prepare the roll-out of the nPA the German government decided to set up a field trial. With the experiences of practical tests the application of the electronic ID concerning the access to eBusiness and eGovernment services in the Internet as well as self-service machines will be prepared, tested and evaluated. The trial started on 1st October 2009 and runs until 30th October 2010. In June 2009 the ministry of Interior selected from over 200 applicants 30 candidates for the field trial containing a broad scope of companies, institutions and governmental agencies. This field trial is supported by a specific competence center (CC nPA). The focus is on suitability for daily use, usability and acceptance. The objective is to create a great number of attractive applications and services – both in the governmental and the commercial sector. In addition to this centrally coordinated and supported field trial, an open field trial was initiated with currently over 200 service providers in spring 2010. The participating citizens received a personalized test eID and a contactless card reader. The user client called "Ausweis-App" is available free of charge for download and supports in different versions all well-established operating systems like Microsoft Windows, Mac OS and Linux.

1.3 The STORK project

The STORK project aims to establish a European eID Interoperability Platform that will allow European citizens to use their national eID to establish new e-relations across borders. The project will test cross-border user authentication by means of five pilot projects that will use existing government services in EU Member States. In time, the number of crossborder services available to European users will increase as more service providers become connected to the platform.

Thus in the future, citizens should be able to start a company, get their tax refund, or obtain their university papers without physical presence; all they will need to access these services is to enter their personal data using their national eID, and the STORK platform will obtain the required guarantee (authentication) from their government.

User-centric Approach = Privacy Guarantee
The role of the STORK platform is to identify a citizen who is in a session with a service provider, and to send his data to this service. Whilst the service provider may request various data items, the citizen always controls the data to be sent. The explicit consent of the owner of the data, the citizen, is always required before his data can be sent to the service provider.

The STORK platform does not store any personal data, so no data can be lost.
This user-centric approach is in line with the legislative requirements of all the various countries involved that oblige concrete measures be taken to guarantee respect of a citizen's fundamental rights, such as his privacy.

The Pilots and their Integration
The STORK interoperability platform will be tested through five pilot projects where it will be integrated into existing applications and tested in real, live situations:

1. Cross-border Authentication Platform for Electronic Services: A demonstrator showing that cross-border electronic services can operate in a number of Member States: The applications include national portals from Austria (help.gv.at), Estonia (eesti.ee), Germany (mein-service-BW), Portugal (portaldocidadao.pt) and the Belgian Limosa service;

2. Safer Chat: Promoting safe use of the Internet by children and young people;

3. Student Mobility: Facilitating people studying abroad in a different Member State;

4. eDelivery: Developing cross-border mechanisms for secure online delivery of documents;

5. Change of Address: Assisting EU citizens move and settle in other EU countries;

6. ECAS-Pilot: European Commission Authentication Service;

Integration in existing eID Infrastructures
Most EU countries have already deployed national electronic citizen cards; citizens are becoming accustomed to them and are beginning to enjoy the benefits they offer. Other countries have opted for simpler solutions based on user-ID and password, sometimes complemented with other identification mechanisms.

The objective of the project is not to replace any existing national infrastructure, but rather to take what is already available and to connect all the various authentication methods with transparency, in such a way that any of these methods will allow users to present their certified personal data to foreign administrations.

2 The architecture and technical infrastructure

The STORK project is divided in several workpackages which firstly define and specify the architecture and secondly implement and run the pilots. Figure 1 shows the structure:

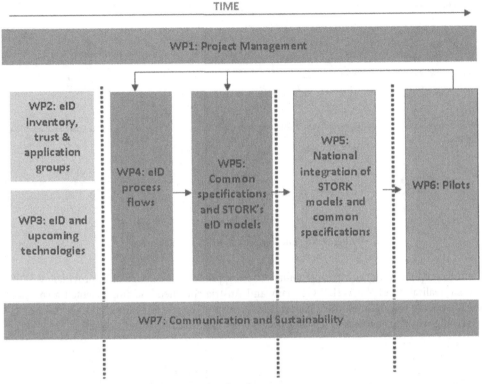

Fig. 1: Workpackage structure

The German participation in STORK is concentrated on both parts of the central workpackage 5, the specification and the implementation/integration and on workpackage 6 containing the pilots. The pilot 1 "cross-border authentication for electronic services" is led by Germany.

Intention of the German participation is the introduction and roll-out of the German eCard framework in Europe creating interest for the German architecture and for a safe and secure eIDM infrastructure in Europe. During the analysis of already existing or just in preparation solutions in European member states two general architecture models could be identified: The PEPS (Pan-European proxy service) and the middleware model. Having experienced that both models should be considered, an additional architecture component was specified to interconnect both models. Figure 2 shows the general architecture:

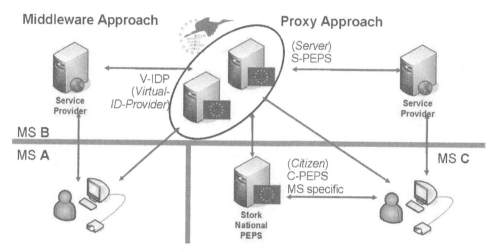

Fig. 2: The middleware and PEPS architecture

Central component for the interoperability of both approaches is the virtual ID provider (V-IDP). For the realisation of the V-IDP Germany and Austria specified and implemented a so called MARS module (Modular Authentication Relay Service). The module offers interfaces to the citizens (plug-ins) and adapters to service providers or centralized PEPSes (plug-ons).

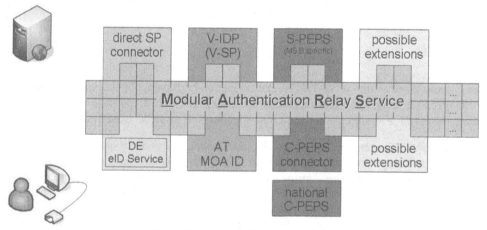

Fig. 3: The configurable MARS module

The pilot 1 contains portals from
- Austria: help.gv.at
- Belgium: limosa.be
- Estonia: eesti.ee
- Germany: mein-service-bw
- Iceland, and
- Portugal: portaldocidadao.pt.

Furthermore, additional member states joined the project in the year 2010 and will participate in pilot 1:

- Finland
- France
- Greece, and
- Lithuania.

The Baden-Württemberg portal service-bw is a running regional portal and has realised the EU service directive. It offers a personalised portal for the citizens at mein-service-bw. Together with T-Systems the portal was enlarged with a registration and authentication function using the nPA. This application is part of the German nPA field trial. In STORK, this development was enlarged again with a function for registration and authentication of non-German citizens holding a national eID. The figure 4 shows the registration page for citizens from other European member states. The relevant pages of mein-service-bw are under construction in English and French versions.

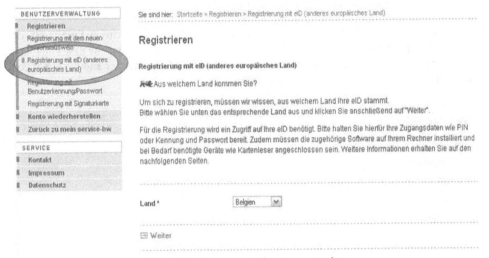

Fig. 4: The German portal mein-service-bw

3 Conclusion

The active and intensive activities from German federal institutions and companies in the preparation, trial and roll-out activities of the nPA together with the German contribution to the STORK project allow the integration of the German eID Solution into the pan-European eID architecture. This guarantees a high level of security and data protection for all citizens. More concrete the STORK infrastructure demonstrates the European dimension and compatibility of the national German eIDM architecture. The unique feature of the German eID solution allows that both citizen and service provider can rely on the identity of their counterpart.

The German view on the importance of a European safe and secure eIDM infrastructure is in line with the view of the European Commission.

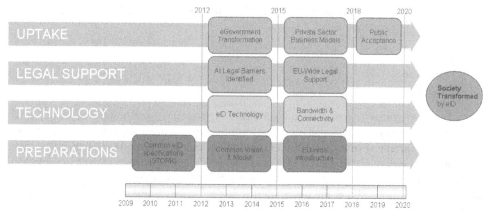

*Aniyan Varghese, EC, Annual European eID Interoperability Conference, 16-17 March 2010, La Hulpe, Belgium

Fig. 5: EC view on role of eIDM in the future

In Germany, various stakeholders and potential service providers follow closely the STORK development and progress. Having in mind that no killer application exists for the nPA in national and/or European context the success story must be based on a large number and variety of governmental and commercial services and applications.

References

ec.europa.eu/idabc
www.eid-stork.eu
www.ccepa.de
www.bsi.de
www.bmi.bund.de
www.service-bw.de

Polish Concepts for Securing E-Government Document Flow

Mirosław Kutyłowski · Przemysław Kubiak

Wrocław University of Technology
{miroslaw.kutylowski | przemyslaw.kubiak}@pwr.wroc.pl

Abstract

One of the basic problems in electronic documents flow in public administration is authentication of documents and fulfilling all related legal and technical requirements. The situation in public administration is in many ways easier that in general flow of legal documents. Here, the citizens and representatives of public bodies are the actors of the process well defined and known in the system.

A number of technical and legal solutions are aimed to make electronic documents flow easier and more reliable. Out of these, the main components are: electronic seal and personal signature.

In this paper we focus on requirements and their technical feasibility concerning personal signatures. The idea is to provide means for signing documents exchanged between citizens and public bodies so that

1. immediate disabling of a signature card is possible, and
2. the signing time is undeniable.

Technical solutions that we propose are based on mediated signatures. In particular, this enables to control ID-card usage against predefined policies (e.g. usage limited to particular time periods, frequency, etc.). In this scenario, a card can be disabled instantly therefore preventing creation of disputable signatures.

In particular, we propose signatures based on hash signatures. For RSA, we propose to embed a deterministic signature based on discrete logarithm problem into padding algorithm. This makes the signatures independent of security of a single algebraic problem.

1 Digital Signatures in Public Administration

Electronic document flow in public administration requires in most situations authentication of digital documents. While modern cryptography provides many effective tools for data authentication, it turns out that choosing appropriate technology is a challenging task from practical point of view.

So far two methods have been considered as suitable for this purpose:

1. holding master copies of documents in a repository,
2. using the framework of qualified electronic signatures.

The first solution can be quite practical provided that the following conditions are fulfilled:

1. it is possible to authenticate the persons getting access to the repository, this concerns the right to access particular data and not necessarily the users identity,
2. the flow of documents is well defined so that it is clear which documents should be stored in the repository.

It turns out that implementing appropriate solutions is nontrivial. Even checking the identity requires a framework such as electronic identity cards – password-based and similar solutions are not reliable enough, as the access can be given to third persons. In particular, there is a danger of coercion. Limiting the rights to specific fields is even more challenging, as privacy of data access should be guaranteed. The technology of restricted identification can be helpful, but still it separates only different application areas.

Using qualified electronic signatures in contacts between citizens and public administration was so far of marginal importance in Poland, due to high costs and lack of interest among the public for buying qualified certificates. The situation has not changed after an obligation for signing reports to social security administration with a qualified signature was introduced.

1.1 Specific Conditions

There are many differences between conditions for flow of legal documents within the frame work defined by civil law and in the framework defined for public administration. The X.509 architecture has been designed having in mind mainly applications within the first framework. Below we describe some important properties of the second framework:

1.1.1 Hierarchical Structure

In the case of public administration all actors of the process are well defined. The structure of public bodies, their interconnections are also well defined. Existing organization structure can be used to define the access rights as well as link the signature verification data with the signers.

The second important issue is that the people submitting legal documents to public bodies are, with exception of some foreigners, known to public administration. Moreover, in most countries one of the roles of the public administration is to provide documents and means (either electronic or non-electronic) by which the citizens can prove their identity.

1.1.2 Multiple Trust Points

In the X.509 approach a certification authority must make a decision based on data provided by the client. However, due to personal data protection rules, possibility to check this data for authenticity is limited. In case of public administration any identity fraud is much more difficult – information can be checked at many independent points. For this reason fraud risk can be significantly reduced.

One of characteristics of administration procedures is that in most cases they involve interaction between the actors of the process – no decision is immediate and irrevocable. So any fraud attempt such as submitting a document with a forged signature is very likely to be detected and appropriate legal consequences drawn.

1.1.3   Role of Time

In proceedings of public administration time plays important role. The deadlines for legal steps are usually well defined. Therefore, it would be desirable to recognize the time of performing certain actions in an undeniable way.

On the other hand, the time does not need to be determined precisely. It is usually sufficient to determine the date of creating a signature. Indirectly, when the signer looses control over a signing device, it is necessary to determine if a signature was created before or after this moment.

1.1.4   Economic Issues

The average number of documents submitted by a citizen to public bodies is as low as just a few a year. So any solution causing either nonnegligible costs or initial effort or personal risk would be non attractive from citizen's point of view. The main advantage is on the side of public administration, where the volume of data processed becomes very high.

1.2 Implementation Requirements

A solution for digital signature in public administration planned in Poland should meet the following properties:

1. the role of a secure signature device should be played by electronic ID card,
2. the status of an ID card (not revoked) should be checked during signing, appropriate procedure must be executed during every signature creation, appropriate means should be technical and not organizational ones,
3. the owner of the card must have possibility to disable the signing functionality temporarily,
4. the signature creation time should be self evident,
5. security should not relay on cryptographic algorithm or a smart card only; instead a combination of independent mechanisms should be used,
6. as signing documents for public administration with an electronic ID is less risky than using qualified electronic signature in relations regulated by civil law, it is possible to use cryptographic and technical mechanisms with lower security level.

Ad 1)
For the ease of future use, a very important issue is to provide appropriate signing devices to the citizens (here a natural solution is an electronic personal ID-card), as well as to representatives and just employees of public administration (in this case, the ID-card should indicate the role of such person, eg. "a police officer", and not his/her identity).

Ad 2)
In the case of personal identification documents there are well-defined revocation procedures that can be easily followed not only by authorities but also by citizens. Therefore a registry containing data of revoked documents is an excellent source of information, when validity of signature is examined. However, the assumption is that appropriate validity checking is done once – during signature creation – and that without interaction with appropriate validation server the signature cannot be created. "Cannot" means here lack of technical possibility and not only lack of permission. So in particular, a stolen electronic identity card cannot be misused for signing.

Ad 3)

Since a kind of interaction with a validation service is enforced during signature creation, additional mechanisms can be easily implemented. In particular the owner of a card should have possibility to disable the card for a certain time (e.g. when she or he undergoes a serious surgery, or just goes for holidays).

In the case of using electronic signature by the employees of public bodies, such mechanism enables particular security features. For example, a card can be immediately disabled, when a given person looses her or his rights to sign documents of a given art. So checking attributes of the signing person can be done automatically at the time of signing by the validation server. Moreover, signing policy may admit signing only during office hours and only at particular locations.

Ad 4)

The main problem in the classical approach based on offline signature cards is impossibility to determine signing time from the signature alone. If a validation server is used as described above, one can insert a timestamp in the signature and check the creation time when required. In order to avoid any manipulation of data, the whole process can be secured by logs based on a hash chain.

Ad 5)

The strength of cryptographic mechanisms cannot be guaranteed for a long period of time. Therefore additional security mechanisms are necessary that would provide proof of authenticity in time horizon that is appropriate for public administration procedures. In general, traces of signing in the system should be enough under normal circumstances.

Ad 6)

Even though the time horizon for electronic documents in public administration must be long, usually there is a lower risk attributed to such documents and, as discussed before, additional mechanisms of checking the data exist. Consequently, even though adequate attention for advances in cryptoanalysis and breaking technical mechanisms for protection of signing devices must be made, the cryptographic mechanisms can still be used despite their potental flaws that can emerge in the future.

2 Mediated Signatures and RSA

The concept of mediated signature is quite simple. Signature creation process cannot be executed alone by the owner of signing keys (or more precisely, by a signature creation device). It is necessary to use also a secret cryptographic material which can be stored on a different device and under control of a different person.

Perhaps the simplest mediated signature scheme is mediated RSA [BDTW01,BoDT04]. Let us assume that n is the public modulus, e is the public verification key and d is the private signing key. The scheme can be modified in the way that the secure signature device stores d', where $d'=d-d''$, and the mediator gets d''. The number d'' can be generated independently from d, for instance as $G(K,ID,n)$, where G is an appropriate keyed hash function, K is a secret key of validation server.

In this scenario, in order to sign a message M, the signer first computes $h=H(M)$, where H is a standard hashing function used for RSA signatures. Then the signer computes

$$s1:= h^{d'} \bmod n$$

and sends its ID, n, $s1$ and h to the validation server. The server reconstructs d'' from the equality $d''=G(K,ID,n)$, computes

$$s2:= h^{d''} \bmod n$$

and finally the RSA signature

$$s:=s1 \cdot s2 \bmod n$$

This basic scheme can be easily extended so that more parties are active in signature creation. For example, if an additional key $\underline{d}$ is stored in the user's desktop computer, then the key d can be modified as follows:

$$d'=d-d''-\underline{d}$$

In this case the PC computes its "share"

$$s3:= h^{d} \bmod n$$

and the final RSA signature is computed as

$$s:=s1 \cdot s3 \cdot s2 \bmod n$$

In this scenario, in order to forge a signature it is necessary to get control over the signature card holding d', break into the PC of the user, and prohibit revoking the card at the validation center. Simultaneous occurrence of these three events is quite unlikely.

The mediated RSA scheme might be further strengthened by choosing the PSS padding [RSA05] for the messages' digests (the padding might be interpreted as a kind of wrapper for the values h) and using an additional signature scheme yielding short signatures of h in place of salt in this padding [BłKK10].

3 Mediated Merkle Signatures

Relying on RSA or signatures based on Discrete Logarithm Problem for creating signatures is risky in the sense that in all cases finding a general method to compute discrete logarithms would break down the system. While this is evident for Discrete Logarithm based systems, for RSA it often escapes our attention. Nevertheless, one can perform the following simple attack. Choose a number $u \gg n$ at random and compute $z=g^u \bmod n$. Then input z into the oracle computing discrete logarithm, getting some value v as the answer. If $\varphi(n)$ has a few prime factors (as recommended), then with a fair probability the numbers u and v differ by the order of the multiplicative group Zn^*. Then we can solve the equation $e \cdot x = 1 \bmod |u-v|$ in order to get the key x that can be used instead of the original signing key.

To mitigate the threat of breaking the system when DLP is broken, signatures based on hash functions can be used as a good alternative. So far they have been regarded theoretically attractive but not practical. The situation has changed with increase of computational power as well as storage size of smart cards. Moreover, it is quite easy to adopt the hash based signatures to mediated signatures scenario.

3.1 Merkle Signatures

3.1.1 Construction Idea

To begin with, let us describe in more detail the building blocks for Merkle Signatures, – the hash signature. They are based on one-wayness of cryptographic hash functions [Lamp79]. A public key is a sequence of values $Y1, Y2, ..., Yn$; the corresponding private key is a sequence $X1, X2, ..., Xn$, where $Yi=H(Xi)$ for each $i{\leq}n$. A signature for a message M with a digest U is a sequence of values Xj for $j{\in}S(U)$, where the set $S(U)$ corresponds to U in a one-to-one way. For instance, in Lamport-Diffie [Lamp79] signatures n is equal twice the binary length of digests U. Denote this length by k. Let ($u1$ $u2$ ... uk) be the binary representation of digest U being signed, then the indexes j of the revealed private keys Xj in the signature of U are calculated as $j=2i+ui$ for $i=1,2,...,k$. This basic idea can be optimized for efficiency: see for instance Winternitz [Merk89] and Reyzin-Reyzin [ReRe02] signatures.

Signatures constructed this way are one-time signatures (OTS): if more than one message is signed using the same sequence $X1, X2, ..., Xn$, then it is possible to combine them to get a signature for a different bitstring. In order to get a more practical solution with possibility to sign multiple documents one can use a general construction converting one-time signatures into a scheme where potentially an unlimited number of signatures can be created. Merkle signature scheme is a solution of this kind.

The basic construction of the Merkle Signature Scheme (MSS) enables to create a fixed number of signatures, say 2^h. First, a set of 2^h pairs (public key, private key) is created. Then, a labelled tree with 2^h leaves is consturcted in the following way. The ith leave corresponds to the ith public key and its label is the hash of this public key. The labels of the inner nodes of the tree are computed so that if a node a has child nodes b and c with labels hb and hc, then its label ha equals $H(hb,hc)$, where H is a strong cryptographic hash function. Once the tree is created, the label of the root of the tree is published as the public key for all signatures to be created with this tree.

Signing a message requires creating a one-time signature using one of the yet unused leaves. Moreover, one has to provide the corresponding public key and a proof that the key have been used when constructing the Merkle tree. For this purpose one has to provide the labels of all nodes that are siblings of the nodes on the path P from the leaf of the public key to the root of the tree. Verification of the signature is then a standard verification of the one-time signature and reconstruction of the labels for all nodes on the path P.

MSS are believed to be very secure: they seem to not rely on some problem having rich (maybe not completely discovered yet) algebraic structure. Recently this belief has been strengthened by the paper [DOTV08], where a variant of the Merkle signatures is presented, and proved to be as secure as the one-time signatures (OTS) are secure and as the hash function used to build Merkle trees is second-preimage resistant. Note that second-preimage resistance is usually much harder to break than collision resistance.

3.1.2 Implementation Issues

First of all, storing all 2^h private keys may seem unfeasible. However, note that the private keys corresponding to the leaves of the tree do not have to be stored after creation of the tree, if they are created with a strong pseudorandom number generator. Then it is possible to reconstruct the keys when required.

The second practical problem is the number of key pairs generated at the set up time (i.e. the value of 2^h). If it is small, then the procedure does not take long, but on the other hand signing capacity might be exhausted too early. The solution to this problem is simple [NaSW05, BGD+06, BDK+07]: instead of a balanced binary tree we prepare a non-balanced hierarhy of trees, where a single subtree T is a full binary tree constructed as before. Each leave u of the top T will be used not for signing a message, but instead for signing a root of a subtree created later and attached at u. The leaves of the bottom trees serve to sign messages. This simple trick requires a slight modification of the verification procedure, but enables creating practically unlimited number of signatures for the same public key. Moreover, when attaching a new subtree one can change the hash algorithm used in this subtree. In this way one can adopt to the changes of cryptographic strength of hash functions.

MSS is also efficient: paper [RED+08] describes an implementation of MSS on a 8-bit micro-controller (Atmel ATmega128, which is a general purpose microcontroller). Memory of the microcontroller has capacity of 10^5 erase/write cycles. This limits height h of the Merkle tree to $h=16$, thus this particular implementation is capable of making 2^{16} signatures verifiable with the root of that tree. Interestingly, as a hash function used in signing the message digest the authors chose a function based on a block cipher (cf. [BlRS02]) instantiated with AES. This choice is a source of very competitive performance of the signature generation. Note that with the progress of technology more write/erase cycles will be available on microcontrollers, see for example smart-card microcontroller [Infi09] claiming even $5 \cdot 10^5$ such cycles. Consequently, the number of signatures that might be generated by the card will not be so limited. What is more, even 2^{16} possible signatures in [RED+08] means that if such a card is issued for a 10-years period, then on average its user has ability to generate more than 17 signatures a day. This is certainly enough for a private person, while automatic server signatures could be based on HSM units. The heaviest part of key generation process for MSS and its variants is the computation of the one-time signature (OTS) keys. Utilizing the scheme from [BDK+07] one can see that for the chosen OTS it is feasible to generate one-time keys on smart cards (which in principle are more resource-constrained than general purpose microcontrollers).

3.2 Mediated Merkle Signatures

Creating a mediated version of MSS is quite easy. The public one-time key Y might be defined not as $Ysigner$ alone, but as concatenation $Ysigner \parallel Yvalid$ where $Ysigner$ and $Yvalid$ are OT public keys created by the signer and the validation center, respectively. Now both parties can make the OT signature of a digest U, and for the public key $Y = Ysigner \parallel Yvalid$ verification path P is generated. As a result, this double-signature might be verified with a single public key beeing the root of the Merkle tree.

Another possibility here is to replace a key pair (X, Y) by the keys $(Xsigner, Xvalid, Y)$, where

$$Y = H(Xsigner) \otimes H(Xvalid)$$

where $\otimes$ denotes the XOR operation, and H is the hash function such as used before. The private key $Xsigner$, is created and held by the signer, while $Xvalid$, is created and held by the validation center. Note that the signer alone cannot create any proof for the public key Y. In deed, any value X' can be claimed as the signer's private key $Xsigner$, as long as $Xvalid$ remains unrevealed.

4 Conclusion

The advances in telecommunication systems prompted an urgent need for systems of electronic document flow in public administration based on mechanisms dedicated for offline data transfer. Mediated signatures, as a concept, provide here a good framework for solving the problems that are inevitable for X.509 based architectures.

It turns out that apart from classical solutions such as RSA-mediated signature, hash based sigantures are potentially quite an atractive alternative. Their practicability becomes more evident in the recent years as a result of huge advances in smart card technology.

5 Acknowledgment

We thank Krystian Matusiewicz, Przemysław Błaśkiewicz, Dariusz Lewicki and colleagues from Trusted Information Consulting for some remarks and discussions. The work presented here was partially financed by Polish Ministry of Science and Higher Education in years 2009-2010, project O R00 0015 07.

References

[BDK+07] Buchmann, Johannes/ Dahmen, Erik/ Klintsevich, Elena/ Okeya, Katsuyuki/ Vuillaume, Camille: Merkle signatures with virtually unlimited signature capacity. In Jonathan Katz/ Moti Yung, editors, ACNS, volume 4521 of LNCS. Springer. ISBN 978-3-540-72737-8, pp. 31-45.

[BDTW01] Boneh, Dan/ Ding, Xuhua/ Tsudik, Gene/ Wong, Chi Ming: A method for fast revocation of public key certicates and security capabilities. In SSYM'01: Proceedings of the 10th conference on USENIX Security Symposium. USENIX Association, Berkeley, CA, USA, pp. 22-22.

[BoDT04] Boneh, Dan/ Ding, Xuhua/ Tsudik, Gene: Fine-grained control of security capabilities. ACM Trans. Internet Techn., 2004. volume 4(1):pp. 60-82.

[BGD+06] Buchmann, Johannes/ Garca, Luis Carlos Coronado/ Dahmen, Erik/ Doering, Martin/ Klintsevich, Elena: CMSS - an improved Merkle signature scheme. In Rana Barua/ Tanja Lange, editors, INDOCRYPT, volume 4329 of LNCS. Springer. ISBN 3-540-49767-6, pp. 349-363.

[BłKK10] Błaśkiewicz, Przemysław/ Kubiak, Przemysław/ Kutyłowski Mirosław: Digital signatures for e-government - a long-term security architecture. Accepted for publication in proceedings of the e-Forensics conference, Shanghai, China, November 10-12, 2010.

[BlRS02] Black, John/ Rogaway, Phillip/ Shrimpton, Thomas: Black-Box Analysis of the Block-Cipher-Based Hash-Function Constructions from PGV. Cryptology ePrint Archive, Report 2002/066, 2002.

[DOTV08] Dahmen, Erik/ Okeya, Katsuyuki/ Takagi, Tsuyoshi/ Vuillaume, Camille: Digital signatures out of second-preimage resistant hash functions. In Johannes Buchmann/ Jintai Ding, editors, PQCrypto, volume 5299 of LNCS. Springer. ISBN 978-3-540-88402-6, pp. 109-123.

[Infi09] Infineon Technologies AG: Chip Card & Security: SLE 66CLX800PE(M) Family, 8/16-Bit High Security Dual Interface Controller For Contact based and Contactless Applications, 2009.

[Lamp79] Lamport, Leslie: Constructing digital signatures from a one way function. Technical Report CSL-98, SRI International Computer Science Laboratory, 1979.

[Merk89] Merkle, Ralph C.: A certied digital signature. In Gilles Brassard, editor, CRYPTO, volume 435 of LNCS. Springer. ISBN 3-540-97317-6, pp. 218-238.

[NaSW05] Naor, Dalit / Shenhav, Amir / Wool, Avishai: One-Time Signatures Revisited: Have They Become Practical? Cryptology ePrint Archive, Report 2005/442, 2005.

[RED+08] Rohde, Sebastian/ Eisenbarth, Thomas/ Dahmen, Erik/ Buchmann, Johannes/ Paar, Christof: Fast hash-based signatures on constrained devices. In Gilles Grimaud/ Francois-Xavier Standaert, editors, CARDIS, volume 5189 of LNCS. Springer. ISBN 978-3-540-85892-8, pp. 104-117.

[ReRe02] Reyzin, Leonid/ Reyzin, Natan: Better than BiBa: Short onetime signatures with fast signing and verifying. In Lynn Margaret Batten/ Jennifer Seberry, editors, ACISP, volume 2384 of LNCS. Springer. ISBN 3-540-43861-0, pp. 144-153.

[RSA05] RSA Laboratories: PKCS#1 v2.1 — RSA Cryptography Standard + Errata, 2005.

Index

A

B

C

D

E

F

G

K

L

M

N

O

P

R

S

Understanding IT

Eberhard Sturm
The New PL/I
... for PC, Workstation and Mainframe
2009. X, 304 pp. with 80 Fig. and Online Service Softc. EUR 59,90
ISBN 978-3-8348-0726-7

Andreas Luszczak
Using Microsoft Dynamics AX 2009
2010. XIV, 341 pp. with 177 Fig. and Online Service. Softc. EUR 39,95
ISBN 978-3-8348-0482-2

Diffenderfer, Paul M.; El-Assal, Samir
Microsoft Dynamics NAV
Jump Start to Optimization
2., rev. Ed. 2008. XII, 304 pp. with 209 fig.
softc. EUR 49,90
ISBN 978-3-8348-0516-4

Karsten Berns | Ewald von Puttkamer
Autonomous Land Vehicles
Steps towards Service Robots
2009. VI, 283 pp. with 246 Fig. and 16 algorithms. Softc. EUR 34,90
ISBN 978-3-8348-0421-1

**VIEWEG+
TEUBNER**
Abraham-Lincoln-Straße 46
65189 Wiesbaden
Fax 0611.7878-400
www.viewegteubner.de

Stand Juli 2010.
Änderungen vorbehalten.
Erhältlich im Buchhandel oder im Verlag.

IT–Sicherheit und Datenschutz

Hans-Peter Königs
IT-Risiko-Management mit System
Von den Grundlagen bis zur Realisierung - Ein praxisorientierter Leitfaden
3., überarb. und erw. Aufl. 2009. XVI, 360 S. mit 88 Abb. und Online-Service.
Geb. EUR 54,90
ISBN 978-3-8348-0359-7

Sebastian Klipper
Konfliktmanagement für Sicherheitsprofis
Auswege aus der "Buhmann-Falle" für IT-Sicherheitsbeauftragte, Datenschützer
und Co
2010. XII, 193 S. mit 63 Abb. und 25 Tab. und Online-Service. (Edition <kes>)
Br. EUR 39,95
ISBN 978-3-8348-1010-6

Heinrich Kersten | Jürgen Reuter | Klaus-Werner Schröder,
IT-Sicherheitsmanagement nach ISO 27001 und Grundschutz
Der Weg zur Zertifizierung
2., akt. und erw. Aufl. 2009. XIV, 299 S. mit 2 Abb. und Online-Service
Br. EUR 49,90
ISBN 978-3-8348-0605-5

Bernhard C. Witt
Datenschutz kompakt und verständlich
Eine praxisorientierte Einführung
2., akt. und erg. Aufl. 2010. XII, 246 S. mit 61 Abb. und Online-Service.
(Edition <kes>) Br. EUR 23,95
ISBN 978-3-8348-1225-4

VIEWEG+ TEUBNER

Abraham-Lincoln-Straße 46
65189 Wiesbaden
Fax 0611.7878-400
www.viewegteubner.de

Stand Juli 2010.
Änderungen vorbehalten.
Erhältlich im Buchhandel oder im Verlag.